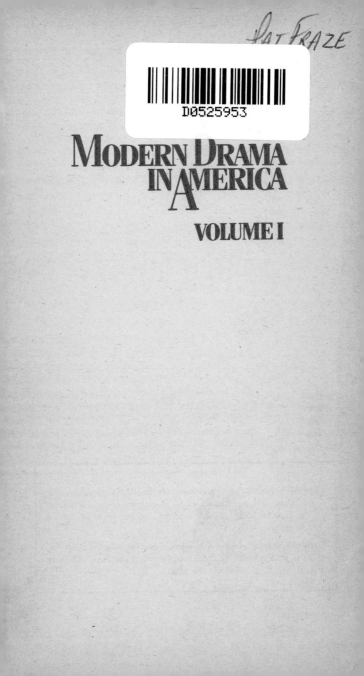

D0525953

MODERN DRAMA
IN AMERICA

VOLUME I

MODERN DRAMA IN AMERICA

VOLUME I

Realism from Provincetown to Broadway 1915-1929

edited by
**Alvin S. Kaufman
& Franklin D. Case**

WASHINGTON SQUARE PRESS
PUBLISHED BY POCKET BOOKS NEW YORK

A WASHINGTON SQUARE PRESS Original Publication

A Washington Square Press Publication of
POCKET BOOKS, a Simon & Schuster division of
GULF & WESTERN CORPORATION
1230 Avenue of the Americas, New York, N.Y. 10020

ISBN: 0-671-44673-8

First Washington Square Press printing September, 1982

10 9 8 7 6 5 4 3 2 1

WASHINGTON SQUARE PRESS, WSP and colophon are
trademarks of Simon & Schuster.

Printed in the U.S.A.

Acknowledgments

Grateful acknowledgment is made for permission to reprint the following material:

Trifles by Susan Glaspell. Reprinted by permission of DODD, MEAD & COMPANY, INC. from *Plays* by Susan Glaspell. Copyright 1920 by Dodd, Mead & Company, Inc. Copyright renewed 1948 by Susan Glaspell.

Anna Christie by Eugene O'Neill. From *The Plays of Eugene O'Neill*, by Eugene O'Neill. Copyright 1922 and renewed 1950 by Eugene O'Neill. Reprinted by permission of Random House, Inc.

The Show-Off by George Kelly. Copyright, 1922 (As a One-Act Play), by George Edward Kelly. Copyright, 1924 (Three-Act Play, Unpublished), by George Kelly. Copyright, 1924, by George Kelly. Copyright, 1949 (In Renewal), by George Edward Kelly. Copyright, 1951 (In Renewal), by George Kelly. Copyright, 1951 (In Renewal), by George Kelly. Reprinted by permission of Samuel French, Inc.

CAUTION: Professionals and amateurs are hereby warned that *The Show-Off*, being fully protected under the copyright laws of the United States of America, the British Empire, including the Dominion of Canada, and all other countries of the Copyright Union, is subject to a royalty. All rights, including professional, amateur, motion pictures, recitation, public reading, radio and television broadcasting and the rights of translation in foreign languages are strictly reserved. Amateurs may give stage production of this play upon payment of royalty of $50.00 Dollars for the first performance and $25.00 Dollars for each additional performance one week before the play is to be given to Samuel French, Inc., at 25 West 45th St., New York, N.Y. 10036, or 7623 Sunset Blvd., Hollywood, Calif., or if in Canada to Samuel French (Canada) Ltd., at 80 Richmond Street East, Toronto M5C 1P1, Canada.

Lucky Sam McCarver by Sidney Howard. Copyright 1924 by Sidney Howard; copyright 1926 by Charles Scribner's Sons; copyright renewed. Reprinted with the permission of Charles Scribner's Sons.

v

To
Dot, Mary and Becky

Contents

Preface

Over the last two generations the American drama has matured as art form and as social barometer. Since the stage has always mirrored the life and times of society, it is not surprising that the mainstream of the American dramatic tradition has been realism.

The realistic form—and realism as a concept—has changed quite radically since it was introduced to the American stage in the late nineteenth century. The first innovators were the playwrights of the "new realism," and we begin our examination of the tradition with their works. Choosing a few plays to represent the many from the period 1915 to 1929 has been difficult; however, there is general agreement in critical circles that the plays of O'Neill, Glaspell, Kelly, Howard and Green are among the most outstanding. Of course, plays by Sherwood, Rice, Barry, Anderson and Behrman could have been included, but space is an obvious limitation. We hope to look at the dramas of some of the latter group in the next volume, and we intend to trace the evolution of the American realistic drama to the present day in subsequent volumes.

We wish to express our gratitude to all those who have assisted us. Particularly we thank Dorothy Kaufman, Mary Jane Case and Peter Sander for their thoughtful reading of the notes, Parker Zellers for his encouragement, and Martha Valentine for typing the manuscript. Our special thanks to our editor, John Thornton, for his intelligent advice and keen editorial skills.

MODERN DRAMA IN AMERICA

VOLUME I

Introduction

Going to the theater may not be as popular a pastime in the United States as watching baseball or football; yet dramatic characters such as Willy Loman, Anna Christie, George and Martha, and Blanche Dubois are almost as well known as our favorite athletes. These characters created by Arthur Miller, Eugene O'Neill, Edward Albee and Tennessee Williams are significant to the American identity. They seem as "real" as any current heroes, and their stage experiences have touched the lives of most of us.

Indeed, the ability of the playwright to make the imaginary seem real is at the center of theater's magic. The playwright, of course, cannot accomplish this sleight of hand alone; it is impossible without the actor, who brings real blood and breath to the stage. Without question, it is the interaction of actor and audience that makes the theater experience possible, but it is the imagination of the playwright that establishes that experience and provides the boundaries for it.

The playwright hopes that what he envisioned in his drama will ultimately be transmitted to the audience by the performers and by the use of various theatrical devices. The manner in which these devices are employed differs from culture to culture. Through the years, theatrical communities have evolved unique stage procedures, or conventions (e.g., the use of masks, elaborate costume pieces, or codified gesture). This method of production is called *conventional* or *ritualistic;* in theater parlance, the term *presentational,* or more commonly, *nonrealistic,* is used. Best known for this style were the ancient Greeks and the Orientals. In Japan the long-surviving Noh theater is an excellent example of this type.

In the presentational theater, the audience is encouraged to remember that it is in a theater observing a series of interrelated or unrelated activities. The actor is rarely a believable character and may change roles at the drop of a hat—or a mask—and is thus akin to a circus performer. Space and objects become whatever the actor–performer intends them to be. In that sense, an actor climbing a ladder could be an astronaut entering a nose cone for a trip to the moon, or Romeo climbing to Juliet's balcony. It could be said that in this case the audience is mostly an observer, primarily involved with the activities on stage rather than with the emotions of the actor. Oftentimes members of the audience may have somewhat different perceptions of the same event.

Various other cultures, however, have presented the drama by creating the illusion of life. In theatrical terminology, this method is called *representational,* or more commonly, *realistic.* In this kind of theater the audience members are made to forget that they are in a theater in order to be transported to a particular environment by the imagination of the actor–performers. In this kind of illusion, much dependent upon scenic embellishment, the audience observes actors making believe that they are characters performing a series of related actions. In realistic theater, the audience becomes lost in the illusion and identifies with the characters through the emotions that are generated.

Theatrical practitioners observe that the contemporary theater is more fluid in the manner of production, and neither presentationalism nor representationalism is absolutely exclusive of the other except in long-enduring cultures such as the Japanese. Such a mixed means of theatrical production can be observed even as far back as the Elizabethan theater. Although very little if any scenery was used on the open platform stage where Shakespeare's plays were done in the dim afternoon light of England (with the audience being told where the scene was occurring by the words and behavior of the actors), there is good reason to believe that the actors tried very hard to create believable people.

Which of these methods, realism or nonrealism, is more successful in communicating the author's intention to the audience has been vitally debated in the American theater since 1915. We do know that no society has employed realism in its drama as pervasively as the United States.

The first playwrights to use realistic elements in their plays began by depicting indigenous characters. Scholars generally agree that Jonathan, a character in *The Contrast* (1787) written by Royall Tyler (1757–1826) and presented at the Park Theatre in New York by the American Company of Comedians, was the first of these types to tread the boards. Tyler, a New Englander himself, so deftly created Jonathan that the character became the prototype of the stage Yankee. He was played so vividly by an English actor named Thomas Wignell (1753–1802) that an acting tradition was initiated that lasted over a hundred years and kept a number of actors well employed. In creating Jonathan, Tyler and Wignell served as reporters by depicting his speech, manner, and dress so well that he was immediately recognized by the audience as a type they knew. After Jonathan appeared, he was soon followed on stage by the Negro, the Irishman, the Indian, the Jew, the Chinaman, the German, the frontiersman, the city tough, and others, each drawn with recognizable manner, speech, and dress. By 1850 most of these types had been portrayed on stage and reflected both the audience's interest in local color as well as changing American society. Thus Americans from all walks of life became a focus for the truly American drama.

Playwrights also addressed their art to activities and behavior drawn from life. For example, William Dunlap (1766–1839), wishing to take his audience on a trip from New York City in his play *A Trip to Niagara*, accomplished this feat by using a device called a diorama that allowed 25,000 square feet of painted canvas rolled onto a large spool to be fed to another spool across the stage, much like film in a camera. As the play's many scenes unfolded, the audience enjoyed the panoramic scenery as well as the farcical play itself, which was populated with a large number of character types who behaved in a manner the audience understood and appreciated.

Thus a kind of superficial realism was achieved, but the ability of the playwright to serve as an accurate reporter was inhibited by his being locked into creating types demanded by his audience. Tradition would not permit a change in playwriting, thus rendering the form moribund. When Tyler wrote *The Contrast,* he was imitating a sentimental version of Sheridan's *School for Scandal*. This bourgeoise genre was the rage of the London stage, and the American theater slavishly imitated English and European forms. The core of the sentimental genre was the concept of poetic justice—that good should be rewarded and evil punished (which is exactly what happens in *The Contrast*). The moral tone was in keeping with Protestant thought, an emerging transcendentalism, and American optimism. Nurturing the concept of poetic justice, William Dunlap, often referred to as the father of American drama and a moralist himself, introduced plays he adapted from Continental playwrights. Dunlap, however, was very adept at changing plot details and characters to satisfy his American audience. David Grimsted, in his striking book *Melodrama Unveiled* (1968), describes this type of drama:

> The person who went to see an early melodrama witnessed the stratagems of the villain, the innocence of the young maiden, the courage of her true love, the kindness of her old and well loved father, and the comic antics of some rustic or servant types. The plot almost invariably centered on the efforts of the villain to rob the girl of her virtue, her fortune or both, and his finally being foiled by Providence and the exertions of the hero. Into the course of these events some full-scaled spectacle was worked, possibly a huge procession of festivity, a thrilling fight or escape, or some tremendous cataclysm, either natural or man made. Such stage effects . . . were the most striking features of these plays. All the while the orchestra played appropriate background music to heighten the suspense in periods of danger and sweeten the sentiment in moments of lull.

As a consequence of this influence, conventional playwriting called for stereotypes based on American characters, a predictable plot with much suspense, action that ended happily, and a theme that supported the morals of the majority of society. Under these circumstances, playwrights were not able to be objective reporters; still, as stage technology improved, at least more lifelike activities could be presented on the stage. As the years passed, imitators of the melodramatic convention, using technology, could create stage catastrophes with such realism that audiences were spellbound. For example, part of the success of two famous melodramas, *Uncle Tom's Cabin* (1858) and *The Octoroon* (1859), derived from spectacular scenes such as Eliza's crossing the ice, and the inclusion of a murder, a suicide, and a ship's burning within a single play. Augustin Daly (1838–1899), producer, director, and author of *Under the Gaslight* (1867), brought sensational realism to its zenith when he had a train roar across the stage and nearly mash its victim into a grisly stew to the terror and delight of the audience.

The Civil War cast a chilling shadow upon the warm sunscape of American optimism. With so much death and destruction striking nearly every part of American life, a cynicism soon became apparent. Older established practitioners such as Augustin Daly tried innovations. In 1871 he adapted and presented the play *Divorce,* based on Anthony Trollope's novel *He Knew He Was Right.* He cleverly Americanized the story by making considerable changes in plot and characters. The dramatic action revealed a theme that emphasized that the only happy marriages are those based on enduring forgiveness. He depicted marriage as a permanent relationship between equals. In order to make his dramatic purpose clear, he planted a modern woman within the undergrowth of conventional melodramatic plot. Played with great verve by Fanny Davenport (1850–1898), the play created a sensation and achieved the longest and most successful run of any play previously produced in New York. Daly was also responsible for introducing Bronson Howard's first play, *Saratoga* (1870).

The rise of Howard and others is coincidental with "the rise of Pinero and Jones . . . with the sudden spread of continental influence . . . over the English-speaking stage," commented the critic Walter Prichard Eaton in 1908. As in the time of Dunlap, Americans based their plays on French and English models, particularly *la pièce bien faite,* "the well-made play," an ingenious theatrical contrivance invented by the Frenchman, Eugène Scribe (1791–1861). Allardyce Nicoll, in his informative book *World Drama* (1950), provides an incisive comment on Scribe's technique:

Being a practicing writer for the theater, Scribe realized that a popular audience wants, in the first instance, a vividly told dramatic tale; he realized, too, that many of the devices used in the telling of theatrical tales in the past no longer suited the changed stages of his time; and he set for himself the task of devising a formula by which narratives of all kinds—melodramatic, comic and farcical—could, with a minimum of effort, be rendered appealing when presented on the boards (p. 488).

And how different was "the well-made play" from the melodrama? It was a question of technique: clear exposition of situation and characters; careful preparation for future events; unexpected but logical reversals; continuing and mounting suspense; all leading to an obligatory scene in which the opposing forces reach the highest point of conflict, and a logical and believable resolution ensues. Scribe's plays also were topical, which suited the growing French middle class. He, however, was not interested in great theatrical art; he was a commercial hack who during his career wrote over four hundred plays. Versions of Scribe's plays and those of his disciple, Victorian Sardou, were very popular in New York.

In England, Tom Robertson (1829–1871) reflected Scribe's accomplishment in France; however, as Nicoll points out, "he not only set forth to write plays in which he tried to reflect the ways of common life; he endeavored to provide for those plays such settings and such interpretation as fitted their lines." Lester Wallack (1820–1888), an important actor–manager, introduced Robertson's plays to America in 1866. George C. D. Odell, in his monumental history of the New York theater, *Annals of the New York Stage* (1936), comments:

> The influence of T. W. Robertson became nearly as great on the American stage as on the English stage. The quiet, refined character of his plays . . . the exquisite home-like settings involved, the naturalness of the dialogue and action, revolutionized the method of writing, acting and setting comedy. (Vol. VIII, p. 130)

Although English playwrights Arthur Wing Pinero (1855–1934) and Henry Arthur Jones (1851–1929) both surpassed Robertson in dramaturgy and depth of thought, their plays did not appear in the United States until the 1890s. It is important to record that Robertson, to some degree, was a thematic writer. His plays were structured and the characters developed about an idea that he had generated from observing society. New figures emerged in the theater who were concerned with the changing attitudes: Bronson Howard (1842–1908); James A. Herne (1839–1901); David Belasco (1853–1931); Edward Harrigan (1845–1911). It is always difficult and somewhat problematic to state what the influence of one writer is on another. We do know, however, that Scribe and Robertson had *some* effect on our stage, and the consequences were an early form of the realistic drama, best revealed in the plays of Bronson Howard.

Bronson Howard, often called the dean of nineteenth-century American playwrights, was the most successful and preeminent dramatist of the age. He made half a million dollars from the production of one of his plays, *The Henrietta,* and he was the first person to support himself totally from playwriting. In that sense, he is our first professional dramatist. His reputation is based on four plays: *The Banker's Daughter* (1878); *Young Mrs. Winthrop* (1882); *The Henrietta* (1887); and *Shenandoah* (1888). Brander Matthews (1852–1929) of Columbia University, first professor to hold a chair in dramatic literature in the United States, noted in a memorial tribute in 1908 that:

it was Bronson Howard who, first of all American playwrights, attained to the compact simplicity and the straightforward directness which this new cosmopolitan formula demands. . . . He knew that the art of the theater, like every other art, can live only by the conventions which allow it to depart from the mere facts of life. . . . Perhaps he first attained his larger ambition in "Young Mrs. Winthrop," to satisfy it more completely in "The Henrietta," which remains today his finest work, the truest and the deepest. Here, indeed, in contradiction to the generally accepted theory that the novel is constantly in advance of the drama in its investigations of society, the dramatist presented a picture of American life and character sharper in outline than any which had then been achieved by any novelist, excepting the author of "Silas Lapham." (*In Memoriam, Bronson Howard* [1910], pp. 34–49)

Accepting the fact that Matthews exaggerated the significance of Howard's contribution, there is enough truth in his accolade to recognize Howard as the first significant realist.

In three different plays, he went beyond the facts by attempting to closely observe two institutions in American society—marriage and business. He poured them into the crucible of his drama, and for the 1880s scorched both rather well. He did use the believable actions of Robertson, and his characters at least cracked the mold of melodrama. In looking back at his work today, the flaws are only too obvious. He still relied on the aside and the soliloquy, devices from the old melodrama, and although he followed Scribe and Robertson in plot methodology, he relied far too heavily on plot. His plays are monumental pieces of carefully organized incident and complication, designed to seem real but obviously ponderous in their invention. A colleague said that "he seldom put pen to paper for the first three months of preparing a play." He had a system of charts drawn upon four-by-six-inch cards, and on each of these cards was elaborated a series of squares much like a chessboard, each card representing a scene from a play. Upon these little chessboards, he worked his characters until each knew his place. At this point dialogue could begin and usually took two years to complete. He was also burdened by current morality. In 1886, at the peak of his career, he was invited by the Shakespere [sic] Club of Harvard University to talk to its members. In his speech Howard observed:

A dramatist should deal, so far as possible, with subjects of universal interest, instead of with such as appeal strongly to part of the audience only . . . a play must be in one way or another "satisfactory" to the audience. This word has a meaning which varies in different countries, and even in different parts of the same country; but whatever audience you are writing for, your work must be "satisfactory" to it. In England and America, the death of a pure woman on the stage is not "satisfactory" except when the play rises to the dignity of tragedy. The death in an ordinary play of a woman who is not pure . . . is perfectly satisfactory, for the reason that it is inevitable. . . . The wife who has once taken the step from purity to impurity can never re-instate herself in the world of art on this side of the grave. . . . (*In Memoriam, Bronson Howard*, pp. 99–100)

Convention, both on stage and off, constricted Howard in his attempt to be a realistic observer and commentator, but he was the first playwright of major stature to make the attempt.

Of all the writers of the period, none were more realistic than William Dean Howells (1837–1920) and Mark Twain (1835–1910), both of whom desperately wanted to be successful playwrights. Though neither realized his desire, Twain did make over seventy thousand dollars from his play *Colonel Sellers,* a contrived farce based on his novel *The Gilded Age,* and Howells wrote at least thirty-six plays, one of which, *A Counterfeit Presentment* (1877), had minimal success. Howells' characters, structure, and diction, that is, his dramaturgy, were generally ahead of anything yet written by an American. His characters spoke simply and honestly, if somewhat excessively; there were no moments of shattering excitement; he abandoned the aside and the soliloquy. His writing for the stage paralleled that of his novels, revealing him to be a careful and minute observer of life. However, as one contemporary critic, G. H. Badger, stated: "Mr. Howells holds himself too far aloof from the real nerve and fiber of our national life—the middle industrious class. His world is too largely that world of gentlemen and ladies of leisure."

James A. Herne has been called the American Ibsen by his biographer, John Perry. Like Ibsen he was an astute, pragmatic man of the theater. Unlike Ibsen, he had a brilliant career as an actor as well as a playwright. After his marriage in 1878 to Katherine Corcoran, one of the most talented and lovely actresses of the day, he wrote a series of plays, with marvelous leading roles for his wife and himself, that entitles him to be ranked as America's pioneer playwright of the nineteenth century. Much of his reputation is based on the play *Margaret Fleming;* however, he wrote three other plays that secured his reputation and brought him a considerable fortune. They were *Drifting Apart* (1888), *Shore Acres* (1892), and *The Reverend Griffith Davenport* (1899). Productions of *Shore Acres* netted a million dollars.

He was employed as an actor in 1859 and immediately changed his name from James A'Herne. He liked playing character roles and played them throughout his career. He stated some years later that the roles he enjoyed playing early in his career were the ones drawn from the novels of Dickens. He intimated that those roles gave him an understanding of everyday life. David Belasco, an early colleague, said that Herne's portrayal of Rip in *Rip Van Winkle* was superior to that of Joe Jefferson, a noted actor. "Jefferson was never the Dutchman; he was the Yankee personating the Dutchman. But James A. Herne's Rip was the real thing." In 1874, with a good offer from Tom Maguire, impresario of San Francisco theater, he went to California. It was a propitious move. He became the leading actor of the company, as well as its stage manager, responsible for directing and managing the productions. More importantly, it was there he met and married "K.C.," as Katherine was called, and in 1874 started his collaboration with David Belasco, a tremendously ambitious and clever man who at age twenty-one had also just joined the company as an actor and assistant to Herne. For the next five years they worked together intimately as colleagues and friends, and in 1879 they collaborated in the writing and production of a play entitled *Chums*, which was almost immediately revised and called *Hearts of Oak*. From the later works of both men it is reasonable to conclude that Herne did most of the writing and Belasco contributed theatrical effect. The latter demonstrated an early genius for inventing and developing realistic bits of action in order to create a superficial illusion of life on stage. For the *Hearts of Oak* production, he used, among other things, real water for rain and a working gristmill, and at one point he had a cat cross the stage, stretch, then drink a saucer of milk.

Hearts of Oak was a melodrama, albeit an unconventional one. If Howard cracked the mold for the portrayal of character on our stage, Herne, began to break it in 1879. He not only avoided using the stereotypical hero or villain, but he often inserted language in the local idiom. Nothing quite like it had been heard on the stage; it was genuine American speech. By 1892 when Herne wrote and produced *Shore Acres*, he had perfected the use of colloquial dialogue. He also had come to despise the melodrama. John Perry reports in his biography:

Herne was caught between two forces: the old popular school of Boucicault and his growing conviction that drama should truthfully mirror the lifestyle of common people. But Gilded Age audiences loved gilded gibberish. They loved romance. They loved oratory. They loved pasteboard plays that didn't make intellectual demands. Herne later wrote: "Seriously, melodrama is valueless to the progress of dramatic art. Seen under the analytical microscope, it is false to almost every aspect and color of life, and eternally comic to the judicious, in its absurdities of perspective and proportion, its grotesqueries of calcium and characterization. Like crimps and crinolines, or the difficult stock tie of our periwig pated grandparents, the melodrama has outlived its day of usefulness." (*James A. Herne, The American Ibsen* [1978], p. 60)

By 1890 Herne had become acquainted with William Dean Howells and had formed a close friendship with another major writer and advanced thinker, Hamlin Garland. All three were living in Boston, which at that time was the Mecca of the literary world in the United States and where Herne recently had produced *Drifting Apart*. Garland was just beginning his career but already had established himself with the leaders of the intellectual community. After seeing *Drifting Apart*, he made it his business to meet Herne; at this time their profitable association began. They went to see European plays by Ibsen, Zola, Sudermann, Tolstoy, Turgenev, and others. Garland introduced Herne to the ideas of Charles Darwin and Herbert Spencer, who were the gods of truth so far as the young novelist was concerned. From their discussions, from his own feelings and observations about American society, and from his relationship with his wife, Herne drew the inspiration for *Margaret Fleming*. The theme was the double standard in marriage, a phenomenon only too obvious to any observer of the times. The idea for the play and his approach to it had been in his mind for some time and was apparent in his earlier plays. The intercourse with Garland sharpened his intuitive abilities. The play was conceived, in terms of action, story, theme, subject, and diction to reveal the truth about many upper-class marriages. His objective was an honest look at man's behavior that would maintain the integrity of artistic expression. He also tried to reject all the old formulas: the use of stereotypes; the big claptrap scenes, and the comfortable, happy endings. For years, as Edith Wharton commented, "our audience wanted to be harrowed (and even slightly shocked) from eight until ten-thirty and then consoled and re-assured before eleven." With *Margaret Fleming,* Herne not only shocked the audience, he mortified and disturbed them. The script itself was so upsetting to theatrical producers that Herne finally in desperation produced, directed, and mounted a production himself that opened in Lynn, Massachusetts, July 4, 1890. According to John Perry, this brief run was warmly received by a "handful of followers, including Garland, another author critic—Thomas Sargent, and a 'party of news and dramatic writers from New York and Boston dailies.'" Encouraged by that response and further supported by Howells and Garland, Herne brought his production to Boston's Chickering Hall about a year later. The storm of protest started. A subsequent run of the play in Boston produced the same result, and a brief run in New York in 1892, produced by a member of the Theatrical Syndicate, created enough furor to have the play withdrawn.

Hamlin Garland's review of the first production appeared in the *Boston Evening Transcript* on July 8, 1890, in which the critic recapitulated the entire plot along with warm praise for the production and performers. The review is of particular importance because all manuscripts of the play have been lost in a fire. The extant version that has been published resembles the play as described by Garland. Between 1890 and 1898, particularly after the debacle in New York, Herne revised the play to make it more acceptable to audiences. Thus today we have a watered-down version of his original potent assault. The major difference is in the ending of the play. In the later version the ailing Margaret, with certain reservations, accepts her philandering husband once again as a mate; the impression is given that their marriage eventually will recover. In the original, Margaret, now blind, rejects her husband, and there seems to be no chance for reconciliation. Both versions include the scene in which Margaret commences to nurse the bastard child of her husband's indiscretion. Even though William Dean Howells objected to a certain "preachiness" in *Margaret Fleming,* he believed that Herne had fulfilled the highest mission of the artist, which was to reveal a moral truth through a mirroring of life on the stage.

Herne's contribution to the development of realism and to the advancement of theatrical art is inestimable. In addition to the melding of dramaturgy with theme, he is the first U.S. dramatist to use naturalistic method, which in a sense is an extension of realism. One of the maxims of the well-made-play form, which was used by both Ibsen and Herne, is the revelation of cause and effect. In *Margaret Fleming* the central figure is suffering from glaucoma and her husband is warned that any shock could produce blindness. In the original version, Margaret starts going blind when she realizes that her husband has been both cruel and unfaithful. The young woman who bears the illegitimate child is not blamed for the indiscretion, for what can be expected from someone living a life of poverty? Philip, Margaret's husband, is blamed because being an educated, responsible married man, he should have had higher standards of conduct. As banal as that may seem today, it was not so then. Today we know that that perception of reality is not accurate; at that time, as Hamlin Garland thought, determinism was law.

Herne also realized that the intimacy of action in *Margaret Fleming* demanded the intimacy of a smaller theater than the usual large houses of the time. When he found a theater in Lynn, Massachusetts, for the first showing of the play, he cleverly disguised its spaciousness and for later performances used the relatively small Chickering Hall in Boston. Upon gathering support for his private production of the play, and with Garland's advice and assistance, he instituted a subscription system. As a direct consequence of the private production, Garland, Howells, and others influenced by Antoine's Théâtre Libre in Paris, started a little theater called The First Independent Theater, in Boston in 1892. The Théâtre Libre, founded in 1887 by André Antoine (1858–1943) for the purpose of presenting naturalistic plays free from commercialism, is the theater that germinated the little-theater movement. The First Independent Theater published a prospectus (of the sort later known as manifestoes):

The objects of the Association are first and in general to encourage truth and progress in American Dramatic Art. Second, and specifically, to secure and maintain a stage whereon the best and most unconventional studies of modern life and distinctly American life, may get a proper hearing.

They were attempting to build an institution which would be independent of the commercial theater. The formation of this theater predated the little-theater movement by more than a decade. Herne's play was the motivating force.

Near the end of his career, Herne published an essay entitled "Art for Truth's Sake." It is one of the most significant statements about dramatic art published in this country during the nineteenth century:

> It is generally held that the province of the drama is to amuse. I claim that it has a higher purpose—that its mission is to interest and instruct. It should not preach objectively, but it should teach subjectively; and so I stand for truth in the drama, because it is elemental, it gets to the bottom of a question. It strikes at unequal standards and unjust systems. It is as unyielding as it is honest. It is as tender as it is inflexible. It has supreme faith in man. It believes that that which was good in the beginning cannot be bad at the end. It sets forth clearly that the concern of one is the concern of all. It stands for the higher development and thus the individual liberty of the human race. (*Arena,* Vol. XVII, pp. 370)

Other writers of this era had also experimented with realistic techniques. Edward Harrigan particularly had been successful in bringing to the stage the city types in his famous series of plays about the Mulligan Guard (1879–84).* Denman Thompson (1833–1911) in 1886 produced *The Old Homestead,* which was, according to Odell, "the outstanding rural drama of the ages and one of the most successful plays of all time. . . . The realistic farm scenes . . . all this material, carefully adjusted to audiences that like the simple and the good" (*Annals of the New York Stage,* Vol. XIII, p. 155). The critic Howard Taubman observed in his book *The Making of the American Theater* (1965):

> Charles Hoyt, who served as a drama and music critic as well as that new thing, a columnist, on the Boston Post,

---

*After the Civil War, small militia groups were formed, indigenous to their neighborhoods. Harrigan, a famous vaudeville performer, influenced by this, created the comic character Mulligan and developed a fictional guard unit about him which become the core for a series of farcical plays.

dealt with everyday scenes and people in a series of farces. . . . His *A Trip to Chinatown* ran at the Madison Square Theater for 650 performances in 1891, 1892 and 1893. (P. 111)

But none of these was able to bring to the stage the totality of the realistic experience that Herne did. Many other contemporary writers followed Herne's example: William Gillette (1855–1937) in *Secret Service* (1895) made action and acting on the stage very believable; Augustus Thomas (1857–1934) experimented with determinism in *The Witching Hour* (1907); Langdon Mitchell (1862–1933) painted realistic, sophisticated people in his incisive and clever *The New York Idea* (1906); the prolific Clyde Fitch (1865–1909) toyed with realistic subjects, themes, and characters in *The Girl with the Green Eyes* (1902) and *The Truth* (1906); William Vaughn Moody (1869–1910), a professor of literature at Harvard, received high acclaim for *The Great Divide* (1906) in which he explored the effect of environment on morals and human behavior; Eugene Walter (1874–1941) in 1908 set New York society on its ear by depicting the life of "a woman of easy virtue" in *The Easiest Way* and for the first time used the word *damn* on the American stage; Rachel Crothers (1878–1958), one of the few successful women playwrights, explored with great objectivity the role of the male and female in marriage in *He and She* (1911); Edward Sheldon (1886–1946) with burning passion exposed injustice in society with *The Nigger* (1909) and *The Boss* (1911). All of these made significant contributions to the realistic play, although it was a case of refining what Herne had already accomplished.

The work of a number of innovative theatrical technicians also helped pave the road to realism. Spectacular realistic effects that were achieved in the melodrama have been mentioned previously. As the technology advanced from painted wings and drops to moving dioramas and box sets, as lighting became more sophisticated with the use of gas and later of electricity, and with Steele MacKaye's invention of the movable stage—permitting entire sets with actors to be changed in forty seconds—it became possible for the stage to approximate someone's parlor or kitchen. David Belasco, who had used the cat in *Hearts of Oak*, in 1909 purchased an entire boarding house and had it rebuilt on the stage of one of his theaters for the final act of Walter's *The Easiest Way*. At another time he had a Childs restaurant duplicated for his production of *The Governor's Lady* (1914). It was also Belasco who conceived of the lighting effects in *Madame Butterfly* (1900), which allowed the audience to believe they were seeing night turn to sunrise. By 1915 a theatergoer in New York, and occasionally in rural America, could be so totally transported by the illusion of reality that had been created by the playwright, actor, and scene technician that he could swear that he was peeping and eavesdropping on the lives of his neighbors. However, that experience would still have been the rare exception. More often, he saw his old friends, the melodramatic characters, dressed in different clothes and occupying different quarters. Actually only the outward appearances had changed.

There were several reasons why "truth," as interpreted by Howells and Herne, was resisted by the theater. First of all, America prior to 1915 was still a very complacent society, and in the theater audiences were not willing to face the "truth." Samuel Johnson observed many years ago, "The stage but echoes back the public voice. / The drama's laws the drama's patrons give, / For we that live to please, must please to live." As a result, theatrical productions are often a compromise between what the playwright and the production team want to do, and what the public will accept. Equally often a compromise has been made between the playwright's intention and what actors and directors believe to be effective theater. The very fact that theater is a joint enterprise requiring cooperation and compromise by a number of dynamic and talented personalities creates tension. Author and wit Truman Capote, while adapting his story *Breakfast at Tiffany's* for the musical theater, commented, "in the theater one is a molecule that has to be joined to other molecules to produce a living, breathing thing. I've done it, but I don't really accept it. That's why I'm not partial to the theater. I just don't function well in team sports."

However, the longest battle that has been waged in the theater has been between art and commerce. The theater has been seen by a large number of people as an opportunity for making money, in short, as a business. Others have idealized it and viewed it as a pure art form. The history of the American theater since 1890 is the story of these two conflicting forces, and between them realism became a whipping boy.

Prior to 1860 management of theatrical ventures was in the hands of theater people, although it was not unusual for the company and/or the physical theater to be supported by local businessmen or financiers. Nevertheless, it was the actor–manager who determined what plays would be produced, who would be in the company, how much money would be spent on advertising and scenery, and so forth. In short, the success or failure of the company depended on the artistic and business acumen of the individual who was the company's leading actor.

In the eighteenth century each actor owned shares in the company, called stocks, and the amount of money an actor made depended on the number of shares he owned plus the success of the company's box office. These companies were known as stock companies, and almost every community of any size could boast the existence of its own producing enterprise. Actors were hired for an entire season, and their employment often depended on their mastery of a number of roles that could be quickly performed on demand. The companies worked on a repertory basis, usually with a different play each night, staying of course within the confines of the plays and roles the group had mastered. Only occasionally was a new play introduced into the repertoire.

By 1800, wages were substituted for shares, the actor–manager determining salaries actually based on the actor's audience-drawing power. In addition to wages, the major actors were allowed benefit performances, in which they presented their most popular roles and received the major portion of those nights' gates. The actor–manager also often engaged "stars" who were on tour, who in the early days of the American theater were almost always English. Depending upon the size of the community, the star performed for a night—or a week—in his most outstanding roles, many of which were from the plays of Shakespeare. As a result, the long run was not really possible within the confines of the stock company. The repertoire of most companies was standardized, and few new plays were introduced. This practice inhibited playwriting in the United States for a number of years until important actors began to look for new roles. Edwin Forrest (1806–1872), the first native-born actor to achieve fame on the stage offered prizes for plays by American writers, and the new plays were integrated with the standard repertoire.

After the Civil War and as a direct consequence of technological advancement, the management and composition of theatrical companies began to change. A network of rails had been developed in the eastern United States to expedite the shipment of war materials; by 1869 even a transcontinental line was in existence. As the eastern cities, New York particularly, became more populated and influential, theatrical activity flourished, and the "combination companies" were born. These companies were established by actor–managers or playwrights (Dion Boucicault [1820–1890], an Irishman who spent many years in the American theater, is a good example. He had a tremendous impact on our drama, theatrical performance, and management.) to present on tour or in residence, a single play. Jack Poggi has stated in his book *Theatre in America* (1968), "By the 1876–77 season there were nearly a hundred combinations on the road; the high point was probably reached in December, 1904, when 420 companies were touring" (pp. 5–6). In later years the combination company became known as the road company. In 1882–83 there were fourteen companies on the road playing Steele MacKaye's *Hazel Kirke*. One effect was the inevitable dissolution of the stock company. Poggi maintains they "were gradually forced out of the theaters. In the season 1871–72 there were fifty permanent stock companies in the larger cities; in 1880 there were only seven or eight" (p. 7). The result was that by 1890 the entire theatrical scene had changed. New York had become the center of the theatrical world in America. The plays that were successful there were duplicated with different casts and scenery and shipped around the country. Actors were hired on a "run-of-the-show contract," which meant that their security depended on one play, and if it closed in rural Iowa, that is where they were left to make their own way back to New York. The hundreds, if not thousands, of theater buildings in existence simply became touring houses for the itinerant companies. The local managers in time became booking agents. It was not long before astute businessmen (some historians have called them financial speculators) saw an opportunity for tremendous profits. Circuits were soon established, and by 1890, as Poggi indicates:

> two agencies controlled a large percentage of the theaters in the country. The firm of A. L. Erlanger and Marc Klaw owned or leased a good number of theaters in important cities and had exclusive booking rights to about two hundred others, mostly one night stands in the Southeast. Charles Forhman, though more famous as a producer, owned several theaters and (in an informal partnership with Al Hayman) ran a booking agency that controlled about three hundred theaters in the West. In 1896, when Klaw and Erlanger joined forces with Forhman and Hayman, and with S. F. Nixon and J. F. Zimmerman—a pair of theater owners who were in control of Philadelphia and surrounding territory—the groundwork was laid for monopoly. . . . (Poggi, *Theatre in America*, p. 10)

The monopoly became known as the Theatrical Syndicate. Although opposition to the Syndicate was vociferous, the only real competition that surfaced was from three brothers, the Shuberts, who quickly developed their own organization. By 1907 the Syndicate and the Shuberts, after a brief period of fierce strife, signed a truce temporarily merging the two organizations. The peace did not last long, and the battles continued. Nevertheless, the theater was now in the absolute control of a few businessmen who determined what plays would be produced, where they would be toured, what actors and actresses would be hired, what theaters would be used, and, therefore, what American audiences would see. The commercial interests had clearly won the first phase of the war.

The result was that audiences saw a great deal of popular entertainment in a number of new theaters. Productions increased in New York from 87 in 1900 to 162 in 1912. By that time, Broadway could boast the existence of forty-five houses for the production of stage shows, which was an increase of about fifteen theaters in a decade and a half. The number of people entering the theatrical profession also increased dramatically. It has been estimated that there were five thousand actors who were called professionals in 1880. By 1912 the *New York Dramatic Mirror* listed over fifteen thousand actors and actresses in the profession. Actually there were many more.

Under the control of the Syndicate and the Shuberts, the actors were treated like pieces of baggage and scenery. Actors were required to undergo long periods of rehearsals without pay, and if their play closed prior to opening, they received no compensation. Actors even had to pay for their own costumes, and extra matinees were added without additional pay. In 1913, as reported by *New York Times* critic Brooks Atkinson in his book *Broadway* (1970), Actors Equity was organized, "for the express purpose of getting the producers to sign a standard contract with minimum pay and basic safeguards against exploitation of actors" (p. 184). Unfortunately, at that time the actors had minimal power for bargaining effectively.

Some actors had other concerns: Minnie Maddern Fiske (1865–1932), for example. She was deeply disturbed by what commercialism had done to the great companies of actors that had existed prior to 1890, best exemplified by the ones maintained by Lester Wallack, Augustin Daly, and A. M. Palmer. Thus, Mrs. Fiske, with her husband, a New York publisher and part-time producer, established her own company in competition with the Syndicate, for whom she refused to work. For six years she kept the ensemble together and alive in spite of constant threats and taunts from the commercial managers. Mrs. Fiske was one of the greatest actresses of the American theater; from the age of three until shortly before her death, she appeared regularly on the stage. She was one of the first performers to play Ibsen, for she was intuitively a naturalistic actress. From 1893 she was a constant champion for realism.

While the New York theaters were burgeoning, all was not well on the road. After 1904 the number of touring companies steadily dwindled. Competition was developing from an advancing technology; the motion-picture camera had an immediate effect on mass-market entertainment. Whereas live entertainers had never had any competition— although there had always been a keen rivalry between the legitimate stage and what was considered "show biz"— suddenly a gadget threatened their very existence.

Thus, just as World War I was underway, the stage was set for a major upheaval in American theater and drama. The first signs of change came from the hinterlands. Already mentioned was the formation of the First Independent Theater in Boston in 1892 as a result of Herne's private production of *Margaret Fleming*. By 1912 the establishment of small independent theaters around the country was foreshadowing a major revolt. This became known as the Little-Theater movement. As Oliver Sayler put it:

> dissatisfaction with the established theater is the cornerstone: revolt—especially communities distant from New York—from the infrequency and inadequacy of travelling companies. . . . The Little Theater was to be an art theater, the utter pole of the commercial stage in financial organization, in plays chosen, and in the manner of presenting and interpreting those plays. It was to set for itself a difficult, impersonal and all but unattainable ideal under which the theater was to be rigorously self-critical as any of the other arts. It would subsist by endowment or, if its independence were sufficiently guaranteed, by subscription. . . . The Chicago Little Theater, under Maurice Browne, professed many of these aims. Founded in 1912 and housed in a nook in the Fine Arts Building seating less than a hundred, it set out to create "a new plastic and rhythmic drama in America." (Oliver Sayler, *Our American Theater* [1923], pp. 114–16)

Other Little Theaters followed immediately in the path being blazed in Chicago—The Philadelphia Little Theater, The Toy Theater in Boston, The Indianapolis Little Theater. Generally, the noncommercial theater movement mushroomed. Between 1912 and 1929 over a thousand such institutions were founded across the country—community theaters, university theaters, rural theaters, settlement-house theaters, and so on. In almost all of these theaters an important emphasis was placed on the manner of presenting plays.

Even prior to the outgrowth of the Little Theaters, other opposition emerged to combat commercialism. In 1910 in Evanston, Illinois, the Drama League of America was founded to encourage the production of good drama and discourage the bad. The organization sponsored the publication of *The Drama,* a quarterly review containing critical and informative articles about theater.

Other experiments developed. One in particular was

fostered by a group of millionaires. Thirty of them each contributed $35,000 for the construction of the New Theater, a large and magnificently equipped plant on Central Park West that opened in 1909. The theater was under the direction of Winthrop Ames, who later opened his own Little Theater in New York. The business manager was one of the three Shubert brothers, Lee, a fact that provides some evidence to support the proposition that the commercial managers did have some artistic standards. They were not totally crass exploiters. (It was Abe Erlanger who brought Herne's *Margaret Fleming* to New York, albeit for a very short run. Charles Frohman spent great sums of money sponsoring artistic enterprises.) The New Theater failed after one season. It was simply too costly a venture, and it catered only to the wealthy and elite.

The revolutionaries who had the greatest impact on commercialism, and who launched the most successful opposition, lived "far" from Central Park West. Some of them resided among the teeming millions of immigrants in lower Manhattan; others lived in Greenwich Village, then often known as Bohemia. They all had one thing in common: they were part of a generation that was turning its back on the past, part of a greater revolution seething in American society, and nowhere was the upheaval more apparent than in the arts:

> It was a restless time. Values were being questioned; dozens of new schools and movements in art were springing up. Cubism was fighting it out with Futurism, and everybody wrote free verse. *The Little Review* was printing "Ulysses" in installments, Gertrude Stein had discovered a new language, the old *Masses* was blazing away at injustice, *The New Republic* was in the first flush of its youth, Stieglitz was making magic with the camera. The International Exhibition had brought modern art to America, and a set of new textbooks had appeared: "Sister Carrie," "The Harbor," "The Spoon River Anthology." (Helen Deutsch and Stella Hannau, *The Provincetown, A Story of a Theater* [1931], p. 5)

During the years 1913–15 in Greenwich Village, many young artists, writers, journalists, lawyers, and others, met at the Liberal Club and the Washington Square Book Store.

The latter was owned by Albert and Charles Boni, who later became successful publishers. The book shop and club were located next door to each other on MacDougal Street. In his autobiography, *The Magic Curtain* (1951), Lawrence Langner tells of the club and its atmosphere:

> The Club itself occupied two large parlors and a sunroom on the first floor, with high ceilings, open fireplaces and magnificent mahogany portals. The rooms were sparsely furnished, the walls covered with paintings of the "art moderne" type, and the current interest in ragtime, which was just being spoken of as a new American art, was represented by an old weather-beaten electric piano that was made to hammer out the popular music of the day whenever the assembled male and female club members felt like publicly hugging one another in what was then known as "modern dancing." The interest displayed by the boys and girls of the group in one another, as demonstrated by the intimacy of their rhythmic embraces, belied the Club's somewhat ostentatious motto, which appeared in quotations on all its literature, that it was "A Meeting Place for Those Interested in New Ideas."

> But even in this new dancing there was, so to speak, a spirit of revolt against the older more formal dances . . . in which the women, encased in stiff corsets, were held away at arms' length by the men, as though to avoid moral contamination by bodily contact. As you clutched your feminine partner and led her through the crowded dance floor at the Club, you felt you were doing something for the progress of humanity, as well as for yourself and, in some cases, for her. Indeed, despite the freedom of thought and the removal of the barriers between the sexes which marked this particular period of our social history, the morals of the young people were stricter than those of thousands who attend country clubs and dance halls throughout the country today. The attitude of young people toward sex was in the nature of a crusade. . . . (Pp. 67–68)

Crusades were waged on many fronts. Frequent visitors and members of the Liberal Club included: Alfred Kreymborg, Vachel Lindsay, Edna St. Vincent Millay, Upton Sinclair, Max Eastman, John Reed, Hutchins Hapgood, Neith Boyce, Floyd Dell, Sinclair Lewis, Susan Glaspell, Inez Haynes, Margalo Gillmore, Art Young, Charles Demuth, Jo Davidson, Lincoln Steffens, Harry Weinberger, Harry Scherman, Gilbert Seldes, Frank Shay, Harold Stearns, George Cram Cook, Helen Westley, and many others. Some of the club members were theater enthusiasts, and from time to time they presented readings of plays. In 1915 and 1916, two theatrical groups were formed from the ranks of the Liberal Club and their friends. The first one was called the Washington Square Players, from its association with the Washington Square Book Store, and the second was known as the Provincetown Players, because it originated on Cape Cod. The founding members of the Washington Square Players included Lawrence Langner, Albert Boni, Ida Rauh, Edward Goodman, Philip Moeller, and Helen Westley. They rented the Band Box Theater on East Fifty-seventh Street off Third Avenue, and immediately published a manifesto:

> . . . The Washington Square Players believe that a higher standard can be reached only as the outcome of experiment and initiative . . . we believe that hard work and perseverance, coupled with ability and the absence of purely commercial considerations, may result in the birth and healthy growth of an artistic theater in this country. . . . We have only one policy in regard to the plays which we will produce—they must have artistic merit. Preference will be given to American plays, but we shall also include in our repertory the works of well-known European authors which have been ignored by the commercial managers. Though not organized for purposes of profit, we are not endowed. Money alone has never produced an artistic theater. We are going to defray the expenses of our productions by the sale of tickets and subscriptions. Believing in democracy in the theater, we have fixed the charge for admission at 50 cents. . . . (Langner, *Magic Curtain*, pp. 94–95)

They concluded by inviting the public to subscribe for ten tickets at five dollars, or to join them as participants in the venture. The first series, all one-act plays and a pantomime, was presented on February 19, 1915. The critic Walter

Prichard Eaton, who was there, described the night's entertainment:

> What happened was surprise, not only to the critics, but to the friends of the Players, who constituted most of that first audience. . . . The plays were "Licensed" by Basil Lawrence (Lawrence Langner), "Eugenically Speaking" by the director, Edward Goodman, and "Interior" by Maeterlinck. The two original plays were frank and racy without any of the offense common to Broadway attempts at frankness and raciness, and "Interior," staged with the help of Robert Edmond Jones at a cost of $35, laid a spell of suggestive visual beauty and haunting mood over the astonished house. The pantomime, "Another Interior" (originally, I believe, a college skit) showed the interior of a human stomach, into which descended various concoctions to the exceeding hurt of its hero, Gastric Juice. If memory serves us, Philip Moeller distinguished himself by his impersonation of a highly colored cordial. It wasn't an important production, though at least it was something the commercial managers would ignore; but it was merry and odd. The acting for the most part, in all the plays, was obviously amateur, even at times fumbling. Certain critics complained of this. But the zest and spirit of the productions, the hushed mood struck by the staging of "Interior," the youthful spirit of adventure which permeated the playhouse, caught everybody's fancy. The next night the theater was sold out, and soon a third weekly performance had to be added. (Walter Prichard Eaton, *The Theater Guild: The First Ten Years* [1929], pp. 23–24)

Thus began the Off-Broadway theater in the United States. During the years 1915–17, the Washington Square Players produced sixty-two one-act plays, including pieces by Eugene O'Neill, Zoe Akins, and Theodore Dreiser. They also produced *The Sea Gull* by Chekhov, *Ghosts* by Ibsen, and *Mrs. Warren's Profession* by Shaw. More important, the Washington Square Players provided theatrical experimentation; to some degree, it relished the unusual. When America entered the Great War in 1917, the Washington Square Players disbanded, only to be reconstituted in 1918 as the Theatre Guild.

Dedicated to building a professional theatrical organization that would be composed of artists presenting outstanding drama, the Guild engineered a unique system of management. Standing behind the organization were six individuals who complemented each other with varied backgrounds, talents, and experiences: Lawrence Langner, the founder, who was a patent attorney by profession; Theresa Helbrun, who served as executive officer; Maurice Wertheim, a banker and financier; Lee Simonson, scene designer; Helen Westley, actress; and Philip Moeller, director. The board met once a week to solve problems and to provide the artistic and financial leadership.

By 1925, the Guild had over twenty thousand subscribers in New York alone, which guaranteed a run of six weeks for every production at the new Guild Theater. Their success at the box office, primarily with European and English plays, allowed them to build a repertory system which had been one of their objectives from the start.

Heading the company were two of the most successful actors of the American theater whose names have been linked together and were synonymous with success—Alfred Lunt and Lynn Fontanne.

Prior to the first offerings of the Washington Square Players, the Neighborhood Playhouse, located in the Henry Street Settlement House, had been formed and was presenting a varied bill of theatrical fare. Officially, the Playhouse opened on February 12, 1915, but the Players, led by Alice and Irene Lewisohn, had already been at work for some three years. Motivated by a desire to assist the large number of immigrants who populated the area near Grand Street and the Bowery in accommodating themselves to the American scene, the Lewisohn sisters quickly discovered that the arts provided a path. In his Introduction to Alice Lewisohn Crowley's *The Neighborhood Playhouse* (1959) Joseph Wood Krutch, commenting on the birth and growth of the Playhouse, states:

The Misses Lewisohn wanted to bring various arts to the East Side, but (and this is perhaps the real secret) they also saw the possibility of eliciting art from it. They saw that it need be no mere matter of anything condescendingly handed down. Those who came to the settlement were not to be merely instructed and presented with "culture." They were to be helped to become the creative artists they potentially were. . . . . It [the Neighborhood Playhouse] was less concerned with intellectualized convictions, with morals, or sociology, or manners, more with song and dance and ritual as direct expressions of the beauty and joy of life; or, as one might sum it up, less interested in drama as literature than in what the theater and the theatrical presentation can accomplish as an independent art. (Pp. xii, xiv)

After 1920, the Neighborhood Playhouse became a semiprofessional producing organization and achieved great fame for two productions: *The Little Clay Cart,* a Sanskrit drama, presented in 1924, and the Jewish, Chassidic drama, *The Dybbuk,* which opened the following season. Both productions fulfilled what Alice Lewisohn had alluded to in commenting on the intensity of the theatrical work in the Neighborhood Playhouse:

the whole concentration upon doing and undoing is designed to experience that intangible, subtle element realizable only as symbol. Though this magical factor eludes all definition it may at times be sensed in the theater through the mood, atmosphere, or imagery of a creative situation. Or again perceived as something which conforms with our senses yet enables us to transcend the immediate or photographic reality. (Crowley, *The Neighborhood Playhouse,* p.xxi)

Alice Lewisohn's words are typical of those of the noncommercial producers of the period. They were searching for an artistic truth, but in a different manner than Herne had. Often the object of their scorn was the photographically real theater that had been developed by Belasco. They were searching for something deeper and more meaningful. Although some theatrical producing organizations, including the Neighborhood Playhouse, focused chiefly on the presentational theater, others such as the most famous of the Little Theaters, the Provincetown Players, first experimented with the "new realism." Roaming around in the dark tunnels of the psyche, those of the Provincetown relentlessly prospected for the truth of human experience and struck the mother lode of American realism.

TRIFLES
by
Susan Glaspell

BACKGROUND

In reading Hutchins Hapgood's *A Victorian in the Modern World* (1939), one is struck by the description of the group that provided the impetus for the Provincetown Players. They were desperate "sensitives" who took to alcohol, nudity, sexual experimentation, attempts at suicide, and other such frenzied behavior. Why? one must ask. The answer lies in their quest for a new realism to be given body and voice in their plays. For them, the cosmos was an utterly cold abyss in which man fumbled about in his conventions without even knowing why. No wonder that Eugene O'Neill chose to live in an abandoned Coast Guard station, or that a wharf would be used as a theater, with the ocean as backdrop. The closer that they could get to the sea—that symbol of emptiness—the better. In this way, Susan Glaspell, O'Neill, and the others could confront and probe the problem of self. For them reality existed only if all the lies of conventional society were exposed and they were allowed to experience every detail of surface life as symbol—to get beyond the horizon's mask to the free self or reality. Without the levels of the unconscious mind being understood in terms of life's symbols, there could be no contact with reality. As Hapgood put it:

> So these few people at Provincetown . . . were inspired with a desire to be truthful to their simple human lives, to ignore if possible, the big tumult and machine and get hold of some simple convictions which would stand the test of their own experience. They felt the need of rejecting

everything, even the Systems of Rejection, and of living as intimately and truthfully as they could; and, if possible, they wanted to express the simple truth of their lives and experience by writing, staging and acting in their own plays. I think they unconsciously took the form of the play, rather than some other form, because of the lifelessness of the theater: here was something obviously needing the breath of life. (P. 394)

George Cram (Jig) Cook, Susan Glaspell, Eugene O'Neill, and others, in attempting "to express the simple truth of their lives and experience," rediscovered a truth that critic Walter Prichard Eaton had spoken: "realism is too integral and too important a part of our modern civilization to be cast aside." Moreover, they proved his prediction that "true realism in the American theater had hardly begun yet."

The Provincetown Players informally started their theatrical ventures in the summer of 1915 in Provincetown, Massachusetts, with the presentation of four one-act plays, one of which, *Suppressed Desires,* by Cook and Glaspell, is still well known. The auspicious beginning, however, took place in the summer of 1916 with the presentation of two one-act plays that have achieved international recognition: O'Neill's *Bound East for Cardiff* and Glaspell's *Trifles.* Both were presented in the tiny, primitive wharf theater, a fish house twenty-five feet square. Glaspell, in her memoir, *The Road to the Temple* (1927), described the night O'Neill's play was shown: "There was a fog . . . the tide was in, and it washed under us and around, spraying through the holes in the floor, giving us the rhythm and the flavor of the sea." She also wrote abut how that theater influenced her writing *Trifles:* "I looked a long time at that bare little stage. After a time the stage became a kitchen. . . . I saw just where the stove was, the table, and the steps going upstairs. The door at the back opened, and the people all bundled up came in. . . ."

At the suggestion of one of the players, John Reed, the group decided to continue their theatrical ventures in New York. On September 5, 1916, the group officially adopted the name of the Provincetown Players and rented a house at 139

MacDougal Street in Greenwich Village. They converted the first floor into a tiny theater measuring fifteen feet by forty-five feet, named it the Playwright's Theatre, and announced to the world:

> . . . The impelling desire of the group was to establish a stage where playwrights of sincere, poetic, literary and dramatic purpose could see their plays in action and superintend their production without submitting to the commercial manager's interpretation of public taste. Equally, it was to afford an opportunity for actors, producers, scenic and costume designers to experiment with a stage of extremely simple resources—it being the idea of the Players that elaborate settings are unnecessary to bring out the essential qualities of a good play. (Deutsch and Hannau, *The Provincetown*, pp. 17–18)

Financed by subscriptions and contributions, the Provincetown Players became enormously successful. The theater drew a regular audience, and the press covered their activities. *The New York Globe* reported in 1917, "There is nothing amateur about their literary qualities. . . . So far as this particular 'little theater' group goes, the members seem not only to write their own plays, but to act and applaud them as well. They are the Sinn Feiners ('ourselves') of the theatrical world."

While a vital audience was growing, so were the number and scope of the productions. This necessitated a move to larger quarters at 133 MacDougal Street, where the Players remained until they disbanded in 1929. Even during the darkest days of World War I, when a pall hung over the Western world, the Playwright's Theatre was determined to produce serious drama. Cook articulated the reasons: "The social justification which we feel to be valid now for makers and players of plays is that they shall help to keep alive in the world the light of imagination. Without it the wreck of the world that was cannot be cleared away, and the new world shaped" (*The Provincetown*, p. 44).

Until 1922, when Jig and Susan decided to take leave of the theater, Jig was the inspirational genius of the organization. During his tenure, the Provincetown Players produced ninety-three plays by forty-seven American playwrights, including all of O'Neill's sea plays, *The Emperor Jones*, *Different*, and *The Hairy Ape,* and a number of his one-act plays. In those six years from 1916 to 1922, nine plays of Glaspell's were seen, and O'Neill and Glaspell made the transition from the one-act to the three-act form. Most of the playwrights of the time had used the one-act form because it was different and therefore part of the rebellion. However, for the Provincetown Players it was also expedient, offering short rehearsals that could be held simultaneously, and brief parts that could be learned quickly. It also provided an opportunity for many eager hands.

In the last year of Cook's leadership, friction developed among the Players, and factions arose:

> One was made up of those who felt that the theater of Jig Cook had outlived its usefulness and that they had come upon new opportunities and duties which might lead quite justifiably into money-making and success. The other sensed that Cook had been forced into sacrificing his ideal, and that those who opposed him did so only because they failed to perceive the true, more-than-theatrical nature of that ideal. There could no longer be any happy meeting of minds here. They had fallen into arguing at cross-purposes. (Ibid., pp. 76–77)

In looking back at the first six years of the Players, Deutsch and Hannau commented that "the playwright was god and Jig Cook was his prophet." They should have added that the Playwright's Theatre was his temple.

While the chief architect for the Provincetown Theater was George Cram Cook, one must agree that his wife, Susan Glaspell, was his inspiration. Her play *Trifles* was evidence of Cook's validity as a seer of the new realism. Because of the importance to American drama of these two Iowans, they deserve a close look.

Susan Glaspell was born on July 1, 1882 (1876, according to a reference in *The Road to the Temple)*, and died on July 27, 1948. Both the Glaspells and the Cooks were of pioneer stock, and Cook's family was well established and known in Davenport. There was the Cook Memorial Library, Cook Memorial Church, Cook Home for Old Ladies, and so on.

Jean Gould, in *Modern American Playwrights* (1966), says: "Susan grew up knowing all about Jig Cook long before he was aware that she existed. She knew that his ancestors, like hers, had been pioneer settlers on the land back of the Mississippi, who built log cabins and became farmers; and she had often heard the legend of the sons and grandsons who became lawyers and bankers to build the thriving town of Davenport" (p. 27). She graduated from Drake University and did graduate work at the University of Chicago, being regarded as a brilliant student. She was a newspaper reporter for two years with the *Des Moines Daily News* and in those years had a variety of assignments including the writing of a sort of "Dear Abby" column. Significantly she covered the case of a woman who had been accused of murdering her husband and mentions being in the woman's house. Surely that must have given her the basis for *Trifles*. She traveled in Europe and the American West before her marriage to Cook on April 14, 1913 in Weehawken, New Jersey. Glaspell thrived on writing short fiction and had a number of short stories published. She also became very well known as a novelist through *The Glory of the Conquered* (1909), *The Visioning* (1911), and *Fidelity* (1915). Though impressive and promising as a novelist, Glaspell turned to playwriting at the urging of her husband. She was awarded the Pulitzer Prize in drama for *Alison's House* (1931). Other plays include *Bernice, Inheritors, The Verge,* and *Chains of Dew*. After her husband's death, she began to write fiction with greater regularity.

Lawrence Langner in *The Magic Curtain* described Glaspell as "a delicate woman with sad eyes and a sweet smile who seemed as fragile as old lace until you talked with her and glimpsed the steel lining beneath the tender surface." Later, Langner describes her husband, George Cook, as "a big, white-haired, pink-faced man with a hearty manner and the appearance of a Roman senator. His secret desire was to dwell on Mount Olympus like an ancient Greek philosopher."

He was known for his generous and kind nature. Susan Glaspell remarks about the care and lengths to which Jig went in designing an elevator for her because of her heart condition. Hutchins Hapgood (one of the Provincetown initiates) recalled that while passing Jig's house one evening, he heard Susan's happy voice cry out from the upstairs bedroom, "Oh, darling, don't bite!" Apparently they were well-mated. Cook himself once remarked that he couldn't endure life without Susan by his side.

Cook was born in 1873 and after attending the State College in Iowa City for three years went to Harvard for his senior year, graduating in 1893. He was a classical Greek scholar and studied abroad at Heidelberg. Returning from Europe, he taught briefly at the State University at Iowa City and then tried farming. He later became literary editor of the *Chicago Evening Post*. In 1922 he went with Susan to live in Greece where he died and was buried on Mount Parnanssus in 1924. A rare disease contracted from an infected dog killed him. In his escape to Greece to search for truth and in his ironic death lurk the motivation for the new realism, as Hutchins Hapgood suggests in *A Victorian in the Modern World:*

> What are we really like, what do we really want, how are we really living, what are the relations actually existing between us? . . . What, to begin with, are we in our personal lives, what are we intimately, what is our real life? . . . The Provincetown movement was, in part, a social effort to live again—spiritually, to recover from discouragement and disappointment, to be free of the poison of self and the poison of the world. (P. 393)

For the Provincetown Players, there was no personal God—only the cryptic matter in which they were imbedded, with its countless physical details. Death, of course, was what lay beyond the mask of physicality. When Jig Cook met his end in a fluke encounter with a sick dog while passionately in search of classical beauty, he unwittingly found the ultimate truth of experience. All things great and small are permanently tinged with fatal irony: that vast symbol of the sea that so overwhelmed him and O'Neill at Provincetown was reduced to a fleck of sputum from a dying dog.

These new playwrights were devoted to exploring the levels of the psyche through the passionate experiences of their characters. Theirs was a no-holds-barred struggle with reality in which comforting illusions were contemptuously cast aside. They were after the very innards of the self. This is abundantly evident in Susan Glaspell's *Trifles*.

TRIFLES

First Performed by the Provincetown Players at the
Wharf Theatre, Provincetown, Mass.,
August 8, 1916

ORIGINAL CAST

GEORGE HENDERSON, *County Attorney*

> Robert Rogers

HENRY PETERS, *Sheriff*   Robert Conville

LEWIS HALE, *A Neighboring Farmer*

> George Cram Cook

MRS. PETERS   Alice Hall

MRS. HALE   Susan Glaspell

SCENE: The kitchen in the now abandoned farmhouse of John Wright, a gloomy kitchen, plainly left without having been put in order—unwashed pans under the sink, a loaf of bread outside the bread-box, a dish-towel on the table—other signs of incompleted work. Door opens rear and enter sheriff followed by county attorney and Hale. The sheriff and Hale are men in middle life, the county attorney is a young man; all are much bundled up and go at once to the store. They are followed by the two women—the sheriff's wife first; she is a slight wiry woman, a thin nervous face. Mrs. Hale is larger and would ordinarily be called more comfortable looking, but she is disturbed now and looks fearfully about as she enters. The women have come in slowly, and stand close together near the door.

COUNTY ATTORNEY: *(Rubbing his hands)* This feels good. Come up to the fire, ladies.

MRS PETERS: *(Takes a step forward and looks around)* I'm not—cold.

SHERIFF: *(Unbuttoning his overcoat and stepping away from the stove as if to mark the beginning of official business)* Now, Mr. Hale, before we move things about, you explain to Mr. Henderson just what you saw when you came here yesterday morning.

35

COUNTY ATTORNEY: By the way, has anything been moved? Are things just as you left them yesterday?

SHERIFF: *(Looking all about)* It's just the same. When it dropped below zero last night I thought I'd better send Frank out this morning to make a fire for us—no use getting pneumonia with a big case on, but I told him not to touch anything except the stove—and you know Frank.

COUNTY ATTORNEY: Somebody should have been left here yesterday.

SHERIFF: Oh—yesterday. When I had to send Frank to Morris Center for that man who went crazy—I want you to know I had my hands full yesterday. I knew you could get back from Omaha by today and as long as I went over everything here myself——

COUNTY ATTORNEY: Well, Mr. Hale, tell just what happened when you came here yesterday morning.

HALE: Harry and I had started to town with a load of potatoes. We came along the road from my place and as I got here I said, "I'm going to see if I can't get John Wright to go in with me on a party telephone." I spoke to Wright about it once before and he put me off, saying folks talked too much anyway, and all he asked was peace and quiet——I guess you know about how much he talked himself, but I thought myself if I went to the house and talked about it before his wife, though I said to Harry that I didn't know as what his wife wanted made much difference to John——

COUNTY ATTORNEY: Let's talk about that later, Mr. Hale. I do want to talk about that, but tell now just what happened when you got to the house.

HALE: I didn't hear or see anything; I knocked at the door, and still it was all quiet inside. I knew they must be up, it was past eight o'clock. So I knocked again, and I thought I heard somebody say "Come in." I wasn't sure, I'm not sure yet, but I opened the door—this door *(jerking a hand backward)* and there in that rocker—*(pointing to it)* sat Mrs. Wright. *(All look at the rocker)*

COUNTY ATTORNEY: What—was she doing?

HALE: She was rockin' back and forth. She had her apron in her hand and was kind of—pleating it.

COUNTY ATTORNEY: And how did she—look?

HALE: Well, she looked queer.

COUNTY ATTORNEY: How do you mean—queer?

HALE: Well, as if she didn't know what she was going to do next. And kind of done up.

COUNTY ATTORNEY: How did she seem to feel about your coming?

HALE: Why, I don't think she minded—one way or other. She didn't pay much attention. I said, "How do, Mrs. Wright, it's cold, ain't it?" And she said "Is it?"—and went on kind of pleating at her apron. Well, I was surprised; she didn't ask me to come up to the stove, or to set down, but just sat there, not even looking at me, so I said, "I want to see John." And then she—laughed. I guess you would call it a laugh. I thought of Harry and the team outside, so I said a little sharp: "Can't I see John?" "No," she says, kind o' dull like. "Ain't he home?" says I. "Yes," says she, "he's home." "Then why can't I see him?" I asked her, out of patience. " 'Cause he's dead," says she. *"Dead?"* says I. She just nodded her head, not getting a bit excited, but rockin' back and forth. "Why—where is he?" says I, not knowing what to say. She just pointed upstairs—like that *(himself pointing to the room above)*. I got up, with the idea of going up there. I walked from there to here—*(pointing)*— then I says, "Why, what did he die of?" "He died of a rope round his neck," says she, and just went on pleatin' at her apron. Well, I went out and called Harry. I thought I might— need help. We went upstairs and there he was—lyin'——

COUNTY ATTORNEY: I think I'd rather have you go into that upstairs, where you can point it all out. Just go on now with the rest of the story.

HALE: Well, my first thought was to get that rope off. It looked—*(stops, his face twitches)*—but Harry, he went up to him, and he said, "No, he's dead all right, and we'd better not touch anything." So we went back down stairs. She was still sitting that same way. "Has anybody been notified?" I asked. "No," says she, unconcerned. "Who did this, Mrs. Wright?" said Harry. He said it businesslike—and she stopped pleatin' of her apron. "I don't know," she says. "You don't *know?*" says Harry. "No," says she. "Weren't you sleepin' in the bed with him?" says Harry. "Yes," says she, "but I was on the inside." "Somebody slipped a rope round his neck and strangled him and you didn't wake up?" says Harry. "I didn't wake up," she said after him. We may have looked as if we didn't see how that could be, for after a minute she said, "I sleep sound." Harry was going to ask her more questions but I said maybe we ought to let her tell her story first to the coroner, or the sheriff, so Harry went fast as he could to Rivers' place, where there's a telephone.

COUNTY ATTORNEY: And what did Mrs. Wright do when she knew that you had gone for the coroner?

HALE: She moved from that chair to this one over here, *(pointing to a small chair in the corner)* and just sat there with her hands held together and looking down. I got a feeling that I ought to make some conversation, so I said I had come in to see if John wanted to put in a telephone, and at that she started to laugh, and then she stopped and looked at me—scared. *(County attorney, who has had his notebook out, makes a note)* I dunno, maybe it wasn't scared. I wouldn't like to say it was. Soon Harry got back, and then Dr. Lloyd came, and you, Mr. Peters, and so I guess that's all I know that you don't.

COUNTY ATTORNEY: *(Looking around)* I guess we'll go upstairs first—and then out to the barn and around there. *(To sheriff)* You're convinced that there was nothing important here—nothing that would point to any motive?

SHERIFF: Nothing here but kitchen things.

COUNTY ATTORNEY: *(Opens the door of a cupboard closet. Gets up on a chair and looks on a shelf. Pulls his hand away, sticky)* Here's a nice mess. *(The women draw nearer)*

MRS. PETERS: Oh, her fruit; it did freeze. *(To county attorney)* She worried about that when it turned so cold. She said the fire'd go out and her jars would break.

SHERIFF: Well, can you beat the woman! Held for murder and worrying about her preserves.

COUNTY ATTORNEY: *(Setting his lips firmly)* I guess before we are through she may have something more serious than preserves to worry about.

HALE: Well, women are used to worrying over trifles. *(The two women move a little closer together)*

COUNTY ATTORNEY: *(With the gallantry of a young politician)* And yet, for all their worries, what would we do without the ladies? *(The women do not unbend. He goes to sink, takes a dipperful of water from pail and pouring it into basin, washes his hands. Starts to wipe them on roller-towel, turns it for a cleaner place)* Dirty towels! *(Kicks his foot against pans under the sink)* Not much of a house-keeper, would you say, ladies?

MRS. HALE: *(stiffly)* There's a great deal of work to be done on a farm.

COUNTY ATTORNEY: *(With conciliation)* To be sure. And yet *(with a little bow to her)* I know there are some Dickson County farmhouses which do not have such roller towels. *(Gives it a pull to expose its full length again)*

MRS. HALE: Those towels get dirty awful quick. Men's hands aren't always as clean as they might be.

COUNTY ATTORNEY: Ah, loyal to your sex, I see. But you and Mrs. Wright were neighbors. I suppose you were friends, too.

MRS. HALE: *(Shaking her head)* I've not seen much of her of late years. I've not been in this house—it's more than a year.

COUNTY ATTORNEY: And why was that? You didn't like her?

MRS. HALE: I liked her all well enough. Farmer's wives have their hands full, Mr. Henderson. And then——

COUNTY ATTORNEY: Yes—?

MRS. HALE: *(Looking about)* It never seemed a very cheerful place.

COUNTY ATTORNEY: No——it's not cheerful. I shouldn't say she had the homemaking instinct.

MRS. HALE: Well, I don't know as Wright had, either.

COUNTY ATTORNEY: You mean that they didn't get on very well?

MRS. HALE: No, I don't mean anything. But I don't think a place'd be any cheerfuller for John Wright's being in it.

COUNTY ATTORNEY: I'd like to talk more of that a little later. I want to get the lay of things upstairs now. *(Moves to stair-door, followed by the two men)*

SHERIFF: I suppose anything Mrs. Peters does'll be all right. She was to take in some clothes for her, you know, and a few little things. We left in such a hurry yesterday.

COUNTY ATTORNEY: Yes, but I would like to see what you take, Mrs. Peters, and keep an eye out for anything that might be of use to us.

MRS. PETERS: Yes, Mr. Henderson. *(The women listen to the men's steps on the stairs, then look about the kitchen)* ✔

MRS. HALE: I'd hate to have men coming into my kitchen,

snooping round and criticizing. (*Arranges pans under sink which the county attorney had shoved out of place*)

MRS. PETERS: Of course it's no more than their duty.

MRS. HALE: Duty's all right, but I guess that deputy sheriff that came out to make the fire might have got a little of this on. (*Gives roller towel a pull*) Wish I'd thought of that sooner. Seems mean to talk about her for not having things slicked up when she had to come away in such a hurry.

MRS. PETERS: (*Going to table at side, lifts one end of towel that covers a pan*) She had bread set. (*Stands still*)

MRS. HALE: (*Her eyes fixed on loaf of bread outside bread-box. Moves slowly toward it*) She was going to put this in there. (*Picks up loaf, then abruptly drops it. In a manner of returning to familiar things*) It's a shame about her fruit. I wonder if it's all gone. (*Gets up on a chair and looks*) I think there's some here that is all right, Mrs. Peters. Yes—here; (*holding it toward the window*) this is cherries, too. (*Looking again*) I declare I believe that's the only one. (*Gets down, bottle in her hand. Goes to sink and wipes it off on the outside*) She'll feel awful bad after all her hard work in the hot weather. I remember the afternoon I put up my cherries last summer. (*Puts bottle on table. With a sigh starts to sit down in rocking-chair. Before she is seated realizes what chair it is; with a slow look at it, steps back. The chair which she has touched rocks back and forth*)

MRS. PETERS: Well, I must get those things from the front room closet. (*Starts to door left, looks into the other room, steps back*) You coming with me, Mrs. Hale? You could help me carry them. (*Both women go out; reappear, Mrs. Peters carrying a dress and skirt, Mrs. Hale following with a pair of shoes*)

MRS. PETERS: My, its cold in there. (*Puts clothes on table, goes up to stove*)

MRS. HALE: (*Holding up skirt and examining it*) Wright was close. I think maybe that's why she kept so much to herself. She didn't even belong to the Ladies' Aid. I suppose she felt she couldn't do her part, and then you don't enjoy things when you feel shabby. She used to wear pretty clothes and be lively, when she was Minnie Foster, one of the town girls singing in the choir. But that was—oh, that was thirty years ago. This all you was to take in?

MRS. PETERS: She said she wanted an apron. Funny thing

to want, for there isn't much to get you dirty in jail, goodness knows. But I suppose just to make her feel more
natural. She said they was in the top drawer in this cupboard. Yes, here. And then her little shawl that always hung
behind the door. (*Looks on stair door*) Yes, here it is.

MRS. HALE: (*Abruptly moving toward her*) Mrs. Peters?

MRS. PETERS: Yes, Mrs. Hale?

MRS. HALE: Do you think she did it?

MRS. PETERS: (*In a frightened voice*) Oh, I don't know.

MRS. HALE: Well, I don't think she did. Asking for an
apron and her little shawl. Worrying about her fruit.

MRS. PETERS: (*Starts to speak, glances up, where footsteps are heard in the room above. In a low voice*) Mr.
Peters says it looks bad for her. Mr. Henderson is awful
sarcastic in a speech and he'll make fun of her sayin' she
didn't wake up.

MRS. HALE: Well, I guess John Wright didn't wake when
they was slipping that rope under his neck.

MRS. PETERS: No, it's strange. It must have been done
awful crafty and still. They say it was such a—funny way to
kill a man, rigging it all up like that.

MRS. HALE: That's just what Mr. Hale said. There was a
gun in the house. He says that's what he can't understand.

MRS. PETERS: Mr. Henderson said coming out that what
was needed for the case was a motive; something to show
anger, or—sudden feeling.

MRS. HALE: (*Standing by table*) Well, I don't see any
signs of anger around here, but (*puts hand on dish-towel in
middle of table, stands looking at table, one half of which is
clean, the other half messy*) It's wiped to here. (*Makes a
move as if to finish work, then turns and looks at loaf of
bread beside the bread-box. Drops towel. In that voice of
coming back to familiar things*) Wonder how they are finding
things upstairs. I hope she had it a little more red-up up
there. You know, it seems kind of *sneaking*. Locking her up
in town and then coming out here and trying to get her own
house to turn against her!

MRS. PETERS: But Mrs. Hale, the law is the law.

MRS. HALE: I s'pose 'tis. (*Unbuttoning her coat*) Better
loosen up your things, Mrs. Peters. You won't feel them
when you go out.

MRS. PETERS: (*Taking off fur tippet, goes to hang it on

hook at back of the room, stands looking at the under part of the small table) She was piecing a quilt. *(Brings large sewing basket to table front and they look at the bright pieces)*

MRS. HALE: It's log cabin pattern. Pretty, isn't it? I wonder if she was goin' to quilt it or just knot it? *(Footsteps have been heard coming down the stairs. The sheriff enters followed by Hale and Henderson)*

SHERIFF: They wonder if she was going to quilt it or just knot it. *(The men laugh, the women look abashed)*

COUNTY ATTORNEY: *(Rubbing his hands over the stove)* Frank's fire didn't do much up there, did it? Well, let's go out to the barn and get that cleared up. *(Exeunt men door rear)*

MRS. HALE: *(Resentfully)* I don't know as there's anything so strange, our takin' up our time with little things while we're waiting for them to get the evidence. *(Sits down, smoothing out block with decision)* I don't see as it's anything to laugh about.

MRS. PETERS: *(Apologetically)* Of course they've got awful important things on their minds. *(Pulls up a chair and sits by the table)*

MRS. HALE: *(Examining another block)* Mrs. Peters, look at this one. Here, this is the one she was working on, and look at the sewing! All the rest of it has been so nice and even. And look at this! It's all over the place! Why, it looks as if she didn't know what she was about! *(After she has said this they look at each other, then start to glance back at the door. After an instant Mrs. Hale has pulled at a knot and ripped the sewing)*

MRS. PETERS: Oh, what are you doing, Mrs. Hale?

MRS. HALE: *(Mildly)* Just pulling out a stitch or two that's not sewed very good. *(Threading a needle)* Bad sewing always made me fidgety.

MRS. PETERS: *(Nervously)* I don't think we ought to touch things.

MRS. HALE: I'll just finish up this end. *(Suddenly stopping and leaning forward)* Mrs. Peters?

MRS. PETERS: Yes, Mrs. Hale?

MRS. HALE: What do you suppose she was so nervous about?

MRS. PETERS: Oh—I don't know. I don't know as she was nervous. I sometimes sew awful queer when I'm just tired. *(Mrs. Hale starts to say something, looks at her, compresses her lips a little, goes on sewing)* Well I must get these things wrapped up. They may be through sooner than we think. *(Piling apron and other things up together)* I wonder where I can find a piece of paper, and string.

MRS. HALE: In that cupboard, maybe.

MRS. PETERS: *(Looking in cupboard)* Why, here's a bird-cage. *(Holds it up)* Did she have a bird, Mrs. Hale?

MRS. HALE: Why, I don't know whether she did or not—I've not been here for so long. There was a man around last year selling canaries cheap, but I don't know as she took one; maybe she did. She used to sing real pretty herself.

MRS. PETERS: *(Glancing around)* Seems funny to think of a bird here. But she must have had one, or why should she have had a cage? I wonder what happened to it.

MRS. HALE: I s'pose maybe the cat got it.

MRS. PETERS: No, she didn't have a cat. She's got that feeling some people have about cats—being afraid of them. My cat got in her room and she was real upset and asked me to take it out.

MRS. HALE: My sister Bessie was like that. Queer, ain't it?

MRS. PETERS: *(Examining cage)* Why, look at this door. It's broke. One hinge is pulled apart.

MRS. HALE: *(Looking too)* Looks as if someone must have been rough with it.

MRS. PETERS: Why, yes. *(Puts cage on table)*

MRS. HALE: I wish if they're going to find any evidence they'd be about it. I don't like this place.

MRS. PETERS: But I'm awful glad you came with me, Mrs. Hale. It would be lonesome for me sitting here alone.

MRS. HALE: It would, wouldn't it? *(Dropping sewing, voice falling)* But I tell you what I do wish, Mrs. Peters. I wish I had come over sometimes when *she* was here. I—*(looking around the room)*—wish I had.

MRS. PETERS: But of course you were awful busy, Mrs. Hale—your house and your children.

MRS. HALE: I could've come. I stayed away because it weren't cheerful—and that's why I ought to have come. I—I've never liked this place. Maybe because it's down in a hollow and you don't see the road. I dunno what it is, but it's a lonesome place and always was. I wish I had come over to see Minnie Foster sometimes. I can see now—*(shakes her head)*

MRS. PETERS: Well, you mustn't reproach yourself, Mrs.

Hale. Somehow we just don't see how it is with other folks until—something comes up.

MRS. HALE: Not having children makes less work—but it makes a quiet house, and Wright out to work all day, and no company when he did come in. Did you know John Wright, Mrs. Peters?

MRS. PETERS: Not to know him; I've seen him in town. They say he was a good man.

MRS. HALE: Yes—good; he didn't drink, and kept his word as well as most, I guess, and paid his debts. But he was a hard man, Mrs. Peters. Just to pass the time of day with him—*(shivers)* Like a raw wind that gets to the bone. *(Pauses, her eye falling on the cage)* I should think she would 'a wanted a bird. But what do you suppose went with it?

MRS. PETERS: I don't know, unless it got sick and died. *(She reaches over and swings the broken door, swings it again, both women watch it)*

MRS. HALE: You weren't raised round here, were you? *(Mrs. Peters shakes her head)* You didn't know—her?

MRS. PETERS: Not till they brought her yesterday.

MRS. HALE: She—come to think of it, she was kind of like a bird herself—real sweet and pretty, but kind of timid and—fluttery. How—she—did—change. *(Silence; then as if struck by a happy thought and relieved to get back to everyday things)* Tell you what, Mrs. Peters, why don't you take the quilt in with you? It might take up her mind.

MRS. PETERS: Why, I think that's a real nice idea, Mrs. Hale. There couldn't possibly be any objection to it, could there? Now, just what would I take? I wonder if her patches are in here—and her things. *(Both look in sewing basket)*

MRS. HALE: Here's some red. I expect this has got sewing things in it. *(Brings out a fancy box)* What a pretty box. Looks like something somebody would give you. Maybe her scissors are in here. *(Opens box. Suddenly puts her hand to her nose)* Why——*(Mrs. Peters bends nearer, then turns her face away)* There's something wrapped up in this piece of silk.

MRS. PETERS: Why, this isn't her scissors.

MRS. HALE: *(Lifting the silk)* Oh, Mrs. Peters—it's *(Mrs. Peters bends closer)*

MRS. PETERS: It's the bird.

MRS. HALE: *(Jumping up)* But, Mrs. Peters—look at it! Its neck! Look at its neck! It's all—other side *to*.

MRS. PETERS: Somebody-wrung-its-neck. *(Their eyes meet. A look of growing comprehension, or horror. Steps are heard outside. Mrs. Hale slips box under quilt pieces, and sinks into her chair. Enter sheriff and county attorney. Mrs. Peters rises)*

COUNTY ATTORNEY: *(As one turning from serious things to little pleasantries)* Well, ladies, have you decided whether she was going to quilt it or knot it?

MRS. PETERS: We think she was going to—knot it.

COUNTY ATTORNEY: Well, that's interesting, I am sure. *(Looking at bird-cage)* Has the bird flown?

MRS. HALE: *(Piling more quilt pieces over the box)* We think the—cat got it.

COUNTY ATTORNEY: *(Preoccupied)* Is there a cat? *(Mrs. Hale glances in a quick covert way at Mrs. Peters)*

MRS. PETERS: Well, not *now*. They're superstitious, you know. They leave.

COUNTY ATTORNEY: *(To Peters, in the manner of continuing an interrupted conversation)* No sign at all of anyone having come from the outside. Their own rope. Now let's go up again and go over it piece by piece. *(They start upstairs)* It would have been someone who knew just the——*(Mrs. Peters sinks into her chair. The two women sit there not looking at one another, but as if peering into something and at the same time holding back. When they talk now it is in the manner of feeling their way over strange ground, as if afraid of what they are saying, but as if they can not help saying it)*

MRS. HALE: She liked the bird. She was going to bury it in that pretty box.

MRS. PETERS: *(In a whisper)* When I was a girl—my kitten—there was a boy took a hatchet, and before my eyes—and before I could get there—*(covers her face an instant)* If they hadn't held me back I would have—*(catches herself, looks upstairs where steps are heard, falters weakly)*—hurt him.

MRS. HALE: *(With a slow look around her)* I wonder how it would seem never to have had any children around. *(Pause)* No, Wright wouldn't like the bird—a thing that sang. She used to sing. He killed that, too.

MRS. PETERS: *(Moving uneasily)* We don't know who killed the bird.

MRS. HALE: I knew John Wright.

MRS. PETERS: It was an awful thing was done in this house that night, Mrs. Hale. Killing a man while he slept, slipping a rope around his neck that choked the life out of him.

MRS. HALE: His neck. Choked the life out of him. *(Her hand goes out and rests on the bird-cage)*

MRS. PETERS: *(With rising voice)* We don't know who killed him. We don't *know*.

MRS. HALE: *(Her own feeling not interrupted)* If there'd been years and years of nothing, then a bird to sing to you, it would be awful—still, after the bird was still.

MRS. PETERS: *(Something within her speaking)* I know what stillness is. When we homesteaded in Dakota, and my first baby died—after he was two years old, and me with no other then——

MRS. HALE: *(Moving)* How soon do you suppose they'll be through, looking for the evidence?

MRS. PETERS: I know what stillness is. *(Pulling herself back)* The law has got to punish crime, Mrs. Hale.

MRS. HALE: *(Not as if answering that)* I wish you'd seen Minnie Foster when she wore a white dress with blue ribbons and stood up there in the choir and sang. *(Suddenly looking around the room)* Oh, I *wish* I'd come over here once in a while! That was a crime! That was a crime! Who's going to punish that?

MRS. PETERS: *(Looking upstairs)* We mustn't—take on.

MRS. HALE: I might have known she needed help! I know how things can be—for women. I tell you, it's queer, Mrs. Peters. We live close together and we live far apart. We all go through the same things—it's all just a different kind of the same thing—*(Brushes her eyes, then seeing the bottle of fruit, reaches out for it)* If I was you I wouldn't tell her her fruit was gone. Tell her it *ain't*. Tell her it's all right. Take this in to prove it to her. She—she may never know whether it was broke or not.

MRS. PETERS: *(Picks up the bottle, looks about for something to wrap it in; takes petticoat from clothes brought from front room, very nervously begins winding that around it. In a false voice)* My, it's a good thing the men couldn't hear us. Wouldn't they just laugh! Getting all stirred up over a little thing like a—dead canary. As if that could have anything to do with—with—wouldn't they *laugh!* (*The men are heard coming down stairs*)

MRS. HALE: (*Muttering*) Maybe they would—maybe they wouldn't.

COUNTY ATTORNEY: No, Peters, it's all perfectly clear except a reason for doing it. But you know juries when it comes to women. If there was some definite thing. Something to show—something to make a story about—a thing that would connect up with this strange way of doing it— (*The women's eyes meet for an instant. Enter Hale from outer door*)

HALE: Well, I've got the team around. Pretty cold out there.

COUNTY ATTORNEY: I'm going to stay here a while by myself. (*To sheriff*) You can send Frank out for me, can't you? I want to go over everything. I'm not satisfied that we can't do better.

SHERIFF: Do you want to see what Mrs. Peters is going to take in?

COUNTY ATTORNEY: (*Goes to table. Picks up apron, laughs*) Oh, I guess they're not very dangerous things the ladies have picked out. (*Moves a few things about, disturbing quilt pieces which cover the box. Steps back*) No, Mrs. Peters doesn't need supervising. For that matter, a sheriff's wife is married to the law. Ever think of it that way, Mrs. Peters?

MRS. PETERS: Not—just that way.

SHERIFF: (*Chuckling*) Married to the law. (*Moves toward front room*) I just want you to come in here a minute, George. We ought to take a look at these windows.

COUNTY ATTORNEY: Oh, windows!

SHERIFF: We'll be right out, Mr. Hale. (*Exit Hale door rear. Sheriff follows county attorney through door left. The two women's eyes follow them out. Mrs. Hale rises, hands tightly together, looking intensely at Mrs. Peters, whose eyes make a slow turn, finally meeting Mrs. Hale's. A moment Mrs. Hale holds her, then her own eyes point the way to the spot where the box is concealed. Suddenly Mrs. Peters throws back quilt pieces and tries to put box in the bag she is wearing. It is too big. She opens box, starts to take bird out, cannot touch it, goes to pieces, stands there helpless. Sound of a knob turning in the other room. Mrs.*)

Hale snatches box and puts it in the pocket of her big coat. Enter county attorney and sheriff.)

COUNTY ATTORNEY: (*Facetiously*) Well, Henry, at least we found out that she was not going to quilt it. She was going to—what is it you call it, ladies?

MRS. HALE: (*Hand against her pocket*) We call it—knot it, Mr. Henderson.

CURTAIN

COMMENTARY

In this play Glaspell works by reflected detail rather than immediate events. The present, in that sense, illuminates the past and allows the story to unfold. It was a new technique in dramaturgy—similar to the use of the flashback, which had been used for the first time on stage by Elmer Rice. Glaspell's title, *Trifles,* not only reveals the theme, but, in a sense, shows the dramaturgy. Although there is significant tension, the dramatic action is understated, and there are no volcanic eruptions of melodrama.

The structure is subtle, and the plot of *Trifles* carefully unfolds in a clear attempt to allow the action to demonstrate the theme. There are three major discoveries: the zany threading on the quilt, the broken bird-cage door, and the bird itself. After they are made, one of the ladies observes: "I wish if they're going to find any evidence they'd be about it." Each of these discoveries is dramatically potent, pointing up the more fundamental aspect of the action. The women in their casual manner finding trifles, discover the truth. The men—particularly the blustering, demeaning, county attorney—find nothing and *never will,* for the women are more clever and hide the evidence. Thus, at the spine of the play is the ever-present battle between the male and the female. Glaspell juxtaposes the arrogant disregard for women by the authoritative men against the defensive and secretive stance of the women, thus providing a fascinating glimpse into the hidden levels of marital conflict, a glimpse that expands into the greater scope of contention between the sexes.

The use of a realistic setting, with its attendant detail, is organic to the meaning of the play. The coldness of the climate and the room intensifies the coldness of the Wrights' marriage and further emphasizes the gap between the sexes. The room's spare quality underscores that of marriage. The use of broken jam jars shows to what level of life the Wrights have fallen. It has both pathos and banality. Here is the new woman in American dramatic literature—canny, alert, and seeming oh-so-simple.

Surely this is a feminist drama, and Glaspell was leading the field. Although Rachel Crothers already had been writing for the theater for several years, none of her plays quite has this power. In *Trifles* there are no compromises. The dialogue is conversational and colloquial—local color in that sense. But how much more mature are these characters than any ever painted by the local colorists! The characters are complex and thoughtful. Glaspell uses the pause, the interruption, the cut-off, abrupt stops and starts—all to create the mood of that Midwest farmland. One believes that one has truly been there in this theater of illusion, carefully modeled with believable characters, action, theme, and dialogue. This is the one-act play at its finest, in a masterful display of situational irony. No wonder Glaspell used it to fashion one of her most successful short stories, *Jury of Her Peers*.

The men—County Attorney George Henderson, Sheriff Henry Peters, and farmer Lewis Hale—feel vastly superior to the women—Mrs. Peters and Mrs. Hale—and are then ironically outwitted by them. To the men these women are fit only to pick up some clothes for the jailed Mrs. Wright. They are thus regarded with cool contempt by the men, who have the truly important task before them of locating evidence with which to convict Mrs. Wright of murder.

Their treatment of the women is akin to the murdered John Wright's handling of his wife, Minnie, which precipitated his murder. When the two women, in a conspiracy of silence, hide the incriminating evidence of the neck-wrung canary, they have tied another knot in the noose that strangled John Wright. By doing so they also make a sad statement about their own marriages. They join hands with Minnie in a deadly sisterhood of marital complaint. And now that no motive can be found for her husband's murder, Minnie will eventually be set free—supposedly to sing once again in the choir. Ironically the women have quilted a pattern of trifles to aid Minnie. We arrive through Glaspell's indirect method at a total understanding of the unseen Minnie and realize why she murdered her husband. Perhaps this was the first appearance on the American stage of this kind of character revelation.

ANNA CHRISTIE
by
Eugene O'Neill

BACKGROUND

When Eugene O'Neill (1888–1953) had his first play produced by the Provincetown Players, he was twenty-eight
years old, but he had already lived a life dangerously packed
with experience. He was the son of the famous star James
O'Neill (1847–1920), who had wasted a creative career but
made much money by playing season after season in the
potboiler *The Count of Monte Cristo*. While his father
toured, Eugene lived in private boarding schools and an
academy until 1906. Thereafter he went to Princeton for one
year, and, supposedly, was dismissed for misconduct. In
1909 he was married secretly, and shortly after had a son;
however, the marriage was unsuccessful, and the young
Eugene spent most of the time wandering abroad as an able
seaman. During those years, as he drifted from place to
place and job to job, he became a heavy drinker and lived in
many flophouses in several port cities, including New York.
In 1912, after his divorce, he learned that he had tuberculosis, and he spent the next five months in a sanitarium reading
dramatic literature—the Greeks, the Elizabethans, Strindberg, and Ibsen.

While in the institution he began writing plays, and after
he was discharged, he enrolled for one year in George Pierce
Baker's drama workshop at Harvard. While there he wrote
Bound East for Cardiff and started several other plays. Later
he had a brief career as a newspaper reporter before he took
to wandering the streets of New York once again as an
emotional and intellectual rebel. He spent much of his time
in Greenwich Village. It was inevitable that he should meet
the people who would form the Playwright's Theatre. He
was intellectually in tune with them even though psychologi-
cally he was a loner. He also despised the commercial

theater, identifying it with the theater of his father. Some years later he said, "my early experience with the theater through my father really made me revolt against it. As a boy I saw so much of the old, ranting, artificial romantic stuff that I always had a sort of contempt for the theater."

After he became a member of the Players, as a worker and as their major playwright, he had a run-in with the old theater in the person of his father. In December 1916, the Players were rehearsing Gene's one-act play *Before Breakfast*. James at sixty-nine, retired from his arduous career and following his son's profession with great interest, offered to help him and the Players. Gene reluctantly agreed, and the results have been recorded in Arthur and Barbara Gelb's memorable biography, *O'Neill* (1960):

> "There was no question of his directing," O'Neill once noted. "I got him down to make suggestions on the acting. He made some I didn't agree with, but also some I thought were fine and which the actors were glad to follow." According to eyewitnesses, Mary Pyne had the sense to do everything James O'Neill told her—grandiloquent gestures, melodramatic inflections and all. And James, gratified, said to her: "You are a most intelligent young actress. I don't need to give you any further instruction." As soon as he had gone, his son redirected her from the beginning to end, and still according to eyewitnesses, mumbled about his father's "old fogey" approach. (Pp. 322–23)

Doubtless the Players, and Jig Cook especially, provided just what O'Neill needed. The Gelbs report that Gene "described Cook as 'a really imaginative man. . . . If I hadn't had the Provincetown Theater, I would have had to write commercial plays . : .' " (p. 315). Thus by 1920 O'Neill was already recognized as a major writer. The Players had produced *The Emperor Jones*, his first full-length play that went beyond realism, and in that same year his first full-length realistic play, *Beyond the Horizon*, was shown on Broadway. He was also looking for someone to produce another full-length play about the sea, on which he had been working for several years. It was originally titled "De Old Devil," which was altered to "Chris," then to "Chris Christopherson," and finally, to *Anna Christie*. After many months of discussion and revisions, George Tyler decided to give *Anna Christie* a tryout in Atlantic City. In the central role of Anna, Tyler cast a young newcomer, Lynn Fontanne. It opened in March 1920, and although audiences did not warm to the play, reviewers did. Even though the production went on to Philadelphia, both Tyler and O'Neill were unhappy with the script. The reception in Philadelphia was mixed, resulting in the script being withdrawn and the production ended.

After Gene was awarded the Pulitzer Prize in June for *Beyond the Horizon,* many other producers wanted to present his plays. Lawrence Langner, one of the directors of the Theatre Guild, was one of these, and he wrote in his autobiography, *The Magic Curtain:*

> I was determined to bring the Theatre Guild and Eugene O'Neill together, but all my early attempts ended in failure. 'Gene, on his side, wanted to work with the Guild. . . . My next attempt was with *Anna Christie.* I had concluded all arrangements with 'Gene for our production of the play, when I had to leave for Europe. On my return I found that some of our temperamental directors had been scrapping with O'Neill as a result of which he withdrew the play and gave it to Arthur Hopkins. (P. 229)

In 1921, when he decided to produce *Anna Christie,* Arthur Hopkins was the most respected of the commercial theatrical producers on Broadway. He was then forty-three and had been a newspaper reporter, a vaudeville press agent, and a booking agent for the Orpheum Circuit. He had produced over a dozen plays and was known for his high ideals and dedication to "admirable" and "consecrated" theater. If, from the hinterlands and Greenwich Village, the Little Theaters led the revolution against the tawdry theater of Broadway, Arthur Hopkins was the rebel within the ranks. In 1914 he discovered Elmer Rice and produced, with George M. Cohan and Sam Harris, Rice's first play, *On Trial.* Hopkins devised the "jack-knife" platforms to execute the quick scene changes the play called for. While the Provincetown Players were creating new dramas downtown, Hopkins was re-creating the classics and discovering new talent uptown. He directed a series of outstanding productions while he was operating the Plymouth Theater during the years 1917–20. They were *Redemption* (an adaptation of

Tolstoy's *The Living Corpse*, 1918), *The Jest* by Sem Bellini
(1919), and *Richard III* by Shakespeare (1920). The productions starred John and Lionel Barrymore, who with their
sister, Ethel, were currently the most famous actors in
America. The brilliant young designer Robert Edmond
Jones executed the scenic, costuming, and lighting designs.
Brooks Atkinson, who was the major critic for the *New York
Times* from 1925 to 1955 reported on the *Richard III* production in his book *Broadway:*

> In order to escape pedantry and the staleness of the past,
> he [Hopkins] eliminated the use of promptbooks at re-
> hearsals, and distributed the sides to the actors in type-
> written form, as if the play were a new one. He staged
> *Richard III* as a melodrama. The opening was one of
> Broadway's most tempestuous occasions. [John] Barry-
> more's Richard was a sardonic, cruel, fiery demon who
> radiated a kind of sinister beauty. He was simultaneously
> winning and repellent. . . . The production and perform-
> ance of *Richard III* were recognized as prologue to a new
> theater that had infinite possibilities. (p. 150)

Hopkins and Jones brought to the stage a kind of honesty,
simplicity, and beauty that had previously been veiled by
directorial pyrotechnics, bombast, and an abundance of
distracting technical effects. Hopkins provided a unique
approach to acting and directing. George Jean Nathan observed:

> he places his trust entirely in a superlatively rigid simplic-
> ity of treatment. He abjures all hocus-pocus, all showy
> pretense. He hires capable actors, tells them briefly what
> the play is about and how he desires them to interpret it,
> and then, with merely a slight touch here, a slight touch
> there, visited upon the picture during the process of
> rehearsal, permits the machine to get underway. No elab-
> orate crossings from left to right, no leaning on mantle-
> pieces, no haltings at doorways—none of the excess bag-
> gage of the Broadway direction. He presents his
> manuscript in the manner of a story simply and easily
> read. (Introduction to *How's Your Second Act?* by Arthur
> Hopkins [1918], pp. 13–14)

Hopkins discovered while working with vaudeville performers that they did not win their effect by "trying but by being." In his autobiography, *To a Lonely Boy,* he states, "the vaudeville actor created, the legitimate actor strutted." Hopkins simply believed in honesty and truth on and off the stage. He also believed in treating actors with courtesy and gentleness. (It was Hopkins who was most responsible, on behalf of management, for the settlement of the first actors' strike, which flared up in 1919 as a result of shabby and overlording treatment by certain managers.)

Robert Edmond Jones (1887–1954) was the first of a group of young artists who ushered in the "new stagecraft" in America (Lee Simonson and Norman Bell Geddes were the others). After leaving Harvard, where he had been classmates with Simonson, Jones went abroad to study Continental theater. Upon returning, he worked briefly with Sam Hume, who was a disciple of Edward Gordon Craig. Politically and artistically rebellious, Jones soon became associated with the Bohemians of Greenwich Village and became close friends with John Reed, Mabel Dodge, and many of the people associated with the Washington Square Players (where Simonson was working) and the Provincetown Players. In fact, he helped both groups in staging many of their productions. Indeed, after George Cram Cook and Susan Glaspell left the Playwright's Theatre, Robert Edmond Jones, Kenneth MacGowan, and Eugene O'Neill took over the management of the theater. They were known as the Triumvirate and for two years were very successful.

From 1915 to 1923 Jones was very active on Broadway; in conjunction with Arthur Hopkins he designed twenty productions. As an exponent of the new stagecraft, he was an avowed enemy of the old realism, with its cluttered stages. In the words of theater critic John Mason Brown, Jones "wanted an imaginative theater, where the knick-knacks of the everyday were to be dropped as the super cargo of the inglorious past, and the few paramount essentials—which had meaning in the theater as well as life—were to be raised to a fresh and glorious significance" (*Upstage* [1930], p. 139). In Jones's hands, the stage became, as Brown observed, "a place of essentials, true to ideas rather than to facts, reflecting not reality, but the shadows reality has cast upon the sensibilities of an artist" (pp. 158–9).

Always attempting to be faithful to the play, and always trying to provide the mood evoked by the playwright, Jones wanted to create an environment on stage to assist the actor. In his esoteric little book, *The Dramatic Imagination,* he wrote, "the sole aim of the arts of scene designing, costuming, lighting is . . . to enhance the natural powers of the actor." Thus, his settings were remarkable for their use of space, simple but meaningful architectural units and light and shadow. He employed varied materials and experimented with many techniques. It was no surprise, therefore, that he became the third member of the production team for *Anna Christie*.

The fourth member was Pauline Lord, who was cast by Hopkins to play Anna. She had been discovered by him and used as one of the leads in a touring company presenting Rice's *On Trial*. Of her acting, Hopkins said that it was "acting that was not acting at all, poignancy that came from deep and troubled wells—Polly is not a fast blooming plant. Her roots are deep and not quickly reached. Without their nourishment, her work is lifeless, but all of the time there are notes in that haunting voice that are unmistakable soundings of the rich flow that is to come." She was an unlikely prospect for the role of Anna, whom O'Neill had described as "tall, blond, fully-developed . . . handsome after a large, Viking-daughter fashion." Polly, as described by the Gelbs, was "thirty-one, delicate, almost fragile, with a tiny waist, small hands and feet, a pale, oval face, and tragic brown eyes." Hopkins said that he cast her because, "to my mind the bewildered innocent prostitute is O'Neill's top character creation, a bitter, deeply compassionate indictment of a snap-judging, ill informed world." O'Neill himself was delighted with her, mainly because she was shy and withdrawn, as he was. Hopkins saw that the success of the play depended on Anna, and therefore that his choice of Polly was crucial. O'Neill and Hopkins watched rehearsals, rarely communicating, and at the end of the last rehearsal, "before the scenery came in, Polly threw her arms around me [Hopkins] and wept, 'that's all I can do with it.' 'I should hope so,' I said, 'nobody could stand much more.' " She did not fail him. The other members of the company were: Frank Shannon as Mat Burke, George Marion as Chris, James C. Mack as "Johnny-the-Priest," and Eugenie Blair as Marthy Owen. Hopkins caught the mood of character in casting. He hired three actors with the names of Reilly, Hansen, and Kelly to portray the sailors.

Anna Christie opened at the Vanderbilt Theater in New York City on November 2, 1921. It played for 177 performances in its first run and won the Pulitzer Prize for the 1920–21 season. After completing its run in New York, the entire production was moved to London, where it opened April 10, 1922. The play was twice adapted to the screen, the more memorable version starring Greta Garbo. The play was revived in 1952 and starred Celeste Holm. In 1957 it was adapted as a musical entitled *New Girl in Town,* with Gwen Verdon.

ANNA CHRISTIE
A Play in Four Acts

CHARACTERS

"Johnny-the-Priest"
Two Longshoremen
A Postman
Larry, *bartender*
Chris Christopherson, *captain of the barge* Simeon
    Winthrop
Marthy Owen
Anna Christopherson, *Chris's daughter*
Three men of a steamer's crew
Mat Burke, *a stoker*
Johnson, *deckhand on the barge*

SCENES

Act I. "Johnny-the-Priest's" saloon near the water front, New York City.

Act II. The barge, *Simeon Winthrop*, at anchor in the harbor of Provincetown, Mass. Ten days later.

Act III. Cabin of the barge, at dock in Boston. A week later.

Act IV. The same. Two days later.

ACT ONE

SCENE: "Johnny-the-priest's" saloon near South Street, New York City. The stage is divided into two sections, showing a small back room on the right. On the left, forward, of the barroom, a large window looking out on the street. Beyond it, the main entrance—a double swinging door. Farther back, another window. The bar runs from left to right nearly the whole length of the rear wall. In back of the bar, a small showcase displaying a few bottles of case goods, for which there is evidently little call. The remainder of the rear space in front of the large mirrors is occupied by half-barrels of cheap whisky of the "nickel-a-shot" variety, from which the liquor is drawn by means of spigots. On the right is an open doorway leading to the back room. In the back room are four round wooden tables with five chairs grouped about each. In the rear, a family entrance opening on a side street.

It is late afternoon of a day in fall.

As the curtain rises, JOHNNY is discovered. "JOHNNY-THE-PRIEST" deserves his nickname. With his pale, thin, clean-shaven face, mild blue eyes and white hair, a cassock would seem more suited to him than the apron he wears. Neither his voice nor his general manner dispel this illusion which has made him a personage of the water front. They are soft and bland. But beneath all his mildness one senses the man behind the mask—cynical, callous, hard as nails. He is lounging at ease behind the bar, a pair of spectacles on his nose, reading an evening paper.

Two longshoremen enter from the street, wearing their working aprons, the button of the union pinned conspicuously on the caps pulled sideways on their heads at an aggressive angle.

FIRST LONGSHOREMAN: (*as they range themselves at the bar*) Gimme a shock. Number Two. (*He tosses a coin on the bar*).

SECOND LONGSHOREMAN: Same here. (JOHNNY *sets two glasses of barrel whisky before them*).

FIRST LONGSHOREMAN: Here's luck! (*The other nods. They gulp down their whisky*).

SECOND LONGSHOREMAN: (*putting money on the bar*) Give us another.

FIRST LONGSHOREMAN: Gimme a scoop this time—lager and porter. I'm dry.

SECOND LONGSHOREMAN: Same here. (JOHNNY *draws the lager and porter and sets the big, foaming schooners before them. They drink down half the contents and start to talk together hurriedly in low tones. The door on the left is swung open and* LARRY *enters. He is a boyish, red-cheeked, rather good-looking young fellow of twenty or so*).

LARRY: (*nodding to* JOHNNY—*cheerily*) Hello, boss.

JOHNNY: Hello, Larry. (*With a glance at his watch*) Just on time. (LARRY *goes to the right behind the bar, takes off his coat, and puts on an apron*).

FIRST LONGSHOREMAN: (*abruptly*) Let's drink up and get

back to it. (*They finish their drinks and go out left.* THE POSTMAN *enters as they leave. He exchanges nods with* JOHNNY *and throws a letter on the bar*).

THE POSTMAN: Addressed care of you, Johnny. Know him?

JOHNNY: (*picks up the letter, adjusting his spectacles.* LARRY *comes and peers over his shoulders.* JOHNNY *reads very slowly*) Christopher Christopherson.

THE POSTMAN: (*helpfully*) Square-head name.

LARRY: Old Chris—that's who.

JOHNNY: Oh, sure. I was forgetting Chris carried a hell of a name like that. Letters come here for him sometimes before, I remember now. Long time ago, though.

THE POSTMAN: It'll get him all right then?

JOHNNY: Sure thing. He comes here whenever he's in port.

THE POSTMAN: (*turning to go*) Sailor, eh?

JOHNNY: (*with a grin*) Captain of a coal barge.

THE POSTMAN: (*laughing*) Some job! Well, s'long.

JOHNNY: S'long. I'll see he gets it. (THE POSTMAN *goes out.* JOHNNY *scrutinizes the letter*) You got good eyes, Larry. Where's it from?

LARRY: (*after a glance*) St. Paul. That'll be in Minnesota, I'm thinkin'. Looks like a woman's writing, too, the old divil!

JOHNNY: He's got a daughter somewheres out West, I think he told me once. (*He puts the letter on the cash register*) Come to think of it, I ain't seen old Chris in a dog's age. (*Putting his overcoat on, he comes around the end of the bar*) Guess I'll be gettin' home. See you tomorrow.

LARRY: Good-night to ye, boss. (*As* JOHNNY *goes toward the street door, it is pushed open and* CHRISTOPHER CHRISTOPHERSON *enters. He is a short, squat, broad-shouldered man of about fifty, with a round, weather-beaten, red face from which his light blue eyes peer short-sightedly, twinkling with a simple good humor. His large mouth, overhung by a thick, drooping, yellow mustache, is childishly self-willed and weak, of an obstinate kindliness. A thick neck is jammed like a post into the heavy trunk of his body. His arms with their big, hairy, freckled hands, and his stumpy legs terminating in large flat feet, are awkwardly short and muscular. He walks with a clumsy, rolling gait. His voice, when not raised in a hollow boom, is toned down to a sly, confidential*

*half-whisper with something vaguely plaintive in its quality.
He is dressed in a wrinkled, ill-fitting dark suit of shore
clothes, and wears a faded cap of gray cloth over his mop of
grizzled, blond hair. Just now his face beams with a too-
blissful happiness, and he has evidently been drinking. He
reaches his hand out to* JOHNNY).

CHRIS: Hello, Yohnny! Have drink on me. Come on,
Larry. Give us drink. Have one yourself. (*Putting his hand
in his pocket*) Ay gat money—plenty money . . .

JOHNNY: (*shakes* CHRIS *by the hand*) Speak of the devil.
We was yust talkin' about you.

LARRY: (*coming to the end of the bar*) Hello, Chris. Put it
there. (*They shake hands*).

CHRIS: (*beaming*) Give us drink.

JOHNNY: (*with a grin*) You got a half-snootful now.
Where'd you get it?

CHRIS: (*grinning*) Oder fallar on oder barge—Irish fallar—he gat bottle vhisky and we drank it, yust us two. Dot
vhisky gat kick, by yingo! Ay yust come ashore. Give us
drink, Larry. Ay vas little drunk, not much. Yust feel good.
(*He laughs and commences to sing in a nasal, high-pitched
quaver*).

"My Yosephine, come board de ship. Long time Ay vait for
you. De moon, she shi-i-i-ine. She looka yust like you.

 Tchee-tchee, tchee-tchee, tchee-tchee, tchee-tchee."
(*To the accompaniment of this last he waves his hand as if he
were conducting an orchestra*).

JOHNNY: (*with a laugh*) Same old Yosie, eh Chris?

CHRIS: You don't know good song when you hear him.
Italian fallar on oder barge, he learn me dat. Give us drink.
(*He throws change on the bar*).

LARRY: (*with a professional air*) What's your pleasure,
gentlemen?

JOHNNY: Small beer, Larry.

CHRIS: Vhisky—Number Two.

LARRY: (*as he gets their drinks*) I'll take a cigar on you.

CHRIS: (*lifting his glass*) Skoal! (*He drinks*).

JOHNNY: Drink hearty.

CHRIS: (*immediately*) Have oder drink.

JOHNNY: No. Some other time. Got to go home now. So
you've just landed? Where are you in from this time?

CHRIS: Norfolk. Ve make slow voyage—dirty vedder—
yust fog, fog, fog, all bloody time! (*There is an insistent ring*

from the doorbell at the family entrance in the back room. CHRIS *gives a start—hurriedly*) Ay go open, Larry. Ay forgat. It vas Marthy. She come with me. (*He goes into the back room*).

LARRY: (*with a chuckle*) He's still got that same cow livin' with him, the old fool!

JOHNNY: (*with a grin*) A sport, Chris is. Well, I'll beat it home. S'long. (*He goes to the street door*).

LARRY: So long, boss.

JOHNNY: Oh—don't forget to give him his letter.

LARRY: I won't. (JOHNNY *goes out. In the meantime,* CHRIS *has opened the family entrance door, admitting* MARTHY: *She might be forty or fifty. Her jowly, mottled face, with its thick red nose, is streaked with interlacing purple veins. Her thick, gray hair is piled anyhow in a greasy mop on top of her round head. Her figure is flabby and fat; her breath comes in wheezy gasps; she speaks in a loud, mannish voice, punctuated by explosions of hoarse laughter. But there still twinkles in her blood-shot blue eyes a youthful lust for life which hard usage has failed to stifle, a sense of humor mocking, but good-tempered. She wears a man's cap, double-breasted man's jacket, and a grimy, calico skirt. Her bare feet are encased in a man's brogans several sizes too large for her, which gives her a shuffling, wobbly gait*).

MARTHY: (*grumblingly*) What yuh tryin' to do, Dutchy— keep me standin' out there all day? (*She comes forward and sits at the table in the right corner, front*).

CHRIS: (*mollifyingly*) Ay'm sorry, Marthy. Ay talk to Yohnny. Ay forgat. What you goin' take for drink?

MARTHY: (*appeased*) Gimme a scoop of lager an' ale.

CHRIS: Ay go bring him back. (*He returns to the bar*) Lager and ale for Marthy, Larry. Vhisky for me. (*He throws change on the bar*).

LARRY: Right you are. (*Then remembering, he takes the letter from in back of the bar*) Here's a letter for you—from St. Paul, Minnesota—and a lady's writin'. (*He grins*).

CHRIS: (*quickly—taking it*) Oh, den it come from my daughter, Anna. She live dere. (*He turns the letter over in his hands uncertainly*) Ay don't gat letter from Anna—must be a year.

LARRY: (*jokingly*) That's a fine fairy tale to be tellin'— your daughter! Sure I'll bet it's some bum.

CHRIS: (*soberly*) No. Dis come from Anna. (*Engrossed by the letter in his hand—uncertainly*) By golly, Ay tank Ay'm too drunk for read dis letter from Anna. Ay tank Ay sat down for a minute. You bring drinks in back room, Larry. (*He goes into the room on right*).

MARTHY: (*angrily*) Where's my lager an' ale, yuh big stiff?

CHRIS: (*preoccupied*) Larry bring him. (*He sits down opposite her.* LARRY *brings in the drinks and sets them on the table. He and* MARTHY *exchange nods of recognition.* LARRY *stands looking at* CHRIS *curiously.* MARTHY *takes a long draught of her schooner and heaves a huge sigh of satisfaction, wiping her mouth with the back of her hand.* CHRIS *stares at the letter for a moment—slowly opens it, and, squinting his eyes, commences to read laboriously, his lips moving as he spells out the words. As he reads his face lights up with an expression of mingled joy and bewilderment*).

LARRY: Good news?

MARTHY: (*her curiosity also aroused*) What's that yuh got—a letter, fur Gawd's sake?

CHRIS: (*pauses for a moment, after finishing the letter, as if to let the news sink in—then suddenly pounds his fist on the table with happy excitement*) Py yiminy! Yust tank, Anna say she's comin' here right avay! She gat sick on yob in St. Paul, she say. It's short letter, don't tal me much more'n dat. (*Beaming*) Py golly, dat's good news all at one time for ole fallar! (*Then turning to* MARTHY, *rather shamefacedly*) You know, Marthy, Ay've tole you Ay don't see my Anna since she vas little gel in Sveden five year ole.

MARTHY: How old'll she be now?

CHRIS: She must be—lat me see—she must be twenty year ole, py Yo!

LARRY: (*surprised*) You've not seen her in fifteen years?

CHRIS: (*suddenly growing somber—in a low tone*) No. Ven she vas little gel, Ay vas bo'sun on vindjammer. Ay never gat home only few time dem year. Ay'm fool sailor fallar. My voman—Anna's mo'der—she gat tired vait all time Sveden for me ven Ay don't never come. She come dis country, bring Anna, dey go out Minnesota, live with her cousins on farm. Den ven her mo'der die ven Ay vas on voyage, Ay tank it's better dem cousins keep Anna. Ay tank it's better Anna live on farm, den she don't know dat ole davil, sea, she don't know fa'der like me.

LARRY: (*with a wink at* MARTHY) This girl, now, 'll be marryin' a sailor herself, likely. It's in the blood.

CHRIS: (*suddenly springing to his feet and smashing his fist on the table in a rage*) No, py God! She don't do dat!

MARTHY: (*grasping her schooner hastily—angrily*) Hey, look out, yuh nut! Wanta spill my suds for me?

LARRY: (*amazed*) Oho, what's up with you? Ain't you a sailor yourself now, and always been?

CHRIS: (*slowly*) Dat's yust vhy Ay say it. (*Forcing a smile*) Sailor vas all right fallar, but not for marry gel. No. Ay know dat. Anna's mo'der, she know it, too.

LARRY: (*as* CHRIS *remains sunk in gloomy reflection*) When is your daughter comin'? Soon?

CHRIS: (*roused*) Py yiminy, Ay forgat. (*Reads through the letter hurriedly*) She say she come right avay, dat's all.

LARRY: She'll maybe be comin' here to look for you, I s'pose. (*He returns to the bar, whistling. Left alone with* MARTHY, *who stares at him with a twinkle of malicious humor in her eyes,* CHRIS *suddenly becomes desperately ill-at-ease. He fidgets, then gets up hurriedly*).

CHRIS: Ay gat speak with Larry. Ay be right back. (*Mollifyingly*) Ay brink you oder drink.

MARTHY: (*emptying her glass*) Sure. That's me. (*As he retreats with the glass she guffaws after him derisively*).

CHRIS: (*to* LARRY *in an alarmed whisper*) Py yingo, Ay gat gat Marthy shore off barge before Anna come! Anna raise hell if she find dat out. Marthy raise hell, too, for go, py golly!

LARRY: (*with a chuckle*) Serve ye right, ye old divil—havin' a woman at your age!

CHRIS: (*scratching his head in a quandary*) You tal me lie for tal Marthy, Larry, so's she gat off barge quick.

LARRY: She knows your daughter's comin'. Tell her to get the hell out of it.

CHRIS: No. Ay don't like make her feel bad.

LARRY: You're an old mush! Keep your girl away from the barge, then. She'll likely want to stay ashore anyway. (*Curiously*) What does she work at, your Anna?

CHRIS: She stay on dem cousins' farm 'till two year ago. Dan she gat yob nurse gel in St. Paul. (*Then shaking his head resolutely*) But Ay don't vant for her gat yob now. Ay vant for her stay with me.

LARRY: (*scornfully*) On a coal barge! She'll not like that, I'm thinkin'.

MARTHY: (*shouts from next room*) Don't I get that bucket o' suds, Dutchy?

CHRIS: (*startled—in apprehensive confusion*) Yes, Ay come, Marthy.

LARRY: (*drawing the lager and ale, hands it to* CHRIS— *laughing*) Now you're in for it! You'd better tell her straight to get out!

MARTHY: (*aggressively*) Wha's that? (*Then, pretending to fly into a rage, her eyes enjoying* CHRIS' *misery*) I'm wise to what's in back of your nut, Dutchy. Yuh want to git rid o' me, huh?—now she's comin'. Gimme the bum's rush ashore, huh? Lemme tell yuh, Dutchy, there ain't a square-head workin' on a boat man enough to git away with that. Don't start nothin' yuh can't finish!

CHRIS: (*miserably*) Ay don't start nutting, Marthy.

MARTHY: (*glares at him for a second—then cannot control a burst of laughter*) Ho-ho! Yuh're a scream, Square-head—an honest-ter-Gawd knockout! Ho-ho! (*She wheezes, panting for breath*).

CHRIS: (*with childish pique*) Ay don't see nutting for laugh at.

MARTHY: Take a slant in the mirror and yuh'll see. Ho-ho! (*Recovering from her mirth—chuckling, scornfully*) A square-head tryin' to kid Marthy Owen at this late day!—after me campin' with barge men the last twenty years. I'm wise to the game, up, down, and sideways. I ain't been born and dragged up on the water front for nothin'. Think I'd make trouble, huh? Not me! I'll pack up me duds an' beat it. I'm quittin' yuh, get me? I'm tellin' yuh I'm sick of stickin' with yuh, and I'm leavin' yuh flat, see? There's plenty of other guys on other barges waitin' for me. Always was, I always found. (*She claps the astonished* CHRIS *on the back*) So cheer up, Dutchy! I'll be offen the barge before she comes. You'll be rid o' me for good—and me o' you—good riddance for both of us. Ho-ho!

CHRIS: (*seriously*) Ay don' tank dat. You vas good gel, Marthy.

MARTHY: (*grinning*) Good girl? Aw, can the bull! Well, yuh treated me square, yuhself. So it's fifty-fifty. Nobody's sore at nobody. We're still good frien's, huh? (LARRY *returns to bar*).

CHRIS: (*beaming now that he sees his troubles disappearing*) Yes, py golly.

MARTHY: That's the talkin'! In all my time I tried never to split with a guy with no hard feelin's. But what was yuh so scared about—that I'd kick up a row? That ain't Marthy's way. (*Scornfully*) Think I'd break my heart to loose yuh? Commit suicide, huh? Ho-ho! Gawd! The world's full o' men if that's all I'd worry about! (*Then with a grin, after emptying her glass*) Blow me to another scoop, huh? I'll drink your kid's health for yuh.

CHRIS: (*eagerly*) Sure tang. Ay go gat him. (*He takes the two glasses into the bar*) Oder drink. Same for both.

LARRY: (*getting the drinks and putting them on the bar*) She's not such a bad lot, that one.

CHRIS: (*jovially*) She's good gel, Ay tal you! Py golly, Ay calabrate now! Give me vhisky here at bar, too. (*He puts down money. LARRY serves him*) You have drink, Larry.

LARRY: (*virtuously*) You know I never touch it.

CHRIS: You don't know what you miss. Skoal! (*He drinks—then begins to sing loudly*).

"My Yosephine, come board de ship——"

(*He picks up the drinks for MARTHY and himself and walks unsteadily into the back room, singing*).

"De moon, she shi-i-ine. She looka yust like you.

      Tchee-tchee, tchee-tchee, tchee-tchee, tchee-tchee."

MARTHY: (*grinning, hands to ears*) Gawd!

CHRIS: (*sitting down*) Ay'm good singer, yes? Ve drink, eh? Skoal! Ay calabrate! (*He drinks*) Ay calabrate 'cause Anna's coming home. You know, Marthy, Ay never write for her to come, 'cause Ay tank Ay'm no good for her. But all time Ay hope like hell some day she vant for see me and den she come. And dat's vay it happen now, py yiminy! (*His face beaming*) What you tank she look like, Marthy? Ay bet you she's fine, good, strong gel, pooty like hell! Living on farm made her like dat. And Ay bet you some day she marry good, steady land fallar here in East, have home all her own, have kits—and dan Ay'm ole grandfader, py golly! And Ay go visit dem every time Ay gat in port near! (*Bursting with joy*) By yiminy crickens, Ay calabrate dat! (*Shouts*) Bring oder drink, Larry! (*He smashes his fist on the table with a bang*).

LARRY: (*coming in from bar—irritably*) Easy there! Don't be breakin' the table, you old goat!

CHRIS: (*by way of reply, grins foolishly and begins to sing*) "My Yosephine, come board de ship——"

MARTHY: (*touching* CHRIS'S *arm persuasively*) You're soused to the ears, Dutchy. Go out and put a feed into you. It'll sober you up. (*Then as* CHRIS *shakes his head obstinately*) Listen, yuh old nut! Yuh don't know what time your kid's liable to show up. Yuh want to be sober when she comes, don't yuh?

CHRIS: (*aroused—gets unsteadily to his feet*) Py golly, yes.

LARRY: That's good sense for you. A good beef stew'll fix you. Go round the corner.

CHRIS: All right. Ay be back soon, Marthy. (CHRIS *goes through the bar and out the street door*).

LARRY: He'll come round all right with some grub in him.

MARTHY: Sure. (LARRY *goes back to the bar and resumes his newspaper.* MARTHY *sips what is left of her schooner reflectively. There is the ring of the family entrance bell.* LARRY *comes to the door and opens it a trifle—then, with a puzzled expression, pulls it wide.* ANNA CHRISTOPHERSON *enters. She is a tall, blond, fully-developed girl of twenty, handsome after a large, Viking-daughter fashion but now run down in health and plainly showing all the outward evidences of belonging to the world's oldest profession. Her youthful face is already hard and cynical beneath its layer of make-up. Her clothes are the tawdry finery of peasant stock turned prostitute. She comes and sinks wearily in a chair by the table, left front*).

ANNA: Gimme a whisky—ginger ale on the side. (*Then, as* LARRY *turns to go, forcing a winning smile at him*) And don't be stingy, baby.

LARRY: (*sarcastically*) Shall I serve it in a pail?

ANNA: (*with a hard laugh*) That suits me down to the ground. (LARRY *goes into the bar. The two women size each other up with frank stares.* LARRY *comes back with the drink which he sets before* ANNA *and returns to the bar again.* ANNA *downs her drink at a gulp. Then, after a moment, as the alcohol begins to rouse her, she turns to* MARTHY *with a friendly smile*) Gee, I needed that bad, all right, all right!

MARTHY: (*nodding her head sympathetically*) Sure—yuh look all in. Been on a bat?

ANNA: No—traveling—day and a half on the train. Had to sit up all night in the dirty coach, too. Gawd, I thought I'd never get here!

MARTHY: *(with a start—looking at her intently)* Where'd yuh come from, huh?

ANNA: St. Paul—out in Minnesota.

MARTHY: *(staring at her in amazement—slowly)* So—yuh're—— *(She suddenly bursts out into hoarse, ironical laughter)* Gawd!

ANNA: All the way from Minnesota, sure. *(Flaring up)* What you laughing at? Me?

MARTHY: *(hastily)* No, honest, kid. I was thinkin' of somethin' else.

ANNA: *(mollified—with a smile)* Well, I wouldn't blame you, at that. Guess I do look rotten—yust out of the hospital two weeks. I'm going to have another 'ski. What d'you say? Have something on me?

MARTHY: Sure I will. T'anks. *(She calls)* Hey, Larry! Little service! *(He comes in)*.

ANNA: Same for me.

MARTHY: Same here. *(LARRY takes their glasses and goes out)*.

ANNA: Why don't you come sit over here, be sociable. I'm a dead stranger in this burg—and I ain't spoke a word with no one since day before yesterday.

MARTHY: Sure thing. *(She shuffles over to ANNA's table and sits down opposite her. LARRY brings the drinks and ANNA pays him)*.

ANNA: Skoal! Here's how! *(She drinks)*.

MARTHY: Here's luck! *(She takes a gulp from her schooner)*.

ANNA: *(taking a package of Sweet Caporal cigarettes from her bag)* Let you smoke in here, won't they?

MARTHY: *(doubtfully)* Sure. *(Then with evident anxiety)* On'y trow it away if yuh hear someone comin'.

ANNA: *(lighting one and taking a deep inhale)* Gee, they're fussy in this dump, ain't they? *(She puffs, staring at the table top. MARTHY looks her over with a new penetrating interest, taking in every detail of her face. ANNA suddenly becomes conscious of this appraising stare—resentfully)* Ain't nothing wrong with me, is there? You're looking hard enough.

MARTHY: *(irritated by the other's tone—scornfully)* Ain't

got to look much. I got your number the minute you stepped in the door.

ANNA: (her eyes narrowing) Ain't you smart! Well, I got yours, too, without no trouble. You're me forty years from now. That's you! (She gives a hard little laugh).

MARTHY: (angrily) Is that so? Well, I'll tell you straight, kiddo, that Marthy Owen never—— (She catches herself up short—with a grin) What are you and me scrappin' over? Let's cut it out, huh? Me, I don't want no hard feelin's with no one. (Extending her hand) Shake and forget it, huh?

ANNA: (shakes her hand gladly) Only too glad to. I ain't looking for trouble. Let's have 'nother. What d'you say?

MARTHY: (shaking her head) Not for mine. I'm full up. And you—— Had anythin' to eat lately?

ANNA: Not since this morning on the train.

MARTHY: Then yuh better go easy on it, hadn't yuh?

ANNA: (after a moment's hesitation) Guess you're right. I got to meet someone, too. But my nerves is on edge after that rotten trip.

MARTHY: Yuh said yuh was just outa the hospital?

ANNA: Two weeks ago. (Leaning over to MARTHY confidentially) The joint I was in out in St. Paul got raided. That was the start. The judge give all us girls thirty days. The others didn't seem to mind being in the cooler much. Some of 'em was used to it. But me, I couldn't stand it. It got my goat right—couldn't eat or sleep or nothing. I never could stand being caged up nowheres. I got good and sick and they had to send me to the hospital. It was nice there. I was sorry to leave it, honest!

MARTHY: (after a slight pause) Did yuh say yuh got to meet someone here?

ANNA: Yes. Oh, not what you mean. It's my Old Man I got to meet. Honest! It's funny, too. I ain't seen him since I was a kid—don't even know what he looks like—yust had a letter every now and then. This was always the only address he give me to write him back. He's yanitor of some building here now—used to be a sailor.

MARTHY: (astonished) Janitor!

ANNA: Sure. And I was thinking maybe, seeing he ain't never done a thing for me in my life, he might be willing to stake me to a room and eats till I get rested up. (Wearily) Gee, I sure need that rest! I'm knocked out. (Then resignedly) But I ain't expecting much from him. Give you a kick when you're down, that's what all men do. *(With sudden passion)* Men, I hate 'em—all of 'em! And I don't expect he'll turn out no better than the rest. *(Then with sudden interest)* Say, do you hang out around this dump much?

MARTHY: Oh, off and on.

ANNA: Then maybe you know him—my Old Man—or at least seen him?

MARTHY: It ain't old Chris, is it?

ANNA: Old Chris?

MARTHY: Chris Christopherson, his full name is.

ANNA: *(excitedly)* Yes, that's him! Anna Christopherson—that's my real name—only out there I called myself Anna Christie. So you know him, eh?

MARTHY: *(evasively)* Seen him about for years.

ANNA: Say, what's he like, tell me, honest?

MARTHY: Oh, he's short and——

ANNA: *(impatiently)* I don't care what he looks like. What kind of is he?

MARTHY: *(earnestly)* Well, yuh can bet your life, kid, he's as good an old guy as ever walked on two feet. That goes!

ANNA: *(pleased)* I'm glad to hear it. Then you think's he'll stake me to that rest cure I'm after?

MARTHY: *(emphatically)* Surest thing you know. *(Disgustedly)* But where'd yuh get the idea he was a janitor?

ANNA: He wrote me he was himself.

MARTHY: Well, he was lyin'. He ain't. He's captain of a barge—five men under him.

ANNA: *(disgusted in her turn)* A barge? What kind of a barge?

MARTHY: Coal, mostly.

ANNA: A coal barge! *(With a harsh laugh)* If that ain't a swell job to find your long lost Old Man working at! Gee, I knew something'd be bound to turn out wrong—always does with me. That puts my idea of his giving me a rest on the bum.

MARTHY: What d'yuh mean?

ANNA: I s'pose he lives on the boat, don't he?

MARTHY: Sure. What about it? Can't you live on it, too?

ANNA: *(scornfully)* Me? On a dirty coal barge! What d'you think I am?

MARTHY: *(resentfully)* What d'yuh know about barges, huh? Bet yuh ain't never seen one. That's what comes of his bringing yuh up inland—away from the old devil sea—where yuh'd be safe—Gawd! *(The irony of it strikes her sense of humor and she laughs hoarsely).*

ANNA: *(angrily)* His bringing me up! Is that what he tells people! I like his nerve! He let them cousins of my Old Woman's keep me on their farm and work me to death like a dog.

MARTHY: Well, he's got queer notions on some things. I've heard him say a farm was the best place for a kid.

ANNA: Sure. That's what he'd always answer back—and a lot of crazy stuff about staying away from the sea—stuff I couldn't make head or tail to. I thought he must be nutty.

MARTHY: He is on that one point. *(Casually)* So yuh didn't fall for life on the farm, huh?

ANNA: I should say not! The old man of the family, his wife, and four sons—I had to slave for all of 'em. I was only a poor relation, and they treated me worse than they dare treat a hired girl. *(After a moment's hesitation—somberly)* It was one of the sons—the youngest—started me—when I was sixteen. After that, I hated 'em so I'd killed 'em all if I'd stayed. So I run away—to St. Paul.

MARTHY: *(who has been listening sympathetically)* I've heard Old Chris talkin' about your bein' a nurse girl out there. Was that all a bluff yuh put up when yuh wrote him?

ANNA: Not on your life, it wasn't. It was true for two years. I didn't go wrong all at one jump. Being a nurse girl was yust what finished me. Taking care of other people's kids, always listening to their bawling and crying, caged in, when you're only a kid yourself and want to go out and see things. At last I got the chance—to get into that house. And you bet your life I took it! *(Defiantly)* And I ain't sorry neither. *(After a pause—with bitter hatred)* It was all men's fault—the whole business. It was men on the farm ordering and beating me—and giving me the wrong start. Then when I was a nurse, it was men again hanging around, bothering me, trying to see what they could get. *(She gives a hard laugh)* And now it's men all the time. Gawd, I hate 'em all, every mother's son of 'em! Don't you?

MARTHY: Oh, I dunno. There's good ones and bad ones, kid. You've just had a run of bad luck with 'em, that's all. Your Old Man, now—old Chris—he's a good one.

ANNA: *(sceptically)* He'll have to show me.

MARTHY: Yuh kept right on writing him yuh was a nurse girl still, even after yuh was in the house, didn't yuh?

ANNA: Sure. *(Cynically)* Not that I think he'd care a darn.

MARTHY: Yuh're all wrong about him, kid. *(Earnestly)* I know Old Chris well for a long time. He's talked to me 'bout you lots o' times. He thinks the world o' you, honest he does.

ANNA: Aw, quit the kiddin'!

MARTHY: Honest! Only, he's a simple old guy, see? He's got nutty notions. But he means well, honest. Listen to me, kid—— *(She is interrupted by the opening and shutting of the street door in the bar and by hearing* CHRIS' *voice)* Ssshh!

ANNA: What's up?

CHRIS: *(who has entered the bar. He seems considerably sobered up)* Py golly, Larry, dat grub taste good. Marthy in back?

LARRY: Sure—and another tramp with her. (CHRIS *starts for the entrance to the back room).*

MARTHY: *(to* ANNA *in a hurried, nervous whisper)* That's him now. He's comin' in here. Brace up!

ANNA: Who? (CHRIS *opens the door).*

MARTHY: *(as if she were greeting him for the first time)* Why hello, Old Chris. *(Then before he can speak, she shuffles hurriedly past him into the bar, beckoning him to follow her)* Come here. I wanta tell yuh somethin'. *(He goes out to her. She speaks hurriedly in a low voice)* Listen! I'm goin' to beat it down to the barge—pack up me duds and blow. That's her in there—your Anna—just come—waitin' for yuh. Treat her right, see? She's been sick. Well, s'long! *(She goes into the back room—to* ANNA) S'long, kid. I gotta beat it now. See yuh later.

ANNA: *(nervously)* So long. (MARTHY *goes quickly out of the family entrance).*

LARRY: *(looking at the stupefied* CHRIS *curiously)* Well, what's up now?

CHRIS: *(vaguely)* Nutting—nutting. *(He stands before the door to the back room in an agony of embarrassed emotion—then he forces himself to a bold decision, pushes open the door and walks in. He stands there, casts a shy glance at Anna, whose brilliant clothes, and, to him, high-toned appearance, awe him terribly. He looks about him with pitiful nervousness as if to avoid the appraising look with which she takes in his face, his clothes, etc.—his voice seeming to plead for her forbearance)* Anna!

ANNA: *(acutely embarrassed in her turn)* Hello—father. She told me it was you. I yust got here a little while ago.

CHRIS: *(goes slowly over to her chair)* It's good—for see you—after all dem years, Anna. *(He bends down over her. After an embarrassed struggle they manage to kiss each other).*

ANNA: *(a trace of genuine feeling in her voice)* It's good to see you, too.

CHRIS: *(grasps her arms and looks into her face—then overcome by a wave of fierce tenderness)* Anna lilla! Anna lilla! *(Takes her in his arms).*

ANNA: *(shrinks away from him, half-frightened)* What's that—Swedish? I don't know it. *(Then as if seeking relief from the tension in a voluble chatter)* Gee, I had an awful trip coming here. I'm all in. I had to sit up in the dirty coach all night—couldn't get no sleep, hardly—and then I had a hard job finding this place. I never been in New York before, you know, and——

CHRIS: *(who has been staring down at her face admiringly, not hearing what she says—impulsively)* You know you vas awful pooty gel, Anna? Ay bet all men see you fall in love with you, py yiminy!

ANNA: *(repelled—harshly)* Cut it! You talk same as they all do.

CHRIS: *(hurt—humbly)* Ain't no harm for your fa'der talk dat vay, Anna.

ANNA: *(forcing a short laugh)* No—course not. Only— it's funny to see you and not remember nothing. You're like—a stranger.

CHRIS: *(sadly)* Ay s'pose. Ay never come home only few times ven you vas kit in Sveden. You don't remember dat?

ANNA: No. *(resentfully)* But why didn't you never come home them days? Why didn't you never come out West to see me?

CHRIS: *(slowly)* Ay tank, after your mo'der die, ven Ay vas avay on voyage, it's better for you you don't never see me! *(He sinks down in the chair opposite her dejectedly— then turns to her—sadly)* Ay don't know, Anna, vhy Ay never come home Sveden in ole year. Ay vant come home end of every voyage. Ay vant see your mo'der, your two bro'der before dey vas drowned, you ven you vas born— but—Ay—don't go. Ay sign on oder ships—go South America, go Australia, go China, go every port all over world

many times—but Ay never go aboard ship sail for Sveden.
Ven Ay gat money for pay passage home as passenger
den—— *(He bows his head guiltily)* Ay forgat and Ay spend
all money. Ven Ay tank again, it's too late. *(He sighs)* Ay
don't know why but dat's vay with most sailor fallar, Anna.
Dat ole davil sea make dem crazy fools with her dirty tricks.
It's so.

ANNA: *(who has watched him keenly while he has been
speaking—with a trace of scorn in her voice)* Then you think
the sea's to blame for everything, eh? Well, you're still
workin' on it, ain't you, spite of all you used to write me
about hating it. That dame was here told me you was captain
of a coal barge—and you wrote me you was yanitor of a
building!

CHRIS: *(embarrassed but lying glibly)* Oh, Ay vork on
land long time as yanitor. Yust short time ago Ay got dis yob
cause Ay vas sick, need open air.

ANNA: *(sceptically)* Sick? You? You'd never think it.

CHRIS: And, Anna, dis ain't real sailor yob. Dis ain't real
boat on sea. She's yust ole tub—like piece of land with
house on it dat float. Yob on her ain't sea yob. No. Ay don't
gat yob on sea, Anna, if Ay die first. Ay swear dat ven your
mo'der die. Ay keep my word, py yingo!

ANNA: *(perplexed)* Well, I can't see no difference. *(Dismissing the subject)* Speaking of being sick, I been there
myself—yust out of the hospital two weeks ago.

CHRIS: *(immediately all concern)* You, Anna? Py golly!
(Anxiously) You feel better now, dough, don't you? You look
little tired, dat's all!

ANNA: *(wearily)* I am. Tired to death. I need a long rest
and I don't see much chance of getting it.

CHRIS: What you mean, Anna?

ANNA: Well, when I made up my mind to come to see
you, I thought you was a yanitor—that you'd have a place
where, maybe, if you didn't mind having me, I could visit a
while and rest up—till I felt able to get back on the job again.

CHRIS: *(eagerly)* But Ay gat place, Anna—nice place.
You rest all you want, py yiminy! You don't never have to
vork as nurse gel no more. You stay with me, py golly!

ANNA: *(surprised and pleased by his eagerness—with a
smile)* Then you're really glad to see me—honest?

CHRIS: *(pressing one of her hands in both of his)* Anna,
Ay like see you like hell, Ay tal you! And don't you talk no

more about gatting yob. You stay with me. Ay don't see you
for long time, you don't forgat dat. *(His voice trembles)*
Ay'm gatting ole. Ay gat no one in vorld but you.

ANNA: *(touched—embarrassed by this unfamiliar emotion)* Thanks. It sounds good to hear someone—talk to me
that way. Say, though—if you're so lonely—it's funny—why
ain't you ever married again?

CHRIS: *(shaking his head emphatically—after a pause)*
Ay love your mo'der too much for ever do dat, Anna.

ANNA: *(impressed—slowly)* I don't remember nothing
about her. What was she like? Tell me.

CHRIS: Ay tal you all about everytang—and you tal me all
tangs happen to you. But not here now. Dis ain't good place
for young gel, anyway. Only no good sailor fallar come here
for gat drunk. *(He gets to his feet quickly and picks up her
bag)* You come with me, Anna. You need lie down, gat rest.

ANNA: *(half rises to her feet, then sits down again)*
Where're you going?

CHRIS: Come. Ve gat on board.

ANNA: *(disappointedly)* On board your barge, you mean?
(Dryly) Nix for mine! *(Then seeing his crestfallen look—
forcing a smile)* Do you think that's a good place for a young
girl like me—a coal barge?

CHRIS: *(dully)* Yes, Ay tank. *(He hesitates—then continues more and more pleadingly)* You don't know how nice
it's on barge, Anna. Tug come and ve gat towed out on
voyage—yust water all round, and sun, and fresh air, and
good grub for make you strong, healthy gel. You see many
tangs you don't see before. You gat moonlight at night,
maybe; see steamer pass; see schooner make sail—see
everything dat's pooty. You need take rest like dat. You
work too hard for young gel already. You need vacation,
yes!

ANNA: *(who has listened to him with a growing interest—
with an uncertain laugh)* It sounds good to hear you tell it.
I'd sure like a trip on the water, all right. It's the barge idea
has me stopped. Well, I'll go down with you and have a
look—and maybe I'll take a chance. Gee, I'd do anything
once.

CHRIS: *(picks up her bag again)* Ve go, eh?

ANNA: What's the rush? Wait a second. *(Forgetting the
situation for a moment, she relapses into the familiar form*

and flashes one of her winning trade smiles at him) Gee, I'm
thirsty.

CHRIS: *(sets down her bag immediately—hastily)* Ay'm
sorry, Anna. What you tank you like for drink, eh?

ANNA: *(promptly)* I'll take a—— *(Then suddenly reminded—confusedly)* I don't know. What'a they got here?

CHRIS: *(with a grin)* Ay don't tank dey got much fancy
drink for young gel in dis place, Anna. Yinger ale—
sas'prilla, maybe.

ANNA: *(forcing a laugh herself)* Make it sas, then.

CHRIS: *(coming up to her—with a wink)* Ay tal you, Anna,
ve calabrate, yes—dis one time because ve meet after many
year. *(In a half whisper, embarrassedly)* Dey gat good port
vine, Anna. It's good for you, Ay tank—little bit—for give
you appetite. It ain't strong, neider. One glass don't go to
your head, Ay promise.

ANNA: *(with a half hysterical laugh)* All right. I'll take
port.

CHRIS: Ay go gat him. *(He goes out to the bar. As soon as
the door closes,* ANNA *starts to her feet).*

ANNA: *(picking up her bag—half-aloud—stammeringly)*
Gawd, I can't stand this! I better beat it. *(Then she lets her
bag drop, stumbles over to her chair again, and covering her
face with her hands, begins to sob).*

LARRY: *(putting down his paper as* CHRIS *comes up—with
a grin)* Well, who's the blond?

CHRIS: *(proudly)* Dat vas Anna, Larry.

LARRY: *(in amazement)* Your daughter, Anna? *(*CHRIS
nods.* LARRY *lets a long, low whistle escape him and turns
away embarrassedly).*

CHRIS: Don't you tank she vas pooty gel, Larry?

LARRY: *(rising to the occasion)* Sure! A peach!

CHRIS: You bet you! Give me drink for take back—one
port vine for Anna—she calabrate dis one time with me—
and small beer for me.

LARRY: *(as he gets the drinks)* Small beer for you, eh?
She's reformin' you already.

CHRIS: *(pleased)* You bet! *(He takes the drinks. As she
hears him coming,* ANNA *hastily dries her eyes, tries to
smile.* CHRIS *comes in and sets the drinks down on the
table—stares at her for a second anxiously—patting her
hand)* You look tired, Anna. Vell, Ay make you take good

long rest now. *(Picking up his beer)* Come, you drink vine. It put new life in you. *(She lifts her glass—he grins)* Skoal, Anna! You know dat Svedish word?

ANNA: Skoal! *(downing her port at a gulp like a drink of whisky—her lips trembling)* Skoal? Guess I know that word, all right, all right!

(The Curtain Falls)

ACT TWO

SCENE: Ten days later. The stern of the deeply-laden barge, *Simeon Winthrop*, at anchor in the outer harbor of Provincetown, Mass. It is ten o'clock at night. Dense fog shrouds the barge on all sides, and she floats motionless on a calm. A lantern set up on an immense coil of thick hawser sheds a dull, filtering light on objects near it—the heavy steel bits for making fast the tow lines, etc. In the rear is the cabin, its misty windows glowing wanly with the light of a lamp inside. The chimney of the cabin stove rises a few feet above the roof. The doleful tolling of bells, on Long Point, on ships at anchor, breaks the silence at regular intervals.

As the curtain rises, ANNA is discovered standing near the coil of rope on which the lantern is placed. She looks healthy, transformed, the natural color has come back to her face. She has on a black oilskin coat, but wears no hat. She is staring out into the fog astern with an expression of awed wonder. The cabin door is pushed open and CHRIS appears. He is dressed in yellow oilskins—coat, pants, sou'wester—and wears high seaboots.

CHRIS: *(the glare from the cabin still in his eyes, peers blinkingly astern)* Anna! *(Receiving no reply, he calls again, this time with apparent apprehension)* Anna!

ANNA: *(with a start—making a gesture with her hand as if to impose silence—in a hushed whisper)* Yes, here I am. What d'you want?

CHRIS: *(walks over to her—solicitously)* Don't you come turn in, Anna? It's late—after four bells. It ain't good for you stay out here in fog, Ay tank.

ANNA: Why not? *(With a trace of strange exultation)* I love this fog! Honest! It's so—— *(She hesitates, groping for a word)* Funny and still. I feel as if I was—out of things altogether.

CHRIS: *(spitting disgustedly)* Fog's vorst one of her dirty tricks, py yingo!

ANNA: *(with a short laugh)* Beefing about the sea again? I'm getting so's I love it, the little I've seen.

CHRIS: *(glancing at her moodily)* Dat's foolish talk, Anna. You see her more, you don't talk dat vay. *(Then seeing her irritation, he hastily adopts a more cheerful tone)* But Ay'm glad you like it on barge. Ay'm glad it makes you feel good again. *(With a placating grin)* You like live like dis alone with ole fa'der, eh?

ANNA: Sure I do. Everything's been so different from anything I ever come across before. And now—this fog—Gee, I wouldn't have missed it for nothing. I never thought living on ships was so different from land. Gee, I'd yust love to work on it, honest I would, if I was a man. I don't wonder you always been a sailor.

CHRIS: *(vehemently)* Ay ain't sailor, Anna. And dis ain't real sea. You only see nice part. *(Then as she doesn't answer, he continues hopefully)* Vell, fog lift in morning, Ay tank.

ANNA: *(the exultation again in her voice)* I love it! I don't give a rap if it never lifts! *(CHRIS fidgets from one foot to the other worriedly.* ANNA *continues slowly, after a pause)* It makes me feel clean—out here—'s if I'd taken a bath.

CHRIS: *(after a pause)* You better go in cabin read book. Dat put you to sleep.

ANNA: I don't want to sleep. I want to stay out here—and think about things.

CHRIS: *(walks away from her toward the cabin—then comes back)* You act funny tonight, Anna.

ANNA: *(her voice rising angrily)* Say, what're you trying to do—make things rotten? You been kind as kind can be to me and I certainly appreciate it—only don't spoil it all now. *(Then, seeing the hurt expression on her father's face, she forces a smile)* Let's talk of something else. Come. Sit down here. *(She points to the coil of rope).*

CHRIS: *(sits down beside her with a sigh)* It's gatting pooty late in night, Anna. Must be near five bells.

ANNA: *(interestedly)* Five bells? What time is that?

CHRIS: Half past ten.

ANNA: Funny I don't know nothing about sea talk—but those cousins was always talking crops and that stuff. Gee, wasn't I sick of it—and of them!

CHRIS: You don't like live on farm, Anna?

ANNA: I've told you a hundred times I hated it. *(Decidedly)* I'd rather have one drop of ocean than all the farms in the world! Honest! And you wouldn't like a farm, neither. Here's where you belong. *(She makes a sweeping gesture seaward)* But not on a coal barge. You belong on a real ship, sailing all over the world.

CHRIS: *(moodily)* Ay've done dat many year, Anna, when Ay vas damn fool.

ANNA: *(disgustedly)* Oh, rats! *(After a pause she speaks musingly)* Was the men in our family always sailors—as far back as you know about?

CHRIS: *(shortly)* Yes. Damn fools! All men in our village on coast, Sveden, go to sea. Ain't nutting else for dem to do. My fa'der die on board ship in Indian Ocean. He's buried at sea. Ay don't never know him only little bit. Den my tree bro'der, older'n me, dey go on ships. Den Ay go, too. Den my mo'der she's left all 'lone. She die pooty quick after dat—all 'lone. Ve vas all avay on voyage when she die. *(He pauses sadly)* Two my bro'der dey gat lost on fishing boat same like your bro'ders vas drowned. My oder bro'der, he save money, give up sea, den he die home in bed. He's only one dat ole davil don't kill. *(Defiantly)* But me, Ay bet you Ay die ashore in bed, too!

ANNA: Were all of 'em yust plain sailors?

CHRIS: Able body seaman, most of dem. *(With a certain pride)* Dey vas all smart seaman, too—A one. *(Then after hesitating a moment—shyly)* Ay vas bo'sun.

ANNA: Bo'sun?

CHRIS: Dat's kind of officer.

ANNA: Gee, that was fine. What does he do?

CHRIS: *(after a second's hesitation, plunged into gloom again by his fear of her enthusiasm)* Hard vork all time. It's rotten, Ay tal you, for go to sea. *(Determined to disgust her with sea life—volubly)* Dey're all fool fallar, dem fallar in our family. Dey all vork rotten yob on sea for nutting, don't care nutting but yust gat big pay day in pocket, gat drunk, gat robbed, ship avay again on oder voyage. Dey don't come home. Dey don't do anytang like good man do. And dat ole davil, sea, sooner, later she svallow dem up.

ANNA: *(with an excited laugh)* Good sports, I'd call 'em. *(Then hastily)* But say—listen—did all the women of the family marry sailors?

CHRIS: *(eagerly—seeing a chance to drive home his point)* Yes—and it's bad on dem like hell vorst of all. Dey don't see deir men only once in long while. Dey set and vait all 'lone. And when deir boys grows up, go to sea, dey sit and vait some more. *(Vehemently)* And gel marry sailor, she's crazy fool! Your mo'der she tal you some tang if she vas alive. *(He relapses into an attitude of somber brooding)*.

ANNA: *(after a pause—dreamily)* Funny! I do feel sort of—nutty, tonight. I feel old.

CHRIS: *(mystified)* Ole?

ANNA: Sure—like I'd been living a long, long time—out here in the fog. *(Frowning perplexedly)* I don't know how to tell you yust what I mean. It's like I'd come home after a long visit away some place. It all seems like I'd been here before lots of times—on boats—in this same fog. *(With a short laugh)* You must think I'm off my base.

CHRIS: *(gruffly)* Anybody feel funny dat vay in fog.

ANNA: *(persistently)* But why d'you s'pose I feel so—so—like I'd found something I'd missed and been looking for—'s if this was the right place for me to fit in? And I seem to have forgot—everything that's happened—like it didn't matter no more. And I feel clean, somehow—like you feel yust after you've took a bath. And I feel happy for once—yes, honest!—happier than I ever been anywhere before! *(As* CHRIS *makes no comment but a heavy sigh, she continues wonderingly)* It's nutty for me to feel that way, don't you think?

CHRIS: *(a grim foreboding in his voice)* Ay tank Ay'm damn fool for bring you on voyage, Anna.

ANNA: *(impressed by his tone)* You talk—nutty tonight yourself. You act 's if you was scared something was going to happen.

CHRIS: Only God know dat, Anna.

ANNA: *(half-mockingly)* Then it'll be Gawd's will, like the preachers say—what does happen.

CHRIS: *(starts to his feet with fierce protest)* No! Dat ole davil, sea, she ain't God! *(In the pause of silence that comes after his defiance a hail in a man's husky, exhausted voice comes faintly out of the fog to port)* "Ahoy!" *(*CHRIS *gives a startled exclamation)*.

ANNA: *(jumping to her feet)* What's that?

CHRIS: *(who has regained his composure—sheepishly)* Py golly, dat scare me for minute. It's only some fallar hail, Anna—loose his course in fog. Must be fisherman's power boat. His engine break down, Ay guess. *(The "ahoy" comes again through the wall of fog, sounding much nearer this time.* CHRIS *goes over to the port bulwark)* Sound from dis side. She come in from open sea. *(He holds his hands to his mouth, megaphone-fashion, and shouts back)* Ahoy, dere! Vhat's trouble?

THE VOICE: *(this time sounding nearer but up forward toward the bow)* Heave a rope when we come alongside. *(Then irritably)* Where are ye, ye scut?

CHRIS: Ay hear dem rowing. Dey come up by bow, Ay tank. *(Then shouting out again)* Dis vay!

THE VOICE: Right ye are! *(There is a muffled sound of oars in oar-locks).*

ANNA: *(half to herself—resentfully)* Why don't that guy stay where he belongs?

CHRIS: *(hurriedly)* Ay go up bow. All hands asleep 'cepting fallar on vatch. Ay gat heave line to dat fallar. *(He picks up a coil of rope and hurries off toward the bow.* ANNA *walks back toward the extreme stern as if she wanted to remain as much isolated as possible. She turns her back on the proceedings and stares out into the fog.* THE VOICE *is heard again shouting "Ahoy" and* CHRIS *answering "Dis vay." Then there is a pause—the murmur of excited voices—then the scuffling of feet.* CHRIS *appears from around the cabin to port. He is supporting the limp form of a man dressed in dungarees, holding one of the man's arms around his neck. The deckhand,* JOHNSON, *a young blond Swede, follows him, helping along another exhausted man similar fashion.* ANNA *turns to look at them.* CHRIS *stops for a second—volubly)* Anna! You come help, vill you? You find vhisky in cabin. Dese fallars need drink for fix dem. Dey vas near dead.

ANNA: *(hurrying to him)* Sure—but who are they? What's the trouble?

CHRIS: Sailor fallars. Deir steamer gat wrecked. Dey been five days in open boat—four fallars—only one left able stand up. Come, Anna. *(She precedes him into the cabin, holding the door open while he and* JOHNSON *carry in their burdens. The door is shut, then opened again as* JOHNSON *comes out.* CHRIS' *voice shouts after him)* Go gat oder fallar, Yohnson.

JOHNSON: Yes, sir. (*He goes. The door is closed again.* MAT BURKE *stumbles in around the port side of the cabin. He moves slowly, feeling his way uncertainly, keeping hold of the port bulwark with his right hand to steady himself. He is stripped to the waist, has on nothing but a pair of dirty dungaree pants. He is a powerful, broad-chested six-footer, his face handsome in a hard, rough, bold, defiant way. He is about thirty, in the full power of his heavy-muscled, immense strength. His dark eyes are bloodshot and wild from sleeplessness. The muscles of his arms and shoulders are lumped in knots and bunches, the veins of his fore-arms stand out like blue cords. He finds his way to the coil of hawser and sits down on it facing the cabin, his back bowed, head in his hands, in an attitude of spent weariness*).

BURKE: (*talking aloud to himself*) Row, ye divil! Row! (*Then lifting his head and looking about him*) What's this tub? Well, we're safe anyway—with the help of God. (*He makes the sign of the cross mechanically.* JOHNSON *comes along the deck to port, supporting the fourth man, who is babbling to himself incoherently.* BURKE *glances at him disdainfully*) Is it losing the small wits ye iver had, ye are? Deck-scrubbing scut! (*They pass him and go into the cabin, leaving the door open.* BURKE *sags forward wearily*) I'm bate out—bate out entirely.

ANNA: (*comes out of the cabin with a tumbler quarter-full of whisky in her hand. She gives a start when she sees* BURKE *so near her, the light from the open door falling full on him. Then, overcoming what is evidently a feeling of repulsion, she comes up beside him*) Here you are. Here's a drink for you. You need it, I guess.

BURKE: (*lifting his head slowly—confusedly*) Is it dreaming I am?

ANNA: (*half smiling*) Drink it and you'll find it ain't no dream.

BURKE: To hell with the drink—but I'll take it just the same. (*He tosses it down*) Ahah! I'm needin' that—and 'tis fine stuff. (*Looking up at her with frank, grinning admiration*) But 'twasn't the booze I meant when I said, was I dreaming. I thought you was some mermaid out of the sea come to torment me. (*He reaches out to feel of her arm*) Aye, rale flesh and blood, divil a less.

ANNA: (*coldly. Stepping back from him*) Cut that.

BURKE: But tell me, isn't this a barge I'm on—or isn't it?

ANNA: Sure.

BURKE: And what is a fine handsome woman the like of you doing on this scow?

ANNA: (*coldly*) Never you mind. (*Then half-amused in spite of herself*) Say, you're a great one, honest—starting right in kidding after what you been through.

BURKE: (*delighted—proudly*) Ah, it was nothing—aisy for a rale man with guts to him, the like of me. (*He laughs*) All in the day's work, darlin'. (*Then, more seriously but still in a boastful tone, confidentially*) But I won't be denying 'twas a damn narrow squeak. We'd all ought to be with Davy Jones at the bottom of the sea, be rights. And only for me, I'm telling you, and the great strength and guts is in me, we'd be being scoffed by the fishes this minute!

ANNA: (*contemptuously*) Gee, you hate yourself, don't you? (*Then turning away from him indifferently*) Well, you'd better come in and lie down. You must want to sleep.

BURKE: (*stung—rising unsteadily to his feet with chest out and head thrown back—resentfully*) Lie down and sleep, is it? Divil a wink I'm after having for two days and nights and divil a bit I'm needing now. Let you not be thinking I'm the like of them three weak scuts come in the boat with me. I could lick the three of them sitting down with one hand tied behind me. They may be bate out, but I'm not—and I've been rowing the boat with them lying in the bottom not able to raise a hand for the last two days we was in it. (*Furiously, as he sees this is making no impression on her*) And I can lick all hands on this tub, wan be wan, tired as I am!

ANNA: (*sarcastically*) Gee, ain't you a hard guy! (*Then, with a trace of sympathy, as she notices him swaying from weakness*) But never mind that fight talk. I'll take your word for all you've said. Go on and sit down out here, anyway, if I can't get you to come inside. (*He sits down weakly*) You're all in, you might as well own up to it.

BURKE: (*fiercely*) The hell I am!

ANNA: (*coldly*) Well, be stubborn then for all I care. And I must say I don't care for your language. The men I know don't pull that rough stuff when ladies are around.

BURKE: (*getting unsteadily to his feet again—in a rage*) Ladies! Ho-ho! Divil mend you! Let you not be making game of me. What would ladies be doing on this bloody hulk? (*As* ANNA *attempts to go to the cabin, he lurches into her path*) Aisy, now! You're not the old Square-head's woman, I suppose you'll be telling me next—living in his cabin with him, no less! *(Seeing the cold, hostile expression on* ANNA'S *face, he suddenly changes his tone to one of boisterous joviality)* But I do be thinking, iver since the first look my eyes took at you, that it's a fool you are to be wasting yourself—a fine, handsome girl—on a stumpy runt of a man like that old Swede. There's too many strapping great lads on the sea would give their heart's blood for one kiss of you!

ANNA: *(scornfully)* Lads like you, eh?

BURKE: *(grinning)* Ye take the words out o' my mouth. I'm the proper lad for you, if it's meself do be saying it. *(With a quick movement he puts his arms about her waist)* Whisht, now, me daisy! Himself's in the cabin. It's wan of your kisses I'm needing to take the tiredness from me bones. Wan kiss, now! *(He presses her to him and attempts to kiss her)*.

ANNA: *(struggling fiercely)* Leggo of me, you big mutt! *(She pushes him away with all her might.* BURKE, *weak and tottering, is caught off his guard. He is thrown down backward and, in falling, hits his head a hard thump against the bulwark. He lies there still, knocked out for the moment.* ANNA *stands for a second, looking down at him frightenedly. Then she kneels down beside him and raises his head to her knee, staring into his face anxiously for some sign of life)*.

BURKE: *(stirring a bit—mutteringly)* God stiffen it! *(He opens his eyes and blinks up at her with vague wonder)*.

ANNA: *(letting his head sink back on the deck, rising to her feet with a sigh of relief)* You're coming to all right, eh? Gee, I was scared for a moment I'd killed you.

BURKE: *(with difficulty rising to a sitting position—scornfully)* Killed, is it? It'd take more than a bit of a blow to crack my thick skull. *(Then looking at her with the most intense admiration)* But, glory be, it's a power of strength is in them two fine arms of yours. There's not a man in the world can say the same as you, that he seen Mat Burke lying at his feet and him dead to the world.

ANNA: *(rather remorsefully)* Forget it. I'm sorry it happened, see? *(Burke rises and sits on bench. Then severely)* Only you had no right to be getting fresh with me. Listen, now, and don't go getting any more wrong notions. I'm on this barge because I'm making a trip with my father. The captain's my father. Now you know.

BURKE: The old Square—the old Swede, I mean?

ANNA: Yes.

BURKE: *(rising—peering at her face)* Sure I might have

known it, if I wasn't a bloody fool from birth. Where else'd you get that fine yellow hair is like a golden crown on your head.

ANNA: (with an amused laugh) Say, nothing stops you, does it? (Then attempting a severe tone again) But don't you think you ought to be apologizing for what you said and done yust a minute ago, instead of trying to kid me with that mush?

BURKE: (indignantly) Mush! (Then bending forward toward her with very intense earnestness) Indade and I will ask your pardon a thousand times—and on my knees, if ye like. I didn't mean a word of what I said or did. (Resentful again for a second) But divil a woman in all the ports of the world has iver made a great fool of me that way before!

ANNA: (with amused sarcasm) I see. You mean you're a lady-killer and they all fall for you.

BURKE: (offended. Passionately) Leave off your fooling! 'Tis that is after getting my back up at you. (Earnestly) 'Tis no lie I'm telling you about the women. (Ruefully) Though it's a great jackass I am to be mistaking you, even in anger, for the like of them cows on the waterfront is the only women I've met up with since I was growed to a man. (As ANNA shrinks away from him at this, he hurries on pleadingly) I'm a hard, rough man and I'm not fit, I'm thinking, to be kissing the shoe-soles of a fine, dacent girl the like of yourself. 'Tis only the ignorance of your kind made me see you wrong. So you'll forgive me, for the love of God, and let us be friends from this out. (Passionately) I'm thinking I'd rather be friends with you than have my wish for anything else in the world. (He holds out his hand to her shyly).

ANNA: (looking queerly at him, perplexed and worried, but moved and pleased in spite of herself—takes his hand uncertainly) Sure.

BURKE: (with boyish delight) God bless you! (In his excitement he squeezes her hand tight).

ANNA: Ouch!

BURKE: (hastily dropping her hand—ruefully) Your pardon, Miss. 'Tis a clumsy ape I am. (Then simply—glancing down his arm proudly) It's a great power I have in my hand and arm, and I do be forgetting it at times.

ANNA: (nursing her crushed hand and glancing at his arm, not without a trace of his own admiration) Gee, you're some strong, all right.

BURKE: *(delighted)* It's no lie, and why shouldn't I be, with me shoveling a million tons of coal in the stokeholes of ships since I was a lad only. *(He pats the coil of hawser invitingly)* Let you sit down, now, Miss, and I'll be telling you a bit of myself, and you'll be telling me a bit of yourself, and in an hour we'll be as old friends as if we was born in the same house. *(He pulls at her sleeve shyly)* Sit down now, if you plaze.

ANNA: *(with a half laugh)* Well—— *(She sits down)* But we won't talk about me, see? You tell me about yourself and about the wreck.

BURKE: *(flattered)* I'll tell you, surely. But can I be asking you one question, Miss, has my head in a puzzle?

ANNA: *(guardedly)* Well—I dunno—what is it?

BURKE: What is it you do when you're not taking a trip with the Old Man? For I'm thinking a fine girl the like of you ain't living always on this tub.

ANNA: *(uneasily)* No—of course I ain't. *(She searches his face suspiciously, afraid there may be some hidden insinuation in his words. Seeing his simple frankness, she goes on confidently)* Well, I'll tell you. I'm a governess, see? I take care of kids for people and learn them things.

BURKE: *(impressed)* A governess, is it? You must be smart, surely.

ANNA: But let's not talk about me. Tell me about the wreck, like you promised me you would.

BURKE: *(importantly)* 'Twas this way, Miss. Two weeks out we ran into the divil's own storm, and she sprang wan hell of a leak up for'ard. The skipper was hoping to make Boston before another blow would finish her, but ten days back we met up with another storm the like of the first, only worse. Four days we was in it with green seas raking over her from bow to stern. That was a terrible time, God help us. *(Proudly)* And if 'twasn't for me and my great strength, I'm telling you—and it's God's truth—there'd been mutiny itself in the stokehole. 'Twas me held them to it, with a kick to wan and a clout to another, and they not caring a damn for the engineers any more, but fearing a clout of my right arm more than they'd fear the sea itself. *(He glances at her anxiously, eager for her approval).*

ANNA: *(concealing a smile—amused by this boyish boasting of his)* You did some hard work, didn't you?

BURKE: *(promptly)* I did that! I'm a divil for sticking it out when them that's weak give up. But much good it did anyone! 'Twas a mad, fightin' scramble in the last seconds with each man for himself. I disremember how it come about, but there was the four of us in wan boat and when we was raised high on a great wave I took a look about and divil a sight there was of ship or men on top of the sea.

ANNA: *(in a subdued voice)* Then all the others was drowned?

BURKE: They was, surely.

ANNA: *(with a shudder)* What a terrible end!

BURKE: *(turns to her)* A terrible end for the like of them swabs does live on land, maybe. But for the like of us does be roaming the seas, a good end, I'm telling you—quick and clane.

ANNA: *(struck by the word)* Yes, clean. That's yust the word for—all of it—the way it makes me feel.

BURKE: The sea, you mean? *(Interestedly)* I'm thinking you have a bit of it in your blood, too. Your Old Man wasn't only a barge rat—begging your pardon—all his life, by the cut of him.

ANNA: No, he was bo'sun on sailing ships for years. And all the men on both sides of the family have gone to sea as far back as he remembers, he says. All the women have married sailors, too.

BURKE: *(with intense satisfaction)* Did they, now? They had spirit in them. It's only on the sea you'd find rale men with guts is fit to wed with fine, high-tempered girls *(then he adds half-boldly)* the like of yourself.

ANNA: *(with a laugh)* There you go kiddin' again. *(Then seeing his hurt expression—quickly)* But you was going to tell me about yourself. You're Irish, of course I can tell that.

BURKE: *(stoutly)* Yes, thank God, though I've not seen a sight of it in fifteen years or more.

ANNA: *(thoughtfully)* Sailors never do go home hardly, do they? That's what my father was saying.

BURKE: He wasn't telling no lie. *(With sudden melancholy)* It's a hard and lonesome life, the sea is. The only women you'd meet in the ports of the world who'd be willing to speak you a kind word isn't woman at all. You know the kind I mane, and they're a poor, wicked lot, God forgive them. They're looking to steal the money from you only.

ANNA: *(her face averted—rising to her feet—agitatedly)* I think—I guess I'd better see what's doing inside.

BURKE: (*afraid he has offended her—beseechingly*) Don't go, I'm saying! Is it I've given you offense with my talk of the like of them? Don't heed it at all! I'm clumsy in my wits when it comes to talking proper with a girl the like of you. And why wouldn't I be? Since the day I left home for to go to sea punching coal, this is the first time I've had a word with a rale, dacent woman. So don't turn your back on me now, and we beginning to be friends.

ANNA: (*turning to him again—forcing a smile*) I'm not sore at you, honest.

BURKE: (*gratefully*) God bless you!

ANNA: (*changing the subject abruptly*) But if you honestly think the sea's such a rotten life, why don't you get out of it?

BURKE: (*surprised*) Work on land, is it? (*She nods. He spits scornfully*) Digging spuds in the muck from dawn to dark, I suppose? (*Vehemently*) I wasn't made for it, Miss.

ANNA: (*with a laugh*) I though you'd say that.

BURKE: (*argumentatively*) But there's good jobs and bad jobs at sea, like there'd be on land. I'm thinking if it's in the stokehole of a proper liner I was, I'd be able to have a little house and be home to it wan week out of four. And I'm thinking that maybe then I'd have the luck to find a fine dacent girl—the like of yourself, now—would be willing to wed with me.

ANNA: (*turning away from him with a short laugh—uneasily*) Why sure. Why not?

BURKE: (*edging up close to her—exultantly*) Then you think a girl the like of yourself might maybe not mind the past at all but only be seeing the good herself put in me?

ANNA: (*in the same tone*) Why, sure.

BURKE: (*passionately*) She'd not be sorry for it, I'd take my oath! 'Tis no more drinking and roving about I'd be doing then, but giving my pay day into her hand and staying at home with her as meek as a lamb each night of the week I'd be in port.

ANNA: (*moved in spite of herself and troubled by his half-concealed proposal—with a forced laugh*) All you got to do is find the girl.

BURKE: I have found her!

ANNA: (*half-frightenedly—trying to laugh it off*) You have? When? I thought you was saying——

BURKE: (*boldly and forcefully*) This night. (*Hanging his*

head—humbly) If she'll be having me. (*Then raising his eyes to hers—simply*) 'Tis you I mean.

ANNA: (*is held by his eyes for a moment—then shrinks back from him with a strange, broken laugh*) Say—are you—going crazy? Are you trying to kid me? Proposing—to me!—for Gawd's sake!—on such short acquaintance? (CHRIS *comes out of the cabin and stands staring blinkingly astern. When he makes out* ANNA *in such intimate proximity to this strange sailor, an angry expression comes over his face*).

BURKE: (*following her—with fierce, pleading insistence*) I'm telling you there's the will of God in it that brought me safe through the storm and fog to the wan spot in the world where you was! Think of that now, and isn't it queer——

CHRIS: Anna! (*He comes toward them, raging, his fists clenched*) Anna, you gat in cabin, you hear!

ANNA: (*all her emotions immediately transformed into resentment at his bullying tone*) Who d'you think you're talking to—a slave?

CHRIS: (*hurt—his voice breaking—pleadingly*) You need gat rest, Anna. You gat sleep. (*She does not move. He turns on* BURKE *furiously*) What you doing here, you sailor fallar? You ain't sick like oders. You gat in fo'c's'tle. Dey give you bunk. (*Threateningly*) You hurry, Ay tal you!

ANNA: (*impulsively*) But he is sick. Look at him. He can hardly stand up.

BURKE: (*straightening and throwing out his chest—with a bold laugh*) Is it giving me orders ye are, me bucko? Let you look out, then! With wan hand, weak as I am, I can break ye in two and fling the pieces over the side—and your crew after you. (*Stopping abruptly*) I was forgetting. You're her Old Man and I'd not raise a fist to you for the world. (*His knees sag, he wavers and seems about to fall.* ANNA *utters an exclamation of alarm and hurries to his side*).

ANNA: (*taking one of his arms over her shoulder*) Come on in the cabin. You can have my bed if there ain't no other place.

BURKE: (*with jubilant happiness—as they proceed toward the cabin*) Glory be to God, is it holding my arm about your neck you are! Anna! Anna! Sure it's a sweet name is suited to you.

ANNA: (*guiding him carefully*) Sssh! Sssh!

BURKE: Whisht, is it? Indade, and I'll not. I'll be roaring it out like a fog horn over the sea! You're the girl of the world and we'll be marrying soon and I don't care who knows it!

ANNA: (*as she guides him through the cabin door*) Ssshh! Never mind that talk. You go to sleep. (*They go out of sight in the cabin.* CHRIS, *who has been listening to* BURKE'S *last words with open-mouthed amazement stands looking after them desperately*).

CHRIS: (*turns suddenly and shakes his fist out at the sea— with bitter hatred*) Dat's your dirty trick, damn ole davil, you! (*Then in a frenzy of rage*) But, py God, you don't do dat! Not while Ay'm living! No, py God, you don't!

(*The Curtain Falls*)

ACT THREE

SCENE: The interior of the cabin on the barge, *Simeon Winthrop* (at dock in Boston)—a narrow, low-ceilinged compartment the walls of which are painted a light brown with white trimmings. In the rear on the left, a door leading to the sleeping quarters. In the far left corner, a large locker-closet, painted white, on the door of which a mirror hangs on a nail. In the rear wall, two small square windows and a door opening out on the deck toward the stern. In the right wall, two more windows looking out on the port deck. White curtains, clean and stiff, are at the windows. A table with two cane-bottomed chairs stands in the center of the cabin. A dilapidated, wicker rocker, painted brown, is also by the table.

It is afternoon of a sunny day about a week later. From the harbor and docks outside, muffled by the closed door and windows, comes the sound of steamers' whistles and the puffing snort of the donkey engines of some ship unloading nearby.

As the curtain rises, CHRIS and ANNA are discovered. ANNA is seated in the rocking-chair by the table, with a newspaper in her hands. She is not reading but staring straight in front of her. She looks unhappy, troubled, frowningly concentrated on her thoughts. CHRIS wanders about the room, casting quick, uneasy side glances at her face, then stopping to peer absentmindedly out of the window. His attitude betrays an overwhelming, gloomy anxiety which has him on tenterhooks. He pretends to be engaged in setting things ship-shape, but this occupation is confined to picking up some object, staring at it stupidly for a second, then aimlessly putting it down again. He clears his throat and starts to sing to himself in a low, doleful voice: "My Yosephine, come board de ship. Long time Ay vait for you."

ANNA: *(turning on him, sarcastically)* I'm glad some-one's feeling good. *(Wearily)* Gee, I sure wish we was out of this dump and back in New York.

CHRIS: *(with a sigh)* Ay'm glad vhen ve sail again, too. *(Then, as she makes no comment, he goes on with a ponder-ous attempt at sarcasm)* Ay don't see vhy you don't like Boston, dough. You have good time here, Ay tank. You go ashore all time, every day and night veek ve've been here. You go to movies, see show, gat all kinds fun—— *(His eyes hard with hatred)* All with that damn Irish fallar!

ANNA: *(with weary scorn)* Oh, for heaven's sake, are you off on that again? Where's the harm in his taking me around? D'you want me to sit all day and night in this cabin with you—and knit? Ain't I got a right to have as good a time as I can?

CHRIS: It ain't right kind of fun—not with that fallar, no.

ANNA: I been back on board every night by eleven, ain't I? *(Then struck by some thought—looks at him with keen suspicion—with rising anger)* Say, look here, what d'you mean by what you yust said?

CHRIS: *(hastily)* Nutting but what Ay say, Anna.

ANNA: You said "ain't right" and you said it funny. Say, listen here, you ain't trying to insinuate that there's some-thing wrong between us, are you?

CHRIS: *(horrified)* No, Anna! No, Ay svear to God, Ay never tank dat!

ANNA: *(mollified by his very evident sincerity—sitting down again)* Well, don't you never think it neither if you want me ever to speak to you again. *(Angrily again)* If I ever dreamt you thought that, I'd get the hell out of this barge so quick you couldn't see me for dust.

CHRIS: *(soothingly)* Ay wouldn't never dream—— *(Then after a second's pause, reprovingly)* You vas gatting learn to svear. Dat ain't nice for young gel, you tank?

ANNA: *(with a faint trace of a smile)* Excuse me. You ain't used to such language, I know. *(Mockingly)* That's what your taking me to sea has done for me.

CHRIS: *(indignantly)* No, it ain't me. It's dat damn sailor fallar learn you bad tangs.

ANNA: He ain't a sailor. He's a stoker.

CHRIS: *(forcibly)* Dat vas million times vorse, Ay tal you! Dem fallars dat vork below shoveling coal vas de dirtiest, rough gang of no-good fallars in vorld!

ANNA: I'd hate to hear you say that to Mat.

CHRIS: Oh, Ay tal him same tang. You don't gat it in head Ay'm scared of him yust 'cause he vas stronger'n Ay vas. *(Menacingly)* You don't gat for fight with fists with dem fallars. Dere's oder vay for fix him.

ANNA: *(glancing at him with sudden alarm)* What d'you mean?

CHRIS: *(sullenly)* Nutting.

ANNA: You'd better not. I wouldn't start no trouble with him if I was you. He might forget some time that you was old and my father—and then you'd be out of luck.

CHRIS: *(with smoldering hatred)* Vell, yust let him! Ay'm ole bird maybe, by Ay bet Ay show him trick or two.

ANNA: *(suddenly changing her tone—persuasively)* Aw come on, be good. What's eating you, anyway? Don't you want no one to be nice to me except yourself?

CHRIS: *(placated—coming to her—eagerly)* Yes, Ay do, Anna—only not fallar on sea. But Ay like for you marry steady fallar got good yob on land. You have little home in country all your own——

ANNA: *(rising to her feet—brusquely)* Oh, cut it out! *(Scornfully)* Little home in the country! I wish you could have seen the little home in the country where you had me in jail till I was sixteen! *(With rising irritation)* Some day you're going to get me so mad with that talk, I'm going to turn loose on you and tell you—a lot of things that'll open your eyes.

CHRIS: *(alarmed)* Ay don't vant——

ANNA: I know you don't; but you keep on talking yust the same.

CHRIS: Ay don't talk no more den, Anna.

ANNA: Then promise me you'll cut out saying nasty things about Mat Burke every chance you get.

CHRIS: *(evasive and suspicious)* Vhy? You like dat fallar—very much, Anna?

ANNA: Yes, I certainly do! He's a regular man, no matter what faults he's got. One of his fingers is worth all the hundreds of men I met out there—inland.

CHRIS: *(his face darkening)* Maybe you tank you love him, den?

ANNA: *(defiantly)* What of it if I do?

CHRIS: *(scowling and forcing out the words)* Maybe—you tank you—marry him?

ANNA: *(shaking her head)* No! (CHRIS'S *face lights up with relief.* ANNA *continues slowly, a trace of sadness in her voice)* If I'd met him four years ago—or even two years ago—I'd have jumped at the chance, I tell you that straight. And I would now—only he's such a simple guy—a big kid—and I ain't got the heart to fool him. *(She breaks off suddenly)* But don't never say again he ain't good enough for me. It's me ain't good enough for him.

CHRIS: *(snorts scornfully)* Py yiminy, you go crazy, Ay tank!

ANNA: *(with a mournful laugh)* Well, I been thinking I was myself the last few days. *(She goes and takes a shawl from a hook near the door and throws it over her shoulders)* Guess I'll take a walk down to the end of the dock for a minute and see what's doing. I love to watch the ships passing. Mat'll be along before long, I guess. Tell him where I am, will you?

CHRIS: *(despondently)* All right, Ay tal him. (ANNA *goes out the doorway on rear.* CHRIS *follows her out and stands on the deck outside for a moment looking after her. Then he comes back inside and shuts the door. He stands looking out of the window—mutters—"Dirty ole davil, you." Then he goes to the table, sets the cloth straight mechanically, picks up the newspaper* ANNA *has let fall to the floor and sits down in the rocking-chair. He stares at the paper for a while, then puts it on table, holds his head in his hands and sighs drearily. The noise of a man's heavy footsteps comes from the deck outside and there is a loud knock on the door.* CHRIS *starts, makes a move as if to get up and go to the door, then thinks better of it and sits still. The knock is repeated—then as no answer comes, the door is flung open and* MAT BURKE *appears.* CHRIS *scowls at the intruder and his hand instinctively goes back to the sheath knife on his hip.* BURKE *is dressed up—wears a cheap blue suit, a striped cotton shirt with a black tie, and black shoes newly shined. His face is beaming with good humor).*

BURKE: *(as he sees* CHRIS—*in a jovial tone of mockery)* Well, God bless who's here! *(He bends down and squeezes his huge form through the narrow doorway)* And how is the world treating you this afternoon, Anna's father?

CHRIS: *(sullenly)* Pooty goot—if it ain't for some fallars.

BURKE: *(with a grin)* Meaning me, do you? *(He laughs)* Well, if you ain't the funny old crank of a man! *(Then soberly)* Where's herself? (CHRIS *sits dumb, scowling, his eyes averted.* BURKE *is irritated by this silence)* Where's Anna, I'm after asking you?

CHRIS: *(hesitating—then grouchily)* She go down end of dock.

BURKE: I'll be going down to her, then. But first I'm thinking I'll take this chance when we're alone to have a word with you. *(He sits down opposite* CHRIS *at the table and leans over toward him)* And that word is soon said. I'm marrying your Anna before this day is out, and you might as well make up your mind to it whether you like it or no.

CHRIS: *(glaring at him with hatred and forcing a scornful laugh)* Ho-ho! Dat's easy for say!

BURKE: You mean I won't? *(Scornfully)* Is it the like of yourself will stop me, are you thinking?

CHRIS: Yes, Ay stop it, if it come to vorst.

BURKE: *(with scornful pity)* God help you!

CHRIS: But ain't no need for me do dat. Anna——

BURKE: *(smiling confidently)* Is it Anna you think will prevent me?

CHRIS: Yes.

BURKE: And I'm telling you she'll not. She knows I'm loving her, and she loves me the same, and I know it.

CHRIS: Ho-ho! She only have fun. She make big fool of you, dat's all!

BURKE: *(unshaken—pleasantly)* That's a lie in your throat, divil mend you!

CHRIS: No, it ain't lie. She tal me yust before she go out she never marry fallar like you.

BURKE: I'll not believe it. 'Tis a great old liar you are, and a divil to be making a power of trouble if you had your way. But 'tis not trouble I'm looking for, and me sitting down here. *(Earnestly)* Let us be talking it out now as man to man. You're her father, and wouldn't it be a shame for us to be at each other's throats like a pair of dogs, and I married with Anna. So out with the truth, man alive. What is it you're holding against me at all?

CHRIS: *(a bit placated, in spite of himself, by* BURKE'S *evident sincerity—but puzzled and suspicious)* Vell—Ay don't vant for Anna gat married. Listen, you fallar. Ay'm a ole man. Ay don't see Anna for fifteen year. She vas all Ay gat in vorld. And now ven she come on first trip—you tank Ay vant her leave me 'lone again?

BURKE: *(heartily)* Let you not be thinking I have no heart at all for the way you'd be feeling.

CHRIS: *(astonished and encouraged—trying to plead persuasively)* Den you do right tang, eh? You ship avay again, leave Anna alone. *(Cajolingly)* Big fallar like you dat's on sea, he don't need vife. He gat new gel in every port, you know dat.

BURKE: *(angrily for a second)* God stiffen you! *(Then controlling himself—calmly)* I'll not be giving you the lie on that. But divil take you, there's a time comes to every man, on sea or land, that isn't a born fool, when he's sick of the lot of them cows, and wearing his heart out to meet up with a fine dacent girl, and have a home to call his own and be rearing up children in it. 'Tis small use you're asking me to leave Anna. She's the wan woman of the world for me, and I can't live without her now, I'm thinking.

CHRIS: You forgat all about her in one veek out of port, Ay bet you!

BURKE: You don't know the like I am. Death itself wouldn't make me forget her. So let you not be making talk to me about leaving her. I'll not, and be damned to you! It won't be so bad for you as you'd make out at all. She'll be living here in the States, and her married to me. And you'd be seeing her often so—a sight more often than ever you saw her the fifteen years she was growing up in the West. It's quare you'd be the one to be making great trouble about her leaving you when you never laid eyes on her once in all them years.

CHRIS: *(guiltily)* Ay taught it vas better Anna stay away, grow up inland where she don't ever know ole davil, sea.

BURKE: *(scornfully)* Is it blaming the sea for your troubles ye are again, God help you? Well, Anna knows it now. 'Twas in her blood, anyway.

CHRIS: And Ay don't vant she ever know no-good fallar on sea——

BURKE: She knows one now.

CHRIS: *(banging the table with his fist—furiously)* Dat's yust it! Dat's yust what you are—no-good, sailor fallar! You tank Ay lat her life be made sorry by you like her mo'der's vas by me! No, Ay svear! She don't marry you if Ay gat kill you first!

BURKE: *(looks at him a moment, in astonishment—then laughing uproariously)* Ho-ho! Glory be to God, it's bold talk you have for a stumpy runt of a man!

CHRIS: *(threateningly)* Vell—you see!

BURKE: *(with grinning defiance)* I'll see, surely! I'll see myself and Anna married this day, I'm telling you. *(Then with contemptuous exasperation)* It's quare fool's blather you have about the sea done this and the sea done that. You'd ought to be 'shamed to be saying the like, and you an old sailor yourself. I'm after hearing a lot of it from you and a lot more that Anna's told me you do be saying to her, and I'm thinking it's a poor weak thing you see, and not a man at all!

CHRIS: *(darkly)* You see if Ay'm man—maybe quicker'n you tank.

BURKE: *(contemptuously)* Yerra, don't be boasting. I'm thinking 'tis out of your wits you've got with fright of the sea. You'd be wishing Anna married to a farmer, she told me. That'd be a swate match, surely! Would you have a fine girl the like of Anna lying down at nights with a muddy scut stinking of pigs and dung? Or would you have her tied for life to the like of them skinny, shriveled swabs does be working in cities?

CHRIS: Dat's lie, you fool!

BURKE: 'Tis not. 'Tis your own mad notions I'm after telling. But you know the truth in your heart, if great fear of the sea has made you a liar and coward itself. *(Pounding the table)* The sea's the only life for a man with guts in him isn't afraid of his own shadow! 'Tis only on the sea he's free, and him roving the face of the world, seeing all things, and not giving a damn for saving up money, or stealing from his friends, or any of the black tricks that a landlubber'd waste his life on. 'Twas yourself knew it once, and you a bo'sun for years.

CHRIS: *(sputtering with rage)* You vas crazy fool, Ay tal you!

BURKE: You've swallowed the anchor. The sea give you a clout once, knocked you down, and you're not man enough to get up for another, but lie there for the rest of your life howling bloody murder. *(Proudly)* Isn't it myself the sea has nearly drowned, and me battered and bate till I was that close to hell I could hear the flames roaring, and never a groan out of me till the sea gave up and it seeing the great strength and guts of a man was in me?

CHRIS: *(scornfully)* Yes, you vas hell of fallar, hear you tal it!

BURKE: *(angrily)* You'll be calling me a liar once too often, me old bucko! Wasn't the whole story of it and my picture itself in the newspapers of Boston a week back? *(Looking CHRIS up and down belittlingly)* Sure I'd like to see you in the best of your youth do the like of what I done in the storm and after. 'Tis a mad lunatic, screeching with fear, you'd be this minute!

CHRIS: Ho-ho! You vas young fool! In ole years when Ay vas on windyammer, Ay vas through hundred storms vorse'n dat! Ships vas ships den—and men dat sail on dem vas real men. And now what you gat on steamers? You gat fallars on deck don't know ship from mudscow. *(With a meaning glance at BURKE)* And below deck you gat fallars yust know how for shovel coal—might yust as vell vork on coal vagon ashore!

BURKE: *(stung—angrily)* Is it casting insults at the men in the stokehole ye are, ye old ape? God stiffen you! Wan of them is worth any ten stock-fish-swilling Swuare-heads ever shipped on a windbag!

CHRIS: *(his face working with rage, his hands going back to the sheath-knife on his hip)* Irish svine, you!

BURKE: *(tauntingly)* Don't ye like the Irish, ye old babboon? 'Tis that you're needing in your family, I'm telling you—an Irishman and a man of the stokehole—to put guts in it so that you'll not be having grandchildren would be fearful cowards and jackasses the like of yourself!

CHRIS: *(half rising from his chair—in a voice choked with rage)* You look out!

BURKE: *(watching him intently—a mocking smile on his lips)* And it's that you'll be having, no matter what you'll do to prevent; for Anna and me'll be married this day, and no old fool the like of you will stop us when I've made up my mind.

CHRIS: *(with a hoarse cry)* You don't! *(He throws himself at BURKE, knife in hand, knocking his chair over backwards. BURKE springs to his feet quickly in time to meet the attack. He laughs with the pure love of battle. The old Swede is like a child in his hands. BURKE does not strike or mistreat him in any way, but simply twists his right hand behind his back and forces the knife from his fingers. He throws the knife into a far corner of the room—tauntingly).*

BURKE: Old men is getting childish shouldn't play with

knives. *(Holding the struggling* CHRIS *at arm's length—with a sudden rush of anger, drawing back his fist)* I've half a mind to hit you a great clout will put sense in your square head. Kape off me now, I'm warning you! *(He gives* CHRIS *a push with the flat of his hand which sends the old Swede staggering back against the cabin wall, where he remains standing, panting heavily, his eyes fixed on* BURKE *with hatred, as if he were only collecting his strength to rush at him again).*

BURKE: *(warningly)* Now don't be coming at me again, I'm saying, or I'll flatten you on the floor with a blow, if 'tis Anna's father you are itself! I've no patience left for you. *(Then with an amused laugh)* Well, 'tis a bold old man you are just the same, and I'd never think it was in you to come tackling me alone. *(A shadow crosses the cabin windows. Both men start.* ANNA *appears in the doorway).*

ANNA: *(with pleased surprise as she sees* BURKE*)* Hello, Mat. Are you here already? I was down—— *(She stops, looking from one to the other, sensing immediately that something has happened)* What's up? *(Then noticing the overturned chair—in alarm)* How'd that chair get knocked over? *(Turning on* BURKE *reproachfully)* You ain't been fighting with him, Mat—after you promised?

BURKE: *(his old self again)* I've not laid a hand on him, Anna. *(He goes and picks up the chair, then turning on the still questioning* ANNA*—with a reassuring smile)* Let you not be worried at all. 'Twas only a bit of an argument we was having to pass the time till you'd come.

ANNA: It must have been some argument when you got to throwing chairs. *(She turns on* CHRIS*)* Why don't you say something? What was it about?

CHRIS: *(relaxing at last—avoiding her eyes—sheepishly)* Ve vas talking about ships and fallars on sea.

ANNA: *(with a relieved simile)* Oh—the old stuff, eh?

BURKE: *(suddenly seeming to come to a bold decision—with a defiant grin at* CHRIS*)* He's not after telling you the whole of it. We was arguing about you mostly.

ANNA: *(with a frown)* About me?

BURKE: And we'll be finishing it out right here and now in your presence if you're willing. *(He sits down at the left of table).*

ANNA: *(uncertainly—looking from him to her father)* Sure. Tell me what it's all about.

CHRIS: *(advancing toward the table—protesting to*

BURKE) No! You don't do dat, you! You tal him you don't vant for hear him talk, Anna.

ANNA: But I do. I want this cleared up.

CHRIS: *(miserably afraid now)* Vell, not now, anyway. You vas going ashore, yes? You ain't got time——

ANNA: *(firmly)* Yes, right here and now. *(She turns to BURKE)* You tell me, Mat, since he don't want to.

BURKE: *(draws a deep breath—then plunges in boldly)* The whole of it's in a few words only. So's he'd make no mistake, and him hating the sight of me, I told him in his teeth I loved you. *(Passionately)* And that's God truth, Anna, and well you know it!

CHRIS: *(scornfully—forcing a laugh)* Ho-ho! He tal same tang to gel every port he go!

ANNA: *(shrinking from her father with repulsion—resentfully)* Shut up, can't you? *(Then to BURKE—feelingly)* I know it's true, Mat. I don't mind what he says.

BURKE: *(humbly grateful)* God bless you!

ANNA: And then what?

BURKE: And then—— *(Hesitatingly)* And then I said—— *(He looks at her pleadingly)* I said I was sure—I told him I thought you have a bit of love for me, too. *(Passionately)* Say you do, Anna! Let you not destroy me entirely, for the love of God! *(He grasps both her hands in his two)*.

ANNA: *(deeply moved and troubled—forcing a trembling laugh)* So you told him that, Mat? No wonder he was mad. *(Forcing out the words)* Well, maybe it's true, Mat. Maybe I do. I been thinking and thinking—I didn't want to, Mat, I'll own up to that—I tried to cut it out—but—— *(She laughs helplessly)* I guess I can't help it anyhow. So I guess I do, Mat. *(Then with a sudden joyous defiance)* Sure I do! What's the use of kidding myself different? Sure I love you, Mat!

CHRIS: *(with a cry of pain)* Anna! *(He sits crushed)*.

BURKE: *(with a great depth of sincerity in his humble gratitude)* God be praised!

ANNA: *(assertively)* And I ain't never loved a man in my life before, you can always believe that—no matter what happens.

BURKE: *(goes over to her and puts his arms around her)* Sure I do be believing ivery word you iver said or iver will say. And 'tis you and me will be having a grand, beautiful life together to the end of our days! *(He tries to kiss her. At first she turns away her head—then, overcome by a fierce im-*

pulse of passionate love, she takes his head in both her hands and holds his face close to hers, staring into his eyes. Then she kisses him full on the lips).

ANNA: *(pushing him away from her—forcing a broken laugh)* Good-by. *(She walks to the doorway in rear—stands with her back toward them, looking out. Her shoulders quiver once or twice as if she were fighting back her sobs).*

BURKE: *(too in the seventh heaven of bliss to get any correct interpretation of her word—with a laugh)* Good-by, is it? The divil you say! I'll be coming back at you in a second for more of the same! *(To CHRIS, who has quickened to instant attention at his daughter's good-by, and has looked back at her with a stirring of foolish hope in his eyes)* Now, me old bucko, what'll you be saying? You heard the words from her own lips. Confess I've bate you. Own up like a man when you're bate fair and square. And here's my hand to you—— *(Holds out his hand)* And let you take it and we'll shake and forget what's over and done, and be friends from this out.

CHRIS: *(with implacable hatred)* Ay don't shake hands with you fallar—not while Ay live!

BURKE: *(offended)* The back of my hand to you then, if that suits you better. *(Growling)* 'Tis a rotten bad loser you are, divil mend you!

CHRIS: Ay don't lose. *(Trying to be scornful and self-convincing)* Anna say she like you little bit but you don't hear her say she marry you, Ay bet. *(At the sound of her name ANNA has turned round to them. Her face is composed and calm again, but it is the dead calm of despair).*

BURKE: *(scornfully)* No, and I wasn't hearing her say the sun is shining either.

CHRIS: *(doggedly)* Dat's all right. She don't say it, yust same.

ANNA: *(quietly—coming forward to them)* No, I didn't say it, Mat.

CHRIS: *(eagerly)* Dere! You hear!

BURKE: *(misunderstanding her—with a grin)* You're waiting till you do be asked, you mane? Well, I'm asking you now. And we'll be married this day, with the help of God!

ANNA: *(gently)* You heard what I said, Mat—after I kissed you?

BURKE: *(alarmed by something in her manner)* No—I disremember.

ANNA: I said good-by. *(Her voice trembling)* That kiss was for good-by, Mat.

BURKE: *(terrified)* What d'you mane?

ANNA: I can't marry you, Mat—and we've said good-by. That's all.

CHRIS: *(unable to hold back his exultation)* Ay know it! Ay know dat vas so!

BURKE: *(jumping to his feet—unable to believe his ears)* Anna! Is it making game of me you'd be? 'Tis a quare time to joke with me, and don't be doing it, for the love of God.

ANNA: *(looking him in the eyes—steadily)* D'you think I'd kid you? No, I'm not joking, Mat. I mean what I said.

BURKE: Ye don't! Ye can't! 'Tis mad you are, I'm telling you!

ANNA: *(fixedly)* No, I'm not.

BURKE: *(desperately)* But what's come over you so sudden? You was saying you loved me——

ANNA: I'll say that as often as you want me to. It's true.

BURKE: *(bewilderedly)* Then why—what, in the divil's name—— Oh, God help me, I can't make head or tail to it at all!

ANNA: Because it's the best way out I can figure, Mat. *(Her voice catching)* I been thinking it over and thinking it over day and night all week. Don't think it ain't hard on me, too, Mat.

BURKE: For the love of God, tell me then, what is it that's preventing you wedding me when the two of us has love? *(Suddenly getting an idea and pointing at* CHRIS—*exasperatedly)* Is it giving heed to the like of that old fool ye are, and him hating me and filling your ears full of bloody lies against me?

CHRIS: *(getting to his feet—raging triumphantly before* ANNA *has a chance to get in a word)* Yes, Anna believe me, not you! She know her old fa'der don't lie like you.

ANNA: *(turning on her father angrily)* You sit down, d'you hear? Where do you come in butting in and making things worse? You're like a devil, you are! *(Harshly)* Good Lord, and I was beginning to like you, beginning to forget all I've got held up against you!

CHRIS: *(crushed—feebly)* You ain't got nutting for hold against me, Anna.

ANNA: Ain't I yust! Well, lemme tell you—— *(She*

glances at BURKE *and stops abruptly)* Say, Mat, I'm s'prised at you. You didn't think anything he'd said——

BURKE: *(glumly)* Sure, what else would it be?

ANNA: Think I've ever paid any attention to all his crazy bull? Gee, you must take me for a five-year-old kid.

BURKE: *(puzzled and beginning to be irritated at her too)* I don't know how to take you, with your saying this one minute and that the next.

ANNA: Well, he has nothing to do with it.

BURKE: Then what is it has? Tell me, and don't keep me waiting and sweating blood.

ANNA: *(resolutely)* I can't tell you—and I won't. I got a good reason—and that's all you need to know. I can't marry you, that's all there is to it. *(Distractedly)* So, for Gawd's sake, let's talk of something else.

BURKE: I'll not! *(Then fearfully)* Is it married to someone else you are—in the West maybe?

ANNA: *(vehemently)* I should say not.

BURKE: *(regaining his courage)* To the divil with all other reasons then. They don't matter with me at all. *(He gets to his feet confidently, assuming a masterful tone)* I'm thinking you're the like of them women can't make up their mind till they're drove to it. Well, then, I'll make up your mind for you bloody quick. *(He takes her by the arms, grinning to soften his serious bullying)* We've had enough of talk! Let you be going into your room now and be dressing in your best and we'll be going ashore.

CHRIS: *(aroused—angrily)* No, py God, she don't do that! *(Takes hold of her arm)*.

ANNA: *(who has listened to* BURKE *in astonishment. She draws away from him, instinctively repelled by his tone, but not exactly sure if he is serious or not—a trace of resentment in her voice)* Say, where do you get that stuff?

BURKE: *(imperiously)* Never mind, now! Let you go get dressed, I'm saying. *(Then turning to* CHRIS) We'll be seeing who'll win in the end—me or you.

CHRIS: *(to* ANNA—*also in an authoritative tone)* You stay right here, Anna, you hear! (ANNA *stands looking from one to the other of them as if she thought they had both gone crazy. Then the expression of her face freezes into the hardened sneer of her experience)*.

BURKE: *(violently)* She'll not! She'll do what I say!

You've had your hold on her long enough. It's my turn now.

ANNA: *(with a hard laugh)* Your turn? Say, what am I, anyway?

BURKE: 'Tis not what you are, 'tis what you're going to be this day—and that's wedded to me before night comes. Hurry up now with your dressing.

CHRIS: *(commandingly)* You don't do one tang he say, Anna! *(ANNA laughs mockingly)*.

BURKE: She will, so!

CHRIS: Ay tal you she don't! Ay'm her fa'der.

BURKE: She will in spite of you. She's taking my orders from this out, not yours.

ANNA: *(laughing again)* Orders is good!

BURKE: *(turning to her impatiently)* Hurry up now, and shake a leg. We've no time to be wasting. *(Irritated as she doesn't move)* Do you hear what I'm telling you?

CHRIS: You stay dere, Anna!

ANNA: *(at the end of her patience—blazing out at them passionately)* You can go to hell, both of you! *(There is something in her tone that makes them forget their quarrel and turn to her in a stunned amazement. ANNA laughs wildly)* You're just like all the rest of them—you two! Gawd, you'd think I was a piece of furniture! I'll show you! Sit down now! *(As they hesitate—furiously)* Sit down and let me talk for a minute. You're all wrong, see? Listen to me! I'm going to tell you something—and then I'm going to beat it. *(To BURKE—with a harsh laugh)* I'm going to tell you a funny story, so pay attention. *(Pointing to CHRIS)* I've been meaning to turn it loose on him every time he'd get my goat with his bull about keeping me safe inland. I wasn't going to tell you, but you've forced me into it. What's the dif? It's all wrong anyway, and you might as well get cured that way as any other. *(With hard mocking)* Only don't forget what you said a minute ago about it not mattering to you what other reason I got so long as I wasn't married to no one else.

BURKE: *(manfully)* That's my word, and I'll stick to it!

ANNA: *(laughing bitterly)* What a chance! You make me laugh, honest! Want to bet you will? Wait 'n see! *(She stands at the table rear, looking from one to the other of the two men with her hard, mocking smile. Then she begins, fighting to control her emotion and speak calmly)* First thing is, I want to tell you two guys something. You was going on 's if one of you had got to own me. But nobody owns me, see?—

'cepting myself. I'll do what I please and no man, I don't give a hoot who he is, can tell me what to do! I ain't asking either of you for a living. I can make it myself—one way or other. I'm my own boss. So put that in your pipe and smoke it! You and your orders!

BURKE: *(protestingly)* I wasn't meaning it that way at all and well you know it. You've no call to be raising this rumpus with me. *(Pointing to* CHRIS) 'Tis him you've a right——

ANNA: I'm coming to him. But you—you did mean it that way, too. You sounded—yust like all the rest. *(Hysterically)* But, damn it, shut up! Let me talk for a change!

BURKE: 'Tis quare, rough talk, that—for a dacent girl the like of you!

ANNA: *(with a hard laugh)* Decent? Who told you I was? (CHRIS *is sitting with bowed shoulders, his head in his hands. She leans over in exasperation and shakes him violently by the shoulder)* Don't go to sleep, Old Man! Listen here, I'm talking to you now!

CHRIS: *(straightening up and looking about as if he were seeking a way to escape—with frightened foreboding in his voice)* Ay don't vant for hear it. You vas going out of head, Ay tank, Anna.

ANNA: *(violently)* Well, living with you is enough to drive anyone off their nut. Your bunk about the farm being so fine! Didn't I write you year after year how rotten it was and what a dirty slave them cousins made of me? What'd you care? Nothing! Not even enough to come out and see me! That crazy bull about wanting to keep me away from the sea don't go down with me! You yust didn't want to be bothered with me! You're like all the rest of 'em!

CHRIS: *(feebly)* Anna! It ain't so——

ANNA: *(not heeding his interruption—revengefully)* But one thing I never wrote you. It was one of them cousins that you think is such nice people—the youngest son—Paul—that started me wrong. *(Loudly)* It wasn't none of my fault. I hated him worse'n hell and he knew it. But he was big and strong—*(pointing to Burke)*—like you!

BURKE: *(half springing to his feet—his fists clenched)* God blarst it! *(He sinks slowly back in his chair again, the knuckles showing white on his clenched hands, his face tense with the effort to suppress his grief and rage)*.

CHRIS: *(in a cry of horrified pain)* Anna!

ANNA: *(to him—seeming not to have heard their interruptions)* That was why I run away from the farm. That was what made me get a yob as nurse girl in St. Paul. *(With a hard, mocking laugh)* And you think that was a nice yob for a girl, too, don't you? *(Sarcastically)* With all them nice inland fellers yust looking for a chance to marry me, I s'pose. Marry me? What a chance! They wasn't looking for marrying. *(As BURKE lets a groan of fury escape him—desperately)* I'm owning up to everything fair and square. I was caged in, I tell you—yust like in yail—taking care of other people's kids—listening to 'em bawling and crying day and night—when I wanted to be out—and I was lonesome—lonesome as hell! *(With a sudden weariness in her voice)* So I give up finally. What was the use? *(She stops and looks at the two men. Both are motionless and silent. CHRIS seems in a stupor of despair, his house of cards fallen about him. BURKE'S face is livid with the rage that is eating him up, but he is too stunned and bewildered yet to find a vent for it. The condemnation she feels in their silence goads ANNA into a harsh, strident defiance)* You don't say nothing—either of you—but I know what you're thinking. You're like all the rest! *(To CHRIS—furiously)* And who's to blame for it, me or you? If you'd even acted like a man—if you'd even had been a regular father and had me with you—maybe things would be different!

CHRIS: *(in agony)* Don't talk dat vay, Anna! Ay go crazy! Ay von't listen! *(Puts his hands over his ears)*.

ANNA: *(infuriated by his action—stridently)* You will too listen! *(She leans over and pulls his hands from his ears—with hysterical rage)* You—keeping me safe inland—I wasn't no nurse girl the last two years—I lied when I wrote you—I was in a house, that's what!—yes, that kind of house—the kind sailors like you and Mat goes to in port—and your nice inland men, too—and all men, God damn 'em! I hate 'em! Hate 'em! *(She breaks into hysterical sobbing, throwing herself into the chair and hiding her face in her hands on the table. The two men have sprung to their feet)*.

CHRIS: *(whimpering like a child)* Anna! Anna! It's lie! It's lie! *(He stands wringing his hands together and begins to weep)*.

BURKE: *(his whole great body tense like a spring—dully and gropingly)* So that's what's in it!

ANNA: *(raising her head at the sound of his voice—with*

extreme mocking bitterness) I s'pose you remember your promise, Mat? No other reason was to count with you so long as I wasn't married already. So I s'pose you want me to get dressed and go ashore, don't you? *(She laughs)* Yes, you do!

BURKE: *(on the verge of his outbreak—stammeringly)* God stiffen you1

ANNA: *(trying to keep up her hard, bitter tone, but gradually letting a note of pitiful pleading creep in)* I s'pose if I tried to tell you I wasn't—that—no more you'd believe me, wouldn't you? Yes, you would! And if I told you that yust getting out in this barge, and being on the sea had changed me and made me feel different about things, 's if all I'd been through wasn't me and didn't count and was yust like it never happened—you'd laugh, wouldn't you? And you'd die laughing sure if I said that meeting you that funny way that night in the fog, and afterwards seeing that you was straight goods stuck on me, had got me to thinking for the first time, and I sized you up as a different kind of man—a sea man as different from the ones on land as water is from mud—and that was why I got stuck on you, too. I wanted to marry you and fool you, but I couldn't. Don't you see how I've changed? I couldn't marry you with you believing a lie—and I was shamed to tell you the truth—till the both of you forced my hand, and I seen you was the same as all the rest. And now, give me a bawling out and beat it, like I can tell you're going to. *(She stops, looking at* BURKE. *He is silent, his face averted, his features beginning to work with fury. She pleads passionately)* Will you believe it if I tell you that loving you has made me—clean? It's the straight goods, honest! *(Then as he doesn't reply—bitterly)* Like hell you will! You're like all the rest!

BURKE: *(blazing out—turning on her in a perfect frenzy of rage—his voice trembling with passion)* The rest, is it? God's curse on you! Clane, is it? You slut, you, I'll be killing you now! *(He picks up the chair on which he has been sitting and, swinging it high over his shoulder, springs toward her.* CHRIS *rushes forward with a cry of alarm, trying to ward off the blow from his daughter.* ANNA *looks up into* BURKE'S *eyes with the fearlessness of despair.* BURKE *checks himself, the chair held in the air).*

CHRIS: *(wildly)* Stop, you crazy fool! You vant for murder her!

ANNA: *(pushing her father away brusquely, her eyes still holding* BURKE'S*)* Keep out of this, you! *(To* BURKE—*dully)* Well, ain't you got the nerve to do it? Go ahead! I'll be thankful to you, honest. I'm sick of the whole game.

BURKE: *(throwing the chair away into a corner of the room—helplessly)* I can't do it, God help me, and your two eyes looking at me. *(Furiously)* Though I do be thinking I'd have a good right to smash your skull like a rotten egg. Was there iver a woman in the world had the rottenness in her that you have, and was there iver a man the like of me was made the fool of the world, and me thinking thoughts about you, and having great love for you, and dreaming dreams of the fine life we'd have when we'd be wedded! *(His voice high pitched in a lamentation that is like a keen)* Yerra, God help me! I'm destroyed entirely and my heart is broken in bits! I'm asking God Himself, was it for this He'd have me roaming the earth since I was a lad only, to come to black shame in the end, where I'd be giving a power of love to a woman is the same as others you'd meet in any hooker-shanty in port, with red gowns on them and paint on their grinning mugs, would be sleeping with any man for a dollar or two!

ANNA: *(in a scream)* Don't, Mat! For Gawd's sake! *(Then raging and pounding on the table with her hands)* Get out of here! Leave me alone! Get out of here!

BURKE: *(his anger rushing back on him)* I'll be going, surely! And I'll be drinking sloos of whisky will wash that black kiss of yours off my lips; and I'll be getting dead rotten drunk so I'll not remember if 'twas iver born you was at all; and I'll be shipping away on some boat will take me to the other end of the world where I'll never see your face again! *(He turns toward the door)*.

CHRIS: *(who has been standing in a stupor—suddenly grasping* BURKE *by the arm—stupidly)* No, you don't go. Ay tank maybe it's better Anna marry you now.

BURKE: *(shaking* CHRIS *off—furiously)* Lave go of me, ye old ape! Marry her, is it? I'd see her roasting in hell first! I'm shipping away out of this, I'm telling you! *(Pointing to* ANNA—*passionately)* And my curse on you and the curse of Almighty God and all the Saints! You've destroyed me this day and may you lie awake in the long nights, tormented with thoughts of Mat Burke and the great wrong you've done him!

ANNA: *(in anguish)* Mat! *(But he turns without another*

word and strides out of the doorway. ANNA *looks after him wildly, starts to run after him, then hides her face in her outstretched arms, sobbing.* CHRIS *stands in a stupor, staring at the floor).*

CHRIS: *(after a pause, dully)* Ay tank Ay go ashore, too.

ANNA: *(looking up, wildly)* Not after him! Let him go! Don't you dare——

CHRIS: *(somberly)* Ay go for gat drink.

ANNA: *(with a harsh laugh)* So I'm driving you to drink, too, eh? I s'pose you want to get drunk so's you can forget—like him?

CHRIS: *(bursting out angrily)* Yes, Ay vant! You tank Ay like hear dem tangs. *(Breaking down—weeping)* Ay tank you vasn't dat kind of gel, Anna.

ANNA: *(mockingly)* And I s'pose you want me to beat it, don't you? You don't want me here disgracing you, I s'pose?

CHRIS: No, you stay here! *(Goes over and pats her on the shoulder, the tears running down his face)* Ain't your fault, Anna, Ay know dat. *(She looks up at him, softened. He bursts into rage)* It's dat ole davil, sea, do this to me! *(He shakes his fist at the door)* It's her dirty tricks! It vas all right on barge with yust you and me. Den she bring dat Irish fallar in fog, she make you like him, she make you fight with me all time! If dat Irish fallar don't never come, you don't never tal me dem tangs, Ay don't never know, and everytang's all right. *(He shakes his fist again)* Dirty ole davil!

ANNA: *(with spent weariness)* Oh, what's the use? Go on ashore and get drunk.

CHRIS: *(goes into room on left and gets his cap. He goes to the door, silent and stupid—then turns)* You vait here, Anna?

ANNA: *(dully)* Maybe—and maybe not. Maybe I'll get drunk, too. Maybe I'll—— But what the hell do you care what I do? Go on and beat it. *(CHRIS turns stupidly and goes out.* ANNA *sits at the table, staring straight in front of her).*

(The Curtain Falls)

ACT FOUR

SCENE: Same as Act Three, about nine o'clock of a foggy night two days later. The whistles of steamers in the harbor can be heard. The cabin is lighted by a small lamp on the table. A suitcase stands in the middle of the floor. ANNA is sitting in the rocking-chair. She wears a hat, is all dressed up as in Act One. Her face is pale, looks terribly tired and worn, as if the two days just past had been ones of suffering and sleepless nights. She stares before her despondently, her chin in her hands. There is a timid knock on the door in rear. ANNA jumps to her feet with a startled exclamation and looks toward the door with an expression of mingled hope and fear.

ANNA: *(faintly)* Come in. *(Then summoning her courage—more resolutely)* Come in. *(The door is opened and* CHRIS *appears in the doorway. He is in a very bleary, bedraggled condition, suffering from the after effects of his drunk. A tin pail full of foaming beer is in his hand. He comes forward, his eyes avoiding* ANNA'S. *He mutters stupidly)* It's foggy.

ANNA: *(looking him over with contempt)* So you come back at last, did you? You're a fine looking sight! *(Then jeeringly)* I thought you'd beaten it for good on account of the disgrace I'd brought on you.

CHRIS: *(wincing—faintly)* Don't say dat, Anna, please! *(He sits in a chair by the table, setting down the can of beer, holding his head in his hands).*

ANNA: *(looks at him with a certain sympathy)* What's the trouble? Feeling sick?

CHRIS: *(dully)* Inside my head feel sick.

ANNA: Well, what d'you expect after being soused for two days? *(Resentfully)* It serves you right. A fine thing— you leaving me alone on this barge all that time!

CHRIS: *(humbly)* Ay'm sorry, Anna.

ANNA: *(scornfully)* Sorry!

CHRIS: But Ay'm not sick inside head vay you mean. Ay'm sick from tank too much about you, about me.

ANNA: And how about me? D'you suppose I ain't been thinking, too?

CHRIS: Ay'm sorry, Anna. *(He sees her bag and gives a start)* You pack your bag, Anna? You vas going——?

ANNA: *(forcibly)* Yes, I was going right back to what you think.

CHRIS: Anna!

ANNA: I went ashore to get a train for New York. I'd been waiting and waiting 'till I was sick of it. Then I changed my mind and decided not to go today. But I'm going first thing tomorrow, so it'll all be the same in the end.

CHRIS: *(raising his head—pleadingly)* No, you never do dat, Anna!

ANNA: *(with a sneer)* Why not, I'd like to know?

CHRIS: You don't never gat to do—dat vay—no more, Ay tal you. Ay fix dat up all right.

ANNA: *(suspiciously)* Fix what up?

CHRIS: *(not seeming to have heard her question—sadly)* You vas vaiting, you say? You vasn't vaiting for me, Ay bet.

ANNA: *(callously)* You'd win.

CHRIS: For dat Irish fallar?

ANNA: *(defiantly)* Yes—if you want to know! *(Then with a forlorn laugh)* If he did come back it'd only be 'cause he wanted to beat me up or kill me, I suppose. But even if he did, I'd rather have him come than not show up at all. I wouldn't care what he did.

CHRIS: Ay guess it's true you vas in love with him all right.

ANNA: You guess!

CHRIS: *(turning to her earnestly)* And Ay'm sorry for you like hell he don't come, Anna!

ANNA: *(softened)* Seems to me you've changed your tune a lot.

CHRIS: Ay've been tanking, and Ay guess it vas all my fault—all bad tangs dat happen to you. *(Pleadingly)* You try for not hate me, Anna. Ay'm crazy ole fool, dat's all.

ANNA: Who said I hated you?

CHRIS: Ay'm sorry for everything Ay do wrong for you, Anna. Ay vant for you be happy all rest of your life for make up! It make you happy marry dat Irish fallar, Ay vant it, too.

ANNA: *(dully)* Well, there ain't no chance. But I'm glad you think different about it, anyway.

CHRIS: *(supplicatingly)* And you tank—maybe—you forgive me sometime?

ANNA: *(with a wan smile)* I'll forgive you right now.

CHRIS: *(seizing her hand and kissing it—brokenly)* Anna lilla! Anna lilla!

ANNA: *(touched but a bit embarrassed)* Don't bawl about it. There ain't nothing to forgive, anyway. It ain't your fault, and it ain't mine, and it ain't his neither. We're all poor nuts, and things happen, and we yust get mixed in wrong, that's all.

CHRIS: *(eagerly)* You say right tang, Anna, py golly! It ain't nobody's fault! *(Shaking his fist)* It's dat ole davil, sea!

ANNA: *(with an exasperated laugh)* Gee, won't you ever

can that stuff? (CHRIS *relapses into injured silence. After a pause* ANNA *continues curiously*) You said a minute ago you'd fixed something up—about me. What was it?

CHRIS: (*after a hesitating pause*) Ay'm shipping avay on sea again, Anna.

ANNA: (*astounded*) You're—what?

CHRIS: Ay sign on steamer sail tomorrow. Ay gat my ole yob—bo'sun. (ANNA *stares at him. As he goes on, a bitter smile comes over her face*) Ay tank dat's best tang for you. Ay only bring you bad luck, Ay tank. Ay make your mo'der's life sorry. Ay don't vant make yours dat way, but Ay do yust same. Dat ole davil, sea, she make me Yonah man ain't no good for nobody. And Ay tank now it ain't no use fight with sea. No man dat live going to beat her, py yingo!

ANNA: (*with a laugh of helpless bitterness*) So that's how you've fixed me, is it?

CHRIS: Yes, Ay tank if dat ole davil gat me back she leave you alone den.

ANNA: (*bitterly*) But, for Gawd's sake, don't you see you're doing the same thing you've always done? Don't you see——? (*But she sees the look of obsessed stubbornness on her father's face and gives it up helplessly*) But what's the use of talking? You ain't right, that's what. I'll never blame you for nothing no more. But how you could figure out that was fixing me——!

CHRIS: Dat ain't all. Ay gat dem fallars in steamship office to pay you all money coming to me every month vhile Ay'm avay.

ANNA: (*with a hard laugh*) Thanks. But I guess I won't be hard up for no small change.

CHRIS: (*hurt—humbly*) It ain't much, Ay know, but it's plenty to keep you so you never gat go back——

ANNA: (*shortly*) Shut up, will you? We'll talk about it later, see?

CHRIS: (*after a pause—ingratiatingly*) You like Ay go ashore look for dat Irish fallar, Anna?

ANNA: (*angrily*) Not much! Think I want to drag him back?

CHRIS: (*after a pause—uncomfortably*) Py golly, dat booze don't go vell. Give me fever, Ay tank. Ay feel hot like hell. (*He takes off his coat and lets it drop on the floor. There is a loud thud*).

ANNA: *(with a start)* What you got in your pocket, for Pete's sake—a ton of lead? *(She reaches down, takes his coat and pulls out a revolver—looks from it to him in amazement)* A gun? What were you doing with this?

CHRIS: *(sheepishly)* Ay forget. Ain't nothing. Ain't loaded, anyvay.

ANNA: *(breaking it open to make sure—then closing it again—looking at him suspiciously)* That ain't telling me why you got it?

CHRIS: Ay'm ole fool. Ay got it when Ay go ashore first. Ay tank den it's all fault of dat Irish fallar.

ANNA: *(with a shudder)* Say, you're crazier than I thought. I never dreamt you'd go that far.

CHRIS: *(quickly)* Ay don't. Ay gat better sense right away. Ay don't never buy bullets even. It ain't his fault, Ay know.

ANNA: *(still suspicious of him)* Well, I'll take care of this for a while, loaded or not. *(She puts it in the drawer of table and closes the drawer).*

CHRIS: *(placatingly)* Throw it overboard if you vant. Ay don't care. *(Then after a pause)* Py golly, Ay tank Ay go lie down. Ay feel sick. (ANNA *takes a magazine from the table.* CHRIS *hesitates by her chair)* Ve talk again before Ay go, yes?

ANNA: *(dully)* Where's this ship going to?

CHRIS: Cape Town. Dat's in South Africa. She's British steamer called Londonderry. *(He stands hesitatingly—finally blurts out)* Anna—you forgive me sure?

ANNA: *(wearily)* Sure I do. You ain't to blame. You're yust—what you are—like me.

CHRIS: *(pleadingly)* Den—you lat me kiss you again once?

ANNA: *(raising her face—forcing a wan smile)* Sure. No hard feelings.

CHRIS: *(kisses her brokenly)* Anna lilla! Ay—— *(He fights for words to express himself, but finds none—miserably—with a sob)* Ay can't say it. Good-night, Anna.

ANNA: Good-night. *(He picks up the can of beer and goes slowly into the room on left, his shoulders bowed, his head sunk forward dejectedly. He closes the door after him.* ANNA *turns over the pages of the magazine, trying desperately to banish her thoughts by looking at the pictures. This fails to distract her, and flinging the magazine back on the table, she springs to her feet and walks about the cabin distract-*

*edly, clenching and unclenching her hands. She speaks
aloud to herself in a tense, trembling voice)* Gawd, I can't
stand this much longer! What am I waiting for anyway?—
like a damn fool! *(She laughs helplessly, then checks herself
abruptly, as she hears the sound of heavy footsteps on the
deck outside. She appears to recognize these and her face
lights up with joy. She gasps)* Mat! *(A strange terror seems
suddenly to seize her. She rushes to the table, takes the
revolver out of drawer and crouches down in the corner, left,
behind the cupboard. A moment later the door is flung open
and* MAT BURKE *appears in the doorway. He is in bad
shape—his clothes torn and dirty, covered with sawdust as if
he had been grovelling or sleeping on barroom floors. There
is a red bruise on his forehead over one of his eyes, another
over one cheekbone, his knuckles are skinned and raw—
plain evidence of the fighting he has been through on his
"bat." His eyes are bloodshot and heavy-lidded, his face
has a bloated look. But beyond these appearances—the
results of heavy drinking—there is an expression in his eyes
of wild mental turmoil, of impotent animal rage baffled by its
own abject misery).*

BURKE: *(peers blinkingly about the cabin—hoarsely)* Let
you not be hiding from me, whoever's here—though 'tis well
you know I'd have a right to come back and murder you. *(He
stops to listen. Hearing no sound, he closes the door behind
him and comes forward to the table. He throws himself into
the rocking-chair—despondently)* There's no one here, I'm
thinking, and 'tis a great fool I am to be coming. *(With a sort
of dumb, uncomprehending anguish)* Yerra, Mat Burke, 'tis
a great jackass you've become and what's got into you at all,
at all? She's gone out of this long ago, I'm telling you, and
you'll never see her face again. *(*ANNA *stands up, hesitating,
struggling between joy and fear.* BURKE'S *eyes fall on* AN-
NA'S *bag. He leans over to examine it)* What's this? *(Joy-
fully)* It's hers. She's not gone! But where is she? Ashore?
(Darkly) What would she be doing ashore on this rotten
night? *(His face suddenly convulsed with grief and rage)* 'Tis
that, is it? Oh, God's curse on her! *(Raging)* I'll wait till she
comes and choke her dirty life out. *(*ANNA *starts, her face
grows hard. She steps into the room, the revolver in her right
hand by her side).*

ANNA: *(in a cold, hard tone)* What are you doing here?
BURKE: *(wheeling about with a terrified gasp)* Glory be to

God! *(They remain motionless and silent for a moment, holding each other's eyes).*

ANNA: *(in the same hard voice)* Well, can't you talk?

BURKE: *(trying to fall into an easy, careless tone)* You've a year's growth scared out of me, coming at me so sudden and me thinking I was alone.

ANNA: You've got your never butting in here without knocking or nothing. What d'you want?

BURKE: *(airily)* Oh, nothing much. I was wanting to have a last word with you, that's all. *(He moves a step toward her).*

ANNA: *(sharply—raising the revolver in her hand)* Careful now! Don't try getting too close. I heard what you said you'd do to me.

BURKE: *(noticing the revolver for the first time)* Is it murdering me you'd be now, God forgive you? *(Then with a contemptuous laugh)* Or is it thinking I'd be frightened by that old tin whistle? *(He walks straight for her).*

ANNA: *(wildly)* Look out, I tell you!

BURKE: *(who has come so close that the revolver is almost touching his chest)* Let you shoot, then! *(Then with sudden wild grief)* Let you shoot, I'm saying, and be done with it! Let you end me with a shot and I'll be thanking you, for it's a rotten dog's life I've lived the past two days since I've known what you are, till I'm after wishing I was never born at all!

ANNA: *(overcome—letting the revolver drop to the floor, as if her fingers had no strength to hold it—hysterically)* What d'you want coming here? Why don't you beat it? Go on! *(She passes him and sinks down in the rocking-chair).*

BURKE: *(following her—mournfully)* 'Tis right you'd be asking why did I come. *(Then angrily)* 'Tis because 'tis a great weak fool of the world I am, and me tormented with the wickedness you'd told of yourself, and drinking oceans of booze that'd make me forget. Forget? Divil a word I'd forget, and your face grinning always in front of my eyes, awake or asleep, till I do be thinking a madhouse is the proper place for me.

ANNA: *(glancing at his hands and face—scornfully)* You look like you ought to be put away some place. Wonder you wasn't pulled in. You been scrapping, too, ain't you?

BURKE: I have—with every scut would take off his coat to me! *(Fiercely)* And each time I'd be hitting one a clout in the mug, it wasn't his face I'd be seeing at all, but yours, and me wanting to drive you a blow would knock you out of this world where I wouldn't be seeing or thinking more of you.

ANNA: *(her lips trembling pitifully)* Thanks!

BURKE: *(walking up and down—distractedly)* That's right, make game of me! Oh, I'm a great coward surely, to be coming back to speak with you at all. You've a right to laugh at me.

ANNA: I ain't laughing at you, Mat.

BURKE: *(unheeding)* You to be what you are, and me to be Mat Burke, and me to be drove back to look at you again! 'Tis black shame is on me!

ANNA: *(resentfully)* Then get out. No one's holding you!

BURKE: *(bewilderedly)* And me to listen to that talk from a woman like you and be frightened to close her mouth with a slap! Oh, God help me, I'm a yellow coward for all men to spit at! *(Then furiously)* But I'll not be getting out of this till I've had me word. *(Raising his fist threateningly)* And let you look out how you'd drive me! *(Letting his fist fall helplessly)* Don't be angry now! I'm raving like a real lunatic, I'm thinking, and the sorrow you put on me has my brains drownded in grief. *(Suddenly bending down to her and grasping her arm intensely)* Tell me it's a lie, I'm saying! That's what I'm after coming to hear you say.

ANNA: *(dully)* A lie? What?

BURKE: *(with passionate entreaty)* All the badness you told me two days back. Sure it must be a lie! You was only making game of me, wasn't you? Tell me 'twas a lie, Anna, and I'll be saying prayers of thanks on my two knees to the Almighty God!

ANNA: *(terribly shaken—faintly)* I can't, Mat. *(As he turns away—imploringly)* Oh, Mat, won't you see that no matter what I was I ain't that any more? Why, listen! I packed up my bag this afternoon and went ashore. I'd been waiting here all alone for two days, thinking may be you'd come back—thinking maybe you'd think over all I'd said—and maybe—oh, I don't know what I was hoping! But I was afraid to even go out of the cabin for a second, honest—afraid you might come and not find me here. Then I gave up hope when you didn't show up and I went to the railroad station. I was going to New York. I was going back——

BURKE: *(hoarsely)* God's curse on you!

ANNA: Listen, Mat! You hadn't come, and I'd gave up

hope. But—in the station—I couldn't go. I'd bought my ticket and everything. *(She takes the ticket from her dress and tries to hold it before his eyes)* But I got to thinking about you—and I couldn't take the train—I couldn't! So I come back here—to wait some more. Oh, Mat, don't you see I've changed? Can't you forgive what's dead and gone—and forget it?

BURKE: *(turning on her—overcome by rage again)* Forget, is it? I'll not forget till my dying day, I'm telling you, and me tormented with thoughts. *(In a frenzy)* Oh, I'm wishing I had wan of them fornenst me this minute and I'd beat him with my fists till he'd be a bloody corpse! I'm wishing the whole lot of them will roast in hell till the Judgment Day— and yourself along with them, for you're as bad as they are.

ANNA: *(shuddering)* Mat! *(Then after a pause—in a voice of dead, stony calm)* Well, you've had your say. Now you better beat it.

BURKE: *(starts slowly for the door—hesitates—then after a pause)* And what'll you be doing?

ANNA: What difference does it make to you?

BURKE: I'm asking you!

ANNA: *(in the same tone)* My bag's packed and I got my ticket. I'll go to New York tomorrow.

BURKE: *(helplessly)* You mean—you'll be doing the same again?

ANNA: *(stonily)* Yes.

BURKE: *(in anguish)* You'll not! Don't torment me with that talk! 'Tis a she-divil you are sent to drive me mad entirely!

ANNA: *(her voice breaking)* Oh, for Gawd's sake, Mat, leave me alone! Go away! Don't you see I'm licked? Why d'you want to keep on kicking me?

BURKE: *(indignantly)* And don't you deserve the worst I'd say, God forgive you?

ANNA: All right. Maybe I do. But don't rub it in. Why ain't you done what you said you was going to? Why ain't you got that ship was going to take you to the other side of the earth where you'd never see me again?

BURKE: I have.

ANNA: *(startled)* What—then you're going—honest?

BURKE: I signed on today at noon, drunk as I was—and she's sailing tomorrow.

ANNA: And where's she going to?

BURKE: Cape Town.

ANNA: *(the memory of having heard that name a little while before coming to her—with a start, confusedly)* Cape Town? Where's that? Far away?

BURKE: 'Tis at the end of Africa. That's far for you.

ANNA: *(forcing a laugh)* You're keeping your word all right, ain't you? *(After a slight pause—curiously)* What's the boat's name?

BURKE: The Londonderry.

ANNA: *(it suddenly comes to her that this is the same ship her father is sailing on)* The Londonderry! It's the same— Oh, this is too much! *(With wild, ironical laughter)* Ha-ha-ha!

BURKE: What's up with you now?

ANNA: Ha-ha-ha! It's funny, funny! I'll die laughing!

BURKE: *(irritated)* Laughing at what?

ANNA: It's a secret. You'll know soon enough. It's funny. *(Controlling herself—after a pause—cynically)* What kind of a place is this Cape Town? Plenty of dames there, I suppose?

BURKE: To hell with them! That I may never see another woman to my dying hour!

ANNA: That's what you say now, but I'll bet by the time you get there you'll have forgot all about me and start in talking the same old bull you talked to me to the first one you meet.

BURKE: *(offended)* I'll not, then! God mend you, is it making me out to be the like of yourself you are, and you talking up with this one and that all the years of your life?

ANNA: *(angrily assertive)* Yes, that's yust what I do mean! You been doing the same thing all your life, picking up a new girl in every port. How're you any better than I was?

BURKE: *(thoroughly exasperated)* Is it no shame you have at all? I'm a fool to be wasting talk on you and you hardened in badness. I'll go out of this and lave you alone forever. *(He starts for the door—then stops to turn on her furiously)* And I suppose 'tis the same lies you told them all before that you told to me?

ANNA: *(indignantly)* That's a lie! I never did!

BURKE: *(miserably)* You'd be saying that, anyway.

ANNA: *(forcibly, with growing intensity)* Are you trying to accuse me—of being in love—really in love—with them?

BURKE: I'm thinking you were, surely.

ANNA: *(furiously, as if this were the last insult—advanc-*

ing on him threateningly) You mutt, you! I've stood enough from you. Don't you dare. *(With scornful bitterness)* Love 'em! Oh, my Gawd! You damn thick-head! Love 'em? *(Savagely)* I hated 'em, I tell you! Hated 'em, hated 'em, hated 'em! And may Gawd strike me dead this minute and my mother, too, if she was alive, if I ain't telling you the honest truth!

BURKE: *(immensely pleased by her vehemence—a light beginning to break over his face—but still uncertain, torn between doubt and the desire to believe—helplessly)* If I could only be believing you now!

ANNA: *(distractedly)* Oh, what's the use? What's the use of me talking? What's the use of anything? *(Pleadingly)* Oh, Mat, you mustn't think that for a second! You mustn't! Think all the other bad about me you want to, and I won't kick, 'cause you've a right to. But don't think that! *(On the point of tears)* I couldn't bear it! It'd be yust too much to know you was going away where I'd never see you again—thinking that about me!

BURKE: *(after an inward struggle—tensely—forcing out the words with difficulty)* If I was believing—that you'd never had love for any other man in the world but me—I could be forgetting the rest, maybe.

ANNA: *(with a cry of joy)* Mat!

BURKE: *(slowly)* If 'tis truth you're after telling, I'd have a right, maybe, to believe you'd changed—and that I'd changed you myself till the thing you'd been all your life wouldn't be you any more at all.

ANNA: *(hanging on his words—breathlessly)* Oh, Mat! That's what I been trying to tell you all along!

BURKE: *(simply)* For I've a power of strength in me to lead men the way I want, and women, too, maybe, and I'm thinking I'd change you to a new woman entirely, so I'd never know, or you either, what kind of woman you'd been in the past at all.

ANNA: Yes, you could, Mat! I know you could!

BURKE: And I'm thinking 'twasn't your fault, maybe, but having that old ape for a father that left you to grow up alone, made you what you was. And if I could be believing 'tis only me you——

ANNA: *(distractedly)* You got to believe it, Mat! What can I do? I'll do anything, anything you want to prove I'm not lying!

BURKE: *(suddenly seems to have a solution. He feels in the pocket of his coat and grasps something—solemnly)* Would you be willing to swear an oath, now—a terrible, fearful oath would send your soul to the divils in hell if you was lying?

ANNA: *(eagerly)* Sure, I'll swear, Mat—on anything!

BURKE: *(takes a small, cheap old crucifix from his pocket and holds it up for her to see)* Will you swear on this?

ANNA: *(reaching out for it)* Yes. Sure I will. Give it to me.

BURKE: *(holding it away)* 'Tis a cross was given me by my mother, God rest her soul. *(He makes the sign of the cross mechanically)* I was a lad only, and she told me to keep it by me if I'd be waking or sleeping and never lose it, and it'd bring me luck. She died soon after. But I'm after keeping it with me from that day to this, and I'm telling you there's great power in it, and 'tis great bad luck it's saved me from and me roaming the seas, and I having it tied round my neck when my last ship sunk, and it bringing me safe to land when the others went to their death. *(Very earnestly)* And I'm warning you now, if you'd swear an oath on this, 'tis my old woman herself will be looking down from Hivin above, and praying Almighty God and the Saints to put a great curse on you if she'd hear you swearing a lie!

ANNA: *(awed by his manner—superstitiously)* I wouldn't have the nerve—honest—if it was a lie. But it's the truth and I ain't scared to swear. Give it to me.

BURKE: *(handing it to her—almost frightenedly, as if he feared for her safety)* Be careful what you'd swear, I'm saying.

ANNA: *(holding the cross gingerly)* Well—what do you want me to swear? You say it.

BURKE: Swear I'm the only man in the world ivir you felt love for.

ANNA: *(looking into his eyes steadily)* I swear it.

BURKE: And that you'll be forgetting from this day all the badness you've done and never do the like of it again.

ANNA: *(forcibly)* I swear it! I swear it by God!

BURKE: And may the blackest curse of God strike you if you're lying. Say it now!

ANNA: And may the blackest curse of God strike me if I'm lying!

BURKE: *(with a stupendous sigh)* Oh, glory be to God, I'm after believing you now! *(He takes the cross from her hand, his face beaming with joy, and puts it back in his pocket. He puts his arm about her waist and is about to kiss her when he stops, appalled by some terrible doubt).*

ANNA: *(alarmed)* What's the matter with you?

BURKE: *(with sudden fierce questioning)* Is it Catholic ye are?

ANNA: *(confused)* No. Why?

BURKE: *(filled with a sort of bewildered foreboding)* Oh, God, help me! *(With a dark glance of suspicion at her)* There's some divil's trickery in it, to be swearing an oath on a Catholic cross and you wan of the others.

ANNA: *(distractedly)* Oh, Mat, don't you believe me?

BURKE: *(miserably)* If it isn't a Catholic you are——

ANNA: I ain't nothing. What's the difference? Didn't you hear me swear?

BURKE: *(passionately)* Oh, I'd a right to stay away from you—but I couldn't! I was loving you in spite of it all and wanting to be with you, God forgive me, no matter what you are. I'd go mad if I'd not have you! I'd be killing the world—— *(He seizes her in his arms and kisses her fiercely).*

ANNA: *(with a gasp of joy)* Mat!

BURKE: *(suddenly holding her away from him and staring into her eyes as if to probe into her soul—slowly)* If your oath is no proper oath at all, I'll have to be taking your naked word for it and have you anyway, I'm thinking—I'm needing you that bad!

ANNA: *(hurt—reproachfully)* Mat! I swore, didn't I?

BURKE: *(defiantly, as if challenging fate)* Oath or no oath, 'tis no matter. We'll be wedded in the morning, with the help of God. *(Still more defiantly)* We'll be happy now, the two of us, in spite of the divil! *(He crushes her to him and kisses her again. The door on the left is pushed open and* CHRIS *appears in the doorway. He stands blinking at them. At first the old expression of hatred of* BURKE *comes into his eyes instinctively. Then a look of resignation and relief takes its place. His face lights up with a sudden happy thought. He turns back into the bedroom—reappears immediately with the tin can of beer in his hand—grinning).*

CHRIS: Ve have drink on this, py golly! *(They break away from each other with startled exclamations).*

BURKE: *(explosively)* God stiffen it! *(He takes a step toward* CHRIS *threateningly).*

ANNA: *(happily—to her father)* That's the way to talk!

(With a laugh) And say, it's about time for you and Mat to kiss and make up. You're going to be shipmates on the Londonderry, did you know it?

BURKE: *(astounded)* Shipmates—— Has himself——

CHRIS: *(equally astounded)* Ay vas bo'sun on her.

BURKE: The divil! *(Then angrily)* You'd be going back to sea and leaving her alone, would you?

ANNA: *(quickly)* It's all right, Mat. That's where he belongs, and I want him to go. You got to go, too; we'll need the money. *(With a laugh, as she gets the glasses)* And as for me being alone, that runs in the family, and I'll get used to it. *(Pouring out their glasses)* I'll get a little house somewhere and I'll make a regular place for you two to come back to— wait and see. And now you drink up and be friends.

BURKE: *(happily—but still a bit resentful against the old man)* Sure! *(Clinking his glass against* CHRIS'S*)* Here's luck to you! *(He drinks)*.

CHRIS: *(subdued—his face melancholy)* Skoal. *(He drinks)*.

BURKE: *(to* ANNA*, with a wink)* You'll not be lonesome long. I'll see to that, with the help of God. 'Tis himself here will be having a grandchild to ride on his foot, I'm telling you!

ANNA: *(turning away in embarrassment)* Quit the kidding now. *(She picks up her bag and goes into the room on left. As soon as she is gone* BURKE *relapses into an attitude of gloomy thought.* CHRIS *stares at his beer absent-mindedly. Finally* BURKE *turns on him)*.

BURKE: Is it any religion at all you have, you and your Anna?

CHRIS: *(surprised)* Vhy yes. Ve vas Lutheran in ole country.

BURKE: *(horrified)* Luthers, is it? *(Then with a grim resignation, slowly, aloud to himself)* Well, I'm damned then surely. Yerra, what's the difference? 'Tis the will of God, anyway.

CHRIS: *(moodily preoccupied with his own thoughts— speaks with somber premonition as* ANNA *re-enters from the left)* It's funny. It's queer, yes—you and me shipping on same boat dat vay. It ain't right. Ay don't know—it's dat funny vay ole davil sea do her vorst dirty tricks, yes. It's so. *(He gets up and goes back and, opening the door, stares out into the darkness)*.

BURKE: *(nodding his head in gloomy acquiescence—with a great sigh)* I'm fearing maybe you have the right of it for once, divil take you.

ANNA: *(forcing a laugh)* Gee, Mat, you ain't agreeing with him, are you? *(She comes forward and puts her arm about his shoulder—with a determined gayety)* Aw say, what's the matter? Cut out the gloom. We're all fixed now, ain't we, me and you? *(Pours out more beer into his glass and fills one for herself—slaps him on the back)* Come on! Here's to the sea, no matter what! Be a game sport and drink to that! Come on! *(She gulps down her glass.* BURKE *banishes his superstitious premonitions with a defiant jerk of his head, grins up at her, and drinks to her toast).*

CHRIS: *(looking out into the night—lost in his somber preoccupation—shakes his head and mutters)* Fog, fog, fog, all bloody time. You can't see vhere you vas going, no. Only dat ole davil, sea—she knows! *(The two stare at him. From the harbor comes the muffled, mournful wail of steamers' whistles).*

CURTAIN

COMMENTARY

According to the Gelbs, O'Neill's biographers, "The reviews of *Anna Christie* were uniformly favorable, although several critics complained about the 'contrived' fourth act and the 'talkiness' of the second. The acting of Miss Lord was praised by all, as was that of George Marion . . . and the production, as a whole, was enthusiastically applauded" (*O'Neill*, N.Y., 1960, p. 478). Alexander Woollcott in the *New York Times* (November 3, 1921) referred to it as "a heavily freighted sea going play." Then, about Pauline Lord, he said: "She gives a telling performance to a rich and salty play that grips the attention with the rise of the first curtain and holds it fiercely to the end." He also had some reservations.

But in this play the part enacted by the sea seems a little forced, a thing of painted canvas, a factor less present and less potent than O'Neill may be guessed to have meant it to be . . . *Anna Christie* might be described as a work which towers above most of the plays in town, but which falls short of the stature and perfection reached by O'Neill in some of his earlier work . . . it has less directness and more dross, and more moments of weak violence than any of its forerunners, it is, nevertheless, a play written with that abundant imagination, that fresh and venturesome mind and that sure instinct for the theater which set this young author apart. . . .

Several critics felt that O'Neill had tacked on a happy ending to *Anna Christie*. And the reviews obviously stung O'Neill to the point where he even sought to answer via the newspaper. A playwright needed good nerves to read Alexander Woollcott's review:

Here, for once, is O'Neill irresolute in the matter of the final scene. Hitherto he has gone to it as unerringly and inevitably as a man goes to the ground who has jumped off the Woolworth building. The last act of *Anna Christie*, however, is full of bogus things and even gives way to the weakness of brandishing a revolver for no other conceivable purpose than that of jouncing the nervous playgoer. . . .

Prior to that burst of hot shrapnel, he had stated the players

occasionally clumsy with a boyish awkwardness. It has one or two moments of feeble violence. It is cluttered up with the rubbish of an earlier play. . . . Its last act shilly shallies. Yet because it is crowded with life, because it has sprung from as fine an imagination as ever worked in our theater, and because it has been wrought by a master of dramatic dialogue, it is worth seeing again and again. It comes to the chronic playgoer like a swig of strong, black coffee to one who has been sipping pink lemonade.

Woollcott then took a parting shot:

The two lovers are interlocked as the final curtain falls. O'Neill seems to be suggesting to the departing playgoers that they can regard this as a happy ending if they are shortsighted enough to believe it and weak-minded enough to crave it. He, at least, has the satisfaction of intimating in his final words that, whereas everything seems cheerful enough at the moment, there is probably no end of misery for everybody hidden just ahead in the enfolding mists of the sea. It is a happy ending with the author's fingers crossed.

It was not Woollcott's overall comments that set O'Neill off, for he thought that the critic had understood and was sympathetic, but he could not let the happy-ending whip-crack go by. His answer was published in the *New York Times* (December 18, 1921), in which he said:

So many people—critics, professional and volunteer—have taken exception to what they allege is the compromising, happy ending to my *Anna Christie* that I feel called upon to make not a defense but an explanation. Evidently—to me at least—these people have ears but are slightly hard of hearing.

First of all, is the ending to *Anna Christie* an ending in the accepted sense at all? Is it not rather a new beginning, with a whole new play, as full of the same pre-ordained human conflict as the last, just starting at the final curtain? Such was my intention, in this type of naturalistic play, which attempts to translate life into its own terms.

O'Neill goes on to defend his ending as a nonending and castigates the attitude of those seeking the neatly packaged morals of an ordinary play:

It may be objected by some stickler for dramatic technique that, after all, the last speeches in the play form an anti-climax, and that the psychology of audiences being what it is, I have no right to expect anything but a general inattention. This point, I grant, is well taken. Nevertheless, those last speeches properly understood are as full of drama as anything in the play. They are not of the stuff of anti-climax. It is only the kiss-marriage-happily-ever-after tradition that makes them so. And it is my business—and that of every playwright worth his or her salt—to drop such doddering old traditions down the manhole—if only to see what happens. In this case the old tradition seems to have bounded back and "beaned" the playwright.

O'Neill then questions whether or not critics of the play aren't simply offended by the likelihood of an ex-prostitute and a sailor getting together in a marriage. Then he thinks the reason might be because the obvious is preferred to the inevitable. He reacts to these suspicions: "But looking deep into the hearts of my people, I say it couldn't be done. It would not have been true." So he refused to compromise with audiences, but chose instead to show them the real world.

Woollcott answers O'Neill's letter with some rather biting comments. He writes:

> The posture of affairs in the final moment of the play is, after all, the posture used by a thousand and one playwrights as a good omen, as a symbol of happiness achieved. That this posture is so regarded by all audiences is an evidence of the pathetically incorrigible hopefulness of the foolish old human race. Over such additional evidence, Mr. O'Neill is free to have a good cry whenever he feels like it. But when he introduces that evidence himself, or at least when he incites it by elaborately contriving the familiar posture of what he likes to call the "kiss-marry-happily-ever-after tradition" of the theatre, he is in no position to rise like the lawyers in court, and say: "I claim surprise." (*New York Times,* December 25, 1921)

Nothing in O'Neill's script suggests a happy ending and one wonders if there was something in the play's direction that gave the impression. Perhaps Hopkins added a gesture or stage picture that O'Neill had not intended—something subtle. Or was it simply a matter of "posture" as Woollcott indicates? There seems to be no satisfactory answer to the matter. But the controversy over the ending of the play disturbed O'Neill for many years and made him believe that the play was a failure. When Joseph Wood Krutch asked, a few years later, to anthologize his early plays, O'Neill replied, "*Anna Christie* must not be among them."

O'Neill apparently was experimenting with plot, trying to avoid the well-made play. The controversy may have stemmed largely from this approach. Surely, one of the earmarks of the realistic–naturalistic play of the nineteenth century and early twentieth century, too, was its tight structure. Much of this can be traced to Scribe, Augier, and Englishmen like Robertson and Pinero. And Bronson Howard, William Dean Howells, and Henry James all wrote at rather great length about the structure of the drama. Howard and James emphasized the careful determining of every event. Clearly one of the advances for which O'Neill worked was the Chekhovian effect of the incidental and accidental. He does use the devices of the past and present with Anna's story. Here, in an approach as old as the Greeks, he shows that man cannot escape his past. This device is deftly employed with Anna and Chris. No matter that Chris left Anna to the land, the sea eventually gets them all. If one sees or feels the sea as a symbol—another development of O'Neill's realism—of fate, we can better discover and appreciate the style and method which he was using.

In the first act, we see Anna as an escapee from the land; in the second act, she is cleansed by the sea. But in the third act she is being entangled by the sea and finally, at the end, trapped by it. It is important to remember, however, that an astute playgoer like Woollcott admits that the effect on the audience of all this was negligible. They were more caught up in the Mat–Anna relationship and were mostly blind and deaf to everything else.

O'Neill's treatment of Anna is also of major interest to students of realism. As pointed out in the Introduction, it would have been impossible in the late nineteenth century to put a character like Anna on the stage. She could only have been accepted if she suffered and died. O'Neill exploded this myth. He did it by presenting a fallen woman as his heroine. Of course, in his heart of hearts she had never really fallen, for her heart was pure. O'Neill was much the romantic at this time on such matters.

The attack on the old models of the perfect woman and the fallen woman had already been partially achieved by Eugene Walter in *The Easiest Way*. At the end of that play, the heroine has lost both her men—the Broadway Lounger, as he was called in those days, who kept her, and the man who really loved her but felt that she could never change. In the end she returns in full sail to the life of the bordello and kept woman. Such characters had to remain in type. O'Neill, however, felt that such women could change and tried to prove it. He had to show that Mat and Anna at least had a chance at happiness, though as he implied, it was highly unlikely to occur.

It is important to remember that O'Neill had a tendency to type. In *Anna Christie,* it is particularly true of Mat, who is an embodiment of the stage Irishman. O'Neill used this artifice in many of his plays. Perhaps it is too obvious. He seems to be trying too hard to characterize by forced dialect and also by trade. The ability of his characters to think and make choices is severely limited. In that sense, he is similar to the writers of local color and an inheritor of the nine-teenth-century stage with its stock types.

Anna Christie begins on a distinctly realistic note with longshoremen entering Jimmy-the-Priest's bar for a drink, a postman arriving with a letter for Chris, and Larry, Jimmy, and Chris bantering over drinks and a cigar. This faithfulness to detail exists throughout, as if the play is merely plain life set simply before us. In this realistic vein, there is the sardonically amusing situation of Chris being captain of a coal barge, the lowliest command job a sailor can have, dully towing tons of darkness through all kinds of weather—mostly fog. Act I is essentially nondramatic, more in the way of establishing realistic color, setting, tone, mood.

In Act II, there is a definite contrast established between realistic barge paraphernalia and romantic health-giving sea mists. Oddly enough, Mat Burke romanticizes Anna's image just as Anna has done with the surface sweetness of the sea. Romance begins in earnest.

The *Simeon Winthrop* is anchored off Provincetown, Massachusetts, possibly as a tribute to George Cook and his wife, Susan Glaspell, who gave O'Neill his start by produc-ing *Bound East for Cardiff* alongside Glaspell's own *Trifles*. In this act, it becomes clear just how allied Anna is to the sea. She feels "clean" in the sea's presence and hears its "call," reflecting her romantic yearning for the sea that pulled her out of the landlocked shallows of Minnesota. Anna is a symbol-in-tandem with the ocean, having her own surface allure. Like a "painted lady," the sea turns out to be a whore underneath, too. The connection between Anna's prostitution and the sailor's life with the sea is unmistakable. O'Neill does not make dozens of unflattering remarks about the sexual behavior of sailors and whores without their having some bearing on his seeing the sea and women together as a mighty force that men must make an accommodation with. Burke and Chris will both go to sea on the *Londonderry,* bound for Cape Town. They have both been reclaimed by the sea through Anna. Ironically this began with Chris and Mat both idealizing Anna, just as she was in the process of idealizing the sea. Chris felt that the sea was after him and not Anna, and if he gave up, the sea would leave Anna alone.

Chris sees his daughter as pure and innocent. Mat thinks of her as a sainted lady. But Burke, who boasts of his physical courage and strength in the face of death itself, quails and turns into marshmallow pudding when confronted with the sexual reality of Anna—that she has slept with hundreds of men as a prostitute. Clearly a strong mind reaches farther than a strong arm. Both men learn the truth about Anna and are about to head out to sea, with neither being able to give up his connection with her. With Anna, as with the sea, they are as oar to lock or rower to wave.

THE SHOW-OFF
by
George Kelly

BACKGROUND

On February 3, 1924, the Provincetown Playhouse, under the management of the Triumvirate of Jones, MacGowan, and O'Neill opened a revival of a famous play of the nineteenth century, Anna Cora Mowatt's *Fashion*. On February 4, 1924, at the Playhouse Theater on West Forty-eighth Street, George Kelly's play, *The Show-Off*, went on the boards. Both plays are excellent examples of a hypothesis that was offered some years ago by Eleanor Flexnor: "American drama was to make its most significant contribution in the critical study of character against a native background" (*American Playwrights, 1918–1938* [1938], p. 28).

Although *Fashion* provides us with some insight about the manners of our ancestors, the play is basically a sentimental farce. The sentimentality is revealed in the treatment of theme—Yankee and Puritan thrift and wholesomeness versus Continental extravagance and deceitfulness. The theme is dramatically enacted by pitting a group of good, clean Americans against a bevy of shifty Continentals and Americans who have forsaken the simple ways of their countrymen. In keeping with the mode of playwriting of the period, many of the characters are broadly exaggerated and caricatured so that more attention is placed on the characters' absurd behavior, thus making the play a farce. When George Kelly appeared on the scene, American comedy was beginning to mature.

George S. Kaufman, the well-known play doctor and master of the "wise crack," had quipped, "Satire's what closes on Saturday night." Yet by the mid 1920s he was the major exponent of the form. After *Dulcy,* written by Kaufman and Marc Connelly, opened in 1921, Alexander Woollcott, in the *New York Times* of August 21, compared the play to English comedy because it had "the pinch of salt of satire to give it flavor, a play wherein the laughter is edged with scorn and the banter is marked by disdainful mockery." It was a time for spoofing, and Kaufman, Connelly, and Woollcott belonged to a group of wits who were known as the "Vicious Circle." They met for lunch each day at the Algonquin Hotel and disdainful mockery was the name of the game they played with precision and wickedness. Primarily composed of writers and journalists, the membership included Franklin P. Adams, Deems Taylor, Robert Benchley, Harold Ross, Heywood Broun, Art Samuels, John Peter Toohey, Brock and Murdock Pemberton, Bill Murray, Robert E. Sherwood, Laurence Stallings, David Wallace, Herman J. Mankiewicz, Dorothy Parker, Jane Grant, Ruth Hale, Beatrice Kaufman, Peggy Wood, Peggy Leech, Margalo Gillmore, Edna Ferber, Neysa McMein as well as the aforementioned playwrights and critic. Margaret Case Harriman said that, "They were no different from any group of plumbers, advertising writers, bankers, or farmers, except for one thing: their minds were born to think of things in an unusual way" (*The Vicious Circle,* N.Y., 1951, p. 19). Not only did they think of things in an unusual way, but they had little or no use for the old ways. Malcolm Goldstein observed in his biography *George S. Kaufman* (1979, p. 75), "Evident throughout the calendar was the new, irreverent, 'debunking' attitude toward the past. Most of the Algonquin writers, not Kaufman and Connelly alone, felt the desire to turn the past upside down. . . ." In doing so, these writers often aimed their barbs at war profiteering and the hypocritical blitz of commerce.

And so George Kaufman and his many play collaborators, armed with the wisecrack, used satire to undermine the establishment. Sometimes they used a broadsword, as in *Animal Crackers* written for the Marx Brothers; other times, the pin prick was sufficient. These writers would have been amused had anyone called them moralists, but moralists they were in the sense that William Dean Howells used the term. George Kelly, however, was a conscious moralist, and in his play *The Show-Off* demonstrated how to wed satirical comedy to realism.

Kelly was born in Philadelphia in 1887, the son of one of the most prominent families in the city. His brother John B. distinguished himself by winning the single- and double-sculling matches in the 1920 Olympic Games. One of John's children, and therefore George's niece, became first a successful actress and then Princess Grace of Monaco. His oldest brother, Walter C., was a well-known vaudeville monologist called the Virginia Judge. George started his theatrical career as an actor when he was about twenty-one years of age, touring with several combination companies. In 1915 he entered vaudeville as an actor and sketch writer. It is perhaps strange for us today to accept the fact that a man who came from a very respected family, who was a devout Roman Catholic and a moralist, could have been a vaudevillian. Of course, that term conjures up visions for most people of cheap song-and-dance acts, magic shows, bawdy comedians, and girlie routines. When the Kelly brothers were on stage, although it is doubtful that they appeared together as a team, vaudeville was one of the less vulgar popular entertainments. Parker Zellers, in his informative book, *Tony Pastor, Dean of the Vaudeville Stage* (1971), indicates that the reform movement in vaudeville started as early as 1865, and Pastor was determined to "attract the patronage of women and families." Between 1915 and 1921, Kelly wrote a series of sketches that were very popular and established him as a capable writer. He rejected the rube-type sketches so typical of the vaudeville circuit, and recalling his vaudeville life some years later commented, "I never wrote down to the vaudeville audiences, I never made any cheap appeals to laughter or to pathos. . . . During the years I appeared, the greatest players in the country were also acting in vaudeville sketches." It should be recalled, as Arthur Hopkins pointed out, that some vaudeville actors were very dedicated and made every attempt to create very believable characters on stage.

Almost all of these sketches are very similar. They have three or four characters drawn from middle-class life, and they examine particular types. Kelly was above all a keen observer of people, with a rare ability to catch the rhythms and sounds of American speech. One of his earliest and most popular sketches, entitled *Finders Keepers,* is a realistic morality play based on the lesson "honesty is the best policy." In the play the central character finds a wallet with a considerable amount of money in it. After several complications, she is forced by her husband to return the money. Before it can be returned, however, she ironically loses it.

The sketch must have had an impact on audiences, for an unusual number of lost items turned up at box offices wherever the sketch played. Perhaps the most famous of the sketches is *Poor Aubrey,* which became the basis for the play *The Show-Off.* In the playlet written about 1920, Kelly already had developed the three major characters and the basic conflict between Aubrey and his mother-in-law.

His first successful full-length play was *The Torchbearers,* presented in 1922, and Foster Hirsch, Kelly's biographer observed:

> Kelly wrote the play, typically, not simply as disinterested entertainment—though it is great fun—but as instructive entertainment; and he laced his burlesque of little-theater amateurishness with the solemn treatise that if we are anything less than complete professionals, we should not participate in plays, for we will only make fools of ourselves and insult the art we are trying so helplessly to practice. Obeying the traditional function of its "satirical comedy" genre, then, *The Torchbearers* ridicules vanity and hypocrisy for purposes of moral correction. (*George Kelly* [1975], p. 51)

Kelly had strict standards in his personal and professional life as well as in his plays. In 1925 he was described as being "tall and not unhandsome" by an interviewer in the *New York Times,* who added:

> He looks more the poet and philosopher than the celebrated Broadway playwright. Unobtrusive, self-effacing and mindful of his own business, he has very few friends and these he picks with great care.

He was not gregarious at all; as a matter of fact, he appears to have been a misogamist. He was a bachelor his entire life, and perhaps a Victorian as far as romance was concerned; at least, he was able to keep his private matters completely secret. He detested having his privacy invaded by the press. As a writer, he was a meticulous craftsman, believing that the playwright was the only person who really understood what had been created, and accordingly he directed all of his own plays. He knew the effect he wanted to achieve and exactly how to get it. Grace Kelly, in an interview, commented about her uncle's stage direction:

> He was quite rigid about his writing and never allowed an actor to change a word of dialogue. If a performer did question what a character said or did, George would explain—often in a quite withering manner—that he knew precisely what the character was about and all that the actor had to do was to follow his direction.

He believed in the "new realism" as a writer, and as a performer. In an interview with a reporter from *Theater Magazine* in 1924, he said:

> I believe that the next few years will see plays which feature character delineation. Universal types will walk the stage. The characters in the new plays will be easily recognizable. They will be far different from the overdrawn, unreal stage creatures of the past. It will not matter whether they are fashioned after a poor chap like the show-off or after a millionaire's son. Human beings are much alike, rich or poor. . . . The trouble is that actors do not get far enough away from—Theater. They do not mix with people who possess a plexus of innumerable influences. Men and women in various walks of life, and in different strata of society, have their individual philosophy, whims, crotchets, mannerisms. If actors are going to faithfully delineate different roles which fall to them, they must understand humanity. . . . If only they could study the art of Stanislavsky and his company. When two actors on the stage in a play he presents glance at each other, while other characters are speaking, that glance is significant, pregnant with meaning. It is intended to convey to the audience a fleeting impression or mood of the moment.

He also believed that a playwright had to be objective. He stated that, "the shadow of the author must never fall across the play," yet he knew that "a writer can achieve complete detachment only when life for him is over."

Obviously Kelly is inconsistent. One can't be a dictatorial director *and* believe in the Stanislavsky system. One can't stand aloof from the play *and* maintain that he is the only one who totally understands it. He must have realized this, for he was too personally involved in his work both as writer and director. Kelly's attitudes, and his creative work as a playwright, raise interesting questions about the craft and method of the realist. He was eminently successful with *The Show-Off*, and it is not an exaggeration to state that no play of the 1920s is more representative of the "new realists." However, Mary McCarthy in her book *Sights and Spectacles* states that Kelly is not a "realist," and her position reflects that of many contemporary critics concerning realism. She for one, and Kelly's biographer for another, cannot accept realism both as a form of playwriting and method of production that can be used to reveal "truths" about our lives and times. The realist for them was limited to reporting. Thus, Mary McCarthy is puzzled by Kelly.

> he is the queerest writer on view in America. His plays though they are set in drawing rooms, are not polite comedies; though they make a fetish of observation, they are not realistic; though they are performed by actors, their complete cast of characters is not listed on the program, their real heroes and heroines being glasses of water, pocketbooks, telephones and after dinner cups. It is difficult to describe a George Kelly play to anyone who has not seen several, simply because it is not like anything else while on the surface it resembles every play one has ever been to. (pp. 97–98)

For her the details of reality that Kelly employed became the major focus of the play. Those details carefully selected and written into the play at exactly the right moment heightened the dramatic action, for example, the ring of the doorbell in *The Show-Off*, or Aubrey's need for a glass of water and his way of drinking it. These details of realistic business, often derided by some critics, are the masterstrokes of the realistic writer, for they underline and carefully emphasize the basic thought or truth behind the dramatic action. Thus, the realistic playwright became more than just a reporter, which everyone thought had been his purpose, that is, to coldly and dispassionately observe. The fact is that Kelly was neither cold nor dispassionate. He was outraged by our materialistic society. His own experiences, whatever they may have been, led him to believe that matrimony and materialism were husband and wife in our society. It was a truth that other people saw as well because his plays were enormously successful. Thus, like O'Neill, Kelly touched all of us with his experiences and made us feel our common humanity.

In spite of his desire to show up American society for what it was, Kelly compromised the ending of his play. His nephew Charles Kelly said that his uncle wanted to be a financial success when he wrote *The Show-Off*, and as a result he changed the ending of the play in order to make Aubrey successful. According to Ward Morehouse, critic and writer, in his book *Matinee Tomorrow* (1949), Kelly did so at the insistence of his producers during the play's tryout stage in Atlantic City. "During the engagement at the shore Miss Stewart persuaded the reluctant Kelly to make a change in an important line, the curtain speech of the final act, which, as changed, made the triumph of the upstart Aubrey over his mother-in-law all the more complete" (p. 199). It is an absolutely false note. In his vaudeville sketch *Poor Aubrey,* no compromise is made. Aubrey is the foolish braggart from beginning to end.

The Show-Off ran for 571 consecutive performances and established Kelly's reputation as a successful playwright. The play has been revived at least four times on Broadway, with the most successful production being staged by the Association of Producing Artists—Phoenix Repertory Company in 1967 starring Helen Hayes and Clayton Corzatte. Three motion pictures were made from the play: one silent version starring Gregory Kelly in 1926; the second starring Spencer Tracy released in 1934; and the final version with Red Skelton in 1947.

In 1926 George Kelly won a Pulitzer Prize for drama with his play *Craig's Wife,* which starred Chrystal Herne, the daughter of James A. (see Introduction, p. 9), in the leading role. His later plays include *Daisy Mayme* (1926), *Behold the Bridegroom* (1927, his personal favorite), *Maggie the Magnificent* (1929), *The Deep Mrs. Sykes* (1945), and *That Fatal Weakness* (1946). He died in Pennsylvania in 1974.

THE SHOW-OFF
A Transcript of Life
in Three Acts

ORIGINAL CAST

As first produced at the Playhouse Theatre, New
York, on February 4th, 1924.

CLARA	Juliette Crosby
MRS. FISHER	Helen Lowell
AMY	Regina Wallace
FRANK HYLAND	Guy D'Ennery
MR. FISHER	C. W. Goodrich
JOE	Lee Tracy
AUBREY PIPER	Louis John Bartels
MR. GILL	Francis Pierlot
MR. ROGERS	Joseph Clayton

ACT ONE

After a slight pause a door out at the left is heard to close,
and then CLARA comes in carrying a fancy box of candy. She
glances about the room and crosses to the kitchen-door at
the right.

CLARA: Anybody out there? (*She crosses back again
towards the left, laying the box of candy on the center-table
as she passes. Upon reaching the parlor-doors, at the left,
she opens them and calls into the parlor.*) You in there,
Mom? (MRS. FISHER *can be heard coming down the stairs.*
CLARA *turns, with a glance toward the hall-door, and moves
over to the mirror above the mantelpiece.* MRS. FISHER
appears in the hall-door and glances in at CLARA.)

MRS. FISHER: Oh, it's *you*, Clara. (*She peers out into the
hall.*)

CLARA: Where is everybody?

MRS. FISHER: I thought I heard that front-door open.

CLARA: Where are they all?

MRS. FISHER: (*Moving towards the parlor-door*). Your
Pop's gone over to Gillespie's for some tobacco: I don't

139

know where Joe is. (*She glances into the parlor, then turns and kisses* CLARA. CLARA *moves down to the chair at the left of the center-table and* MRS. FISHER *moves over to the kitchen-door at the right.*) I don't know how you can stand that fur on you, Clara, a night like this.

CLARA: It's rather cool out.

MRS. FISHER: (*Calling out through the kitchen-door*). You out there, Joe?

CLARA: (*Sitting down*). He isn't out there.

MRS. FISHER: (*Turning around to the cellar-door at her left*). He must be around here somewhere; he was here not two minutes ago, when I went upstairs. (*Opening the cellar-door and calling down.*) You down there, Joey?

JOE: (*From the cellar*). Yes.

MRS. FISHER: All right. (*Closes the cellar-door.*)

JOE: What do you want?

MRS. FISHER: (*Turning to the cellar-door again*). What?

JOE *and* CLARA, *speaking together.*

JOE: What do you want?

CLARA: He sez, "What do you want?"

MRS. FISHER: (*Opening the cellar-door again*). I don't want anything; I was just wonderin' where you were. (*She closes the cellar-door and comes a step or two forward, fastening an old-fashioned brooch that she wears on the front of her dress.*) He spends half his time down in that cellar foolin' with that old radio thing. He sez he can make one himself, but I sez, "I'll believe it when I see it."

CLARA: There's some of that candy you like.

MRS. FISHER: (*Crossing to the center-table*). Oh, did you bring me some more of that nice candy? (*Beginning to untie the ribbon around the candy.*) I never got a taste of that last you brought.

CLARA: Why not?

MRS. FISHER: Why,—Lady Jane took it away with her down to the office, and never brought it back. She sez the girls down there et it. I sez, "I guess you're the girl that et it." She sez she didn't, but I know she did.

CLARA: Well, I hope you'll keep that out of sight, and don't let her take that too.

MRS. FISHER: (*Opening the candy*). Oh, she won't get her hands on this, I can promise you that. Let her buy her own candy if she's so fond of it.

CLARA: (*Opening the "Delineator"*). She won't *buy* much of *anything,* if she can get hold of it any *other* way.

MRS. FISHER: Oh, isn't that lovely! Look Clara—(*Tilting the box of candy towards* CLARA.) Don't that look nice?

CLARA: Yes, they do their candy up nice.

MRS. FISHER: (*Gingerly picking up the cover of lace paper*). That looks just like Irish point lace, don't it? (CLARA *nods yes.*) I think I'll put that away somewhere,—in a book or something. My, look at all the colors—look Clara—did you ever see so many colors?

CLARA: It's pretty, isn't it?

MRS. FISHER: It's beautiful—seems a pity to spoil it. Do you want a bit of it, Clara?

CLARA: Not now, Mom.

MRS. FISHER: I think I'll take this pink one here. I *like* the pink ones. (*She picks up the box and the lid and moves around to the chair at the right of the table.*) Mind how they all have this little fancy paper around them. You'd wonder they'd bother, wouldn't you?—just for a bit of candy. (*She tastes the candy and chews, critically.*) That's nice candy, isn't it?

CLARA: Yes, *I* like bonbons.

MRS. FISHER: (*Sitting down*). I do too—I think I like them better than most anything. (*Putting the box of candy down on the table.*) I'm sorry these are not all bonbons.

CLARA: (*Looking up from the "Delineator"*). They *are* all bonbons—(*Her Mother looks at her.*) There's nothing else in there.

MRS. FISHER: Oh, are they!—I thought only the pink ones were the bonbons.

CLARA: No, they're all bonbons.

MRS. FISHER: Well, that's lovely. I can eat any one of them I like, then, can't I? (*She sits back in her chair and rocks and chews.*) How is it you're not home to-night, Clara?

CLARA: Frank had to go to a dinner of some kind at the Glenwood Club; so I thought I'd stay in town and get something. He said he might call for me here around eight o'clock. I was in anyway about my lamp.

MRS. FISHER: (*Rocking*). Men are always going to dinners somewhere. Seems to me they can't talk about anything unless they've got a dinner in front of them. It's no wonder so many of them are fat.

CLARA: (*Turning a page of the "Delineator"*). Where's Amy,—upstairs?

MRS. FISHER: Yes, she's gettin' dressed. I was just hookin' her when you came in.

CLARA: Is she going out?

MRS. FISHER: I don't know whether she is or not,—I didn't hear her say. (*Leaning a bit towards* CLARA, *and lowering her voice.*) But it's Wednesday night, you know.

CLARA: Is that fellow still coming here?

MRS. FISHER: Oh, right on the dot—such as he is. Sunday nights too now, as well as Wednesdays. It looks like a steady thing. And you never in your life heard anybody talk so much, Clara—I don't know how she stands him. Your Pop can hardly stay in the room where he is. I believe in my heart that's the reason he went over to Gillespie's to-night—so he wouldn't be listenin' to him.

CLARA: Doesn't she take him into the parlor?

MRS. FISHER: She does, yes; but she might just as well leave him out here; for he's not in there five minutes till he's out here again—talkin' about Socialism. That's all you hear,—Socialism—and capital and labor. You'd think he knew somethin' about it. And the Pennsylvania Railroad. He's always talkin' about that, too. That's where he works, you know. I don't know what he does down there. He sez himself he's head of the freight department; but as I sez to our Joe, I sez, "I don't know how *he* can be head of *anything,* from the talk of him. Joe sez he thinks he's a nut. And your Pop told him right to his face here last Sunday night—that he didn't know the meanin' of the *word* Socialism. (*She checks herself and gets up.*) I'd better not be talkin' so loud,—he's apt to walk in on us. (*She moves up towards the hall-door and glances out.*) He's a great joker, you know—That's what he did last Sunday night. (*Coming forward again to a point above the center-table.*) I never got such a fright in my life. Your Pop and me was sittin' here talkin', just the way we are now, when, all of a sudden, I glanced up, and there he was,—standin' in the doorway there, doin' this (*She points her forefinger and thumb at* CLARA *and wiggles her thumb.* CLARA *laughs faintly*)—as though he was a bandit, you know. Well,—I thought the breath'd leave my body. Then he sez, "Haha!—that's the time I fooled you!" I don't know how long he'd been standin' there. But, as luck'd have it, we wasn't talkin' about him at the time: altho we *had* been talkin' about him not five minutes before. I don't know whether he heard us or not, for I don't know how long he'd been standin' there. I hope he did: it'd just be the price of him, for bein' so smart. (*With a glance toward the hall-door, and speaking very confidentially.*) But, you know, what'd kill you, Clara, you can't say a *word* about him in front of her. (CLARA *moves*.) Oh, not a word. No matter what he sez, she thinks it's lovely. When Joe told her here the other night he thought he was a nut, she just laughed, and said that Joe was jealous of him—because *he* could express himself and *he* couldn't. (CLARA *smiles*.) You never *heard* such talk. And, you know, Clara, *I* think he wears a wig. (CLARA *laughs*.) I do, honestly. And our Joe sez he thinks he does too. But when I asked *her* about it here one mornin', I thought she'd take the head right off me. You never *seen* anybody get themselves into such a temper. She sez, "It's a lie," she sez, "he *don't* wear a wig." She sez, "People always say somethin' like that about a fellow that makes a good appearance." But, *I* think he does, just the same; and the first chance I get I'm goin' to take a good look. (*She moves around to her chair again, at the right of the table*.) He often sits right here, you know, under this light, while he's talkin'; (*Selecting another piece of candy*) and I'm goin' to look close the very first chance I get. (*She sits down.*) *I* can tell a wig as good as anybody. (*She rocks and looks straight out, chewing.*) She won't make a liar out of me.

AMY: (*From the head of the stairs*). Mom, did you see anything of that blue bar-pin of mine?

MRS. FISHER: (*Calling back to her*). Which blue bar-pin?

AMY: Well now, how many blue bar-pins have I got?

MRS. FISHER: I don't know how many you've got, and I don't care! (*Turning back again and speaking rather to herself*.) So don't be botherin' me about it. (*Calling up to* AMY *again*.) If you can't find it, go look for it. (*She resumes her rocking and her chewing*.) She thinks all she's got to do is come to the head of them stairs and holler and everybody'll jump.—But she'll get sadly left.—I've got somethin' else to do besides waitin' on her. (*She takes another bite of candy, and turns casually to* CLARA.) Did you *get* your lamp yet?

CLARA: No, that's what I was in town to-day about. The girl sez they haven't been able to match the silk till yesterday.

MRS. FISHER: I wish I could get somethin' done to that one of mine there in the parlor; the wire's right out through the silk in two places.

CLARA: Why doesn't Amy take it in some day (MRS. FISHER *makes a sound of amusement*)—when she's going to work?

MRS. FISHER: Why don't she! It's all Amy can do to take *herself* into work these days. I've almost got to *push* her out the door every morning.

CLARA: Couldn't she take it over at lunch-time?

MRS. FISHER: She sez she hasn't time at lunch-time.

CLARA: Oh, she has so time.

MRS. FISHER: Of course she has.

CLARA: It's only at Ninth and Chestnut, and she's at Eighth.

MRS. FISHER: That's what I told her. I sez, "I bet if it was somethin' for yourself you'd have plenty of time." (*Leaning towards* CLARA.) But, you know,—what *I* think, Clara—*I* think she's meetin' this fellow at lunch-time. Because in the mornin's here she stands fixin' herself there in front of that glass till it's a wonder to me she don't drop on the floor. And whenever you see them gettin' very particular that way all of a sudden—there's somethin' in the wind. I sez to her the other mornin', when she was settlin' herself there till I got tired lookin' at her, I sez, "You must be goin' to see him to-day, ain't you?" And she sez, "He must be on your mind, isn't he?" "No," I sez, "but by the looks of things, I think he's on yours. And," I sez, "maybe after you get him you won't think he was worth all the bother you went to." Because, you know, Clara, she don't know a *thing* about him; except that he works in the Pennsylvania freight office—I believe he *did* tell her that much. But *she* don't know whether he works there or not. He could tell her anything; and she'd believe it (*Taking another bite of candy and settling herself in her chair*)—before she'd believe me.

CLARA: That's where he works (*Her Mother looks at her sharply*)—at the Pennsylvania freight office.

MRS. FISHER: How do you know?

CLARA: Frank knows him.

MRS. FISHER: Frank Hyland?

CLARA: Yes,—he sez he eats his lunch at the same place, there at Fifteenth and Arch.

MRS. FISHER: And, does he say he knows him?

CLARA: Yes. He sez he's seen him around there for a long time. I've often heard him speak of him, but I didn't know it was the same fellow. Frank always called him Carnation Charlie. He sez he's always got a big carnation in his buttonhole.

MRS. FISHER: (*Tapping the table conclusively*). That's the one; he's always got it on when he comes here, too.

CLARA: Frank sez he's never seen him without it.

MRS. FISHER: I haven't either. And I believe in my heart, Clara, that's what's turned her head. (CLARA *smiles*.) You often see things like that, you know. The worst fool of a man can put a carnation in his coat or his hat over one eye, and half a dozen sensible women'll be dyin' about him.

CLARA: Well, Frank sez this fellow's absolutely *crazy*.

MRS. FISHER: That's what your Father sez.

CLARA: He sez they kid the life out of him down around the restaurant there.

MRS. FISHER: Well, he don't know who Frank Hyland *is*, does he?

CLARA: No, Frank didn't tell him. He sez he just happened to get talking to him the other day and he mentioned that he was calling on a girl up this way named Fisher. So then Frank found out what his right name was, and when he came home he asked me about him.

MRS. FISHER: Well, is he sure it's the same fellow?

CLARA: He told him his name was Piper.

MRS. FISHER: (*With finality*). That's the name—Aubrey Piper. I don't know where he got the Aubrey from; *I* never heard of such a name before, did you?

CLARA: Yes, I've heard the name of Aubrey.

MRS. FISHER: (*Rocking*). Well, I never did. Sounds to me more like a place than a name. (AMY *can be heard coming down the stairs*.) Here she comes. (*She snatches up the box of candy and puts it under her apron*.)

CLARA: Don't say anything, now.

MRS. FISHER: It'd be no use. (*Trying to be casual*.) What color are you havin' your lamp-shade made, Clara?

AMY: (*Hurrying in at the hall-door*). Mom, you *must*

have seen something of that bar-pin of mine; I can't find it anywhere. (*She tosses a beaded bag onto the center-table and turns to the mantelpiece and looks for the bar-pin.*)

MRS. FISHER: (*Abstractedly*). I saw a pin of yours in one of the drawers in the buffet there a few days ago, I don't know whether it's there yet or not.

AMY: (*Hurrying across to the buffet at the right*). How's it *you're* not home to-night, Clara? (*She starts to rummage in the buffet-drawers.*)

CLARA : (*Casually*). I had my dinner in town.

AMY: Is that parlor all right, Mom?

MRS. FISHER: Certainly it's all right.

AMY: Well, did you side it?

MRS. FISHER: (*Sharply*). Certainly I sided it.

AMY: All right, Mom, don't make a speech about it.

MRS. FISHER: (*Considerably ruffled*). No, but you'd think the way she sez it that I sat here all day with my two hands as long as each other. (AMY *finds the pin and slams the drawer shut, leaving various ends of tape and pieces of lace hanging out. Then she starts back towards the mirror over the mantelpiece.*) Did you find it?

AMY: (*Disrespectfully*). Yes.

MRS. FISHER: (*Rising, still holding the candy under her apron, and stepping over to the buffet*). It's a wonder you wouldn't leave these drawers the way you found them. She does that every time she goes near this buffet. (*She puts the various odds and ends back into the drawers and closes them.*) She's in such a great rush lately.

AMY: (*Settling herself at the mirror*). Isn't that a new dress on you, Clara?

CLARA: Yes.

MRS. FISHER: (*Coming back to her chair*). I'd like to see the kind of house you'll keep.

AMY: Well, I hope it won't be anything like this one, I'll tell you that.

MRS. FISHER: (*Stopping halfway to her chair*). Oh, go easy, lady! You might be very glad to have half as good, if you live long enough. (*Continuing to her chair, and looking keenly at* CLARA's *dress.*) I thought I hadn't seen that dress on you before. (*She sits down.*)

CLARA: No, I only got it last week.

MRS. FISHER: Stand up there till I see it. (CLARA *gets up and takes a couple of steps towards the left, pulling down her skirt, then turns around to her left and faces her Mother.* AMY *comes down to the center-table, looking sharply at* CLARA'S *dress.*)

CLARA: I got it at a sale in Strawbridge's. (AMY *opens her beaded purse on the table and looks at herself critically in the little inside mirror; then adds a touch of powder.*)

MRS. FISHER: It's a nice length.

CLARA: I didn't have to have a thing touched on it.

MRS. FISHER: That's what I was tellin' you about the other day, Amy.—Do you see the way that dress hangs?

AMY: Yeh.

MRS. FISHER: (*Speaking directly to* CLARA). There was a dress on Queen Mary in last Sunday's Ledger that I was sayin' to Amy I thought'd look good on me. And it had all buttons up and down the front, the way that has.

CLARA: (*Coming back to her chair*). A lot of the new dresses are made that way.

MRS. FISHER: How much was it?

CLARA: (*Sitting down*). Forty-two seventy-five. (AMY *starts to polish her nails.*)

MRS. FISHER: (*Turning away, with a lift of her eyes to Heaven*). You must have plenty of money.

AMY: Mom, where'd you put those roses I brought home?

MRS. FISHER: They're out there in the dining-room. (AMY *starts towards the right.*) I put them in some water. (AMY *goes out; and* MRS. FISHER *rocks for a second or two; then she turns and calls after* AMY.) I think it's time you lit the light in that parlor, Amy, if that fellow of yours is comin' here to-night. (*She rocks a little bit more, then turns casually to* CLARA.) What time is it by your watch there, Clara? (*With a glance toward the mantelpiece at the back.*) That old clock of ours is stopped again.

CLARA: (*Looking at her wrist-watch*). Quarter past eight.

MRS. FISHER: (*Getting up suddenly*). I must tell her. (*The box of candy lands on the floor.*) My God, there goes the candy! Pick that up, Clara, I can't stoop; and put it out of sight. (*Going towards the door up at the right.*) It's a wonder I didn't do that while she was in here. (*Calling out after* AMY.) Amy!

AMY: Yes?

MRS. FISHER: Clara sez it's a quarter past eight by her watch;—you'd better get some kind of a light in that parlor if that fellow's comin'. (*She moves back towards her chair, then speaks in a very subdued tone to* CLARA.) She brings flowers home with her from the city now, every night he's coming. She must have flowers for him in the parlor. (*She sits down.*) I told her, I sez, "I bet it'd be a long time before you'd bring any flowers home from the city to me."

CLARA: That's another new dress on *her* to-night, isn't it?

MRS. FISHER: (*Straightening the magazines on the table*). She's had it about a week.

CLARA: What's she getting so many new dresses for lately?

MRS. FISHER: Heaven knows, I don't.

CLARA: That's the fourth I've seen on her since Easter.

MRS. FISHER: Tryin' to make him think she's rich, I guess. I told her the other night she might not get so many after she gets him.

AMY: (*Entering from the right, carrying a vase of roses, and crossing directly to the parlor-doors at the left*) You need another box of matches out there, Mom.

MRS. FISHER: Is that box of matches gone already?

AMY: Pretty near. (*She goes into the parlor.*)

MRS. FISHER: I swear I don't know where all the matches go to;—seems to me all I do is buy matches. (AMY *strikes a match in the parlor.*) Be careful of them lace curtains there, now, Amy, if you're goin' to light that lamp. (*The lamp is lit in the parlor; and* AMY *closes the parlor-doors.*)

CLARA: (*Rising and handing her Mother the box of candy, which she has been holding since she picked it up from the floor*) I think I'll go, before he comes.

MRS. FISHER: (*Rising*) You'd better, unless you want to be here all night. (CLARA *moves up to the looking-glass over the mantelpiece, and* MRS. FISHER *crosses to the buffet with the candy.*) For if he ever starts talkin', you'll never get out. (*She puts the candy into one of the drawers, then starts across towards the hall door, up at the left.*) You wouldn't mind, you know, if he'd stay in there in the parlor;—but the minute ever he hears a voice out here, he's out like a jumpin'-jack. (AMY *can be heard coughing out in the hallway, and, as* MRS. FISHER *passes back of* CLARA, CLARA *half turns and suggests with a movement of her hand that* AMY *might overhear her.*) Oh, he's not here yet; you'd know it if he was. (*She peers keenly out into the hallway, then turns and tiptoes back to* CLARA, *and speaks in a very low tone.*) She stands out there in the vestibule until she sees him get off the trolley, then she comes in and lets him ring, so he won't think she's been waitin' for him. *(She tiptoes back and peers out into the hallway again, and* CLARA *moves over to the right, adjusting her neck-piece.* MRS. FISHER *comes back to the center-table.*) You never seen anybody so crazy about a fellow.

CLARA: Well, I think somebody ought to tell her about him, Mom.

MRS. FISHER: *(Folding the ribbon and the paper from the candy-box)* What's the good of tellin' her;—she'd only give you a look if you said anything about him.

CLARA: Well, I'd say it anyway, whether she gave me a look or not; for, remember what I'm telling you, Mom, it's *you* that'll have them on your hands if she takes him. *(Her Mother looks at her sharply.)*

MRS. FISHER: *I'll* have them on my hands?

CLARA: *(Turning to her Mother)* Well now, who else *will*, Mom? You couldn't leave her out on the street; and that's exactly where she'll land if she takes *him;* for you know how long Amy could get along on a hundred and fifty dollars a month.

MRS. FISHER: Takes more than that to keep herself, never name a house and a husband.

CLARA: Well, that's exactly what he gets, for he's only a clerk down there.

MRS. FISHER: He told her he was the head of the department.

CLARA: He's a clerk, Mom,—like a hundred others down there: Frank knows what he does.

MRS. FISHER: *(Moving a step or two nearer to* CLARA*)* Well, why don't *you* say something to her, Clara?

CLARA: Now, you know how much attention she'd pay to anything I'd say.

MRS. FISHER: *(With measured definiteness)* She won't pay any attention to what anybody sez.

CLARA: Especially if she knew it was Frank Hyland that said it.

MRS. FISHER: She thinks everybody's jealous of him; and jealous of *her* because she's gettin' him. So let her get him. If she makes her bed, let her lie in it.

CLARA: *(Looking straight out)* Well, that's the trouble, Mom; it isn't always the person that makes the bed that lies *in* it.—Very often somebody else has to lie in it.

MRS. FISHER: *(Turning back to the table)* Well, it'll be nobody around here, I can promise you that.

CLARA: *(Turning to the buffet-mirror)* Maybe not.

MRS. FISHER: No maybe about it.

CLARA: But you know what *you* are, Mom, where Amy's concerned.

MRS. FISHER: *(Taking a step towards CLARA)* Why, don't be silly, Clara. Do you think your Father'd be listenin' to that rattle-brain here every night?

CLARA: *(Turning and speaking directly to her Mother)* He has to listen to him now, doesn't he—or go out, as he did tonight. *(The front-door closes. They both turn and glance in the direction of the hallway.)* Maybe this is Frank now. *(There is a slight pause, then FRANK HYLAND comes in, and comes forward to the center-table.)*

MRS. FISHER: Hello, Frank.

HYLAND: Hello, Mother. Hello, Clara. *(He puts his hat down on the table.)*

CLARA: I was just going; I thought maybe you weren't coming.

HYLAND: *(Looking at his watch)* I couldn't get away from there until nearly eight o'clock.

MRS. FISHER: Frank,—Clara sez you know this fellow that's comin' to see our Amy.

HYLAND: Who, Piper?

MRS. FISHER: Yes—the one that does so much talkin'.

HYLAND: Yes. I know him. *(He moves to the left and sits down on the arm of the Morris-chair.)*

MRS. FISHER: I think he's crazy, Frank; *(HYLAND makes a sound of amusement)* I do, honestly; and Pop and Joe sez they think he is, too.

CLARA: Mom sez he told Amy he was head of the freight department, Frank.

MRS. FISHER: He did, honestly, Frank; and she believes him. But Clara sez *you* say he's only a clerk down there.

CLARA: That's all he is, Mom.

MRS. FISHER: He isn't head of the freight department, is he, Frank? *(FRANK sits looking away off, dreamily.)*

CLARA: Frank—

HYLAND: *(Turning)* I beg your pardon, what did you say, dear?

MRS. FISHER: He isn't head of the freight department down there, is he?

HYLAND: No, he's just one of the clerks.

MRS. FISHER: *(Turning to CLARA)* Now, you see that—and she'd only laugh at you if you told *her* that. *(Turning back to HYLAND.)* How much do them freight-clerks get a month, Frank?

(HYLAND *is gazing out of the window at the left.*)

CLARA: Frank, Mom is talking to you.

HYLAND: *(Turning)* Oh, I beg your pardon, what did you say, Mother?

MRS. FISHER: I say, how much do them freight-clerks get a month?

HYLAND: Why,—about a hundred and forty or fifty dollars,—I don't know exactly; but not any more than that. *(His eyes wander to the window again.)*

MRS. FISHER: What are we goin' to do about it, Frank?—It looks like a steady thing. He comes Wednesday and Sunday nights now—and if she ever takes him, she'll be the poorest woman in this city. You know how our Amy spends money. *(Turning to CLARA.)* She's got seven pairs of shoes up in that hall-closet.

HYLAND: *(Abstractedly)* Amy certainly does let her money fly. (MRS. FISHER *gives him a stony look.*)

MRS. FISHER: Well, if she does she earns it. She might as well have a good time now while she's young;—God knows what's ahead of her. *(The front door-bell rings,—a series of funny little taps.)* Here he is now, I know his ring. *(She steps up to the mantelpiece and glances out into the hallway.)*

CLARA: *(Turning towards the kitchen-door)* We'll go out the side-door. Come on, Frank. (HYLAND *rises and picks up his hat from the table, as he crosses below it.*)

HYLAND: Good-night, Mother. (MRS. FISHER *is too occupied with her interests out in the hallway.*) Do you want to go to a picture, Clara?

CLARA: *(Going out at the right)* I don't care.

HYLAND: *(Following her)* It's only about twenty after eight. *(He glances at his watch.)*

CLARA: We can get the second show at Broad and Columbia Avenue.

MRS. FISHER: (*Following them out*) Frank, I wish you'd talk to Amy some time, and tell her what you told me; she won't believe *me*.

HYLAND: I don't suppose she'd believe me, either, Mother.

AUBREY: (*Out at the front-door*) Right on the job!

AMY: Hello!

AUBREY: The pride of old West Philly! (*He laughs a bit, boisterously.*)

AMY: I'll take your hat, Aubrey.

AUBREY: Anything to please the ladies. (*The front-door closes.*) The boy rode off with many thanks, and many a backward bow. (*He laughs again, rather wildly.* MRS. FISHER *tiptoes into the room from the right and stands listening, keenly.*) Do you know, I think I'll have to get hold of an airship somewhere, Amy, to come out here to see you.

AMY: It *is* quite a trip for you, isn't it?

AUBREY: Just one shining hour and a half, if you say it quick; by the little old Brill special. And how is the Mother? (MRS. FISHER'S *face hardens, and a door closes. Then she tiptoes over to the double-doors at the left and listens.* AUBREY'S *voice can be heard fairly distinctly from beyond the doors.*) Say, Amy—wasn't that hold-up in last night's paper somewhere out this way?

AMY: Yes, it was right over here on Erie Avenue. (MR. FISHER *appears in the hall-door and stands, looking with amusement at his wife. He takes an old pipe and tobacco-pouch from the pocket of his knit-jacket and starts to fill the pipe.*)

AUBREY: A doctor's house, wasn't it?

AMY: Yes, Doctor Donnelly's. They got nearly two thousand dollars.

AUBREY: I don't believe that, Amy.

AMY: Why not?

AUBREY: I don't believe there's that much money *in* North Philadelphia. (*He roars with laughter.* MR. FISHER *gives his wife a little dig in the ribs and makes a sound like a startled cat. She starts violently, smothering a little shriek.*)

MRS. FISHER: Oh, you frightened me! (MR. FISHER *continues to the center-table and sets his newspaper down.*)

MR. FISHER: You ought to be pretty nearly frightened to death by this time, oughtn't you? (*He replaces the tobacco-pouch in his pocket.*)

MRS. FISHER: Well, it's no wonder I'd be.

MR. FISHER: You've been jumpin' that way ever since I knew you.

MRS. FISHER: Well, what do you come pussy-footin' in that way for, when you know how nervous I am?

MR. FISHER: I didn't come pussy-footin' in at all.

MRS. FISHER: You did so, or I'd have heard you.

MR. FISHER: You *would* have heard me, if you weren't so busy listenin' to somethin' that's none of your business.

MRS. FISHER: Well, it'll be somethin' of my business if you go spillin' any of that dirty old tobacco on my nice new table-cloth, I tell you that. (*She resumes her listening at the door, and* MR. FISHER *brushes the tobacco from the table-cloth.*)

MR. FISHER: I'm not spillin' any of it. (*There's a burst of laughter from* AUBREY *in the parlor, and* MR. FISHER *looks toward the parlor-door.*) Who's in there—Windy? (MRS. FISHER *nods, yes, and the old man moves down at the right of the center-table, picking up the newspaper and reaching into his vest-pocket for his spectacles.*) What's he doin', laughin' at some more of them West Philadelphia jokes of his? (*He sits down to read, in the chair at the right of the table, and* MRS. FISHER *comes tiptoeing towards the chair at the left of the table.*)

MRS. FISHER: (*In a lowered tone*) He was astin' Amy about that robbery over at Doctor Donnelly's yesterday mornin'; and when she told him the bandits got away with nearly two thousand dollars, he said it couldn't be true, because there wasn't that much money *in* North Philadelphia.

MR. FISHER: (*With mock laughter*) Ha! Ha! Ha!

MRS. FISHER: (*Returning to the parlor-doors to listen*) Shush! (*There's a Ha! Ha! Ha! from the parlor from* AUBREY, *and the old man looks quickly and distrustfully in that direction.* AUBREY *continues to laugh.*)

MR. FISHER: (*Settling himself to read*) I'll bet there wouldn't have to be much money up this way to be more than *he's* got. (*There's a sound of hammering in the cellar.* MRS. FISHER *hurries across to the cellar-door.*)

AUBREY: (*In the parlor*) You know, I discovered to-night, Amy, that I can save a full fifteen minutes on this trip over here, by transferring up Twenty-ninth to the Lehigh Avenue car, instead of going on in and up Nineteenth.

MRS. FISHER: *(Opening the cellar-door and calling down, in a subdued voice)* Joe! Stop that hammering down there, we can't hear our ears up here. *(The old man gives a hard chuckle.* MRS. FISHER *tiptoes back towards the parlor-doors, looking at her husband stonily.)* What ails *you?*

AMY: *(In the parlor)* It *is* hard to get out here, unless you use the Park trolley. I hear some people say that's a great deal quicker. *(*MRS. FISHER *listens keenly again with her ear against the parlor-door.)*

AUBREY: I don't know how they ever found this place.

AMY: I don't know how *you* ever found *West* Philadelphia.

AUBREY: Lot of people think they haven't found it *yet.* *(He bursts into violent laughter.)* Lost somewhere between the Schuylkill River and Darby. *(He laughs some more. The old man looks piercingly over his spectacles at his wife.)*

MR. FISHER: *(Almost shouting)* Come away from there, Josie! *(*MRS. FISHER *is startled almost to death. She places her hand on her bosom and moves away from the door towards the center of the room.)* Don't be listenin' to that damned blatherskite.

MRS. FISHER: *(Trying to be casual)* I wasn't listenin' to him;—I was just seein' what he was sayin'. *(She moves up to the little stand between the hall-door and the mantelpiece and picks up her knitting-bag.* AMY *is very much amused at something* AUBREY *has just said in the parlor.* MRS. FISHER *glances toward the parlor-doors, then comes down to her husband's right, and, with another glance toward the door, speaks very confidentially.)* He was astin' Amy how she ever found this part of town to live in; and she was astin' him how *he* ever found *West* Philadelphia. He sez West Philadelphia ain't *been* found yet,—that it's lost somewhere between the Schuylkill River and Darby. *(She moves over to the arm-chair at the right, in front of the window, and sits down.)*

MR. FISHER: I wish to God *he'd* get lost some night, somewhere between here and the Schuylkill River.

MRS. FISHER: *(Taking the needles and the pink wool out of the knitting-bag)* What'd kill you, too, you know, he always dies laughin' whenever he gets off one of them bum jokes.

MR. FISHER: Somebody's got to laugh.

AUBREY: *(From the parlor)* Ha! Ha! That's the time I

fooled you, Amy! Leave it to me to put it right over the plate. (AMY *has quite a laughing fit in the parlor. Her Mother looks narrowly toward the parlor-doors until* AMY *has finished laughing.*)

MRS. FISHER: He's got Amy laughin' now, too. (*She commences to knit; and there is a slight pause. Then she glances at the clock on the mantelpiece.*) That old clock has stopped again, Neil.

MR. FISHER: (*Without moving*) Needs fixin'.

MRS. FISHER: It's *been* fixed twice,—don't do no good. (*There is a pause, and* MRS. FISHER *sighs.*) I think it's terrible lonesome not to hear the clock—it's too still in a room.—It always sounds to me like soap-bubbles meltin'.

MR. FISHER: H'm—here's a fellow here's been left a quarter of a million dollars, and he won't take it.

MRS. FISHER: (*Sharply*) What's the matter with him?

MR. FISHER: Nothin' at all's the matter with him—he just won't take it.

MRS. FISHER: (*Resuming her knitting*) He mustn't be in his right mind, poor boy. I wisht somebody'd leave *me* a quarter of a million dollars.

MR. FISHER: You wouldn't know what to do with it if they did.

MRS. FISHER: Well, I know *one* thing I'd do with it; and that'd be to have somethin' done to that old heater of ours downstairs, and not be freezin' to death all *next* winter, the way I was last. (AUBREY *laughs in the parlor.* MRS. FISHER *glances toward the parlor-doors; then shifts her knitting.*) Every sweater I start I swear it'll be the last—and then I start right in on another. (*She gives a faint little laugh and looks at her husband; but he's reading; so she subsides and continues to knit. Suddenly she stops and rests her knitting in her lap, and thinks; then turns to* MR. FISHER.) Well now, what becomes of money like that, Neil, that people won't take?

MR. FISHER: (*Squinting at her over his glasses*) What'd you say?

MRS. FISHER: I say, what becomes of money that people won't take that way?

MR. FISHER: (*Resuming his paper*) Why, nothing at all becomes of it;—they just come and get it. (*She looks at him steadily.*)

MRS. FISHER: Who does?

MR. FISHER: The people that won't take it. *(MRS. FISHER is puzzled for a second.)*

MRS. FISHER: *(Resuming her knitting)* Well, I'll bet if they left it to *me* they wouldn't have to come and take it.

MR. FISHER: *(Looking at her again with a shade of irritation)* Who wouldn't have to come and take it?

MRS. FISHER: *(Losing her temper)* Why, the people that won't take it!

MR. FISHER: What are you talkin' about, Josie, do you know?

MRS. FISHER: Yes, I do know very well what I'm talkin' about!—but I don't think *you* do.

MR. FISHER: Let me read this paper, will you?

MRS. FISHER: *(Knitting rapidly)* Go ahead and read it!— I'm sure I don't want to talk to you. It was you that started talkin' to me—readin' about that young man that took the money. *(JOE comes up from the cellar, carrying some kind of a radio-arrangement on a flat base-board and a screwdriver.)* Joe, I'm goin' to have that light took out of that cellar, if you don't stop spendin' all your time down there.

JOE: *(Holding his work under the table-lamp to look at it closely)* You don't want me hammerin' up here, do you?

MRS. FISHER: I don't want you hammerin' anywhere. I want you to go out at night and get some air, and not be cooped up in that dusty old cellar. *(There's a violent burst of laughter from AUBREY in the parlor. JOE glances toward the parlor-doors, then turns, with something of distress in his expression, to his Mother.)*

JOE: Who's *in* there—the Pennsylvania Railroad?

MRS. FISHER: Yes, and he's got about as much sense as yourself.

JOE: *(Moving around to the chair at the left of the center-table and sitting down)* You won't say that when you're sittin' here listenin' to the Grand Opera. *(He starts to tighten the small screws in the base-board.)*

MRS. FISHER: I won't be listenin' to it, don't fret—I got somethin' else to do besides listenin' to a lot of dagoes singin'.

MR. FISHER: *(Looking over at JOE's radio-arrangement)* What is it?

MRS. FISHER: He sez when he gets that radio-thing finished, I can sit here and listen to the Grand Opera.

MR. FISHER: *(Resuming his paper)* What's that, them singin' people?

MRS. FISHER: Yes—them that goes away up high, you know—that Clara has on her Victrola. *(The parlor-door opens, and* AMY *comes out, walking on air.)*

AMY: Oh, it's all right if you let it run for a minute. *(She crosses to the right to the kitchen-door, glancing at herself in the mantelpiece-mirror as she pauses.)*

MRS. FISHER: What's the matter?

AMY: Nothing; Aubrey wants a drink of water. *(She goes out at the right.)*

MRS. FISHER: *(With a significant sound)* Oh.

AUBREY: *(Coming out of the parlor)* Stay right where you are, folks, right where you are. *(He moves to the mirror over the mantelpiece.)* Just a little social attention,—going right out again on the next train. *(He surveys himself critically in the mirror, touching his tie and toupé gingerly.* MRS. FISHER *gives him a smouldering look, and* JOE *looks at his Father.* AUBREY *turns from the mirror, and indicates his reflection with a wide gesture.)* There you are, Mother! Any woman's fancy, what do you say? Even to the little old carnation. *(He gives the table a double tap with his knuckles, then laughs, and moves up towards the kitchen-door, and calls out to* AMY.*)* Come on, Amy, step on the United Gas out there; customer in here waiting for the old aqua pura. *(Moving down to* MR. FISHER'S *right.)* Man's got to have something to drink—how about it, Pop? *(He gives* MR. FISHER *a slap on the right shoulder.)* You'll stay with me on that, won't you? *(He laughs and moves up to the mirror again. Old man* FISHER *is very much annoyed.)* Yes, sir. *(Coming forward again at the right.)* I want to tell those of you who have ventured out this evening, that this is a very pretty little picture of domestic felicity. *(He laughs a little and looks from one to the other, patronizingly; but nobody pays the slightest attention to him.)* Father reading,—Mother knitting; *(*MRS. FISHER *withers him with a quick look.)* But then, Mama is *always* knitting. *(She knits rapidly and* AUBREY *laughs, and moves up and across back of the table.)* And little old Tommy Edison over here, working eighteen hours a day to make the rich man richer and the poor man poorer. *(He gives* JOE *a tap on the back, then moves back again towards* MR. FISHER.*)* What about it, Popcorn? *(Slaps him on the back.)* Shake it up! Right or raving?

MR. FISHER: *(Starting to his feet violently)* God damn it, let me alone! And keep your hands to yourself. *(He crosses below the center-table and up to the hall-door.)* I never saw such a damn pest in my life! *(He goes up the stairs bristling with rage, and muttering to himself.* AUBREY *is vastly amused. He leans on the back of* MR. FISHER'S *chair and roars with laughter.)*

AUBREY: Sign on the dotted line! And little old Popsy-Wopsy getting sore and going to leave us flat. *(He laughs again considerably; then turns to* MRS. FISHER.*)* Nevertheless, and notwithstanding, Mrs. Fisher, I'd like to mention that the kid from West Philadelphia is giving the growing boy the said and done. *(He indicates* JOE *with a waving gesture.* AMY *comes in from the right with a glass of water. He turns and acknowledges her with even a wider gesture.)* And there she is herself, and not a moving picture. *(AMY extends the glass of water, laughing, and with a touch of self-consciousness.)* Blushing as she gave it, looking down—at her feet so bare, and her tattered gown. *(AMY giggles, and her Mother looks sharply at* AMY'S *shoes.* AUBREY *takes the glass of water and turns to* MRS. FISHER.*)* How's that, Mother Fisher? Can't beat that little old Willie Shakespeare, can you? No, sir,—I'd like to tell the brothers that that little old Shakespeare party shook a wicked spear. *(He laughs at his own comedy, and* AMY *is immeasurably delighted.)* Well, here's laughter, ladies! and, *(Turning to* JOE*)* Mr. Marconi,— my best regards to you. *(He drinks.)*

AMY: I'm afraid it's not very cold. *(He just raises his hand, signifying that it's perfectly satisfactory.)*

MRS. FISHER: Why didn't you let it run?

AMY: I did, but it doesn't seem to get any colder.

AUBREY: *(Handing the glass back to* AMY*)* Very nice indeed. And a sweeter draught, from a fairer hand was never quaffed.

AMY: *(Flipping her hand at him)* Oh, you! *(She goes out at the right again with the empty glass.)*

AUBREY: *(Laughing a bit)* Thank you very much. *(He turns and moves across above the table towards* JOE, *drawing a gaily-bordered handkerchief from his breast-pocket and touching it to his lips.)* Yes, sir, Mr. Joseph, I want to tell you you're wasting time; for when you're all through, they'll offer you twenty cents for it, and sell it for twenty million. *(He punctuates this last remark with a series of patronizing taps on* JOE's *back)*—Take it or leave it—sign on the dotted line. *(He taps his knuckles on the table, and moves back again to* MRS. FISHER's *left.)* Yes, sir,—that's exactly what they did to little old yours truly here. Twenty Lincoln Anacondas, for a formula that would have solved the greatest problem before the Industrial Chemical world to-day. *(*AMY *comes in from the right, and, looking at* AUBREY *wonderingly, moves across towards the left.* AUBREY *moves forward and across in front of the table towards* JOE.) A formula to prevent the rusting of iron and steel. *(*JOE *gets up and moves up and around above the table towards the kitchen-door at the right.)* A solution of Vanadium and Manganese, to be added to the metal in its molten state; *(*JOE *stops and looks back at him)* instead of applied externally as they have been doing.

JOE: What did you say, Aubrey?

AUBREY: I said, a simple combination of chemical elements, to be added to the metal in its *molten* state, instead of applied externally as they have been doing.

JOE *and* AUBREY, *speaking together.*

JOE: *(Speaking to his Mother)* Mom, do you know anything about that little screw-driver with the black handle?

AUBREY: But,—simply because it was discovered by a working-man—that they saw they couldn't buy—

MRS. FISHER: Do you mean the one you fixed the sewing machine with?

JOE *and* AUBREY, *speaking together.*

JOE: Yes, that little short one with the black handle.

AUBREY: They gave it the swinging door. *(*AMY *moves over to the parlor-doors.)*

MRS. FISHER *and* AUBREY, *speaking together.*

MRS. FISHER: I think I saw it on that shelf out there, over the sink. And now, don't go upsettin' everything out there.

AUBREY: They'd rather go on paying a million dollars a year *(*JOE *goes out, and* AUBREY *follows him to the kitchen-door)*—to paint their steel and iron structures throughout the country, than pay *me*.

MRS. FISHER: Do you see it, Joe?

AUBREY: *(Coming down to* MRS. FISHER's *left)* And do you know *why*, Mrs. Fisher?

JOE: *(Answering his Mother from the kitchen)* No!

AUBREY: Then, I'll tell you. Because I work for my living. That's the said and done on the whole business. *(*MRS.

FISHER *starts to put her things into the knitting-bag, preparatory to getting up.)* Keep them poor and get them married; and then, *(He looks away off)* as my darling old Mother used to say, "You've got them on their beams and hinges."

MRS. FISHER: *(Getting up)* I don't see that anybody's tryin' to make anybody get married if they don't want to. *(She passes up to the kitchen-door, putting her knitting-bag on the buffet as she goes.)*

AUBREY: *(Following her up)* But they *do* want to, Mrs. Fisher,—but the capitalist wants to stop them.

MRS. FISHER: *(Turning at the kitchen-door and speaking directly to him)* Well, I guess it'd be just as well to stop *some* of 'em. *(She goes out.)*

AUBREY: *(Calling after her through the kitchen-door)* Ah, don't go back on little old William Jennings Bryan, Mother Fisher. Life, liberty and the pursuit of happiness, you know. *(He turns and comes forward at the right again, laughing a little.)* Sign on the dotted line.

AMY: *(Trying to conceal her temper)* Come on in here, Aubrey.

AUBREY: *(Starting towards her)* Yes, sir, Amy, I want to tell you it's the poor man that gets it every time. I put a question up to Secretary Mellon, in a letter six weeks ago— that absolutely stumped him, because I haven't had a line from him since. (AMY *is smiling into his eyes. He passes in front of her and goes into the parlor. The curtain commences to descend slowly.* AMY *looks darkly toward the kitchen-door, and stamps her foot with temper; then follows* AUBREY *into the parlor.)* I simply asked him to what extent his proposed program of Income Tax Revision would affect the great American Railroad Employé. *(The curtain is down.)*

THREE HOURS PASS

THE CURTAIN RISES AGAIN

MRS. FISHER *is sitting at the right of the table asleep, her knitting lying in her lap; and* JOE, *sitting at the left of the table, is endeavoring to pass the tip of a wire through a small eyelet on the base-board.* AMY *starts to play the piano in the parlor; and, after the usual introduction,* AUBREY *begins to sing, "Rocked In the Cradle Of The Deep," in a heavy bass voice.*

AUBREY: *(Singing)*

"Rocked in the cradle of the deep,
    I lay me down,—in peace to sleep—
Secure I rest upon the wave,
    For Thou alone—

(MRS. FISHER starts slightly and wakens. JOE *glances at her.* AUBREY *continues.)*

has the power to save."

MRS. FISHER: Where'd you put it? What? Did you say something? *(AUBREY continues to sing.)*

JOE: Not a thing, Mom.

MRS. FISHER: *(Brushing back her hair)* I must have been dozin'.

JOE: You've been dead.

MRS. FISHER: What?

JOE: Since half-past nine. *(MRS. FISHER becomes conscious of* AUBREY *singing.)*

MRS. FISHER: What time is it now, Joe? *(The singing becomes louder, and* MRS. FISHER *rises, with her eyes fastened on the parlor-door.)* Is that him singin' in there?

JOE: *(Reaching into his belt-pocket for an Ingersoll watch)* The old Scientific American himself. A quarter of twelve.

MRS. FISHER: My God! what's he startin' to sing at this hour for! *(She steps to the buffet at the right and puts her knitting-bag into one of the drawers.)*

JOE: Talent should never be suppressed at any time, Mother.

MRS. FISHER: It's a wonder Amy wouldn't have sense enough to stop him. *(She slams the buffet-drawer shut, and starts across towards the parlor-doors.)* I never saw a man yet that didn't think he could sing. Put that thing away, now, Joe, you've been at it long enough. And see that that back is locked. I don't think Amy has any idea what time it is or she'd shut him up.

JOE: Let the young man express himself. *(He gets up and*

crosses below the table towards the right, and up to the kitchen-door.)

MRS. FISHER: Oh, I wouldn't care if he bawled his head off, as far as I'm concerned—I'd be glad if he did; but I don't want him to waken your Father. *(She steps up to the hall-door and listens, at the foot of the stairs.)* And that's what he'll be doin' the first thing you know, and then the fat'll be in the fire for sure. *(AUBREY reaches a high note, and JOE and his Mother stand looking at each other. Then JOE bursts out laughing.)* Ain't that terrible, Joe? Do you think I ought to tell Amy what time it is? .

JOE: No, give the boy a chance. *(AUBREY finishes on a high note and holds it.)* Hurray! *(AUBREY can be heard applauding himself. JOE applauds, also.)*

MRS. FISHER: *(Frantically, and going towards JOE)* Shush, Joe!

JOE: *(Going out through the door at the right)* Sign on the dotted line!

MRS. FISHER: Don't encourage him, for God's sake, Joe, he's bad enough as it is.

MR. FISHER: *(Shouting from the head of the stairs)* Josie!

MRS. FISHER: *(Rushing back towards the hall-door on her tiptoes)* Yes?

MR. FISHER: What the devil's goin' on down there! Do you know what time it is?

MRS. FISHER: *(Trying to pacify him)* Why, Joe was just cuttin' up here a minute ago.

MR. FISHER: What's Amy playin' the piano for, at this time of the night?

MRS. FISHER: *(Trying not to be heard in the parlor)* Why, her and Joe was just foolin'—

MR. FISHER: Damn funny kind of foolin', at this time of night! The neighbors'll be wonderin' what kind of a house we're keepin' here!

MRS. FISHER: Well, they've stopped it now, Neil.

MR. FISHER: Well, tell them to see that it's *kept* stopped! And get them lights out down there and go to bed! It's nearly twelve o'clock.

(MRS. FISHER turns and looks at the parlor-doors. Then there's a burst of wild laughter from AUBREY. This decides MRS. FISHER. She steps resolutely towards the doors with the ostensible purpose of opening them, but, before she can

reach the knob, the door is yanked open from the inside, and AMY *steps out, looking resentfully at her.)*

AMY: What's the matter?

MRS. FISHER: *(A trifle disconcerted)* Why,—a—I was just comin' to tell you to be sure and put them lights out; I'm just goin' up—it's nearly twelve o'clock.

AUBREY: *(Thrusting his head and shoulders out through the door)* I am also just about to take my reluctant leave, Mrs. Fisher.

MRS. FISHER: *(Trying to be polite)* Well, I don't want to hurry you, but—

AUBREY: In fact, the recent outburst was in the nature of a farewell concert. *(He breaks into a wild laugh and draws back into the parlor; and* MRS. FISHER, *with a series of frantic gestures, intended to convey to* AMY *the imminence of her Father at the head of the stairs, steps back out of the range of the parlor-door.* AMY *makes an impatient movement of her body, and stamps her foot, then flounces into the parlor and slams the door.)* The little old song at twilight, you know, Mother Fisher—to soothe the savage breast. *(He gives vent to another gale of laughter; and* MRS. FISHER *stands petrified, expecting to hear her husband again.)*

MRS. FISHER: *(As* AUBREY'S *laugh subsides)* The damn fool! *(She crosses to the right of the kitchen-door and calls out to* JOE*)*. Joe!

JOE: Yeh?

MRS. FISHER: You'd better bring Gypsy Queen in and put her in the laundry there; she was shiverin' when I opened the door this mornin'. I think it's too cold for her on that back porch yet a while. *(She moves a little back towards the center of the room.)*

JOE: *(Out at the right)* Come on in here, Gypsy! Come on. *(He whistles.)*

MRS. FISHER: *(Turning around to her left and looking back towards the kitchen-door)* Ain't she there?

JOE: I don't see her.

MRS. FISHER: *(Calling in a high voice)* Where *are* you, Gypsy?

JOE: Here she is. Come on in here, Gypsy! Come on! That's the old gypsy kid. *(The door out at the right closes.)*

MRS. FISHER: *(Going a step nearer the kitchen-door)* Go into that laundry there, Gypsy.

JOE: Come back here, Gypsy!

MRS. FISHER: Make her go in there, Joe.

JOE: *(Stamping his foot)* Gypsy!

MRS. FISHER: *(Stamping her foot at the kitchen-door)* Go back there, Gypsy! You bad girl! And go into that laundry this minute—

JOE: There she goes.

MRS. FISHER: And don't let me hear a sound out of you when you get in there either, or I'll come right straight out and give you what I gave you last Sunday afternoon. *(A door closes.)* You better put the ketch on that door, Joe, or she'll be pushin' it open again; she wants to lay out here on this rug. *(Going nearer to the door again, and calling.)* Now, you remember what I told you, Gypsy; and don't let me have to speak to you again. *(Turning and moving across the room to the left.)* Your Father has her spoiled. *(A door out in the hallway at the left opens, and AMY can be heard laughing. MRS. FISHER stops dead in the middle of the room and listens.)*

AUBREY: *(Calling from the hallway)* Good-night, Mrs. Fisher. *(MRS. FISHER turns and darts back into the cellar-alcove at the right.)*

AMY: *(In the hallway)* I guess she's gone up. Aubrey.

AUBREY: *(Coming in at the hall-door, poising on one toe, hat and cane in hand, and looking about the room)* Montreal, Mother. *(MRS. FISHER flattens herself against the wall at the head of the cellar-stairs, and listens with a stony expression.)*

AMY: I don't think she's in there, Aubrey.

AUBREY: And silence was her answer. *(He laughs wildly, turns, and starts out into the hallway again.)* Right you are, Amy—*(Glancing up the stairs).* On the right side she is sleeping. *(He goes laughing out into the hallway.)*

JOE: *(Coming in from the kitchen, mimicking AUBREY'S laugh.)* Ha! Ha! Ha! *(He passes his Mother without seeing her.)*

MRS. FISHER: *(Coming out of the alcove)* Shush! Don't let him hear you, Joe. *(JOE turns and looks at his Mother, then continues across to the left to the hall-door.)*

JOE: Is he goin'?

MRS. FISHER: *(Following JOE to the center of the room)* At last! *(JOE glances out into the hallway.)* Don't let him see you, now, Joe, or we'll have him here for another hour.

JOE: *(Starting up the stairs)* I'm goin' to bed.

MRS. FISHER: Joe!

JOE: *(Leaning back and looking)* What?

MRS. FISHER: Come here! (AMY *can be heard giggling in the hallway.* JOE *comes back to his Mother.*)

JOE: What?

MRS. FISHER: *(Very confidentially)* What was that he was sayin' here to-night, about discoverin' something to keep rust out of iron and steel?

JOE: *(Very much amused)* Wasn't that a scream.

MRS. FISHER: That's what *you're* always talkin' about, ain't it?

JOE: Yes, I was talkin' to *him* about it one night here, while he was waitin' for Amy to come down; and he's forgot where he heard it.

MRS. FISHER: Can you imagine!

JOE: I was wonderin' if you were gettin' that to-night.

MRS. FISHER: No, it never struck me till afterwards.

JOE: *(With a shade of seriousness)* Did you get what he said to-night, Mom?

MRS. FISHER: Now, you know I never pay any attention to what he sez.

JOE: *(Turning away laughing)* He's a bird. *(He goes to the hall-door and looks out into the hall.)*

MRS. FISHER: Don't let him see you, now, Joe.

JOE: The vestibule-door's shut. *(He goes up the stairs. His Mother follows him to the hall-door.)*

MRS. FISHER: You'd better close that window at the head of your bed, Joe, and not have it blowin' in on you all night. *(She glances out into the hallway, then steps to the parlor-door, opens it quietly and glances in, and starts across towards the right. The front-door closes out in the hallway, then the vestibule-door.* MRS. FISHER *glances over her right shoulder towards the hallway, then continues to the kitchen-door. Just as she reaches the kitchen-door and glances out, the parlor-door is flung open and* AMY *comes in. She takes a couple of steps towards the middle of the room, then stands still, looking bitterly at her Mother.* MRS. FISHER *speaks without looking at her.)* Did you put that light out in there?

AMY: *(In a quiet rage)* That was a *nice* trick you people did to-night! *(Her Mother turns and looks at her.)*

MRS. FISHER: What?

AMY: Everybody walking out of the room, while Aubrey was talking.

MRS. FISHER: What did you *want* us to do, sit here all night listenin' to him?

AMY: You wouldn't have *had* to sit here all night listening to him; he was only in here five minutes.

MRS. FISHER: (*Moving back towards the center-table*) That's no thanks to him; he'd have been here till mornin' if somebody didn't do somethin'.

AMY: (*Swinging to the mirror over the mantelpiece*) I was never so mortified in my life.

MRS. FISHER: (*Standing above the center-table*) Oh, don't waste your sympathy, Amy! He don't have to have anybody listen to him; he'd talk to the wall if there wasn't anybody else around.

AMY: (*Coming forward at her Mother's right*) What did Pop get into such a temper about?

MRS. FISHER: (*Getting mad*) Because he hit him on the back!

AMY: That was a lot to get mad about.

MRS. FISHER: Well, he's always hittin' *somebody!*—on the back—or the shoulder—or someplace else. And your Father *said* the next time he did it he'd walk out of the room!—He can't say two words *together* without *hittin'* somebody someplace.

AMY: Well, I'll bet you won't get a chance to insult him *again*, Mom, I'll tell you that. (*She flounces down to the arm-chair at the extreme right.*)

MRS. FISHER: Then, let him stop his silly talk! and he won't get insulted. Sign on the dotted line! every two minutes. And talkin' about Shakespeare. (*She crosses to the parlor-door.*) What kind of goin' on is that for a sensible man. (*She slams the parlor-door shut, and moves up to the hall-door to listen for* MR. FISHER.) It's no wonder our Joe sez he's a nut!

AMY: Oh, everybody's a nut with the people around here!

MRS. FISHER: (*Coming back towards the center-table*) Oh, it ain't only the people around here that sez it; everybody that knows him sez it. (AMY *makes a sound of derisive amusement.*) You needn't laugh, for it's true.

AMY: (*Turning sharply to her Mother*) Who do *you* know that knows him?

MRS. FISHER: I know Frank Hyland. (AMY *is puzzled for the fraction of a second.*)

AMY: You mean Clara's *husband?*

MRS. FISHER: Yes, I mean Clara's *husband.*

AMY: Oh, don't make up a lie, Mom! Frank Hyland never saw Aubrey Piper.

MRS. FISHER: Oh, didn't he!

AMY: No, he didn't.

MRS. FISHER: Well now, my lady, you're so smart, he knows him better than you do.

AMY: I don't believe it.

MRS. FISHER: Doesn't matter whether you believe it or not, he knows him just the same; he's been lookin' at him for years, down at that restaurant at Fifteenth and Arch, where he eats his lunch. And he sezs he's as crazy as a *bass-singer.*

AMY: (*Whirling on her Mother*) I suppose that's what Clara was here to tell you, was it?

MRS. FISHER: What does it matter *who* was here to tell it, Amy, if it's true.

AMY: (*Stepping up close to her Mother*) Well now, listen, Mom, I want to tell you something right now! You tell our Clara for me the next time you see her, to mind her own damn business—(*She taps the back of the chair twice with her knuckles, emphasizing the words "damn" and "business"*) as far as Aubrey Piper is concerned.

MRS. FISHER: (*Before* AMY *has finished speaking*) Oh, don't fly into a temper, if anybody speaks to you! (*She turns and crosses hurriedly in the hall-door to listen.*)

AMY: (*Stamping her foot*) Well then, don't speak to me about things that *put* me in a temper!

MRS. FISHER: You're not frightenin' anybody around here. (*She looks up the stairs and listens.*)

AMY: No, and nobody around here is frightening *me,* either—Our Clara took who *she* wanted. And I guess you took who *you* wanted. (MRS. FISHER *moves steadily forward at the left to a point in front of the lower left-hand corner of the center-table.*) And if I want Aubrey Piper I'll take *him!*

MRS. FISHER: (*Taking* AMY'S *tone*) Well, take him then!—and the sooner the better; for it's a pity to spoil two houses with you. (*She leans forward a little on the table and speaks with a steady precision.*) Only remember this, Amy,—if you *do* take him,—be sure that you keep him—and that—he—

keeps—you. (AMY *looks at her keenly.*) And don't be comin' around here cryin' for your *Pop* to keep you.

AMY: (*With a sound of amused derision, and flouncing down to the arm-chair at the right*) Don't make me laugh.

MRS. FISHER: You can laugh all you like; there's a lot of that kind of laughin' goin' on these days. But they change their tune as soon as the rent begins to come due; and it's the Mothers and Fathers that has to listen to the changed tune. But nothin'll do but they'll get married.

AMY: (*Pinning her Mother with a quick look*) *You* got married, didn't you?

MRS. FISHER: Yes I did.

AMY: (*Turning away again*) Well—

MRS. FISHER: To a man that was able to keep me.

AMY: (*Back to her Mother again*) And how do *you* know that Aubrey Piper wouldn't be able to keep *his* wife?

MRS. FISHER: Because I know what he *earns*;—(*She strikes the table with her fist*) and it isn't enough.

AMY: (*Stamping her foot*) Oh, don't go making up things, Mom!—You don't know anything *about* what he earns.

MRS. FISHER: (*With measured emphasis*) He earns a hundred and fifty dollars a month and not a penny more, for Frank Hyland sez so.

AMY: What does Frank Hyland know about it?

MRS. FISHER: He knows what he does!—His business takes him in there all the time.

AMY: And what does he say he does?

MRS. FISHER: Why, he sez he's a clerk, of course—(*AMY makes a sound of amusement*) like a hundred others down there.

AMY: That shows how much he knows about it.

MRS. FISHER: But I suppose he told you he *owns* the Pennsylvania Railroad.

AMY: Well, I'd take his word before I'd take Frank Hyland's. (*Her Mother looks at her narrowly, and there is a pause.*)

MRS. FISHER: (*Significantly*) *Why* would you take *his* word before you would take Frank Hyland's?

AMY: Well, why shouldn't I?

MRS. FISHER: (*Losing her temper*) Because he's a fool!—of a blatherskite.

AMY: That's only your opinion, Mom.

MRS. FISHER: It's the opinion of everybody that ever

listened to him. But you'd believe *him* before you'd believe the word of a steady sensible man.

AMY: I don't know anything about Frank Hyland.

MRS. FISHER: You know he's been your brother-in-law for five years; and what do you know about this other clown?

AMY: Well, what do you *want* to know about him?

MRS. FISHER: I don't want to know *anything* about him; I *know* all I want to know about him. But before I'd get the name of havin' a fellow comin' to see *me* steady, there's a few things I'd want to know about him, I'll tell you that. (*She turns away and takes a step towards the back of the room.*)

AMY: I've told you where he lives and where he works,— what else do you want to know about him?

MRS. FISHER: There's no use talkin' to you, Amy.

AMY: No, and there's no use talking to you, either.

MRS. FISHER: (*Turning to her sharply*) This fellow's got you so crazy mad about him, that I believe you'd take him if you knew he had a wife and family somewhere, and not two cents in his pocket. (*She moves towards the mantelpiece at the back, removing her spectacles.*)

AMY: Well, I guess we'd get along some way even if I did.

MRS. FISHER: All right.

AMY: Everybody else does.

MRS. FISHER: (*Turning upon* AMY *in a rage, and wiping the glasses in her apron*) That's the kind of talk that leaves them livin' in garrets! And back at their jobs ten days after the weddin'.

AMY: Oh, you talk as though everybody that was married was starving to death.

MRS. FISHER: (*Lifting the glasses towards* AMY *with a quiet, knowing gesture*) There are ways of starvin' to death, Amy, besides not gettin' enough to eat. (*With a change to great shrewdness of tone and manner.*) And the funny part of it is, Amy,—like a lot of others, you're very shrewd about money while you're at home, as far as what you give your Mother and Father is concerned; but the minute some clown, with a flower in his coat and patent-leather shoes, winks at you, you seem to forget there's such a thing in the world as a ton of coal. (*Crossing suddenly above the table towards amy in quite a surge of temper.*) And then it's just as Clara sez, it's your *people* that has to come to the rescue.

AMY: *(Furiously)* I wish I'd been here while she was talking! I bet I'd a told her a thing or two!

MRS. FISHER: Oh, you needn't try to turn it onto Clara;—she wasn't talkin' at all.

AMY: *(Stamping her foot)* She *must* have been talking!

MRS. FISHER: She simply asked me where you were!—and I told her you were gettin' dressed—that this fellow was comin' here to-night: so then she told me that Frank Hyland knew him, and where he worked, and what he got and all about him. *(She turns away and moves to the left. There is a slight pause.)*

AMY: *(Half crying)* I'd just take him for *spite* now. (MRS. FISHER *comes to a stop, and turns slowly—and looks at her.)*

MRS. FISHER: Well, let me tell *you,* Amy—the day a girl that's used to spendin' money the way you do, takes a thirty-five-dollar-a-week man,—the only one she's spitin' is herself. *(She moves slowly to the mantelpiece at the back and puts her glasses down definitely, then turns and starts to remove her apron.)* There'll be no more permanent waves after that—*(She rolls her apron up)* you can make up your mind to that. *(She flings the rolled apron onto the sofa at the right of the mantelpiece, and commences to unfasten the old-fashioned brooch in the front of her house-dress.)* Nor fifty-five dollar beaded dresses, neither.

AMY: *(In a crying temper)* Well, I'd never bother anybody around here if I needed anything, I'll tell you that.

MRS. FISHER: Maybe you won't.

AMY: I won't,—you needn't worry.

MRS. FISHER: *(With a bitter levelness)* Time'll *tell* that, Lady Jane; I've heard the likes of you before. *(She detaches the brooch and goes to the hall-door, glances out into the hallway, then turns and looks back at* AMY.*)* Put out that light and go to bed, it's twelve o'clock. *(She goes up the stairs.* AMY *stands for a second, fuming, over at the right; then she swings suddenly to the middle of the room and stops, with her hands on her hips, irresolute. Then she comes forward and stands above the table, thinking. As she clasps her hands together she becomes conscious of the ring in her hand. She tiptoes to the hall-door, stands listening for a second, then looks up. Then she hurries back to the center-table, looks at the ring, slides it onto the third finger of her left-hand and holds it so that the diamond will catch the light from the chandelier. But, the reflection is evidently unsatis-*

factory; so, with a furtive glance toward the hall-door, she shifts her position to a point nearer the table-lamp and holds her hand so that the ring will reflect that light. The curtain commences to descend slowly; and she stands, holding her hand at arm's length, lost in the melting wonder of her engagement ring.)

(The Curtain Falls)

ACT TWO

SCENE: Same as preceding Act, six months later, about five-thirty on a Monday afternoon. MRS. FISHER is sitting in the arm-chair below the buffet, over at the right, listening in on the radio. Suddenly the front-door closes with a bang, and she starts, and looks in the direction of the hall-door. AUBREY bounces into the room, very much done up, with the traditional carnation, as usual, and comes forward, putting his hat down on the table.

AUBREY: Hello, Mother—Amy here? *(He steps to the mirror at the back and gives himself a critical touch here and there.)*

MRS. FISHER: *(Commencing to remove the listeners)* Our Amy?

AUBREY: Yes, have you seen anything of her?

MRS. FISHER: *(Rising)* No, I haven't seen anything of her. *(She places the listeners on the buffet, and signs off.)*

AUBREY: *(Turning from the glass)* Wonder where she is?

MRS. FISHER: Isn't she home?

AUBREY: No, I just came by there.

MRS. FISHER: *(Picking up her knitting-bag from the buffet)* She hasn't been here today.

AUBREY: She was saying this morning she thought she'd go out looking for a house today; I suppose she hasn't got back yet. *(He gives the chair at the left of the center-table a double tap with his cane as he crosses down to the window at the left.)* I wanted to take her out to the Automobile Show to-night; I got the loan of Harry Albright's car.

MRS. FISHER: *(Moving to the chair at the right of the center-table)* Did you say she was out lookin' for a house?

AUBREY: *(Moving back, towards her)* Yes, we've got to get out of that place we're in. The LePage printing people have bought the whole block: they're going to put up a new building there.

MRS. FISHER: *(Standing with her hand on the back of the chair)* How soon do you have to get out?

AUBREY: Soon as we can find a place, I suppose. I understand they want to begin tearing down there about the first of the year.

MRS. FISHER: I'm afraid you won't find it so easy to get a place as reasonable as that again in a hurry. *(She sits down.)*

AUBREY: I don't *want* a place as reasonable as that, if I can get something better. *(He plants himself at the left of the table and looks away off, with a dreamy narrowing of his eyes, and balancing himself on his toes.)* I want a home—something with a bit of ground around it—where I can do a bit of tennis in the evening—*(He makes a couple of leisurely passes at an imaginary tennis-ball)* if I feel like it.

MRS. FISHER: *(Beginning to knit on a green sweater)* Well, if you do you'll pay for it.

AUBREY: That is exactly what I expect to do, Mother Fisher, not giving you a short answer,—that is exactly what I expect to do. *(He gives the table a double tap with the cane.)* But, I want what I'm paying for, I'll tell you that. No more of the old first-of-the-month business for this bambino. He's all washed up, and signed on the dotted line. *(He moves up to the mirror at the back.)*

MRS. FISHER: They're not puttin' *up* any more houses, from what I can hear.

AUBREY: Be yourself, now, Mother Fisher, be yourself.

MRS. FISHER: Well, where *are* they?

AUBREY: You ought to go out along the Boulevard some Sunday,—see what they're doing out there.

MRS. FISHER: Well, there's no danger of you goin' out along the Boulevard, except for a walk.

AUBREY: *(Moving to the hall-door and glancing out into the hallway)* Lot of people out that way, Mother.

MRS. FISHER: Well, if there is they're payin' more than you're able to pay.

AUBREY: Man's got to live somewhere, Mother. *(He swings forward to the window down at the left, and stands whistling to the canary.)*

MRS. FISHER: Well, if he's wise, he'll live where he's able to pay for it;—unless he wants to be breakin' up half a dozen times a year—like a lot of them are doin'. Makin' a big show.

Buyin' ten thousand dollar houses, and puttin' fifty dollars down on them. *(He turns to her.)* Besides, you haven't got any furniture for a house, even if you got one—unless you want to be sittin' on the floor.

AUBREY: The matter of furniture nowadays, Little Mother, is a very inconsequential item, from what I can gather.

MRS. FISHER: You ought to price it sometime when you're in the city, and see how unconsequent it is.

AUBREY: *(Settling himself for a golf shot, using his cane for a club)* I've investigated the matter very thoroughly, Mrs. Fisher, and I find that there are at least fifteen first-class establishments right here in this city that will furnish a man's house from garret to garage, and give him the rest of his life to pay for it. *(He hits the imaginary golf-ball, and pretends to follow it straight out with his eyes.)*

MRS. FISHER: They'd need to give some of them the rest of their lives, at the rate they're goin' now.

AUBREY: Give the growing boy a chance, Mrs. Fisher, give the growing boy a chance. You know what Mr. L. D. Brophy of the American Can Company said in the September number of the American Magazine, don't you?

MRS. FISHER: No, I don't.

AUBREY: Well, I'll tell you. (MRS. FISHER *shifts her knitting, giving him a wearied glance.*) He said, "I would say, to that innumerable host of young men, standing on the threshold of life, uncertain, and, mayhap, dismayed—as they contemplate the stress of modern industrial competition, 'Rome was not built in a day'." Those were his very words, I wouldn't kid you, and I think the old boy's got it right, if you ask me. *(He moves up to the hall-door again and glances out.)*

MRS. FISHER: What are *you* goin' out to the Automobile Show for?

AUBREY: *(Turning and coming forward again)* Repeat the question, Mrs. Fisher, if you please.

MRS. FISHER: I say, what are you goin' out to the *Automobile* Show for?

AUBREY: *(Coming to a point above the center-table)* Ha! Married five months ago today, Mother; got to celebrate the happy event. Besides, one never knows what a day will bring, in the way of an opportunity to satisfy a long-felt want. And since she knocks but once—*(He taps his cane on*

the table, causing MRS. FISHER *to start slightly)* at each
man's door, the kid here doesn't want to miss his chance by
any uncertainty as to just what choo-choo he prefers. (MRS.
FISHER *turns with an annoyed expression, to find him pointing at her with his forefinger and thumb. He laughs at her
annoyance.)* Well, got to run along now, Mother, and see if
Amy's back at the house yet. *(He picks up his hat from the
table and starts for the hall-door.)*

MRS. FISHER: What'll I tell her if she comes here after
you're gone?

AUBREY: *(Stopping at the door)* Why, tell her I've got the
loan of Harry Albright's car, and I want her to see that new
Jordan Six that I was telling her about, out at the Show. And
that I'll be at Childs' at Fifteenth and Chestnut until eight
o'clock. *(He looks at his Ingersoll.)*

MRS. FISHER: Fifteenth and Chestnut?

AUBREY: That's the said and done, Mother. *(He laughs
boisterously.)* The old Café Infanté. *(He laughs again.)*
Olive oil, Mother. *(He goes out the hall-door, breaking into
another laugh, and in a second the front-door closes with a
bang, causing* MRS. FISHER *to start again, and look irritat-
edly toward the hall-door. Then she resumes her knitting.
The parlor-door opens and* AMY *drifts in, and starts across
towards the chair at the left of the table.)*

AMY: Hello! *(*MRS. FISHER *starts again.)*

MRS. FISHER: Oh, you frightened me, Amy—walkin' in
that way like a ghost! When did you come in?

AMY: *(Sitting down, with a wearied air)* A couple of
minutes ago—I've been in the parlor.

MRS. FISHER: Why, your man just left here, didn't you
see him?

AMY: No, I heard him when I came in—I went in the
parlor.

MRS. FISHER: He's lookin' for you—He sez he wants you
to go to some kind of an Automobile Show with him.

AMY: I know; I don't want to go; I'm too tired.

MRS. FISHER: What's he doin' about his supper?

AMY: I told him this morning to get something in town; I
knew I wouldn't be home till late. *(*MRS. FISHER *resumes her
knitting; and there is a slight pause.)*

MRS. FISHER: He sez you've got to get out of that place
you're in.

AMY: Yes, they're going to tear those houses down.

That's what I was doing today—looking around for some-place.

MRS. FISHER: Did you see anything?

AMY: I saw a couple of places that were fair, but they want too much money.

MRS. FISHER: I'm afraid that's what you'll find, Amy, wherever you go.

AMY: Thirty-eight dollars a month—for a little two-story house—that didn't even have a front porch.

MRS. FISHER: Well, you're surely not lookin' for a house, Amy, are you?

AMY: Yes, if I can find one.

MRS. FISHER: And have you any idea what they're askin' for houses these days?

AMY: Well, Aubrey sez he *will* not live in rooms any longer.

MRS. FISHER: What the devil does it matter *what he* sez! He don't know what he's sayin' half the time, anyway. It's *you* that has to stretch the money, and it'll only go so far; and the money that *he* gets won't cover any forty-dollar rents, you can make up your mind to that right now, before you go any further. And that's what you'll be asked to pay, Amy, remember I'm tellin' you.

AMY: He doesn't want to pay rent—he wants to buy.

MRS. FISHER: What on, thirty-two dollars a week?

AMY: He sez he can put it into a new building society that he heard about, over in Frankford.

MRS. FISHER: Wouldn't he have to pay the building society?

AMY: Well, he wouldn't have to pay it all at once.

MRS. FISHER: There'd be more onces than he'd be able to meet. I thought *you* had a *little* sense, but you're nearly as bad as him.

AMY: No, but you talk awfully silly, Mother; you'd think everybody that was married was living out in the street.

MRS. FISHER: That's where a good many of them would be livin', Amy, only that somebody belongin' to them is givin' them a hand. Money'll only go so far, and I've been keepin' house too long not to know just how far that far is. Nobody can tell *me*.

AMY: There was a girl down in our office that was married, just before I was married, and the fellow she married didn't even get as much money as Aubrey gets; he got about twenty-five a week—he was a guard in the Corn Exchange Bank; and *they* bought a house, out in Kensington, and they say it's beautiful.

MRS. FISHER: She's back at her job, though, isn't she?

AMY: *(With reluctant admission)* She never left her job.

MRS. FISHER: Well,—that's how she's doin' it. You told me yourself there were five girls in your office that have married within the last two years. Do you think they're hanging over books nine hours a day because they *like* it? And you haven't got any furniture even if you got a house.

AMY: Oh, you can always get furniture.

MRS. FISHER: You can if you pay for it. And I don't know how you expect to do all these wonders later on, when you find it so hard to make ends meet now, with only the rent of two rooms to pay for. You're everlastin' borrowin' from me as it is.

AMY: I always pay you, don't I?

MRS. FISHER: You do when you get it. But, that's not the point, Amy; it's that what you get one week don't last you till the next.

AMY: The reason I was short last week, Aubrey bought that new overcoat.

MRS. FISHER: And next week it'll be something else.

AMY: Well, a man can't be shabby, Mom, in a position like Aubrey's. He sez he's got nearly eighty clerks down there in his department; and he sez unless he sets some kind of an example of personal appearance, he sez there are some of them down there that'd come in in overalls.

MRS. FISHER: *(Laying her knitting on the table and looking keenly at* AMY*)* How is it, Amy, that a girl like you—that was smart enough to keep books, has so little sense when it comes to what some man tells you? (AMY *looks at her Mother steadily.)*

AMY: Who do you mean, Aubrey?

MRS. FISHER: Yes.

AMY: Why, what does he tell me that I have so little sense about?

MRS. FISHER: That he has eighty clerks under him.

AMY: So he has.

MRS. FISHER: And gets thirty-two dollars a week?

AMY: He gets thirty-two fifty. (MRS. FISHER *resumes her knitting, shaking her head hopelessly.)* Well now, Mom, you know yourself what the Pennsylvania Railroad pays its men.

MRS. FISHER: I don't know what anybody pays anybody.

AMY: Well, the Pennsylvania Railroad is notorious. Aubrey sez that only that a couple of things haven't panned out just right with him, he'd have left them *long* ago. He sez they just try to break your spirit. He sez that's one of the main reasons why he pays so much attention to his clothes.—He sez he just wouldn't *please* them.

MRS. FISHER: How much did he pay for that overcoat?

AMY: Twenty-eight dollars. (MRS. FISHER *raises her eyes to Heaven.*) Oh, he didn't have to pay it all at once; the man said on account of it being so near Christmas he could let it go till the first of February.

MRS. FISHER: I guess he'll be wantin' a suit, now, the first you know, to go with the overcoat.

AMY: No, his suit's all right,—yet a while. But this suit of mine is beginning to go; I've worn it till I'm tired looking at it.

MRS. FISHER: People can't *get* things so handy once they're married.

AMY: I thought I'd be able to put something away out of this week, toward a suit; but I don't know where the money went to:—it just seemed to go. Honestly, I had exactly *twelve cents* in my purse when Aubrey gave me his pay.

MRS. FISHER: I don't know what'll become of you, Amy, if ever you have a houseful of children to keep. (AMY *sits looking at nothing, with a rather troubled expression about the eyes, and her Mother continues to knit. Suddenly* AMY *bursts into tears.* MRS. FISHER *looks at her: then she gets up quietly, laying her knitting on the table, and crosses in front of the table to her—and lays her hand on her arm.*) Now, there's no use a startin' that kind a thing, now, Amy; for it won't do you a bit of good. (*She continues across.*)

AMY: I don't know what I'm going to do, Mom—I'm nearly crazy.

MRS. FISHER: (*Turning*) I'll tell you what you're goin' to do, Amy, if you're a wise woman—You're goin' to realize that you're married; and that you've got some kind of a house to keep up; and just how much money you're goin' to get each week to keep it up *on;* and then suit your ideas accordin'. And if you don't, you'll have plenty of cryin' to do. And you'll have nobody to thank but yourself, for you had nothing but impudence for them that tried to tell you— how many beans made five. (*The front-door is heard to close.)* I guess this is your Father. Go into the parlor there, and don't let him see you cryin'. (AMY *rises and steps quickly across and through the parlor-doors at the left into the parlor; and* MRS. FISHER *crosses above the center-table to the buffet and puts her knitting into one of the drawers.* CLARA *appears in the hall-door.)*

CLARA: What's the matter? (MRS. FISHER *turns and looks at her.)*

MRS. FISHER: There's nothing at all the matter.

CLARA: What did Joe telephone me for?

MRS. FISHER: *Our* Joe, do you mean?

CLARA: Yes; Bertha said he telephoned the house about four o'clock and told her to tell me to come right over home as soon as I came in.

MRS. FISHER: Well, I'm sure *I* don't know what he'd want you for, Clara; he didn't leave any word with me for you this morning.

CLARA: *(Coming forward towards the center-table)* I was over paying my Electric, and just got back; so I came right over; I thought maybe something was wrong here, and he was calling from next door.

MRS. FISHER: No, he hasn't been home here today. (CLARA *puzzles for a second, then tosses her purse onto the table.)*

CLARA: I wonder what he wanted me for. *(She turns to the mirror at the back and touches her hat.)*

MRS. FISHER: Is that girl at your house sure it was our Joe?

CLARA: *(Coming back to the table)* She said it was; and I suppose she knows his voice,—she's often answered the 'phone when he's called. *(She picks up a book from the table and glances casually at it.)*

MRS. FISHER: Well, maybe he wants to see you about something; I'd wait a while; he'll be here at six.

CLARA: *(Looking suddenly at her Mother)* Maybe he's heard some news about that formula that those people are interested in.

MRS. FISHER: *(Coming over to the table)* Oh, I guess he'll be an old man before he ever hears anything from that. *(She folds and settles various things on the table, and* CLARA *glances through the book. Then, as she moves over to settle the upper left-hand corner of the table-cover, she gives* CLARA *a little push.)* Look out of my way, Clara, till I fix this cloth. (CLARA *just moves without lookng up from the book.*) That's a book Joe brought home last night: about that woman that was left up on the North Pole. He sez it's very nice. I've got to put those potatoes on, for your Father's supper; he'll be here around six. (*She moves to the door at the right.*)

CLARA: (*Standing at the left of the table, still looking at the book*) Did you know that Amy's got to get out of those rooms she's in?

MRS. FISHER: (*From the kitchen*) Yes.

CLARA: They're going to tear those houses down.

MRS. FISHER: (*Coming back into the room*) So she was telling me.

CLARA: (*Moving to the chair at the left of the table*) What's she going to do, (*Tossing the book onto the table*) come in here to live? (*She sits down.*)

MRS. FISHER: Now, that's a sensible question for you to ask, Clara;—you know how much she's comin' in here to live.

CLARA: (*Commencing to remove her gloves*) I don't know where else she'll go,—with rents the way they are now;—unless she goes back to work.

MRS. FISHER: She'll have to look around.

CLARA: What good will it do her to look around—she certainly won't find anything as reasonable as where she is now: and when she's not able to pay that, how does she expect to pay any more? (*The parlor-door is whipped open and* AMY *is standing between the curtains looking tight-lipped at* CLARA.)

AMY: How do *you* know I'm not able to pay my rent where I am?

MRS. FISHER: (*Moving towards the hall-door*) Now, don't start a fight, Amy, your Pop'll be in here any minute. (*She looks out into the hallway.*)

AMY: (*Speaking to her Mother, and indicating* CLARA *with a gesture*) No, but I'd like to know what business it is of hers whether I can pay my rent or not. I don't see that anybody's asking *her* to pay it for me.

CLARA: (*Very sure of her ground*) It's a bit late in the day to talk that way, Amy; your husband's been to Frank Hyland *twice* already to pay it for you. (AMY *looks at her aghast, and* MRS. FISHER *comes forward between them.*) It's time you quit this posing in front of me; *I* know how you're fixed better than you do yourself. *(She turns sharply away and flings her gloves onto the table.)*

AMY: *(Almost crying)* Now, do you hear that, Mom!

MRS. FISHER: Stop your talk, Amy! Do you want your Father to walk in and hear you?

AMY: *(Lowering her voice, but still speaking with angry rapidity)* She sez that Aubrey Piper's been to Frank Hyland twice, for the loan of *our* rent.

CLARA: So he has.

AMY: You're a liar! *(MRS. FISHER gives her a slap on the back; and there is a vibrant pause. Then AMY moves down towards the window at the left and bursts out crying.)*

MRS. FISHER: *(With controlled excitement)* Will you stop when I speak to *you!* *(There is a pause.)* What kind of talk do you call that! *(She steps to the hall-door again and glances out into the hallway.)*

AMY: *(Whirling again upon CLARA)* Well, that's what she is! Aubrey Piper never asked Frank Hyland for a cent in his life.

CLARA: He's asked him a dozen times, and got it, too; till I put a stop to it.

MRS. FISHER: *(Coming forward again, and speaking with authority)* Now, that'll do, Clara!—I don't want to hear another word—out of either one of you—I had enough of that when the two of you were at home.

AMY: Well, I'll make her prove what she sez about Aubrey Piper, just the same!

CLARA: It's very easily proved. Just come over to the house some night and I'll show you a few of his letters.

AMY: What do you do, open them?

CLARA: I do now, yes,—since I found out who they're from.

MRS. FISHER: *(Keenly)* Do you mean to tell me, Clara, that he's writin' to Frank Hyland for money?

AMY: No, he doesn't do anything of the kind, Mom, that's another of her lies!

MRS. FISHER: *(Before AMY has finished speaking)* I'm not talkin' to you, Amy.

AMY: She just makes those things up.

CLARA: I make them *up!*

AMY: *(Crying)* Yes!

CLARA: And I've got at least twelve letters right in my bureau-drawer this minute that he's written within the last two months.

MRS. FISHER: What does he write letters for?

CLARA: For money—so he can pay seven dollars for a seat out at the football game—as he did Thanksgiving afternoon,—Frank saw him there.

MRS. FISHER: Why don't he just ast Frank Hyland for the money when he sees him, instead of writin' to him?

CLARA: I suppose he thinks a written request is more appropriate, coming from one of the heads of the Pennsylvania Railroad.

MRS. FISHER: How much does he ast for, when he asts him?

CLARA: There was one a couple of weeks ago, for three hundred. (AMY *makes a sound of bitter amusement, and turns away.*)

MRS. FISHER: (*Aghast*) Three hundred dollars?

CLARA: That's what the letter said. (MRS. FISHER *turns and looks at* AMY.)

MRS. FISHER: What would he have wanted three hundred dollars for, Amy?

AMY: Oh, ask her, Mom; she's good at making things up. (*She sweeps towards the parlor-doors.*)

MRS. FISHER: (*Taking a step or two after her*) Oh, you wouldn't believe it, even if it was true, if it was against him.

AMY: Well, I wouldn't believe *her,* anyway. (AMY *slams the parlor-door with a bang.*)

MRS. FISHER: (*Raising her voice*) You wouldn't believe your own Mother,—never name your sister. (*She turns to* CLARA.) She flew at *me* like a wild-cat, when I told her he wore a wig. I guess she knows it herself by this time.

CLARA: She's for *him,* Mom; and the sooner you get that into your head the better.

MRS. FISHER: (*Moving towards the right, above the table*) I know very well she is, you needn't tell me. And she'd turn on everyone belongin' to her for him. The idea of askin' anybody for three hundred dollars. (*She continues towards the kitchen-door, fuming; then turns.*) I suppose he wanted to buy an automobile or something. That's where he is tonight, out at the Automobile Show—and not two cents in his pocket—like a lot of others that'll be out there I guess— And I'll bet he'll be doin' more talk out there than them that'll buy a dozen cars.

CLARA: I think that's what he *did* want the money for.

MRS. FISHER: I wouldn't surprise me,—the damned fool. (*She steps to the mantelpiece and glances out into the hallway.)* It'd be fitter for him to be thinkin' about getting' a house to live in.

CLARA: He doesn't think he *needs* to think about that; he thinks he's coming in here.

MRS. FISHER: *(Turning sharply, on her way back to the kitchen-door)* Comin' in here *to live*, do you mean?

CLARA: That's what he told Frank, the day before yesterday.

MRS. FISHER: Well, he's very much mistaken if he does, I can tell you that. I'd like to be listenin' to that fellow seven days in the week. I'd rather go over and live with your Aunt Ellie in Newark.

CLARA: *(Rising, and picking up her gloves from the table)* Well, that's about what you'll have to do, Mom, if you ever let them in on you. *(She stands looking straight out, unfastening her neck-piece.)*

MRS. FISHER: I won't let them in one me, don't fret. Your Father 'ud have something to say about that.

CLARA: *(Slipping off her neck-piece)* Pop may not always *be* here, Mom. *(She turns around to her left and moves to a point above the table, and puts her fur and gloves down.)*

MRS. FISHER: Well, I'll be here, if he isn't; and the furniture is mine. And there's very little danger of my walkin' off and leavin' it to any son-in-law. *(The front-door closes.)* I guess this is your Pop now, and I haven't even got the kettle on. *(She hurries out at the right.* CLARA *glances at the hall-door, and* JOE *appears in it, and stands for the fraction of a second, irresolute.)*

JOE: Where's Mom?

CLARA: Out in the kitchen,—why?

JOE: *(Motioning to her, causing the paper to drop from his hand)* Come here,—don't let her hear your. *(*CLARA *steps towards him, with a shade of apprehension in her face and manner.)* Listen, Clara—Pop had some kind of a stroke this afternoon at his work.

CLARA: *Pop* did?

JOE: They found him layin' in front of one of the boilers.

CLARA: Oh, my God!

JOE: I tried to get you on the 'phone about four o'clock.

CLARA: I know—I came right over as soon as I came in.

JOE: *You* better tell Mom. *(He starts for the stairs, and* CLARA *turns towards the kitchen-door.)*

CLARA: *(Turning sharply back again)* Joe!

JOE: *(Stopping abruptly on the first step of the stairs)* What?

CLARA: Where's Pop now?

JOE: They took him to the Samaritan Hospital. I just came from there—they telephoned me to the office.

CLARA: Well, is he very bad?

JOE: *I* think he's done.

CLARA: Oh, don't say that, Joe!

JOE: That's what the Doctor at the Hospital sez.—He hasn't regained consciousness since three o'clock. So you'd better tell Mom to get her things on and go right down there. I've got to change my clothes; I went right up there from work. *(He starts up the stairs; and* CLARA *moves vaguely towards the kitchen-door. She stops and stands looking toward the kitchen in a controlled panic of indecision. Then, abruptly she whirls round and steps quickly back to the hall-door.)*

CLARA: *(In a subdued voice)* Joe!

JOE: What?

CLARA: That Samaritan Hospital's at Broad and Ontario, isn't it?

JOE: Yes. *(She turns slowly and looks out, irresolute. Then she stoops down abstractedly and picks up the newspaper that* JOE *dropped. The parlor-door opens sharply and* AMY *stands looking at her apprehensively. Their eyes meet.)*

AMY: What is it? *(*MRS. FISHER *appears in the door at the right, drying an agate-ware plate.)*

MRS. FISHER: Wasn't that your Pop that came in, Clara? *(*CLARA *makes a deft, silencing gesture with her left hand to* AMY, *and moves towards the center-table.)*

CLARA: No, it wasn't, Mom, it was the boy with the paper.

MRS. FISHER: *(Coming further into the room to see the clock)* I wonder what's keepin' him; he's late to-night. *(*CLARA *leans against the center-table, keeping her face averted from her Mother.)* He's nearly always here before this. *(She moves back again towards the kitchen.)*

AMY: *(Crossing quickly down to* CLARA'S *left)* What is it, Clara?

MRS. FISHER: *(Turning and looking at* CLARA*)* What's the matter with her? *(*CLARA *tries to control her feelings.)*

AMY: I don't know what's the matter with her, Mom! Something *Joe* just told her—he's just gone upstairs.

MRS. FISHER: *(Coming forward apprehensively at* CLARA'S *right)* What is it, Clara,—somethin' about your Father? Is that what you're cryin' for?

AMY: Why don't you tell her, Clara?

MRS. FISHER: Go to the foot of the stairs, Amy, and call Joe. *(*AMY *steps towards the foot of the stairs.)* Something's happened to your Father, I know it.

CLARA: *(Moving a step or two towards her Mother)* Now, it's nothing to get upset about, Mom; he just took a little spell of some kind at his work this afternoon, and they had to take him to the hospital. *(*AMY *comes forward eagerly, and crosses to a point below the table.)* Joe just came from there, and he sez we'd better get our things on right away and go down there. *(*MRS. FISHER *sways a step forward, letting the agate-ware plate slide from her hands to the floor.* AMY *steps towards her Mother, lifting the chair from the right of the table and guiding her Mother into it.)* Here, sit down here, Mom.

MRS. FISHER: *(Slightly dazed)* What is it she's sayin' happened to your Father, Amy? *(*AMY *passes back of the chair to her Mother's right, and* CLARA *comes to her left.)*

CLARA: Now, it's nothing to get excited about, Mom; it might be just a little heart-attack or something that he took. *(She takes the towel from her Mother's hand and hands it to* AMY.*)* Put this over there. *(*AMY *turns to the buffet.)*

MRS. FISHER: There was never anything the matter with your Father's heart, Clara.

CLARA: Well, it's pretty hot in there where he works, you know that. *(*MRS. FISHER *shakes her head up and down, knowingly.)* And men at Pop's age are always taking little spells of some kind.

MRS. FISHER: *(With a long, heavy sigh)* Ah, I guess it's a stroke, Clara.

CLARA: It might not be, Mom, you can't tell.

MRS. FISHER: That's how his two brothers went, you know.

CLARA: Amy, you'd better go to the telephone next door and tell Frank Hyland I won't be home. *(*AMY *hurries across towards the hall-door, and* CLARA *follows her, continuing her instructions.)* If he isn't home yet, tell Bertha to tell him to come right down to the Samaritan Hospital as soon as he comes. And tell Johnny Harbison to go to the corner for a taxi. (*The front-door closes after* AMY, *and* CLARA *steps back to her Mother's side.*)

MRS. FISHER: Is that where your Father is, Clara, the Samaritan Hospital.

CLARA: Yes; it's right down there near where he works, at Broad and Ontario.

MRS. FISHER: (*Starting to cry*) Your poor Father—I wonder what happened to him. (CLARA *reflects her Mother's sentiment.*)

CLARA: (*Picking up the plate*) Now, there's no use looking on the dark side of it already, Mom.

MRS. FISHER: No, but me gettin' his supper out there, and him not comin' home to it at all. And maybe *never* comin' home to it again, Clara, for all we know.

CLARA: He'll be home again, Mom—Pop is a strong man. (*She puts the plate on the buffet.*)

MRS. FISHER: (*Suddenly*) I guess he's dead, now, and you're not tellin' me.

CLARA: (*Coming to her Mother's left*) He isn't dead, Mom; I'd have told you if he was.

MRS. FISHER: What did Joe say?

CLARA: Just what I told you; that he'd had a spell of some kind.

MRS. FISHER: Well, why didn't he tell me! What's he doin' upstairs, anyway?

CLARA: He's changing his clothes; he's got to go right back down there again.

MRS. FISHER: He's cryin' I guess. You know, it'll kill our poor Joe, Clara, if anything happens to your Father.

CLARA: He sez we'd better go right down there, too, Mom; so you'd better go upstairs and fix yourself up a bit. Give me your apron.

MRS. FISHER: (*Rising and commencing to remove her apron*) I don't know whether I'll be able to dress myself now or not; my hands are like lead.

CLARA: You don't need to get all dressed up, Mom—just put on your black-silk waist; that skirt's good enough. (*She goes towards the door at the right with the apron and goes out.*)

MRS. FISHER: (*Taking the comb from the back of her head and commencing to comb her hair*) Well, I'm not goin' down there lookin' like a dago woman.

CLARA: *(Coming quickly in again)* Nobody'll see you in the dark. *(She picks up the plate and towel from the buffet and straightens the runner.)*

MRS. FISHER: *(Moving aimlessly about in front of the mantelpiece)* It won't be dark in the *hospital;* unless somethin' happens to the lights. (CLARA *goes out again.*) Put that gas out under them potatoes, Clara, I just lit it. And you'd better pick up this room a bit while I'm upstairs, you don't know who might be comin' here if they hear about your Father. *(She stops and looks helplessly about the room.)* Oh, dear, Oh, dear, Oh, dear! I don't know what I'm doin'. *(*CLARA *comes in again.)* Take all them papers off that table, Clara, and put them in the kitchen.

CLARA: *(Crossing to the table and folding and gathering up the various papers)* You'd better bring your umbrella down with you, Mom, when you go up,—it looked like rain when I came in.

MRS. FISHER: Oh, and I let our Amy take my rubbers the last day she was here, and she *never* brings anything back.

CLARA: *(Taking the papers out into the kitchen)* You won't need rubbers.

MRS. FISHER: Oh, I get my feet all wet, when I don't have rubbers. *(She is facing the hall-door, fastening the old-fashioned brooch at her throat.* AUBREY *frames himself in the door, with a bandage around his head, and looking a bit battered.)* My God, what happened to *you,* now!

AUBREY: *(Coming forward at the left, removing his hat)* It's beginning to rain. *(He places his hat and cane on the table, and stands in front of the table removing his gloves.)*

MRS. FISHER: *(Following him with her eyes)* Never mind the rain, the rain didn't do that to you. *(She comes forward at his left.* CLARA *comes in and stands over near the door at the right, looking at him.)* I guess you ran into somebody, didn't you?

AUBREY: *(With a shade of nonchalance)* Don't get excited, Mother,—just a little misunderstanding on the part of the traffic-officer.

MRS. FISHER: You don't mean to tell me that you ran into a traffic-officer! (CLARA *comes forward at the right.*)

AUBREY: Control, now, Little Mother, I assure there is no occasion for undue solicitation. *(He turns and sees* CLARA.*)* Good evening, Mrs. Hyland.

CLARA: Hello! What happened to your head?

MRS. FISHER: You look like a bandit.

AUBREY: The veriest trifle, Mrs. Hyland—just a little spray from the wind-shield.

MRS. FISHER: Where's the car you borrowed? Smashed, I guess, ain't it?

AUBREY: The car I borrowed, Mother Fisher, is now in the hands of the bandits of the law. The judicial gentlemen, who have entered into a conspiracy with the regulators of traffic—to collect fines from motorists—by ordering them to go one way—and then swearing that they told them to go another.

MRS. FISHER: Never mind your fancy talk, we've heard too much of that already! I want to know who you killed,—or what you did run into; for I know you ran into somethin'. And where's the automobile that someone was fool enough to lend you?

AUBREY: The automobile, Little Mother, is perfectly safe—parked and pasturing—in the courtyard of the Twenty-second and Hunting Park Avenue Police Station.

MRS. FISHER: Did you get arrested, too?

AUBREY: I accompanied the officer as far as the station-house, yes; and I told them a few things while I was there, too, about the condition of traffic in this city.

MRS. FISHER: I guess they told you a few things, too, didn't they?

AUBREY: Beg pardon?

MRS. FISHER: (*Starting abruptly for the hall-door*) Never mind; you're welcome.

CLARA: You'd better change your shoes, Mom; you can't go down there with those.

MRS. FISHER: (*Pointing toward the cellar-door*) See if my long black coat's in the cellar-way there. (CLARA *goes quickly to the cellar-door, opens it, and looks for the coat.*) That fellow's got me so upset I don't know what I'm doin'. (*She goes out the hall-door and to her left, up the stairs.* AUBREY *moves over to the chair at the right, where* MRS. FISHER *collapsed, and sits down,—quite ruffled in his dignity.* CLARA *closes the cellar-door and, with a glance toward the hall-door, comes quickly forward at* AUBREY'S *left.*)

CLARA: What did they do, fine you, Aubrey?

AUBREY: They were all set to fine me; but when I got through with them they didn't have a leg to stand on. So they tried to cover themselves up as gracefully as possible, by trumping up a charge against me of driving an automobile without a license.

CLARA: What did they do, take the automobile *away* from you?

AUBREY: Nothing of the sort; they simply complied with the usual procedure in a case of this kind—which is to release the defendant on bond, pending the extent of the victim's injuries.

CLARA: Was there somebody injured?

AUBREY: The traffic-cop that ran into me, yes.

CLARA: For God's sake, couldn't you find anybody but the traffic-cop to run into!

AUBREY: I did not run into him, Mrs. Hyland—you don't understand the circumstances of the case.

CLARA: Well, I understand this much about them—that they can give you ten years for a thing like that. And it'd just serve you right if they did, too. Borrowin' people's automobiles, and knowing no more about running them than I do. *(She turns away to her right and moves across above the table towards the hall-door.)*

AUBREY: No time like the present to learn, Mrs. Hyland.

CLARA: *(Turning to him sharply).* Well, you'll very likely have plenty of time, from now on,—if that officer is seriously injured. *(She continues over and down to the window at the left, where she draws the drape aside and looks anxiously down the street for the taxi.)*

AUBREY: He was faking a broken arm around there when I left—But it's a wonder to me the poor straw-ride wasn't signed on the dotted line; for he ran head on right into me.

CLARA: *(Crossing back towards him, in front of the Morris-chair).* Was *he* in a car, too?

AUBREY: No, he was jay-walking—trying to beat me to the crossing, after giving me the right of way.

CLARA: Where did this thing happen?

AUBREY: Broad and Erie Avenue, I wouldn't kid you.

CLARA: Did they take the cop to the hospital?

AUBREY: Yes, we took him over there in the car.

CLARA: Did they let *you* run it?

AUBREY: Repeat the question, Mrs. Hyland.

CLARA: You heard me,—I don't need to repeat it. And take that silly-looking bandage off your head, before Amy sees you; and don't frighten the life out of her. *(She steps up to the hall-door and glances out.)* She's got enough to worry her now without looking at you. *(AUBREY rises, and, detaching the handkerchief from around his head, moves across to a point above the center-table.)*

AUBREY: Is my wife here?

CLARA: She's next door, telephoning, yes; and she'll be back in a minute. *(Coming forward a step or two at the left.)* Pop just had a stroke of some kind at his work this afternoon, Joe just told us.

AUBREY: What are you doing, kidding me?

CLARA: *(Starting to cry).* No, of course I'm not kidding you! What would I be kidding you about a thing like that for? *(She crosses down and across in front of the center-table. The front-door closes.)*

AUBREY: Where is he now?

CLARA: They took him to the Samaritan Hospital; we're just going down there. *(AMY appears in the hall-door, and stands looking questioningly at AUBREY.)*

AMY: What's the matter, Aubrey? *(He turns and looks at her.)*

AUBREY: *(Extending his arm and hand in a magnificent gesture).* Well! *(AMY comes forward to her husband.)* The old kid herself!

AMY: What is it, Aubrey?

AUBREY: *(Taking her in his arms).* Nothing in the world but this, Baby. *(He kisses her affectionately.)*

CLARA: Did you get Frank on the 'phone, Amy? *(MRS. FISHER can be heard hurrying down the stairs.)*

AMY: *(Crossing above AUBREY and speaking directly to CLARA).* He wasn't home yet; I told the girl to tell him as soon as he came in.

MRS. FISHER: *(Coming through the hall-door, and tossing her little knit-jacket onto the small stand at the left of the mantelpiece.)* Clara, is that automobile-cab here yet?

CLARA: It'll be here in a minute, Mom.

MRS. FISHER: What do you think of this fellow, Amy,— runnin' wild through the city breakin' policemen's bones! We didn't have enough trouble without that—with your poor Father layin' dead for all we know,—down in the Jewish hospital. *(She starts to cry and steps down to the window at the left to look out for the taxicab.)* It's enough to make a body light-headed.

CLARA: Where's your coat, Mom?

MRS. FISHER: *(Turning to her).* Isn't it there in the cellar-way?

CLARA: No, I just looked.

MRS. FISHER: *(Going up to the hall-door).* It must be upstairs. Joe!

AMY: *(At* AUBREY'S *right).* I thought you were out at the Automobile Show, Aubrey.

MRS. FISHER: *(At the foot of the stairs).* Listen, Joe—

AUBREY: I had a little mix-up at Broad and Erie Avenue.

AMY: You didn't get hurt, did you?

MRS. FISHER *and* AUBREY, *speaking together.*

MRS. FISHER:—Throw down my long black coat; you'll find it on a hook there in the hall-closet. *(She starts for the buffet.)*

AUBREY:—Nothing but a scratch or two, here on my forehead, from the glass in the wind-shield. Just a little shake-up.

MRS. FISHER: *(Stopping and turning sharply at the right of the center-table).* He nearly killed a traffic-officer!—That's how much of a little shake-up it was. *(She continues to the buffet, where* CLARA *is standing.)* Get out of my way, Clara, till I get a clean handkerchief out of here. *(She pushes* CLARA *out of her way and opens the left-hand drawer of the buffet and rummages for a handkerchief.* CLARA *passes across in front of the center-table to the window at the left.)*

AMY: You *didn't*, Aubrey, did you?

AUBREY: Certainly not, Amy—your Mother's raving. *(*MRS. FISHER *finds the handkerchief, slams the drawer shut and turns.)*

MRS. FISHER: The man's in the hospital!—I don't know what more you want. *(The big black coat lands at the foot of the stairs with a thud, causing* MRS. FISHER *to start nervously; then she hurries across at the back towards the hall-door, tucking the folded handkerchief at her waist.)*

AMY: Is he, Aubrey?

AUBREY: Do you think I'd be here, Kid, if he was?

MRS. FISHER: *(On the way over).* You wouldn't be here, only that someone was fool enough to bail you out; instead of lettin' you stay in where you couldn't be killin' people. *(*CLARA *has stepped up to the foot of the stairs and picked the coat up immediately it fell, and now stands holding it for her Mother to put on; but* MRS. FISHER *disregards her, going* *straight out to the foot of the stairs and calling shrilly up to* JOE.) Joe, why don't you tell a body when you're goin' to throw a thing down that way, and not be frightenin' the life out of people! *(She comes back into the room again and* CLARA *assists her.* AMY *stands above the center-table looking wide-eyed at* AUBREY, *who sways forward at the left, and, crossing below the center-table to the chair at the right, where he has been previously seated, sits down.)*

CLARA: Aren't you going to put on another waist, Mom?

MRS. FISHER: No, this one is good enough—I'll keep the coat buttoned up. Put that collar inside.

AMY: *(In a lowered tone).* Are you out on bail, Aubrey?

AUBREY: They always bail a man in a case like this, Amy; they've got my car on their hands.

MRS. FISHER: *(Buttoning the coat, and moving to the mirror over the mantelpiece).* Get my hat, will you, Clara?

CLARA: *(Starting for the hall-door).* Where is it, upstairs?

MRS. FISHER: No, it's in the parlor there, inside the top of the Victrola. *(CLARA comes back and goes into the parlor.)*

AMY: Why didn't you bring the car back with you, Aubrey?—That fellow might want it tomorrow.

AUBREY: I'll have it for him all right; I've got to call around there for it Monday morning at ten o'clock. *(MRS. FISHER turns sharply from her primping at the mirror.)*

MRS. FISHER: I guess you've got to go down there to a hearing Monday morning at ten o'clock,—(AMY *turns and looks at her Mother)* and pay your fine! *(Speaking directly to* AMY.) I guess that's the automobile he's got to call for. *(CLARA hurries out of the parlor brushing the dust off an old black hat, with a bunch of cherries on it.)*

CLARA: I'd better go out and get a whisk-broom and dust this, Mom.

MRS. FISHER: *(Turning to her nervously).* No, never mind, it's good enough, give it to me.

CLARA *(Crossing below her Mother, to the right).* Your coat needs dusting. *(She takes a whisk-broom from a hook just inside the kitchen-door.)*

AMY: How much did they fine you, Aubrey?

AUBREY: They didn't fine me at all.

MRS. FISHER: *(Settling her hat).* They'll do that Monday.

AUBREY: Time'll tell that, Mother Fisher. *(CLARA hurries back and starts brushing her Mother's coat.)*

MRS. FISHER: And you'll pay it, too, or go to jail; and it'ud just be the price of you.

AUBREY: They didn't seem very anxious to do any fining today, after I got through telling it to them.

MRS. FISHER: Am I all right, Clara?

AUBREY: I took a slam at the Pennsylvania Railroad, too, while I was at it.

MRS. FISHER: You're always takin' slams at somethin'; that's what's leavin' you under bail right now. Are you ready, Clara? *(She hurries to the foot of the stairs.)*

CLARA *(Hurrying back to the kitchen with the whisk-broom).* Yes, I'm ready.

AUBREY: Never mind about that, Mother Fisher.

MRS. FISHER: *(Calling up the stairs).* Are you goin' down there with us, Joe?

JOE: *(From upstairs).* Comin' right down. *(MRS. FISHER comes in to the mantelpiece and picks up her gloves. CLARA hurries in from the kitchen again to the center-table and picks up her neck-piece and gloves.)*

AUBREY: Only don't be surprised if you hear of a very quiet little shake-up very soon—in the Department of Public Safety.

MRS. FISHER: Are you warm enough with that coat, Clara?

CLARA: Yes, I'm all right. How about the umbrella?

MRS. FISHER: I think it's out there in the hall-rack; look and see. *(CLARA hurries out into the hallway, and MRS. FISHER stands putting on her gloves. AMY crosses to AUBREY's left.)*

AMY: *(Very quietly).* How much bail did they put you under, Aubrey?

AUBREY: One thousand berries, Amy. *(MRS. FISHER looks over at them keenly.)*

AMY: A thousand dollars!

AUBREY: That's regulation—*(AMY turns and gives her Mother a troubled look, and MRS. FISHER moves forward at the left to a point where she can see AUBREY.)* A little chicken-feed for the stool-pigeons.

MRS. FISHER: Did *he* say they put him under a thousand dollars' bail?

AUBREY: That's what I said, Mrs. Fisher, one thousand trifles—I wouldn't kid you.

MRS. FISHER: You wouldn't kid anybody that'd listen to

you for five minutes. And who did you get to *go* a thousand dollars bail *for* you?

AUBREY: Don't be alarmed, Little Mother,—I saw that the affair was kept strictly within the family.

MRS. FISHER: What do you mean?

AUBREY: Your other son-in-law—was kind enough to come forward. (CLARA *hurries in from the hallway with the umbrella, and comes forward at the extreme left.*)

MRS. FISHER: Clara's husband!

AUBREY: That's the gentleman, Mrs. Fisher,—Mr. Francis X. Hyland.

MRS. FISHER: (*Helplessly*). My God! (*She turns around to her right till she locates* CLARA.) Do you hear that, Clara?

CLARA: What?

MRS. FISHER: He got Frank Hyland to go his bail for a thousand dollars.

CLARA: (*Looking bitterly at* AUBREY). What did you do, write him another letter?

AUBREY: That was not necessary, Mrs. Hyland, not giving you a short answer. Your husband was fortunate enough to see the whole affair from the trolley-car. He was just returning from his business, and happened to be on the trolley-car that ran into me.

MRS. FISHER: How many more things ran into you,—besides traffic-cops and trolley-cars! I suppose a couple of the buildin's ran into you too, didn't they? (JOE *hurries in from the hall-door buttoning his overcoat.*)

JOE: Are you ready, Mom?

CLARA: (*Going up to the hall-door*). Yes, we're ready. (JOE *comes forward at the extreme left, looking questioningly from one to the other.* CLARA *goes out into the hall.*)

AUBREY: You'll find out all about that Monday morning, Mrs. Fisher.

MRS. FISHER: (*Moving up towards the hall-door*). Well, see that nothin' else runs into you between now and Monday.

JOE: What's the matter?

MRS. FISHER: We don't want Frank Hyland losin' any thousand-dollar bills on account of you.

JOE: What's happened, Mom?

MRS. FISHER: (*Turning to* JOE, *and pointing at* AUBREY *with a wide gesture.*) Why, this crazy Jack here's been runnin' into everything in the city but ourselves; and he got himself arrested; and Frank Hyland had to bail him out for a thousand dollars. *(She starts to cry.)*

JOE: What were you doin', Aubrey, joy-ridin'?

MRS. FISHER: No!—he was trolley-ridin',—and traffic-cop-ridin',—and every other kind of ridin',—in an automobile that he borrowed.

CLARA: *(Hurrying in from the hallway).* I think I see that taxi coming, Mom.

MRS. FISHER: *(Starting towards the hall-door).* Come on here, Joe. *(*JOE *crosses up at the left of the center-table to the mirror over the mantelpiece, looking disapprovingly at* AUBREY. AUBREY *rises and strolls over to a point in front of the center-table.)* How do we get down there, Clara?

CLARA: Right down Erie Ave.

AUBREY: Too bad I left that car down there at the Station House, I could have run you down there. *(They all turn and look at him; and* MRS. FISHER, *with poison in her right eye, moves forward at the left of the center-table, with a level, ominous slowness.)*

MRS. FISHER: *You* wouldn't run *me* down there,—don't fret—not if you had a thousand cars. There's enough of us in the hospital as it is. *(*AUBREY *simply regards her from a great height.)* And don't you come down there neither;—for you'd only start talkin', and that'd finish Pop quicker than a stroke. *(There's a startling hoot from the taxicab horn outside, which almost throws* MRS. FISHER *from her balance.)*

CLARA: *(Going out).* Come on, Joe.

JOE: *(Following her out).* Ain't you comin' down to the hospital, Amy?

MRS. FISHER: *(Going out).* No, you'd better stay here, Amy,—there'd better be some one of us here—or that fellow'll be runnin' into somethin' else. You ought to have somethin' heavier on you than that fur, Clara. *(*AUBREY *sits down at the left of the center-table.)*

CLARA: *(In the hallway).* I'm all right, we'll be down there in a few minutes.

MRS. FISHER: Have you got your coat buttoned up good, Joe? *(The front-door closes after them.* AMY *turns from the hall-door, where she has been standing, seeing them out, and comes forward to the back of the chair at the left of the center-table, where* AUBREY *is sitting.)*

AMY: Where's your toupé, Aubrey? *(Touching the sticking-plasters on his forehead.)*

AUBREY: In my pocket here.

AMY: *(Stroking his hair)*. Is your head hurting you?

AUBREY: *(Reaching for her hand and drawing it down over his left shoulder)*. Not a bit, Honey—just a couple of little scratches. *(He kisses her hand. She raises her eyes and looks straight ahead, with a troubled expression.)*

AMY: Aubrey, what do you think they'll do to you down there Monday?

AUBREY: Now, don't you worry about that, Sweetheart; I'll be right there if they try to pull anything. *(She moves over thoughtfully towards the upper right-hand corner of the center-table. Then a new thought occurs to her, and she turns her head and looks at him narrowly.)*

AMY: You hadn't had anything to drink, had you, Aubrey?

AUBREY: *(Looking at her quickly)*. Who, me?

AMY: I mean I thought somebody might have treated you or something.

AUBREY: *(Making a statement)*. I had a glass of Champagne six months ago with a friend of mine in his suite at the Ritz-Carlton Hotel, and I haven't had a drink of anything since.

AMY: You better take off your overcoat, Aubrey; we'll have to stay here till they get back. *(He gets up and commences to remove the overcoat.)*

AUBREY: Yes, I guess we will.—I wonder how your Father is.

AMY: *(Taking the overcoat from him)*. Pretty bad I guess,—or they wouldn't have sent for Joe. *(She takes the coat up to the sofa at the right of the mantelpiece, and AUBREY takes a huge cigar from his vest-pocket and feels for a match.)* I'll get you a match, Aubrey. *(She goes out into the kitchen, and AUBREY moves to a point above the center-table, biting the tip of his cigar.)*

AUBREY: I thought I had some here, but I guess I haven't. Did they send for Joe?

AMY: Yes, they telephoned for him, to the place where he works.

AUBREY: Your Mother said it was a stroke.

AMY: *(Entering with some matches)*. I guess that's what it is, too; his two brothers died that way.

AUBREY: *(Taking the matches from her)*. I'm sorry to hear that, Amy. But, you mustn't worry, now, Kid.

AMY: It isn't only that I'm worried about, Aubrey;—I'm

thinking about you—Monday. (*She takes hold of the lapels of his coat and almost cries.*)

AUBREY: (*Putting his arm around her*). Now, listen to me, Baby—you know I'd tell you, don't you, if there was anything to worry about.

AMY: But, they're getting awfully strict in this city; there's been so many automobile accidents lately.

AUBREY: They're only strict, Honey, when a man's driving under the influence of liquor. (*There's a slight pause, and* AMY *thinks hard.*)

AMY: What if that traffic-cop is hurt bad, Aubrey?

AUBREY: It'd only be a fine for reckless driving, even if they could prove it *was* reckless driving; and *I* can prove it was the copper's fault. (*Detaching himself from her.*) So they'll very likely be *apologizing* to me around there Monday morning, instead of fining me. (*He moves across and down to the window at the left,—with ever so slight a touch of swagger.*)

AMY: Oh, I wouldn't care if they only fined you, Aubrey; because I could go back to work until it was paid.

AUBREY: (*Looking out the window*). You'll never go back to work, Kid, while I'm on the boat.

AMY: I wouldn't mind it, Aubrey.

AUBREY: Not while you're my wife, Amy. (*He half turns to her, with considerable consequence.*) I'd rather leave the Pennsylvania Railroad *flat;* and go out and take one of the jobs that have been offered me where they pay a man what he's worth.

AMY: You don't think they might do anything else to you, do you, Aubrey?

AUBREY: (*Turning to her*). Oh, they might try to take away my license.

AMY: You haven't *got* a license, have you?

AUBREY: (*Turning back to the window.*) No, I neglected to attend to it this year.

AMY: They can fine you for that, can't they?

AUBREY: Driving an automobile without a license, you mena?

AMY: Yes.

AUBREY: Sure—they can fine you for anything unless you know how to beat them to it. (*He strikes the match on the arm of the Morris-chair at his right.* AMY *rests her hands on the center-table, and looks straight out, wretchedly.*)

AMY: *(Tonelessly).* What is it they send them to prison for, Aubrey? *(He is just holding the lighted match to the cigar, and, consequently, is unable to answer her immediately. The front door-bell rings. She glances apprehensively in the direction of the hall-door, then meets his eyes.)* I wonder who that is.

AUBREY: *(Tossing the burnt match into the window at his left.)* Do you want me to answer it?

AMY: I wish you would, Aubrey; it might be something about Pop. *(He crosses in front of the Morris-chair and up at the left of the center-table to the mirror over the mantelpiece, where he stands settling his tie and vest.* AMY *turns to the couch and gathers up his coat, then steps forward to the center-table and picks up his hat and the bandage that he took off his head.)*

AUBREY: *(Touching the plasters on his forehead.)* Does my head look all right?

AMY: *(Glancing at him, as she goes towards the hooks at the head of the cellar-stairs).* Yes, it's all right, Aubrey.

AUBREY: Wait a minute—*(He steps to her side and takes the carnation from the buttonhole of his overcoat, then steps back to the mirror and fixes it in his sack-coat.)*

AMY: Hurry up, Aubrey. *(The door-bell rings again.)*

AUBREY: *(Going out into the hallway).* All right—all right. *(*AMY *hangs the overcoat and hat up, then turns, opens the cellar-door, and tosses the bandage down the cellar-stairs. Then she crosses quickly to a point in front of the mantelpiece and listens intently.)*

GILL: *(At the front-door).* Good evenin'.

AUBREY: Good evening, sir.

GILL: Is this where Mr. Fisher lives?

AUBREY: This is Mr. Fisher's residence, yes, sir. What can I do for you?

GILL: Why, I got some things of his here that the boss ast me to leave.

AUBREY: Oh, just step inside for a minute. Getting a little colder I think. *(The front-door closes.)*

GILL: Well, we can look for it any time, now.

AUBREY: Will you just step in this way, please? *(*AUBREY *enters from the hallway.)* There's a gentleman here, Amy, with some things belonging to your Father. Just come right in. *(*AUBREY *comes forward a few steps at the left; and* GILL *enters.)*

GILL: Good evenin'.

AMY: Good evening.

AUBREY: This is my wife, Mrs. Piper.

GILL: *(Nodding)*. How do you do. *(*AMY *nods.)*

AUBREY: Mrs. Piper is Mr. Fisher's daughter. The rest of the folks have gone down to the hospital.

GILL: I see. *(Turning to* AMY*)*. Have you *heard* anything from the hospital yet?

AMY: Not yet, no.

AUBREY: We didn't know anything about it at all, till fifteen minutes ago.

GILL: It's too bad.

AUBREY: Those hospitals won't tell you anything.

AMY: Do you work with my Father?

GILL: No, ma'am, I'm a twister on the second floor. But, one of the machinist's-helpers that works with your Father knows I live out this way, so he ast me to stop by with these things on me way home. *(He crosses towards* AMY*, with a hat and overcoat, and a more or less discolored lunch-box.)*

AMY: *(Taking the things)*. Thanks ever so much.

GILL: There's just the <u>overcoat and hat,</u> and his lunch-box.

AMY: Thanks.

GILL: McMahon sez if he comes across anything else he'll let me know.

AMY: *(Crossing to the sofa with the things)*. No, I don't imagine there's anything else.

GILL: If there is, I'll bring it up.

AMY: Well, that's very nice of you; I'm ever so much obliged to you. *(She comes back towards* GILL*.)*

AUBREY: Who is this McMahon?

GILL: He's one of the machinist's-helpers down there.

AUBREY: I see.

AMY: Were you there when my Father was taken sick?

GILL: No, ma'am, I wasn't. I don't think there was anybody there, to tell you the truth. McMahon sez he was talkin' to him at a quarter of three, and he sez when he came back from the annex at three o'clock, he found Mr. Fisher layin' in front of number five.

AUBREY: *(With a suggestion of professionalism)*. Very likely a little touch of Angina Pectoria. *(*GILL *looks at him.)*

GILL: The doctor down there sez he thought it was a stroke.

AUBREY: Same thing.

AMY: Won't you sit down, Mr.—a—

GILL: No, thank you, ma'am, I can't stay; I've got to get along out home. (*There's a rapping out at the right. They all look in the direction of the kitchen.*)

AMY: Oh, I guess it's Mrs. Harbison—I'll go. (*She goes out at the right.*)

AUBREY: (*Crossing above* GILL *towards the right*). Don't stand out there talking, now, Amy, with nothing around you. (*Surveying himself in the buffet-mirror at the right.*) Do you live up this way, Governor?

GILL: No, sir, I live out Richmond way.

AUBREY: I see.

GILL: I take number thirty-two over Allegheny Avenue.

AUBREY: (*Turning and moving over towards the center-table.*) Too bad my car's laid up, I could run you out there.

GILL: Oh, that's all right; the trolley takes me right to the door.

AUBREY: I had to turn it in Thursday to have the valves ground.

AMY: (*Appearing in the kitchen-door*). I'm wanted on the telephone, Aubrey; I'll be right in. Will you excuse me for a minute?

GILL: That's all right, ma'am; I'm goin' right along me-self.

AUBREY: Very likely some word from the Hospital.

GILL: I hope it ain't any bad news.

AUBREY: Well, you've got to be prepared for most any-thing, Governor, when a man gets up around the old three-score mark.

GILL: That's true, a lot of them push off about that age.

AUBREY: Especially when a man's worked hard all his life.

GILL: Yes, I guess Mr. Fisher's worked pretty hard.

AUBREY: Not an excuse in the world for it, either.—I've said to him a thousand times if I've said to him once, "Well, Pop, when are you going to take the big rest?" "Oh," he'd say, "I'll have lots of time to rest when I'm through." "All right," I'd say, "go ahead; only let me tell you, Pop, you're going to be through ahead of schedule if you don't take it soon."

GILL: Well, I guess it comes pretty hard on a man that's been active all his life to quit all of a sudden.

AUBREY: Well, he wouldn't have to quit exactly.—I mean, he's a handy man; he could putter around the house.

There are lots of little things here and there that I'm not any too well satisfied with. *(He glances around the room.)*

GILL: Is Mr. Fisher's wife livin'?

AUBREY: Yes, she's here with us too.

GILL: Well, that makes it nice.

AUBREY: Well, it's a pretty big house here; so when I married last June, I said, "Come ahead, the more the merrier." *(He laughs a little.)*

GILL: 'Tis a pretty big house this.

AUBREY: Yes, they don't make them like this anymore, Governor. Put up by the McNeil people out here in Jenkintown.

GILL: Oh, yes.

AUBREY: They just put up the twenty of them—kind of sample houses—ten on that side and ten on this. Of course, these on this side have the southern exposure,—so a man's got to do quite a bit of wire-pulling to get hold of one of these.

GILL: You've got to do some wire-pullin' to get hold of *any* kind of a house these days.

AUBREY: Well, I have a friend here in town that's very close to the city architect, and he was able to fix it for me.

GILL: *(Glancing toward the window, at the left)*. It's a nice street.

AUBREY: Nice in summer.

GILL: I was surprised when I saw it, because when I ast a taxicab-driver down here where it was, he said he never heard of it.

AUBREY: *(Looking at him keenly)*. Never heard of Cresson Street?

GILL: He said not.

AUBREY: *(With pitying amusement)*. He must be an awful straw-ride.

GILL: I had to ast a police officer.

AUBREY: Well, I'll tell you, Governor,—I don't suppose they have many *calls* for taxicabs out this way. You see, most everybody in through here has his own *car*.

GILL: I see.

AUBREY: Some of them have a half dozen, for that matter. *(He laughs, a bit consequentially.)*

GILL: *(Starting for the parlor-doors)*. There certainly is plenty of them knockin' around.

AUBREY: All over the ice. *(Aubrey indicates the hall-door.)* This way, Governor.

GILL: (*Turning towards the hall-door*). Oh, excuse me.

AUBREY: (*Moving towards the hall-door*). Those doors go into the parlor.

GILL: I see. (*He turns at the hall-door*). A fellow was tellin' me over here in the cigar store that there was quite a smash-up about a half hour ago down here at Broad and Erie Avenue.

AUBREY: That so?

GILL: He sez there was some *nut* down there runnin' into everything in sight. He sez he even ran into the traffic-cop; and broke his arm. Can you imagine what they'll *do* to that guy, knockin' the traffic-cop down!

AUBREY: What was the matter with him, was he stewed?

GILL: *No,*—the fellow in the cigar store sez he was just a *nut*. He sez they didn't know where he got hold of this car; he sez it didn't belong to him. I guess he picked it up somewhere. They took it away from him and pinched him. (*Starting to go out.*) So I guess he won't be runnin' into anything else for a while.

AUBREY: (*Following him out*). Traffic's in pretty bad shape in this town right now.

GILL: Certainly is. Why, a man's not safe walkin' along the sidewalk, these days. I hope your wife'll hear some good news.

AUBREY: Well, while there's life there's hope, you know.

GILL: That's right. No use lookin' on the dark side of things. (AMY *enters from the right, with a wide-eyed, wan expression, and comes slowly down to the center-table.*)

AUBREY: Where do you get your car, Governor?

GILL: Why, I can get one right at the corner here, and transfer.

AUBREY: Oh, that's right, so you can. Well, we're ever so much obliged to you.

GILL: Don't mention it.

AUBREY: Good-night, sir.

GILL: Good-night. (*The door closes.*)

AUBREY: (*Coming in from the hall-door*). When did you come in, Amy? (*He stops to look at himself in the mantel-piece-mirror.*)

AMY: (*Without turning*). I came in the side-door; I thought that man'd be still here.

AUBREY: (*Coming down to her*). Well, Kid, what's the good word?

AMY: (*Breaking down*). Aubrey, Pop is dead. (*She buries*

her face in the lapel of his coat. He takes her in his arms, looks straight ahead, and there is a long pause—during which AMY *cries hard.)*

AUBREY: Don't let it get you, Honey—you have nothing to regret; and nothing to fear. The Kid from West Philly'll never go back on you,—you know that, don't you, Baby? *(She continues to cry.)* You know that, don't you, Amy? *(She doesn't answer him.)* Amy?

AMY: What?

AUBREY: You know I'm with you, don't you?

AMY: Yes. *(He kisses her hair affectionately.)*

AUBREY: Don't cry, Honey; the old man's better off than we are. He knows all about it now. *(He kisses her again; then detaches himself and moves over and down at the left of the center-table.)*

AMY: What do you think we ought to do, Aubrey?

AUBREY: There's nothing at all that you can do that I can see, Sweetheart; except to sit tight till the folks get back. They'll be down there themselves in a few minutes, and they'll know all about it.

AMY: They said that Pop died at a quarter of six.

AUBREY: Was that the Hospital on the telephone?

AMY: Yes.

AUBREY: *(Moving up to a point above the center-table again).* Something we ought to have in here, Amy; a telephone—not be letting the whole neighborhood in on our business. *(*AMY *leans on the back of the chair at the right and cries softly.)* Now, pull yourself together, Sweetheart. *(He crosses to her and puts his arm around her shoulders.)*

AMY: This is where Pop always used to sit in the evening.—It'll seem funny not to see him here anymore. *(She breaks down again.)*

AUBREY: *(After a slight pause).* The old gent had to go sometime. *(He passes back of her, comes forward at the right and stands, looking at the tip of his cigar.)* Your Mother'll have you and me to comfort her now. *(He strolls across below the center-table and stops, thinking profoundly.* AMY *sinks down on the chair dejectedly.)*

AMY: I don't know how Mom'll keep this house going now, just on Joe's pay.

AUBREY: Why don't you say something to your Mother about letting *us* come in here? She'll need a man in the house. And my salary'ud cover the rent.

AMY: Mom doesn't have to pay rent, Aubrey,—she owns this house. Pop left it to her. He made his will out the week after we were married. (AUBREY *looks at her keenly.*) Clara got him to do it.

AUBREY: Who's the executor, do you know?

AMY: Clara is. (AUBREY *nods comprehendingly.*)

AUBREY: (*Looking away off*). Too bad your Father didn't make *me* the executor of that will;—I could have saved him a lot of money. (*He replaces the cigar in his mouth.*)

AMY: I suppose he thought on account of Clara being the oldest.

AUBREY: I wonder why your Father never *liked* me.

AMY: Pop never said he didn't like you, Aubrey.

AUBREY: I always tried to be clubby with him. I used to slap him on the back whenever I spoke to him.

AMY: Pop was always very quiet.

AUBREY: And the Kid from West Philly had too much to say. Well,—forgive and forget.—It's all over now.—And the old man can be as quiet as he likes. (AMY *cries again, and there is a pause.* AUBREY *stands smoking.*)

AMY: (*Pulling herself together and getting up*). You haven't had anything to eat tonight yet, have you, Aubrey?

AUBREY: (*Coming out of his abstraction, and sauntering up at the left of the center-table.*) Don't worry about me, Sweetheart.

AMY: (*Going to the buffet-drawer at the right for an apron*). I'll get you something.

AUBREY: It'll be all the same at the finish,—whether I've had my dinner or not. (*He rests his fist on the table, throws his head back, and looks to the stars.*) "Sic transit gloria mundi." And we never get used to it. (*He moves across to the upper right-hand corner of the center-table.*) The paths of glory lead but to the grave. (*He stops again, leans on the table and looks out and away off.*) And yet we go on,—building up big fortunes—only to leave them to the generations yet unborn. Well, (*He moves forward to the chair at the right*)—so it goes. (*He sits down, throws one leg across his knee, and shakes his head up and down slowly.*) And so it will *always* go, I suppose. "Sic transit gloria mundi."

AMY: (*Standing at his right*). What does that mean, Aubrey, "Sic transit gloria mundi"?

AUBREY: (*Casually*). It's an old saying from the French—meaning, "we're here to-day, and gone tomorrow."

AMY: *(Looking out, wretchedly).* I'm worried about to-morrow, Aubrey. *(He looks at her.)*

AUBREY: What are you worried about, Sweetheart?

AMY: I mean Monday.

AUBREY: *(Extending his hand towards her).* Now,—"sufficient unto the day is the evil thereof,"—you know that, don't you, Baby? *(She takes his hand and moves over to the back of his chair.)*

AMY: But, you didn't have a license, Aubrey. And if that traffic-officer should be seriously injured——

AUBREY: Don't you worry about that, Sweetheart;—we're here today; and if he's seriously injured,—we'll know all about it Monday. *(The curtain commences to descend slowly.)* "Sic transit gloria mundi."

(The Curtain Falls)

ACT THREE

SCENE: Same as preceding Act—the following Monday, about four o'clock in the afternoon. MRS. FISHER is seated at the right of the center-table, in black, watching MR. ROGERS, the insurance agent, opposite her, writing on various papers. CLARA, also in mourning, is standing back of her Mother's chair, watching MR. ROGERS.

ROGERS: *(Handing MRS. FISHER an insurance receipt).* Now, will you just sign that, Mrs. Fisher. Right on that line there. *(He hands her his fountain-pen.)*

MRS. FISHER: *(After a sincere attempt to write with the fountain-pen).* It won't write.

CLARA: Press on it a bit, Mom.

MRS. FISHER: I *am* pressin' on it.

ROGERS: Just let me have it a second, Mrs. Fisher. *(She hands him the pen.)*

MRS. FISHER: I never saw one of them fountain-pens yet that'd write.

ROGERS: *(Holding the pen out and shaking it, in an attempt to force the ink forward.)* They cut up a little once in a while. *(MRS. FISHER looks keenly to see if her carpet is being stained.)*

MRS. FISHER: I gave one to my son the Christmas before last, and it's been in that drawer there from that day to this.

ROGERS: *(Handing her the pen again).* There we are. I think you'll find that all right.

MRS. FISHER: Right here?

ROGERS: That's right. *(He commences to collect his papers.)*

MRS. FISHER: *(Writing).* It's writin' now all right.

ROGERS: It's usually pretty satisfactory. *(She hands him the receipt, and he hands her another.)* And that one also, Mrs. Fisher, if you please.

MRS. FISHER: In the same place?

ROGERS: Yes; right on the dotted line. It's just a duplicate. *(She looks at him sharply, then signs it and hands it back to him; and he puts it into his wallet.* MRS. FISHER *looks distrustfully at the point of the fountain-pen.)*

MRS. FISHER: Here's the pen.

ROGERS: Thank you. *(He signs a check and looks at it.)*

MRS. FISHER: *(Half-turning towards the cellar-door).* See if that cellar-door is closed, Clara, I feel a draught from somewhere. *(CLARA goes and sees that the door is closed.)*

ROGERS: *(Handing a check).* There you are, Mrs. Fisher, one thousand dollars.

MRS. FISHER: Thank you. *(CLARA comes forward again.)*

ROGERS: *(Collecting his things).* That's money we like to pay, Mrs. Fisher, and money we don't like to pay.

MRS. FISHER: No, things are never very pleasant when this kind of money is bein' paid.

ROGERS: *(Rising, and putting his wallet into his inside-pocket.)* Well, at least, it doesn't make things any less pleasant, Mrs. Fisher.

MRS. FISHER: *(Rising).* No, I'm sure I don't know what a lot of folks'ud do without it.

ROGERS: Pretty hard to make a good many of them see it that way, Mrs. Fisher.

MRS. FISHER: *(Moving around to a point above the table).* Yes, I guess we don't think much about trouble when we're not havin' it.

ROGERS: Lot of people think they're never going to have trouble; *(*MRS. FISHER *shakes her head knowingly)* and never going to need a dollar.

MRS. FISHER: They're very foolish.

ROGERS: Very foolish indeed.

MRS. FISHER: Everybody'll have trouble if they live long enough.

ROGERS: Yes, indeed.

MRS. FISHER: Well now, what do I do with this check, Mr. Rogers?

ROGERS: Why, you can deposit it if you like, Mrs. Fisher, or have it cashed—just whatever you like.

CLARA: Frank'll get it cashed for you, Mom, downtown.

MRS. FISHER: I'm not used to thousand-dollar checks, you know, Mr. Rogers.

ROGERS: I'm not very used to them myself, Mrs. Fisher, except to pay them out to somebody else. (*He laughs a little.*)

MRS. FISHER: Well, will you take this, then, Clara, and give it to Frank Hyland?

CLARA: (*Advancing*). Yes; I'll give it to him to-night, Mom. (ROGERS *moves to the window at the left and takes a paper from his pocket.*)

MRS. FISHER: Don't go layin' it down somewhere, now, and forgettin' where you left it,—the way you're always doin' with your gloves.

CLARA: (*Crossing to the buffet where her purse is lying*). I'll put it in my purse here. (MRS. FISHER *comes forward at the right of the Morris-chair*).

ROGERS: (*Turning and coming back a little from the window*). Oh, by the way, Mrs. Fisher—would you give this to your son-in-law, Mr. Piper? (*He hands her the paper.*)

MRS. FISHER: What is it?

ROGERS: Why, it's a little explanation of some of the features of a very attractive *accident* policy that our company has brought out recently;—and I was talking to Mr. Piper about it the day I called for Mr. Fisher's policy. He seemed to be very much interested. In fact, I find that people are usually a little more susceptible to the advantages of a good insurance policy, when they actually see it being paid to somebody else. Now, that particular policy there—is a kind of combination of accident and life-insurance policy,—as well as disability and dividend features. In fact, we contend that there is no investment on the market today (CLARA *sits down in the arm-chair at the right window*) that offers the security or return that that particular policy described there does. The thing is really almost benevolent.

MRS. FISHER: How much is it for?

ROGERS: Why, we *have* them as low as ten thousand

dollars; but the policy that Mr. *Piper* was most interested in, was one of our fifty-*thousand*-dollar policies. (CLARA *laughs faintly, and her Mother looks over at her.*)

MRS. FISHER: (*Turning back to* ROGERS). It's no wonder she's laughin', Mr. Rogers; for if you knew Mr. Piper as well as she knows him, you'd laugh too. He has just about as much notion of takin' out a fifty-thousand-dollar insurance policy as I have. And just about as much chance of payin' for it.

ROGERS: Why, he seemed very much interested, Mrs. Fisher.

MRS. FISHER: He was showin' off, Mr. Rogers, what he's always doin'. Why, that fellow don't make enough salary in six months—to pay one year's premium on a policy like this. So, if I was you, I'd just put this paper right back in my pocket, for you're only wastin' it to be givin' it to him.

ROGERS: (*Taking the paper*). Seems rather funny that he'd talk about it at all,—I mean, if he had no idea of taking it.

MRS. FISHER: He never has any idea when *he* talks, Mr. Rogers—that's the reason he talks so much; it's no effort. That's the reason he's gettin' thirty-two dollars a week, down here in the Pennsylvania Freight Office. And it's a wonder to me they give him *that* much, after listenin' to him for five minutes.

ROGERS: It's particularly funny, because I spoke to Mr. Piper first about one of our ten-thousand-dollar policies; but he didn't seem to be interested in anything but the *fifty*-thousand-dollar life and *accident* policy.

MRS. FISHER: Well, I can understand him being interested in the accident part of it, after last Monday. I suppose you heard about him runnin' into everything here last Monday evening, didn't you? Down here at Braod and Erie Avenue.

ROGERS: Oh, was that Mr. Piper?

MRS. FISHER: That was him. He ran into a traffic-cop, and broke his arm.

ROGERS: Yes, I saw that in the paper; but the name was spelled Pepper in my paper.

MRS. FISHER: Well, it was spelled Piper in our paper.

ROGERS: Well, what did they do about that, Mrs. Fisher?

MRS. FISHER: Why, he's down there today, at the Magistrate's, gettin' his hearin'. God knows what they'll do with him; for he didn't own the car he was drivin', and didn't have a license to drive it.

ROGERS: Well, that's very unfortunate.

MRS. FISHER: But, he'll very likely tire the Magistrate out so with his talk, that the man'll discharge him just to get rid of him.

ROGERS: *(Laughing)*. I'm afraid Mr. Piper won't want to see *me* today when he comes back.

MRS. FISHER: He may not *be* back, for six months.

ROGERS: *(Starting for the hall-door)*. Oh, well, let's hope it won't be anything like that. Good-afternoon, Mrs. Hyland.

CLARA: *(Rising)*. Good-afternoon, Mr. Rogers. *(He goes out into hallway.)*

ROGERS: Good-afternoon, Mrs. Fisher.

MRS. FISHER: Good-afternoon, Mr. Rogers. *(Calling after him from the hall-door.)* Will you close that vestibule-door tight after you, Mr. Rogers——

ROGERS: Yes, I will, Mrs. Fisher.

MRS. FISHER: This hallway gets awful cold when that vestibule-door isn't shut tight. *(A door closes in the hallway, then another door. And then MRS. FISHER turns, removing her glasses, and moves towards the mantelpiece.)* I'm glad you were here; I don't understand them insurance papers. *(She puts her glasses on the mantelpiece.)*

CLARA: *(Moving to the chair at the right of the center-table)*. What do you think you'll do with that money, Mom?

MRS. FISHER: Why, I think I'll just put it into a bank somewhere; everything is paid. And then I'll have something in my old days. *(She comes forward to the chair at the left of the center-table.)*

CLARA: Do you want me to put the check right into the bank?

MRS. FISHER: No,—I want to see the money first. *(She sits down.)* But, can you imagine that clown, Clara, takin' up that man's time talkin' about a fifty-thousand-dollar policy; and him in debt to his eyes.

CLARA: *(Sitting down)*. What does it matter, Mom; you can never change a man like Piper.

MRS. FISHER: No, but I hate to see him makin' such a fool of Amy; and of all of us,—with his name in all the papers, and the whole city laughin' at him.

CLARA: He doesn't mind that, he likes it.

MRS. FISHER: But, Amy's married to him, Clara,—that's the trouble.

CLARA: Amy doesn't mind it either, Mom, as long as it's Aubrey.

MRS. FISHER: Well, she ought to mind it, if she's got any pride.

CLARA: *(Looking straight ahead, wistfully).* She's in love with him, Mom—she doesn't see him through the same eyes that other people do.

MRS. FISHER: You're always talkin' about love; you give me a pain.

CLARA: Well, don't you think she is?

MRS. FISHER: How do *I* know whether she is or not? I don't know anything about when people are in love; except that they act silly—most everybody that I ever knew that was. I'm sure *she* acted silly enough when she took *him.*

CLARA: She might have taken worse, Mom. *(MRS. FISHER looks at her; and CLARA meets the look.)* He does his best. He works every day, and he gives her his money; and nobody ever heard of him looking at another woman.

MRS. FISHER: But, he's such a rattle-brain, Clara.

CLARA: Oh, there are lots of things that are harder to put up with in a man than that, Mom. I know he's terribly silly, and has too much to say, and all that, but,—I don't know, I feel kind of sorry for him sometimes. He'd so love to be important; and, of course, he never will be.

MRS. FISHER: Well, I swear I don't know how Amy stands the everlastin' talk of him. He's been here now only a week, and I'm tellin' you, Clara, I'm nearly light-headed. I'll be glad when they go.

CLARA: I'd rather have a man that talked too much than one of those silent ones. Honestly, Mom, I think sometimes if Frank Hyland doesn't *say* something I'll go out of my mind.

MRS. FISHER: What do you want him to say?

CLARA: Anything; just so I'd know he had a voice.

MRS. FISHER: He's too sensible a man, Clara, to be talkin' when he has nothin' to say.

CLARA: I don't think it's so sensible, Mom, never to have anything to say.

MRS. FISHER: Well, lots of men are that way in the house.

CLARA: But there are usually children there,—it isn't so bad.

MRS. FISHER: Well, if Amy ever has any children, and they have as much to say as their Father, I don't know what'll become of her.

CLARA: She'll get along some way; people always do.

MRS. FISHER: Leanin' on somebody else,—*that's* how they get along.

CLARA: There are always the Leaners and the Bearers, Mom. But, if she's in love with the man she's married to,— and he's in love with her,—and there are children——

MRS. FISHER: I never saw a married woman so full of love.

CLARA: I suppose that's because I never had any of it, Mom. (*Her Mother looks over at her.*)

MRS. FISHER: Don't your man love you? (CLARA *looks straight out, shaking her head slowly.*)

CLARA: He loved someone else before he met me.

MRS. FISHER: How do you know?

CLARA: The way he talks sometimes.

MRS. FISHER: Why didn't he marry her?

CLARA: I think he lost her. I remember he said to me one time—"Always be kind, Clara, to anybody that loves you; for," he said, "a person always loses what he doesn't appreciate. And," he said, "it's a *terrible* thing to lose love." He said, "You never realize what it was worth until you've lost it." I think that's the reason he gives Piper a hand once in a while,—because he sees Amy's in love with him, and he wants to make it easy for her; because I have an idea he made it pretty hard for the woman that loved him. (MRS. FISHER *leans back and rocks slowly.*)

MRS. FISHER: Well, a body can't have everything in this world, Clara. (*There is a pause: and* CLARA *touches her handkerchief to her eyes. Then the front-door closes softly, and* MRS. FISHER *gets up.*) Maybe this is them now. (*She moves up to the hall-door.* AMY *comes in, looking wearied. She is in mourning.*) What happened, Amy? (AMY *wanders down to the chair at left of table and sits down, and her Mother follows her down at the left.*) Where's Aubrey Piper?

AMY: He's coming.

CLARA: Is Frank with him?

AMY: Yes.

MRS. FISHER: Where are they?

AMY: Aubrey stopped at the corner to get some cigars.

CLARA: What happened down there?

AMY: Oh, a lot of talk.

MRS. FISHER: (*Leaning towards her, solicitously*) Are you sick?

AMY: No.

MRS. FISHER: Well, you look sick.

AMY: I have a headache; we had to wait there so long.

CLARA: Why don't you take off your hat? (AMY *starts to remove her hat.*)

MRS. FISHER: Will I make you a cup of tea?

AMY: No, don't bother, Mom; I can get it myself.

MRS. FISHER: (*Going towards the right door*) It won't take a minute. (AMY *takes her handkerchief from her bag.* CLARA *glances toward the right door.*)

CLARA: (*In a subdued tone*) What did they do to Aubrey?

AMY: (*Confidentially*) Fined him—a thousand dollars. Don't let Mom know. Recklessness, and driving without a license.

CLARA: Did Frank pay it?

AMY: Yes; I told him I'd be responsible for it.

CLARA: How can *you* ever pay him a thousand dollars, Amy?

AMY: I can go back to work for a while. I can always go back to the office. (CLARA *moves.*) Well, it was either that or six months in jail. And Frank said we couldn't have that.

CLARA: Was there anybody there that we know?

AMY: I didn't see anybody.

CLARA: Was the traffic-cop there?

AMY: Yes, there were fourteen witnesses. The traffic-cop's arm was broken. The fellow that owned the car was there, too.

CLARA: When do you think you'll go back to work?

AMY: (*After a troubled pause*) As soon as I get settled. There's no use in my going back now; I'd only have to be leaving again pretty soon. (CLARA *looks at her.*)

CLARA: Does Mom know?

AMY: No, I haven't told her. (*There is a pause.* CLARA *gets up; and, with a glance toward the kitchen-door, moves around and crosses towards the left, above the center-table. She stops back of* AMY'S *chair and looks at her for a second compassionately; then she steps forward and lays her hand on her shoulder.*)

CLARA: Don't worry about it, Amy. (*She moves towards the window at the left.*) I wish to God it was me. (*There is a murmur of voices at the front-door; then* AUBREY'S *laugh rings through the house.* AMY *rises quickly, picks up her hat from the table, and signifies to* CLARA, *with a gesture, that she will go into the parlor.* CLARA *moves across in front of the center-table.*)

AUBREY: *(Entering, all dressed up, and with a little flourish of his cane to* CLARA*)* Hello, Clara!

CLARA: Hello.

AUBREY: *(Hanging up his hat and cane on the hooks at the head of the cellar-stairs)* Where's Amy?

CLARA: She's just gone in the parlor there. *(*FRANK HYLAND *appears in the hall-door and comes forward to the chair at the left of the table.)*

HYLAND: Hello! *(*AUBREY *crosses to the parlor, removing his gloves.)*

AUBREY: You in there, Amy?

AMY: Yes. *(He goes into the parlor; and* CLARA *moves across above the center-table to* HYLAND'S *left.)*

CLARA: How is it you didn't go back to the office, Frank? *(*AUBREY *hurries out of the parlor again and across to the hooks, removing his overcoat.* MRS. FISHER *appears in the kitchen-door, and stands, looking at him.)*

HYLAND: It was so late when we got through down there I didn't think it was worth while.

AUBREY: Hello, Mother.

MRS. FISHER: I see you're back again. *(He hangs up his overcoat.)*

AUBREY: Right on the job, Mother,—doing business at the old stand. *(He takes the carnation from the overcoat and fastens it in the sack-coat.* MRS. FISHER *comes forward at the right.)*

HYLAND: Hello, Mother!

MRS. FISHER: Hello, Frank.

HYLAND: You're lookin' good, Mother.

MRS. FISHER: Well, I'm not feelin' good, Frank, I can tell you that.

HYLAND: What's the trouble?

MRS. FISHER: Why, I'm troubled to think of all the bother you've been put to in this business.

HYLAND: Don't worry about that, Mother—we've got to have a little bother once in a while.

MRS. FISHER: What did they do down there today, Frank?

HYLAND: Why,—they——

AUBREY: *(Coming forward, adjusting the carnation)* I'll tell you what they *tried* to do.

MRS. FISHER: Oh, shut up, you! Nobody wants to hear what you've got to say about it at all. *(*CLARA *crosses above the Morris-chair and looks out the window at the left.)*

AUBREY: Well, I *told* them down there what I had to say about it, whether they wanted to hear it or not. (*He goes up to the mirror at the back.*)

MRS. FISHER: I guess they let you go just to get rid of you. (*He turns to his left and looks at her; then starts for the parlor-doors.*)

CLARA: Why don't you take your coat off, Frank? (AUBREY *goes into the parlor, looking back over his shoulder at his Mother-in-law, who has not taken her eyes off him.*)

HYLAND: (*Looking at his watch*). I've got to meet that fellow at North Philadelphia Station at four o'clock.

MRS. FISHER: (*Coming a step or two nearer to the table*). What did they say to that fellow down there today, Frank?

HYLAND: Why, nothing very much, Mother—just a little reprimand, for driving without a license.

MRS. FISHER: Didn't they fine him at all, for breakin' that man's arm?

HYLAND: A little bit, not very much.—You see, that was more or less in the nature of an accident.

MRS. FISHER: How much was it?

HYLAND: Now, Mrs. Fisher, as Aubrey says, "It's all washed up, and signed on the dotted line." (*He laughs.*)

MRS. FISHER: How much was it, Clara, do *you* know?

CLARA: He hasn't told me, Mom.

MRS. FISHER: Well, I'll bet you paid it, Frank, whatever it was; for I know he didn't have it. (*She sits at the right of the table.*)

HYLAND: (*Rising*). Well, you know, it's getting near Christmas, Mother—got to give some kind of a little present here and there.

MRS. FISHER: Well, I don't think it's right that you should have to be goin' around payin' for that fellow's mistakes.

HYLAND: (*Standing up a bit toward the hall-door, putting on his gloves*). That's about all any of us is doin' in this world, Mother—payin' for somebody's mistakes—and somebody payin' for ours, I suppose.

MRS. FISHER: Well, it don't seem right to me.

HYLAND: Well, I'll tell you, Mother—when you've made a couple of mistakes that *can't* be paid for, why, then you try to forget about them by payin' for the kind that can. (*He makes a little pallid sound of amusement. And there is a pause.* MRS. FISHER *rocks back and forth.*)

CLARA: Will you be home for dinner to-night, Frank?

HYLAND: *(coming suddenly out of an abstraction).* What'd you say?

CLARA: I say, will you be home for dinner to-night?

HYLAND: *(Picking up his hat from the table).* I don't think so; I'll very likely have to go to dinner with *him. (He goes towards the hall-door.)* Good-bye, Mother.

MRS. FISHER: Good-bye, Frank.

HYLAND: *(Going out into the hallway).* Good-bye, dear. *(CLARA wanders up to the hall-door and looks out after him).*

CLARA: Good-bye. *(The vestibule-door is heard to close. And there is a significant pause; during which CLARA stands looking wistfully out into the hallway).*

MRS. FISHER: *(Rising, and moving to a point above the table).* Listen, Clara. *(CLARA comes towards her).*

CLARA: What?

MRS. FISHER: Didn't he tell you how much they fined Aubrey?

CLARA: No, he didn't, Mom, really.

MRS. FISHER: Didn't *she* tell you, while I was out puttin' the tea on?

CLARA: *(Moving forward to the chair at the left of the table).* Well now, what does it matter, Mom? You won't have to pay it. *(She sits down.)*

MRS. FISHER: Well, I'll find out; it'll very likely be in the evening paper.

CLARA: Well, I wouldn't say anything to Amy about it, even if it is; she has enough to bother her now.

MRS. FISHER: Well, she brought it on herself if she has:— nobody could tell her anything.

CLARA: Well, there's nothing can be done by fighting with her, Mom.

MRS. FISHER: *(With conviction).* There's nothing can be done by *anything,* Clara,—when once the *main* thing is done. And that's the marriage. That's where all the trouble starts—gettin' married.

CLARA: If there were no marriages, Mom, there'd be no world.

MRS. FISHER: *(Moving around to the chair at the right of the table again).* Oh, everybody sez that!—if there were no marriages there'd be no world.

CLARA: Well, would there?

MRS. FISHER: Well, what if there wouldn't? *(She sits down.)* Do you think it'd be any worse than it is now? I think there'll be no world pretty soon, anyway, the way things are goin'. A lot of whiffets gettin' married, and not two cents to their names, and then throwin' themselves on their people to keep them. They're so full of love before they're married. You're about the only one I've *heard* talkin' about love *after* they were married. It's a wonder to me you have a roof over you; for they never have, with that kind of talk. Like the two in the parlor there—that has to *kiss* each other, every time they meet on the floor. *(She bristles for a second or two; and then there is a silence.)*

CLARA: *(Quietly)*. Amy's going to have a child, Mom. *(Her Mother looks at her.)*

MRS. FISHER: How do you know?

CLARA: She told me so.

MRS. FISHER: *(Softening a bit)*. Why didn't she tell me?

CLARA: I suppose she thought it'd start a fight.

MRS. FISHER: *(Indignant again)*. I don't know why it'd start a fight; *I* never fight with anybody; except him: and I wouldn't fight with *him* only for his impudence.

CLARA: Has Amy said anything to you about coming in here to live?

MRS. FISHER: She said something to me the night your Father was laid out, but I wasn't payin' much attention to her.

CLARA: I think you ought to let her come in here, Mom. *(Her Mother looks at her)*. She'd be company for you, now that Pop is gone. And you don't know what day Joe might take a notion to get married.

MRS. FISHER: What's changed *your* ideas so much about lettin' her come in here? You were very much against it when she was married.

CLARA: I'd be against it now, if things around here were the way they were then. You didn't even own this house, Mom, when Amy was married; it was Pop's; and I knew if anything ever happened to him, and there was no will,—you might not find it so easy to order anybody out of it.

MRS. FISHER: It isn't that I'd mind lettin' Amy come in here, Clara,—but I wouldn't like to please him; for I know the first thing *I'd* know, he'd very likely be tellin' somebody that he'd let *me* come in. (CLARA *smiles faintly*). Oh, I wouldn't put it past him; he's told bigger lies than that. And if I ever found out that he said *that*,—he'd go out of here inside of five minutes, bag and baggage. *(The front door-bell rings.)* See who that is, Clara. *(They rise; and* CLARA *goes out—into the hallway, and* MRS. FISHER *crosses below the table to the parlor-doors.)* Are you in there, Amy? *(She opens the door.)*

AMY: Yes; what is it, Mom?

MRS. FISHER: This kettle's boilin' out here, if you want a cup of tea.

AMY: All right, Mom, I'll be right out.

MRS. FISHER: *(Crossing to the kitchen-door).* I'm goin' to make it right away, so you'd better come out if you want it hot. *(She goes out at the right.)*

AMY: *(Coming out of parlor).* Do you want a cup of tea, Aubrey? *(She crosses to the mirror over the mantelpiece and touches her hair.)*

AUBREY: *(Coming out of the parlor).* No, thanks, Honey, I don't care for any just now. *(He strolls to the hall-door, glances out, then moves to* AMY'S *side and puts his hands on her shoulders and kisses her affectionately. Then he pats her on the shoulder. She moves towards the kitchen-door.)*

AUBREY: *(Patting her hand).* Everything'll be all right, Kid. You know me. *(She goes out into the kitchen, and he settles himself at the mirror over the buffet at the right).*

CLARA: *(In the hallway).* Yes, I think it is myself. *(Appearing in the hall-door.)* Just come right in, I'll call my Mother. Is she out in the kitchen, Aubrey?

AUBREY: *(Turning).* Yes, she's getting some tea. *(GILL appears in the hall-door.)*

GILL: Well, you needn't bother, Ma'am, if she's busy. I just wanted to leave this watch.

AUBREY: How do you do.

GILL: How do you do. *(CLARA stops and looks back at the watch.)*

AUBREY: And how is the young man?

GILL: I can't complain.

CLARA: Is that my Father's watch?

GILL: Yes, Ma'am. Are you Mr. Fisher's daughter?

CLARA: Yes. Close that door, Aubrey, will you?— I don't want Mom to see it. *(To* GILL.) I'd rather my Mother wouldn't see it. *(She takes the watch, and* AUBREY *closes the kitchen-door.)*

GILL: That's right.

CLARA: I believe she gave him this watch when they were married. *(AUBREY comes forward again, at the right.)*

GILL: Yes, it'd make her feel bad.

CLARA: Thanks ever so much.

GILL: McMahon didn't notice it when he was gettin' the rest of Mr. Fisher's things together.

CLARA: I see.

GILL: He said it was hangin' under the time-chart, back of number five.

AUBREY: This is the gentleman that brought Pop's lunch-box home.

CLARA: Oh, is that so?

GILL: I stopped by the day Mr. Fisher died.

CLARA: Did you work with my father?

GILL: No, Ma'am; I'm a twister; but I live out this way.

AUBREY: How is it you're not working today, Governor?

GILL: Mondays and Tuesdays is my earlies as a rule.

AUBREY: I see.

GILL: But the hunkies don't always get the stuff up to us. You got to keep right after them. Well, I guess I'll be gettin' along. *(He starts for the parlor-doors, then remembers that that is not the way out, and turns to his left towards the hall-door.)*

CLARA: I'm ever so much obliged to you, for bringing this watch up.

GILL: *(Turning to her, at the hall-door)*. Oh, that's all right. I'm only sorry for the reason I have to do it.

CLARA: Yes, it was very sad.

GILL: Mr. Fisher was a hard-workin' man.

CLARA: I suppose he worked *too* hard, for his age.

GILL: Yes, I guess he did.

CLARA: You couldn't stop him, though

GILL: No, that's what your brother-in-law here was sayin' the day I was here. He was tellin' me about all the times *he* tried to get him to quit, and take a rest. *(AUBREY turns to the buffet-mirror)*. But, I guess when a man's worked as hard all his life as Mr. Fisher did, it ain't so easy for him to quit.

CLARA: No, I guess not.

GILL: *(Stepping a little forward again)*. *I* didn't know that was you, Mr. Piper, that was in that automobile smash-up that I was tellin' you about that day I was here.

AUBREY: *(Turning)*. That so?

GILL: I didn't know it till I saw your picture in the paper the next day.

AUBREY: What paper did you see it in?

GILL: I saw it in the Record.

AUBREY: Wasn't a very good picture of me, was it?

GILL: I knew it was you, though, the minute I saw it.

AUBREY: A friend of mine loaned me his car while mine was laid up, and something went wrong with the steering-gear.

GILL: How did you make out about that traffic-cop?

AUBREY: Oh, I squared that up all right.

CLARA: Where do you live up here, Mr. a—

GILL: I live out Richmond way. I'd like to get a house over this way more, on account of bein' a little nearer my work, but I don't see much chance.

CLARA: No, I don't know of any vacant houses around here right now.

GILL: No, your brother-in-law was tellin' me about the time *he* had gettin' hold of *this* one. (AUBREY *turns to the buffet-mirror again and smooths his toupé with considerable precision.*) Well, I'll be gettin' along. (*He starts out into the hallway.*)

CLARA: (*With a bitter look over her shoulder at* AUBREY, *and following* GILL *out into the hallway*). Well, thanks, ever so much, Mr. a— (*She puts the watch back of the statuette on the little stand at the left of the mantelpiece.*)

GILL: Don't mention it.

CLARA: I'm sure Mother'll be glad to have this watch. (AUBREY *turns and looks after them. Then, with a glance toward the kitchen-door, he moves carefully to the mantelpiece and tries to see what is going on at the front-door.*)

GILL: Yes; she might as well have it as one of them hunkies down there.

CLARA: Can you open it?

GILL: Yes, I got it. Good-bye.

CLARA: Good-bye; and thank you.

GILL: You're welcome. (*The front-door closes; and* AUBREY *glides hastily for the parlor-doors, in an attempt to avoid* CLARA;—*but just as he reaches the parlor-doors, she appears in the hall-door, and, with a quick glance toward the kitchen-door, comes forward to the back of the Morris-chair.*)

CLARA: Come here, Aubrey, I want to talk to you. (*He turns towards her, with an attempt at nonchalance.*) What do you mean by telling people that this is your house?

AUBREY: I didn't tell anybody it was my house.

CLARA: You *must* have told this man, or he wouldn't have said so.

AUBREY: What do you think I am, a liar?

CLARA: Yes, I do; one of the best I know.

AUBREY: Well, ask Amy what I said to him, she was here when I was talking to him.

CLARA: *(Before he has finished speaking).* I don't have to ask anybody anything!—you were lying to him here to-day, right in front of me.

AUBREY: *(With a shade of challenge in his manner).* What'd I say?

CLARA: That you'd fixed the automobile thing up.

AUBREY: It's fixed up, isn't it?

CLARA: *You* didn't fix it up. *(There is a slight pause, during which* AUBREY, *his dignity considerably outraged, moves forward and crosses in front of her to the front of the center-table, where he stops.* CLARA *moves down at the right of the Morris-chair to a point near him.)* You'd have gone to jail for six months only for Frank Hyland. And telling this man that you tried to persuade Pop to stop working.

AUBREY: *(Over his left shoulder).* So I did.

CLARA: When?

AUBREY: I didn't say it to him. But I told Amy he ought to stop. And I think he'd be right here to-day if he'd taken my advice.

CLARA: He wouldn't be right here to-day if he'd stopped expecting *you* to keep him. *(He moves further over to the right; and she follows him.)* And now, listen to me, Aubrey; I want to talk seriously to you. You've made a lot of trouble for us since you've been in this family; and I want you to stop it. There's no reason my husband, because he happens to have a few dollars, should be going around paying *your* bills.

AUBREY: *(Half-turning to her.)* What do you want me to do?

CLARA: I want you to stop telling *lies;* for that's about all everything you do amounts to. Trying to make people believe you're something that you're not;—when if you'd just stop your talking and your showing-off, you *might* be the thing that you're trying to make them believe you are. *(She glances toward the kitchen-door, and then speaks to him again, in a slightly lower tone.)* Your wife's going to have a child one of these days, Aubrey, and you want to pull yourself together and try to be sensible, like the man of a family *should* be. You're smart enough;—there's no reason why a fellow like you should be living in two rooms over a barber shop. I should think you'd have more respect for your wife. (*She turns and moves a few steps up towards the kitchen-door.*)

AUBREY: A man doesn't stand much chance of getting ahead, Clara, when the boss has got a grudge against him.

CLARA: (*Turning sharply to her right, and moving to the upper right-hand corner of the center-table*). Well, stop your silly talk, and get rid of that carnation, and the boss might get rid of his grudge. (*She glances toward the kitchen-door again, leans across the table towards him, and lowers her voice.*) But, what I wanted to tell you was this, Aubrey,—I've asked Mom to let you and Amy come in here; and she sez she wouldn't mind it only that she knows that the first thing she'd *hear* is that you'd told someone that you'd taken *her* in. And, you see, that's exactly what you've done already,—to this man that brought the watch. If I told Mom that there'd be war.

AUBREY: Are you going to tell her?

CLARA: (*With authoritative levelness*). I'm going to put that up to you. And the very first time I hear that you've told anybody that this is *your* house,—I'll see to it that you'll get a house that *will* be your own. (AUBREY *smiles, a bit smugly, and looks at her out of the sides of his eyes.*)

AUBREY: I guess your Mother'ud have something to say about that, Clara.

CLARA: (*With a measured evenness*). Well, the only thing that needs to worry you, is what *I'll* have to say about it. (AUBREY'S *smugness begins to fade—into a questioning narrowness.*) This is my house—Pop left it to me; so that Mom'ud always have a roof over her. For he knew how long she'd have it if Amy ever got round her. And if Amy ever got hold of it, he knew what she'd do if it ever came to a choice between you and Mom.

AUBREY: What are you doing, kidding me? (CLARA *holds his eyes steadily for a fraction of a second.*)

CLARA: I'm giving you a tip;—see that you keep it to yourself. (AUBREY *withdraws his eyes slowly and looks straight out, weighing his new bit of intelligence carefully in his mind.*) Be wise, now, Aubrey—you've got a chance to sit *in* here and live like a human being; and if you throw it away, you'll have nobody to blame but yourself. *(There is a sound at the front-door of a newspaper being thrown into the vestibule, and a man's voice says, "Paper!" Then the front-door is heard to close.)* Open that door there, Mom'll be wondering what it's doing shut. *(She crosses up to the hall-door and goes out for the newspaper.* AUBREY *stands for a second thinking; and then* AMY *opens the kitchen-door and comes in. She glances about the room.)*

AMY: Where's Clara, Aubrey?

AUBREY: I think she's out on the front porch. *(AMY glances toward the hall-door, then turns to her husband.)* How are you feeling?

AMY: All right, I just had some tea. Listen, Aubrey,— *(She takes hold of the lapels of his coat.)* Mom said we could come in here to live.

AUBREY: Yes, I got Clara to fix it up.

AMY: She said we could have *my* room.

AUBREY: Is it a front room?

AMY: No, it's that one at the head of the stairs.

AUBREY: Will we put that bureau of ours in there?

AMY: I think the one that's in there is better-looking. Let's go up and see. *(She starts up towards the hall-door.)*

AUBREY: *(Following her).* You look nice in black, Amy.

AMY: *(Glancing in the mantelpiece-mirror as she passes it).* This is the dress that Clara gave me. *(CLARA appears in the hall-door with the evening paper in her hand.)*

CLARA: It's in the paper here about that trial today. *(AMY takes the paper.)* Keep it out of sight and don't let Mom see it.

AMY: *(Going out the hall-door and to her left up the stairs).* I'll take it upstairs. *(CLARA moves down towards the center-table, and* AUBREY *crosses above her towards the hall-door. As he passes her he excludes her with a look.)*

AUBREY: *(Calling after* AMY *as he starts up the stairs).* Has it got my picture in it? *(CLARA looks after him, rather hopelessly.* MRS. FISHER *comes in from the kitchen and moves down to the buffet at the right for her knitting-bag.)*

MRS. FISHER: You goin' to stay here for supper to-night, Clara?

CLARA: Yes, I might as well, Mom; Frank won't be home. I think I'll run in next door and tell Bertha I won't be home. *(She starts towards the kitchen-door.)*

MRS. FISHER: *(Crossing up to the mantelpiece for her spectacles)*. Yes, you'd better; she'll be expectin' you. Put somethin' around you.

CLARA: *(Stopping at the hooks at the head of the cellar-stairs)*. Is there something here?

MRS. FISHER: Put that old raincoat of Joe's around you; it's good enough. *(She moves forward to the chair at the right of the center-table.)* And go to the side-door, Clara; and don't be bringin' Mrs. Harbison to the front. *(She sits down and puts on her spectacles; and CLARA shakes the old raincoat out and puts it around her shoulders.)* I told Amy she could have that side room upstairs.

CLARA: She might as well be using it, Mom.

MRS. FISHER: But I know I'm not goin' to hit it with *him*.

CLARA: Well, it's better to be fighting than lonesome, Mom. *(She goes out at the right, and MRS. FISHER takes a purple sweater that she's working on, out of the knitting-bag. A door out at the right closes after CLARA. MRS. FISHER commences to knit, when suddenly there is a shout of laughter from AUBREY upstairs. MRS. FISHER freezes instantly into a stony stillness, and listens narrowly. There is another gale of laughter from AUBREY, and this decides MRS. FISHER. She puts her knitting back into the bag, very definitely, puts the bag on the table, gets up and marches resolutely across in front of the table and up to the hall-door. Just as she reaches the hall-door, with the ostensible purpose of reminding AUBREY that this is not his house, there is another roar from him. AMY can be heard laughing this time, also. MRS. FISHER subsides, and thinks. She appears to suddenly realize the futility of all remonstrances against the irresponsibility of AUBREY; and, after a thoughtful pause, to accept the situation. And as she moves back across the room, in front of the mantelpiece, to resume her chair at the right of the table, she seems a little older. Just as she reaches a point above the center-table, the front-door closes, with a bang. She starts nervously, and steps back to the mantelpiece to peer out into the hallway.)*

MRS. FISHER: Is that you, Joe?

JOE: *(From the hallway)*. Yes.

MRS. FISHER: *(Continuing to her chair at the right of the table)*. It's a wonder you wouldn't take the door off the hinges, and be done with it. (JOE *hurries in from the hallway.*)

JOE. How did they make out down there to-day, Mom? *(He tosses the evening paper onto the center-table, and continues on over and up to the hooks at the head of the cellar-stairs, to hang up his hat and overcoat.)*

MRS. FISHER: *(Sitting down).* Who do you mean, Aubrey Piper?

JOE: Yes. Are they back yet?

MRS. FISHER: They're upstairs.

JOE: What'd they do to him?

MRS. FISHER: They fined him.

JOE: How much?

MRS. FISHER: *(Taking her knitting out of the bag).* I don't know; they wouldn't tell me. Frank paid it. But, I'll find out; it'll very likely be in the evening paper. *(JOE comes forward to the center-table.)*

JOE: *(Picking up the paper from the table.)* It isn't in this paper, I looked.

MRS. FISHER: I'll find out.

JOE: But there's something else in to-night's paper, Mom.

MRS. FISHER: *(Knitting).* What?

JOE: *(Indicating a certain point on the paper).* Just cast your eyes on this, right here.

MRS. FISHER: *(Looking casually).* What is it?

JOE: *(Reading).* "Philadelphia Youth Makes Important Chemical Discovery. Mr. Joseph Fisher of North Philadelphia Perfects Rust-Preventive Solution." *(He gives his Mother a squeeze and a kiss.)*

MRS. FISHER: *(Startled, and giving him a little slap).* Stop it, Joe! *(He laughs exultantly, strikes the palms of his hands together, and strides across above the table towards the left.)* Did they buy the thing from you, Joe?

JOE: *(Turning to her, at the left of the center-table).* One hundred thousand dollars, Mother! They signed for it this afternoon in the lawyer's office. *(He becomes aware that the shoe-lace of his right shoe is untied, and puts his foot up on the chair to tie it.)*

MRS. FISHER: *(Leaning towards him).* The Meyers and Stevens people?

JOE: Yeh. They sent for me to come over there this afternoon about two o'clock, so I knocked off and got hold of Farley right away, and we went over there. And they had the contracts all drawn up and everything.

MRS. FISHER: What did you say about a hundred thousand dollars, Joe?

JOE: That's what they paid for it this afternoon, on account;—(*He starts across above the center-table and up to the hooks again at the right, removing his coat*) then they're to market it for me from their laboratories, and give *me* half the net.

MRS. FISHER: (*Talking over her right shoulder*). What's the net?

JOE. (*Hanging his coat up*). Whatever's left after all expenses are paid. (MRS. FISHER *tries to encompass the situation.*)

MRS. FISHER: I guess they'll see that there ain't much left, won't they?

JOE: (*Coming forward again to the center-table*). Why, there'll be a fortune out of this thing, Mom. Have you any idea what a rust-preventive means as an industrial chemical problem? Why, they'll make a million dollars out of this, within the next five years. (*He moves over to the left, removing his tie.*)

MRS. FISHER: Well, how much of that are you goin' to get, Joe?

JOE: I'll get the same as they get, that's the contract.

MRS. FISHER: A million dollars?

JOE: Easy, I got a hundred thousand today. (MRS. FISHER *shifts her eyes and tries to concentrate.*)

MRS. FISHER: How many noughts is a hundred thousand?

JOE: (*Coming back to her left, taking a pencil from his vest-pocket*). It's a one, (*He leans over the table and writes it on the margin of the newspaper*) and two noughts, and three more noughts. (MRS. FISHER *looks at it closely.* JOE *replaces the pencil in his pocket and moves across again towards the left.*) They paid that today on account. I knew it was coming, though; their head chemist out at Bristol told me six weeks ago it was all set. I've got to go over there to their offices right away; they made an appointment for the newspaper and magazine people over there at five o'clock. (*He starts for the hall-door.*) I've got to talk to them.

MRS. FISHER: Did they give you any of the money, Joe?

JOE: (*Stopping at the hall-door*). A hundred thousand dollars, sure.

MRS. FISHER: Not in money, though?

JOE: *(Laughing, and coming back towards the center-table).* Not in dollar bills, no; they gave me a check for it.

MRS. FISHER: Where is it?

JOE: Farley has it in his safe, down in the office.

MRS. FISHER: How much do you have to give *him*, half of it?

JOE: No, he's not a partner, he's just my lawyer. I give him five per cent of all monies received. *(He moves forward at the left of the center-table.)*

MRS. FISHER: How much will that be?

JOE: Well, that was five thousand dollars right off the bat, to-day. Pretty soft for that bird. When I first talked to him he wanted to stick me for ten per cent; but I nailed that quick; I knew what this was goin' to be worth.

MRS. FISHER: What are you goin' to do now, Joe, stop workin'?

JOE: No, of course not, I'm not goin' to stop working; I've got that oil-paint thing on the carpet, now.

MRS. FISHER: Well, won't you have to go to Washington or someplace?

JOE: *(Rolling his tie up on his finger, and stuffing it into his vest-pocket.)* No, that's all been attended to. But I'll tell you, Mom—I might go to Trenton.

MRS. FISHER: New Jersey?

JOE: Yes.

MRS. FISHER: Not to live, surely?

JOE: I might—till I put this oil-paint thing through.

MRS. FISHER: Well, I think you'd be very foolish, Joe, to go to Trenton at *your* age.

JOE: *(Removing his cuff-links and dropping them into his vest-pocket).* Well, the Meyers and Stevens people made me a proposition this afternoon that looks pretty good. They've got one of the most perfectly equipped experimenting laboratories in the world, just outside of Trenton; and it's open day and night; and that's what I want. I'd have had this rust-preventive through six months sooner, if I could have had the use of a laboratory somewhere at night. So they want me to go up there on a salary, with a first look at anything I strike; but I didn't want to say anything until I talked to *you*.

MRS. FISHER: What do you mean?

JOE: I mean, I wouldn't like the idea of goin' away, and leavin' you alone in the house.

MRS. FISHER: *(Resuming her knitting).* Oh, you go ahead, Joe,—if it's for your good. Never mind me,—I'll get along some way.

JOE: I don't like the idea of leavin' you here alone.

MRS. FISHER: Nearly every Mother is left alone, Joe, if she lives long enough. *(JOE looks straight out and thinks.)*

JOE: I was wonderin', Mom,—why Amy couldn't come in here: she seems to be havin' a pretty tough time of it. *(There is a slight pause, during which MRS. FISHER knits.)*

MRS. FISHER: She's *in* here already; and her man with her.

JOE: I mean, to stay.

MRS. FISHER: They're goin' to stay;—she can have that room at the head of the stairs. *(She stops knitting and thinks, looking steadily at the floor in front of her.)* They'll have to live somewhere; and I guess it'll have to be here. It's just as our Clara said here one night,—I remember it as if it was yesterday. She said, "Remember what I'm telling you, Mom,—it's *you* that'll have them on your hands if she takes him." And I suppose that's true. She made her bed,—and I guess it's me that'll have to lie in it.

JOE: *(Starting up and across towards the hooks at the head of the cellar-stairs, to get a paper out of his coat-pocket).* They want me to go to Trenton right away.

MRS. FISHER: What would you do, Joe, come home over Sundays?

JOE: Sure, it's only thirty-eight miles from here.

MRS. FISHER: *(Astonished.)* Is that all the further Trenton is from Philadelphia?

JOE: *(Starting across towards the left to the hall-door, removing his vest).* That's all.

MRS. FISHER: It always seemed very far away to me. I guess it's the name.

JOE: I'm goin' up to get fixed up a bit before I go over to that office.

MRS. FISHER: *(Suddenly putting her knitting on the table, preparatory to getting up).* Well, listen, Joe!

JOE: *(Stopping, with his foot on the first step of the stairs).* What?

MRS. FISHER: *(Getting up and moving across in front of the center-table).* Come here. *(JOE comes down to her left.)* Don't say anything about this to him, Joe, or he'll be wantin' to go up and talk to the newspaper men, too. *(JOE laughs faintly, then looks away off and thinks.)*

JOE: You know, Mom,—I kinda feel that there's some-thin' comin' to that nut out of this thing.

MRS. FISHER: How do you mean?

JOE: *He* gave me an idea here one night.

MRS. FISHER: *(Seizing him suddenly by both arms).* Well, for God's sake, don't tell *him* that, Joe!—or, as sure as you live, he'll be tellin' everybody that he done the whole thing.

JOE: You remember the night he was saying' here about bein' at work on a solution for the prevention of rust in iron and steel?

MRS. FISHER: Yes.

JOE: Well, you know, I'd been tellin' him somethin' about it a week or so before—

MRS. FISHER: Yes, you told me.

JOE: While he was waitin' here for Amy one night.

MRS. FISHER: Yes.

JOE: Well, he forgot that night he was tellin' *me* about it that it was me that had been tellin' *him* about it; and he got it mixed.

MRS. FISHER: That's the way he does with everything.

JOE: And it was the way he got it mixed, Mom, that gave me the idea. *He* said,—that it was a combination of chemical elements to be added to the metal in its *molten state,* instead of applied *externally,* as they *had* been doin'. And I *landed* on it—the way Howe did when he dreamed of puttin' the eye in the point of the needle instead of the other end. That was exactly what *I'd* been doin'—applying the solution *exter-nally*—in a mixture of paint. But the next day, I tried adding parts of it to the molten state of the metal, and it did the trick. Of course, he didn't know what he was sayin' when he said it—

MRS. FISHER: He never does.

JOE: And he didn't know anything about the solution-formula—But it was the way he got what I'd been tellin' him *twisted,* Mom,—that put the thing over.

MRS. FISHER: Well, that's no credit to him, Joe.

JOE: I know.

MRS. FISHER: He was only blowin' when he said it.

JOE: Sure.

MRS. FISHER: He don't know what a formala means. And I'd have told him where he heard it, too, if I'd been you.

JOE: *(Thoughtfully).* I'd like to give him a little present of some kind. *(His Mother looks at him sharply.)*

MRS. FISHER: What would you give him a present for?

JOE: *(Breaking into a little laugh).* For makin' a mistake.

MRS. FISHER: That's all everybody's doin' around here,—givin' that fellow presents for makin' mistakes. That's what Frank Hyland said here to-day, when I ast him why he paid his fine. He said, "Oh, you've got to give a little present here and there once in a while." There's no use tryin' to be sensible anymore.

JOE: I'd like to give him *somethin'. (She looks at him again keenly, and thinks for a second.)*

MRS. FISHER: I'll tell you what you can do, Joe, if you're so anxious to *give* him somethin'.—Find out what fine Frank Hyland paid for him this afternoon, and tell him you're goin' to give him that. But don't tell him what you're givin' it to him *for,* Joe, or we won't be able to live in the house with him. And don't give him money, Joe; for he'd only be goin' from one room to another here in an automobile. And don't give it to her neither, Joe; for she'll only hand it right over to him.—Give it to me. *(JOE looks at her.)* And I'll give it to them when I think they need it. *(A door closes out at the right; and JOE steps up towards the mantelpiece to look off.)* That's Clara; she's been next door telephonin'. *(She turns to her left and picks up her knitting from the table and sits down again. CLARA comes in, slipping off the raincoat.)*

JOE: Hello!

CLARA: *(Hanging the raincoat up on the hook).* How's it you're home so early, Joe? *(AUBREY enters from the hall-door, smoking a cigar.)*

JOE: The long threatening has come at last!

CLARA: *(Coming forward, looking at him seriously).* What?

JOE: The big news.

CLARA: The steel thing? *(JOE laughs.)* Did they buy it, Joe?

JOE: One hundred thousand dollars!—first payment—they gave me the check this afternoon.

CLARA: Joe, you're not telling me the truth!

AUBREY: *(Coming forward).* Something about the invention Joe?

JOE: Hello, Aubrey!

CLARA: *(Coming down to her Mother's right).* Did they, Mom?

JOE *and* MRS. FISHER, *speaking together.*

MRS. FISHER:——So he sez.

JOE:——They bought it this afternoon.

CLARA: Isn't that wonderful!

AUBREY: *(Extending his hand to* JOE*)*. Congratulations!

JOE: *(Laughing)*. Thanks.

AUBREY: So we put it over! (MRS. FISHER *poisons him with a look.)*

JOE: To the tune of one hundred thousand clackers. *(He swings above* AUBREY *towards the hall-door.)*

AUBREY: *(Turning and following him)*. No kidding?

JOE: *(Running up the stairs)*. The check's in the safe, down in the lawyer's office.

AUBREY: *(Calling up the stairs after him)*. Well, Kid, you know what I always told you!

JOE *and* CLARA, *speaking together*.

JOE: —Leave it to you to call the turn, Aubrey.

CLARA: *(Running up to the hall-door)*. Joe! Come here and tell us something about it.

JOE: *(Calling back)*. I've got to get dressed, Clara, I'll tell you about it later. (AUBREY *comes forward at the left, laughing; but suddenly he becomes conscious of* MRS. FISHER'S *left eye, and his laugh freezes into a detached gaze out the window at the left.)*

MRS. FISHER: *(Speaking to* CLARA*)*. He's got to go down to see them people that bought the thing from him.

CLARA: *(Coming forward to the center-table)*. Why, what will Joe *do* with all that money, Mom?

MRS. FISHER: *(Knitting)*. Heaven knows, I don't.

CLARA: Have you any idea how much a hundred thousand dollars is?

MRS. FISHER: Joe sez it's a one and two noughts, and then three more noughts.

CLARA: Why, it's a fortune!

MRS. FISHER: Well, he brought it on himself; he'll have to tend to it; I'm sure I won't.

AUBREY: *(Coming towards the center-table from the left)*. If he's a *wise bird,* he'll let *me* handle that money for him. (MRS. FISHER *pins him with a look, and her knitting slides to her lap.) I* could give him a couple of very fly tips on that.

MRS. FISHER: *(With dangerous steadiness)*. He don't want *your* tips; nor your *taps* neither. We *know* about one tip *you* gave a man, and his arm has been in a sling ever since. (CLARA *picks up the "Delineator" from the table and moves over to the right to the buffet, to look at the styles.)*

AUBREY: That's all right, Mrs. Fisher; but if he's a wise

Bimbo,—he'll take the drooping left, (*He lowers the lid of his left eye, very mysteriously.*) and I'll *double* that money for him, within the next two weeks; (MRS. FISHER *resumes her knitting.*) and give him an extra pair of trousers.

MRS. FISHER: I guess he'd *need* an extra pair of trousers, if he was sittin' around waitin' for *you* to double his money for him.

AUBREY: Well, I'm telling you, Mother,—he's an awful straw-ride if he doesn't get in on some of that copper-clipping that those people are writing me about. (*She looks at him, hard.*)

MRS. FISHER: What is it, a copper mine this time?

AUBREY: 'Tain't a mine at all,—it's a mint.

MRS. FISHER: What are they writin' to *you* about it for?

AUBREY: They're writing to everybody.

MRS. FISHER: They must be. (*She resumes her knitting.*)

AUBREY: Prospective Investors—They hear a man's got a few dollars laying around idle, and they get in touch with him.

MRS. FISHER: Well, nobody's heard that you have any dollars layin' around idle, have they?

AUBREY: (*With a touch of consequence*). Oh,—I don't know,—they may have. (MRS. FISHER *stops knitting and leans towards him, stonily,—her left elbow resting on the table.*)

MRS. FISHER: Listen, Boy,—if you've got any dollars layin' around idle, it'd be fitter for you to pay Frank Hyland the money he paid to keep you out of jail, than to be lookin' around for an investment for it—in some old copper mine, out in God-Knows-Where—that you don't know no more about than them that's writin' to you about it. (*She knits again, indignantly.*)

AUBREY: I know a whole lot about this proposition, Mrs. Fisher; and so do a lot of other people. Why,—they say they can see enough copper in those rocks, right now, to keep this thing going for the next ten years.

MRS. FISHER: (*Almost violently*). They *shoot* that in there.

AUBREY: Shoot copper into solid rocks, eh?

MRS. FISHER: (*Putting her knitting down on the table and picking up the newspaper that* JOE *has left there*). That's what I said. (AUBREY *turns away, with a gesture of helplessness, and moves across in front of the Morris-chair to the window at the left.*) I read all about just how they do it, in a magazine not two weeks ago. (*Looking at the paper.*) Then they shoot a lot of letters to the likes of you, and you *shoot off* about it.

AMY: (*Entering hurriedly from the hall-door and coming forward to the center-table*). Mom, is it true what Joe sez about the invention?

MRS. FISHER: (*Looking sharply at something in the paper*). Here it is in the paper. (AUBREY *moves across above the Morris-chair towards the center-table.*)

AMY: Isn't that wonderful, Aubrey? (AUBREY *nods and smiles.*)

MRS. FISHER: (*To* CLARA). I thought our Joe said it wasn't *in* here.

CLARA: (*Moving a step or two from the buffet*). What is it?

AMY: (*Leaning over her Mother's left shoulder, looking at the paper*). What does it say, Mom?

MRS. FISHER: (*Reading*). Mad Motorist Fined One Thousand Dollars for Reckless Driving. (AUBREY *glides forward and crosses in front of the Morris-chair to the window at the left again.* AMY *straightens up and gives a distressed look at* CLARA, *who suggests, with a nod, that she go into the kitchen.*) Mr. Aubrey Piper, of 903 Lehigh Avenue, was arranged today before Magistrate Lister of the 22nd and Huntington Park Avenue Police Station, to answer to the charge of having disregarded traffic-signals at Broad Street and Erie Avenue last Monday evening; resulting in rather serious injuries to Mr. Joseph Hart, a traffic-officer. The defendant was fined one thousand dollars for recklessness, disregard of traffic-signals, and operating an automobile without a license. (*She lowers the paper to her lap and looks at* AUBREY.)

AUBREY: (*Turning from the window, and with a magnificent gesture*). That's the law for you. (*He folds his arms and leans on the back of the Morris-chair, looking straight out.*)

MRS. FISHER: What do you think of that, Clara?

CLARA: (*Moving to the arm-chair below the buffet at the right*). Well, it's all over now, Mom—Frank paid it.

MRS. FISHER: What did he pay it *for*?

CLARA: (*Sitting down*). Well, it was either that or go to jail, Mom; and you wouldn't want that, on account of Amy. (*She opens the "Delineator."*)

MRS. FISHER: Well, Frank Hyland didn't have to pay it— (*She sits looking straight out, fuming*) Amy's got a Mother. (*Turning sharply to* CLARA.) And you take that thousand-dollar insurance check that I gave you and give it to him as soon as ever you see him. I don't want Frank Hyland goin' around payin' out thousand-dollar bills on account of this clown. (*She looks bitterly at* AUBREY, *who looks at her with an expression as though he were trying to come to some conclusion as to the most effectual means of putting her in her place.*) It's bad enough for *me* to have to do it.

CLARA: (*Calling to* AMY). Amy.

AMY: (*From the kitchen*). What?

CLARA: Come here a minute. (MRS. FISHER *puts the newspaper back onto the table and resumes her knitting.* AUBREY *strolls over and sits down at the left of the center-table, reaching for the newspaper which* MRS. FISHER *has just put down.* AMY *comes in from the kitchen.*)

AMY: What?

CLARA: Here's that skirt I was telling you about. (AMY *comes forward to* CLARA'S *left and they look at a certain skirt in the "Delineator."* AUBREY *deposits some ashes from his cigar on the little tray on the table, then sits back, takes a pair of tortoise-shell rimmed glasses, with a black-tape attachment for over the ear, from his vest-pocket, and settles them on his nose. His Mother-in-law gives him a look.*)

AUBREY: Was that Insurance man here to-day? (AMY *opens the left-hand drawer of the buffet and takes out a package of Life-Savers. She takes one herself, then offers* CLARA *one;* CLARA *takes it; and the two continue their discussion of the styles in the "Delineator."*)

MRS. FISHER: What do you want to know for?

AUBREY: (*Glancing over the evening paper*). Nothing,—I was just wondering if he got around this way to-day.—Did he leave a paper here for me?

MRS. FISHER: (*Knitting*). He *wanted* to; but I told him not to waste his time—(AUBREY *looks at her narrowly*) talkin' to *you* about fifty-thousand-dollar policies.

AUBREY: Well, what about it?

MRS. FISHER: (*Looking at him*). Nothin' at *all* about it; only the man was laughin' up his sleeve at you.

AUBREY: Is that so?

MRS. FISHER: What else *could* he do? He knows you haven't the faintest idea of takin' out any such policy.

AUBREY: How do you know he does?

MRS. FISHER: Because he knows you're only a clerk; and that you don't get enough salary in *six months*—to pay one year's premium on a policy like that.

AUBREY: What were you doing, handing out a line of gab about my business?

MRS. FISHER: (*Quietly knitting again*). You haven't got any business for anybody to hand out a line of gab about— that I ever heard of. (AMY *moves slowly across above the center-table towards the left, picking up a newspaper.*)

AUBREY: Well, whether I have any line of business or not, it isn't necessary for you to be gabbing to perfect strangers about it.

MRS. FISHER: (*Getting mad*). Then, you stop gabbin' to people about fifty-thousand-dollar policies!—On your thirty-two dollars a week. (*Turning to him furiously.*) I told him *that*, too.

AMY: (*Touching* AUBREY *on the left shoulder, as she passes back of him.*) Keep quiet, Aubrey.

MRS. FISHER: So he'd know how much attention to pay to you the *next* time you start. (AMY *moves forward to the Morris-chair at the left and sits down.*)

AUBREY: What else did you tell him?

MRS. FISHER: I told him the truth!—whatever I told him.—And I guess that's more than can be said for a whole lot *you* told him. (*She knits again.*)

AUBREY: (*Resuming his paper*). A man'ud certainly have a swell chance trying to make anything of himself around *this* hut. (MRS. FISHER *stops knitting, and leans her elbow on the table.*)

MRS. FISHER: Listen, Boy,—any time you don't like this *hut*, you go right straight back to Lehigh Avenue to your two rooms over the dago barber shop. And I'll be glad to see your heels.

CLARA: Stop talking, Mom.

MRS. FISHER: Nobody around here's tryin' to stop you from makin' somethin' of yourself.

AUBREY: No, and nobody's trying to help me any, either; only trying to make me look like a *pin-head*—every chance they get.

MRS. FISHER: Nobody'll have to try very hard to make *you* look like a *pin-head;* your own silly talk'll do that for you, any time at all.

AUBREY: I suppose it's silly talk to try to make a good impression.

MRS. FISHER: (*Turning to him and speaking definitely*). Yes; it's silly to try to make an impression of any kind; for the only one that'll be made'll be the right one,—and that'll make itself.

AUBREY: Well, if you were out in the world as much as *I* am, you'd very soon see how much easier it is for a fellow to get along—if people think he's got something.

MRS. FISHER: Well, anybody that'ud listen to *you* very long'ud know you *couldn't* have very much.

AUBREY: Is that so.

MRS. FISHER: (*Tersely*). You heard me. (CLARA *rises and moves towards her Mother.*)

AUBREY: (*Reaching over to dispose of some more cigar-ashes*). People that are smart enough to be able to make it easier for you——

CLARA: Aubrey,—that'll do. (*He is silenced; and resumes his paper.* CLARA *shows her Mother a particular pattern in the "Delineator."*) Mom, that'd look good for that new black crepe de chine of yours, No. 18, there in the middle.

MRS. FISHER: But, I wouldn't want that bunch of fullness like that right there, Clara. (JOE *enters hurriedly from the hall-door, wearing a clean shirt and collar, and with his face washed and hair combed.*)

CLARA: Well, you're always saying you look too thin; and I think—Joe, tell me something about the invention.

JOE: (*Crossing quickly to the hooks at the right for his coat*). They telephoned for me this afternoon about two o'clock, and I got hold of Farley and we went right over there. And they had the contracts all drawn up and everything.

CLARA: (*Having moved up towards the hooks with him*). Well, did they really give you a hundred thousand dollars for it? (AUBREY *gets up and moves around and up to the upper-left hand corner of the table.*)

JOE: (*Coming forward, putting on his coat*). Check's in the safe, down in Farley's office.

AUBREY: (*Flicking some ashes from his cigar*). Joe!— what do you think we ought to do with that money? (JOE *tries to hide his laughter, and steps down to his Mother's right; and* CLARA *comes forward and leans on the buffet.*)

JOE: You know, it was a funny thing, Mom,—when I first talked to the Meyers and Stevens people, I was only to get *fifty* thousand dollars advance; and when I went up there to-day they had the contracts all made out for a *hundred* thousand.

AUBREY: And they're getting away with murder at that.

MRS. FISHER: *(Turning to him impatiently)*. Oh, keep still, you!—You don't know anything about this at all.

AUBREY: I made *them* think I knew something about it.

MRS. FISHER: You made *who* think?

AUBREY: The Meyers and Stevens people.

JOE: What are you talkin' about, Aubrey, do you know?

AUBREY: Certainly, I know what I'm talking about. *I* went to see those people, last Saturday afternoon, after you told me they'd talked to you.

JOE: *(Crossing towards him, to a point above the center-table)*. And, what'd you do up there?

AUBREY: Why, I told them,—that they'd have to double the advance, if they wanted to do business with us.

MRS. FISHER: And, what business was it of yours?

AUBREY: Well,—I'm Joe's guardian, ain't I?

MRS. FISHER: Who told you you were?

AUBREY: Well,—he's got to have somebody tend to his business, doesn't he?—He's only a lad.

MRS. FISHER: Well, he doesn't need *you* to tend to his business for him.—He tended to his business long before he ever saw *you*.

AUBREY: He never landed a hundred thousand dollars, though, till he saw me, did he?

JOE: Well, what did you say to them, Aubrey?

AUBREY: Why,—I simply told them that your Father was dead,—and that I was acting in the capacity of *business*-adviser to you: and that, if this discovery of yours was as important as you had led me to believe it was, they were simply taking advantage of your youth by offering you fifty thousand dollars for it. And that I refused to allow you to negotiate further—unless they doubled the advance, market it at their expense, and one half the net—*sign* on the dotted line. *(He flicks more ashes from his cigar.)*

JOE: Well, did they know who you were?

AUBREY: I told them—that I was head of the house here; (MRS. FISHER *grips the edge of the table, threateningly*) and that I was also connected with the Pennsylvania Railroad.

MRS. FISHER: It's too bad they didn't know what you do down there; and call your bluff.

AUBREY: I beat them to it; I called theirs first. *(He strolls towards the left, with a bit of swagger.)*

JOE: Well, I certainly have to give you credit, Aubrey; that's the way the contract reads.

AUBREY: *(Strolling back again).* I told it to them; and I told it to your lawyer, too.

JOE: I'll have to give you a little present of some kind out of this, Aubrey.

AUBREY: *(Dismissing the suggestion with a touch of ceremony).* You'll not give *me* any present, Joe;—give it to your Mother. *(He strolls over to the left again).* She'll need it more than I will. *(He comes forward at the left of the Morris-chair.)* Amy,—have you got the financial page there?

AMY: *(Handing him the newspaper).* Is this it, Aubrey?

AUBREY: *(Taking it).* Thank you. *(He crosses in front of her to the chair at the left of the center-table and sits down.* AMY *gets up, looking at him wonderingly.)*

AMY: Aubrey, you're wonderful!

AUBREY: *(Settling himself to look over the bond market).* A little bit of bluff goes a long way sometimes, Amy.

AMY: Isn't he wonderful, Mom? *(*MRS. FISHER *prepares to resume her knitting.)*

MRS. FISHER: *(After a long sigh).* God help *me*, from now on. *(The curtain descends slowly, with* AMY *standing lost in admiration of the wonder of* AUBREY. *When the curtain rises again* AUBREY *is reading,* MRS. FISHER *is knitting,* CLARA *is sitting reading the "Delineator," over on the arm of the arm-chair at the right,* JOE *is putting on his overcoat and hat at the mantelpiece-mirror, and* AMY *is sitting in the Morris-chair at the left, just looking at* AUBREY.)

CURTAIN

COMMENTARY

Kelly subtitled *The Show-Off* "A Transcript of Life," which gives a clear indication of his intent to be as faithful to life in his characterizations as possible. Stephen Porter, who directed a 1967 revival of the play, said: "Characters this vivid and dialogue this truthful deserve the most respectful and honest ensemble acting we can provide." And Alexander Woollcott wrote of Kelly in the same attitude of respect: "He has written with almost flawless art—in the living idiom of our life and time—wise, deliciously malicious and piteously true." The reviews champion *The Show-Off* as being true to life and very funny. Indeed, as comedy it qualifies as a gem of hilarious fun that moves brilliantly along with quips, repartee, plenty of situational irony, and smartly drawn characterizations. Its satire is clearly visible.

On a sociological level the play is interesting as an example of the grasping, up-and-coming middle class of the 1920s with its notions of sudden wealth and satisfaction in achieving the American dream. For these people there is no romantic "green light" far out across the bay such as beckoned to Gatsby. What they see is a set of keys to a huge house, a car, and perhaps a little power boat to sweeten the dullness of married life. Like some member of the Inquisition, Kelly stretches the middle class out on the torture rack of his satiric jibes and practically destroys it with ridicule. He hated the pettiness of middle-class life and ruthlessly attacked it. Joseph Wood Krutch wrote of Kelly, "Vulgarity offends him, not only aesthetically, but morally as well, and the kind of meanness which he sees most commonly in men and women strikes him always as a sort of vulgarity of the soul." *The Show-Off* attacks that meanness of soul in the middle class.

The character of Aubrey Piper as the show-off son-in-law is one of the best-written comic characters of the period. The comic power of the play is rooted in letting the character "take off." Aubrey, who is based on the traditional stage Yankee (the boaster–hayseed), is transformed into a Philadelphia "hick." But beneath that is a picture of every little

237

guy in America who wants to succeed but ultimately fails. Aubrey wants to have that house because it suggests the craving for possessions of the middle class; he has a hunger for the crass world the house symbolizes. That very value is, of course, a cliché. But Aubrey, with his pat phrases, is himself the ultimate cliché and becomes devastatingly funny. The character is easily identified with and is both pitied and feared. His comic breadth spans the structure of the play, crisscrossing from one situation and character to another. In some way or other, he touches every event.

Aubrey, with all odds against him, through sheer bravado parlays his poor-relation status into one of strength and prominence. The comedy of the play is primarily an outgrowth of the contrast between the buffoon, Aubrey, and the shrewd, nagging mother. She finds him totally unacceptable but must grant him admission to the family merely because he's married into it—a rather common calamity in families.

Having been ridiculed by nearly all of the family for his obvious pretentiousness and tendency to lie at the drop of anyone's hat, he stumbles into a contract negotiation that he turns into a stunning success for his brother-in-law. There's no holding him now, and the play ends on a comic highlight in which it is obvious that Aubrey has "arrived."

The extraordinary comic element of Aubrey's car accident in which he ran down a traffic cop who was giving him directions is wonderfully comic. Aubrey simply doesn't take directions from anyone; rather, he gives them as a freewheeling spirit, as irrepressible as he is delightful. Even Mrs. Fisher and Clara, her daughter, eventually give way to his energy and resignedly accept his newly acquired position as hopeless braggart of the family.

The set is very important to the play's success, and the one not-so-successful staging in 1950 may have failed because it used an arena stage that failed to establish the rigid, solid middle class the playwright had as his central target.

All the elements of action, theme, setting, dialogue, and character meld into that unbreakable fist of unity that the new realists aimed at. Kelly certainly shows that he is a master at portraying the bourgeoisie, and *The Show-Off* is a satirical paradigm of middle-class society. It is also brilliant comedy.

LUCKY SAM McCARVER
by
Sidney Howard

BACKGROUND

Midway through the 1920s, the nation was well out of the economic recession of 1920–22, and the "Golden Twenties" were reflected in stock prices, which had doubled on Wall Street in five years. Financial boom was in the atmosphere and Broadway was no exception. During the 1925–26 season (July 1 through June 30), 255 different productions, musicals, and plays, were presented at seventy-five different theaters. In a little over a decade, thirty new theaters had been built, and the activity on the Rialto had increased by almost one hundred productions per year. Perhaps these figures will be more meaningful if one compares them with subsequent data:

Year	Productions	Theaters
1935–36	135	53
1945–46	76	36
1955–56	56	30
1965–66	68	36
1975–76	60	34

In the 1927–28 season, seventy theaters were used to house 264 productions. The 1925–26 season established the high-water mark for theatrical production along the Great White Way.

"Theater weeks" is a more reliable guide to measure activity. A theater week is defined as a production occupying one theater for one week. For the 1925–26 period, the number of active theater weeks was 2806—an all-time record. For 1935–36, it was 1299; 1945–46, 1420; 1955–56, 1239; 1965–66, 1229; and for 1975–76, it was 1136.

Even though the theater seasons of the mid-1920s were the most prosperous and prolific, they were not necessarily the most prodigious or prestigious as far as the drama was concerned. In reading Burns Mantle's commentaries (the Best Play series) on each of these seasons, one can conclude that escapist entertainment, sometimes cheap and tawdry, was the most frequently presented theatrical *pièce de résistance*. In spite of that, challenging and unconventional works were being produced more and more often. For the first time since 1909, when he started selecting the best plays on Broadway, Burns Mantle chose ten American plays for the 1924–25 season, including *Desire Under the Elms* by O'Neill, *What Price Glory?* by Maxwell Anderson and Laurence Stallings, *Minick* by George Kaufman and Edna Ferber, and *They Knew What They Wanted* by Sidney Howard. For the next season, he included *Craig's Wife* by George Kelly, *The Great God Brown* by O'Neill, and *The Butter and Egg Man* by Kaufman. Writing in *The Nation* in January 1925, Joseph Wood Krutch commented that "no playwright who had anything important to say has failed to receive an attentive hearing . . . it means that the current dramatic tradition has established itself. . . ." And what was the tradition? Krutch called it "realism, irony and iconoclasm."

Sidney Howard, more than any other writer of the 1920s, mastered the emerging tradition. Between 1924 and 1926, four of his best-known plays—*They Knew What They Wanted, Lucky Sam McCarver, Ned McCobb's Daughter,* and *The Silver Cord*—were produced on Broadway, and his reputation as the "major writer of social drama" was confirmed. As Walter Meserve, a leading scholar of American drama, has observed, Howard is a true descendant of Bronson Howard, James A. Herne, and Eugene Walter. "Into this stream of American drama, Sidney Howard launched his plays and by so doing, added an imagination and talent which, guided by a new sense of realism, gave social drama a new dignity and position in the eyes of the audiences and critics, both in America and abroad."

Howard was born in Oakland, California, in 1891 of Irish stock. He graduated from the University of California in 1915 with an A.B. degree, and after a brief bout with tuberculosis, like O'Neill, he enrolled at Harvard, where he studied with Sam Hume and George Pierce Baker. Years later, Howard said that he learned from Baker to "write what you know to be true about your characters, and write nothing that you know not to be true."

In 1916, being an idealist, he joined the French forces as an ambulance driver, and when America entered World War I, he became a fighter pilot and saw considerable action. Sidney Howard White, one of his biographers, commented about his war experiences: "He was marked for life, one might say, as the sensitive young man who had seen too much of social devastation and military ineptness. It was the making of a realist in the theater."

After the war, he became a reporter and writer for journals and magazines including *Life, Collier's, The New Republic,* and *Hearst's International.* Between 1920 and 1924, he wrote a number of articles that would be best described as muckraking. It was during this time that he also began his career as a playwright. He started by translating and adapting plays, which he continued to do throughout his career, and one of his finest plays, *Paths of Glory* (1935), is an adaptation of a novel by Humphrey Cobb. His first original play, *Swords,* a romantic verse drama, was presented in 1921, and its reception, as well as his own reaction, precluded him from writing verse plays again. He then adapted a series of short plays written by the French realist, Charles Vildrac, whose plays in subject and style convinced Howard, as White reports, to "avoid the fads of expressionism and sensationalism and simply write of everyday men and women." Thus, impressed by Vildrac and drawing from his own experiences as a crusading reporter, he wrote the four plays that brought him fame and a Pulitzer Prize (for *They Knew What They Wanted,* 1924).

During the late 1920s he went to Hollywood, and he is well remembered for being the screen writer of *Arrowsmith* (1932), *Dodsworth* (1936), and *Gone With the Wind* (1939). During the 1930s, he continued to write, collaborate on, and adapt a number of plays, including *The Late Christopher Bean* (1932), *Alien Corn* (1933), *Dodsworth* (1934), *Yellow Jack* (1934), and *The Ghost of Yankee Doodle* (1937). In

1939, along with Robert Sherwood, Maxwell Anderson, Elmer Rice, and S. N. Behrman, he organized and managed the Playwrights' Company, which had been formed to give playwrights greater freedom from commercial managers and pressures. His brilliant and still-budding career was cut short when at age forty-eight he was crushed to death by a tractor on his farm in Massachusetts.

One of his closest friends was the critic and historian Barrett H. Clark, who wrote a great deal about Howard's career, including an article entitled "His Voice Was American," which appeared in *Theater Arts* in 1949. In recounting the playwright's contribution to the American drama, he first presented the reader with a glimpse of the man:

> he was the most completely alive man, the most multitudinous and abounding person with whom I ever had anything to do . . . his way of bursting into a room as if he had just descended from the clouds, and his wholly unconscious and deferential way of getting things done in a hurry . . . he had a knack for getting close to people of all kinds; he was always ready for a fight, providing he could take quick and summary action; he stood up for oppressed minorities. He fought literary and political censorship; he spoke French and Italian and a little German; he wrote a good deal of passable verse; he loved music and painting . . . he was devoted to children, his own, his friends', anyone's. He thrived on work. . . .

Most of all, Clark wanted people to know of Howard's great need to transfer to the stage his convictions and beliefs about American society. Knowing that he was a fine reporter and a keen observer, Clark believed that Howard was particularly well equipped to speak for America through "our newly born, and so promising, native drama." Howard was interested in the personal reactions of people, their private moods and ways, rather than merely being concerned with abstract ideas. His plays reflect this, even when they do have a clear "social message."

In *Lucky Sam McCarver,* he spoke of a society that was experiencing an economic boom yet was full of doubt and pessimism. Disillusioned by a disappointing peace after great sacrifices for the war effort, Americans became cynical and intolerant, leading to the worshiping of success. Cynicism and money precipitated a hedonistic binge brought on, to a great degree, by the Eighteenth Amendment, which prohibited the manufacture, sale, or use of alcoholic beverages. Although the Prohibition Age was conceived during the war years to conserve grain and to demonstrate our ability at self-sacrifice, it became an issue that only too well demonstrated the fissure in American society. Prohibition was a last gasp on the part of a large segment of our society to hold on to the morality of the past, while the speak-easy became the symbol for the debunkers. It was a time which ushered in corruption and gangsterism, and the theme song was:

> My sister she works in the laundry,
> My father sells bootlegger gin,
> My mother she takes in the washing,
> My God! how the money rolls in!

When Sidney Howard wrote *Lucky Sam McCarver,* he was married to the actress Clare Eames whom he had met in 1921 when she played the leading role in his play *Swords.* During the period of their marriage, 1922–28 (they were separated in 1928 and divorced in 1930), he was undoubtedly influenced by her ability as a performer and by her personality. She played the leading role of Carlotta in the production of *Lucky Sam McCarver* as well as the title role in his next play, *Ned McCobb's Daughter.* Later she starred in the London production of *The Silver Cord.* Lawrence Langner of the Theatre Guild, the organization that produced most of Howard's plays in those years (excluding *Lucky Sam McCarver*) and by whom Clare had been hired as a member of the acting company, described her as "tall, distinguished and vibrant, with features and mannerisms which reminded one of Queen Elizabeth." She was from Cleveland, and Langner reports that she "swept us all off our feet with her brilliant acting, directing and sheer joy of living." In spite of that energy, she was not physically strong, and her health was a critical issue during much of her marriage to Howard. She died shortly after their divorce.

Lucky Sam McCarver opened at the Playhouse on October 21, 1925, and closed after twenty-nine performances, much to the disappointment of the author, who considered this play his favorite. Out of his frustration with the general reaction, he wrote a long preface to *Lucky Sam McCarver* that is a major commentary on the American theater of that time, and also is a clear statement about his craft, particularly why and how *Lucky Sam McCarver* was written:

> *Lucky Sam McCarver* . . . set out to present some detached episodes from the lives of an imaginary man and an imaginary woman who should, between them, represent the two most spectacular extremes of the American social pendulum as it swings, in all its shoddiness of standard and philosophy across the handsome horizon of this handsome city of New York. . . .
>
> I determined also to stick as closely as I was able to "the value and significance of flesh"—in other words, to ask of the life I was reporting no more concessions than my limited skill as a reporter forced me to ask. I was resolved, for example, that my characters should, throughout the play, do and say what they would, as people have done and said, rather than what the dramatic situation might seem to require of them. I did not, furthermore, make any attempt at a theatrical simplification of the motives of my characters. No one, in life, ever does anything for any single reason; I cannot see why people in plays should be as singleminded as audiences like to have them. . . .
>
> I tried to make a real man out of my Sam by omitting his heroics whenever I was tempted to indulge them, and a real woman of my Carlotta by emphasizing her good qualities along with her faults. . . .
>
> I wrote my two people as close to life as I was able. (Pp. viii, ix, x, xi)

LUCKY SAM McCARVER
(1925)

ORIGINAL CAST

Cast of the original production as presented at the Playhouse, in New York City, on October 21, 1925, by Messrs. William A. Brady, Jr., and Dwight Deere Wyman, in association with John Cromwell.

GEORGE, *the House Manager*	At the	Robert Craig
DAN, *the Doorman*	Club	Guy Nichols
OSCAR, *the Jazz*	Tuileries	Charles Tazewell
SAM McCARVER		John Cromwell
SERGEANT HORAN, *of the Force*		Eric Jewett
COUNT LENTELLI, *of the Prohibition Unit*		James H. Bell
MAX, *the Head Waiter*	Also at	Craig Williams
DOLLY, *the Hostess*	the Club	Gladys Coburn
JIMMIE, *the Dancing Partner*	Tuileries	Philip Leigh
ARCHIE ELLIS		Gerald Hamor
CARLOTTA ASHE, *his cousin*		Clare Eames
BURTON BURTON		Austin Fairman
MONTGOMERY GARSIDE		William Wellford
ANNIE		Augusta Haviland
THE PRINCESS STRÁ		Hilda Spong
PIETRO		George Piani
CARTER ASHE		Montague Rutherford
TUDOR RAEBURN		Lew Martin
MIRIAM HALE		Rose Hobert
"PUDGE"		Philip Leigh

Settings designed by Jo Mielziner.
Gowns by Herman Patrick Tappe.
"Ave Maria" foxtrot arranged by Con Conrad.
Production directed by the author.

SCENES

First in the house manager's office of the Club Tuileries, New York. New Year's Eve.

Then in the salon of Sam McCarver's apartment on Park Avenue. Three months later.

Then in the salons of the Palazza Strá in Venice. The following July.

Then in the sitting-room of an Upper West Side apartment. The following March.

All in the present day.

ACT ONE

SCENE: The office of the house manager of a New York resort known as "The Club Tuileries." A shapeless room which gives the impression of having been crowded into the entresol. One door leads, presumably, into the lobby of the establishment. The other leads into the corridor off which the boxes open. When this door is ajar the music comes up more loudly from the dance floor, and one can see into a box, and beyond the box into an impression of lights and decorations signifying gaiety. The office is furnished with a desk, swivel-chair, other chairs, wash-stand and mirror, a cooler for ice-water, and a telephone. Its decorations suggest the business side of night life.

GEORGE, the house manager, a thoroughly barbered young man who wears a dinner coat which is the latest in snappiness, lounges in the door which gives on the box corridor. DAN, the doorman, a bulky Irishman in the conventional doorman's uniform great-coat, is spread over two chairs. The jazz orchestra is distinctly audible.

DAN: *(continuing the conversation)* Yessir, I've knowed Sam McCarver these twenty year if I've knowed him a day, an' a finer, smarter, luckier chap I've *never* knowed! (GEORGE *pays no attention. There is a pause filled by the dance-music.* OSCAR *enters by the other door. He is the Hebraic leader of the Tuileries Dance Orchestra, breezy, pomaded, self-satisfied. He wears a dinner-coat with a low collar, which allows ample room for his heavy chins. At the moment he is busily thrusting a gardenia into his button-hole.)*

OSCAR: *(as he enters)* Hello, George! Sam down yet? *(At the sound of his voice,* DAN *turns and regards him malevolently.* GEORGE *hears him, too, and closes the rear door, thus reducing the sound of the dance-music.)*

GEORGE: How's that?

OSCAR: Sam. Is he down yet?

GEORGE: Sam stopped off at the Ranch House to give the show the once over.

OSCAR: How's it going?

GEORGE: Rotten.

OSCAR: What did I tell him? I said to Sam: "Sam, you're branchin' out too much."

DAN: *(under his breath)* Th' hell you did!

OSCAR: *(a glance, merely, in* DAN'S *direction)* "What this town wants is dance-music," I said. "Dance-music like the kind I give 'em."

GEORGE: I just been listenin' to the boys. They're gettin' so they can play pretty fair without you.

OSCAR: There's a difference when I take hold.

GEORGE: It's a pity there's only one of you.

DAN: One's enough.

GEORGE: Shut up, Dan. What was it you was sayin', Oscar?

OSCAR: What I said to Sam. "Keep me here, Sam," I said, "an' I'll keep the crowd here. Shows is no go."

GEORGE: *(absorbed in his finger-nails)* Shows is shows. Some of 'em goes an' some of 'em flops. What the hell!

DAN: Music ain't what it used to be.

OSCAR: I don't like to make suggestions, Dan, but you ought to be on the door. Don't you know it's eleven-thirty?

GEORGE: Go on, Dan. You can't gas here *all* night.

DAN: I'd like to know if anybody around this here joint has got any better right to gas in Sam McCarver's office than old Dan has?

OSCAR: New Year's Eve is no time for people in our business to be anywhere but on the job.

GEORGE: Now, don't get that way. New Year's Eve is bad enough without you two makin' it any worse, scrappin'.

DAN: Th' hell wid New Year's Eve these days.

GEORGE: Oh, sure, th' hell with everything these days.

DAN: An' me half dead wid standin' in th' snow an' wet, night after night, night after night, chasin' taxicabs for wild wimmin'!

OSCAR: We know all about that.

DAN: *(continuing on his favorite theme)* If I had half-way good sense, I'd be quittin' Sam McCarver to-morrow.

OSCAR: Why don't you?

DAN: It 'ud be a fine thing for me to go off an' leave Sam at the mercy of a jazz-crazy Broadway high-binder like yourself.

GEORGE: *(quieting* OSCAR *with a gesture)* Sam 'ud break your back if you tried it. Yeah, an' he'll break your back if he don't find you on the door when he comes in.

DAN: *(no stopping him)* Oh, will he! After all I done for him! I first knowed Sam when he was no better'n a runt, rustlin' drinks an' pickin' up towels for a Turkish bath in Hoboken. It was me started him out in life, gettin' him th' first respectable job he ever had, washin' glasses for a Democratic bar on Grand Street.

GEORGE: Some job!

DAN: It was me put him into th' fightin' game, makin' him me promoter an' manager in th' days of me prime. It was me set him up in th' first place he ever run for himself, which was a business lunch on Liberty Street, as ye know very well. An' d'ye know what I could wish? *(By this he stands magnificently erect.)* I could wish this here Cloob Tuileries hadn't never been heard of. I could wish Sam McCarver an' me was back in Oliver Street or Grand Street, or any old street away from this God-forsaken Broadway. An' as for you an' your jazz, Oscar, it not only offends me religion, but it turns me stomach, God forgive ye! I'll be gettin' to work. *(He goes by the side door.)*

OSCAR: *(exploding)* What the . . . !

GEORGE: *(quieting him)* You have to put up with Dan around here, Oscar. He's been Sam's body-guard for a good many years, now.

OSCAR: You'd think he was Sam's special wet-nurse. Where'd you get the suit?

GEORGE: *(preening)* Like it?

OSCAR: Yeah. Not bad. Where'd you get it?

GEORGE: *(he rises to give us a better view)* Birnheimer. You know.

OSCAR: Oh! Hand me down, eh?

GEORGE: Like hell! Made to order.

OSCAR: *(it is worthy of his attention after all)* What'd it set you back?

GEORGE: Ninety.

OSCAR: That all Birnheimer sets you back for makin' a "tuck" to order?

GEORGE: Well, he knocked off something for me.

OSCAR: Sure. . . . Well, he makes a nice job if it is conservative.

GEORGE: I like 'em conservative.

OSCAR: Sure. For ninety bucks you can't expect too much. It's a nice fit, too.

GEORGE: Yeah.

OSCAR: *(concluding his inspection)* Yes. . . . It's a nice fit. . . . How's the crowd?

GEORGE: Fillin' in, I guess.

OSCAR: Anybody special?

GEORGE: Dunno.

OSCAR: Sam got a party?

GEORGE: *(ducking for a glimpse of himself in the mirror)* Couldn't say.

OSCAR: That Ashe woman?

GEORGE: Couldn't say.

OSCAR: Well, I don't blame him. She's got looks an' style an' money to burn.

GEORGE: Last I heard she was in Atlantic City.

OSCAR: How do you size 'em up, George? Sam an' Ashe?

GEORGE: *(at the wash-stand, touching up his hair and tie)* I don't.

OSCAR: I never would have expected to see Sam McCarver lose his head over any woman.

GEORGE: I wouldn't fret.

OSCAR: She's got her divorce.

GEORGE: Has she?

OSCAR: Saw it in the paper yesterday. Third, isn't it?

GEORGE: Guess so. Third or fourth.

OSCAR: What do you bet she divorced Ashe to marry Sam?

GEORGE: *(turning scornfully from the mirror)* Say, do you know who her father was?

OSCAR: *(an indignant note)* Certainly I do. I knew old

man Ellis well. I used to play for her parties when she was a débutante.

GEORGE: And you think she'd marry Sam? What a chance!

OSCAR: Why not? She's tried everything else.

GEORGE: That may be.

OSCAR: I'll bet he's sleepin' with her.

GEORGE: Don't he wish he could!

OSCAR: Then what's she doin' here every night in Sam's box?

GEORGE: Don't ask me.

OSCAR: Well, if you feel that way about it!

GEORGE: I do.

OSCAR: All right.

(*A sudden pause.* GEORGE *looks at his watch.*)

GEORGE: What time you goin' on, Oscar?

OSCAR: Just before the big noise. I wish to hell Sam 'ud come. I want to ask him . . . How do *you* think they'll take "Ave Maria" as a foxtrot?

GEORGE: I'll bite. What is it?

OSCAR: It's a hymn.

GEORGE: If it's a good tune they'll take it.

OSCAR: Well, if Sam says to go, I'm puttin' it on just after the big noise. It's just about the cutest thing you ever heard. (SAM MCCARVER *enters precipitately by the door from the lobby. He is thirty-six years old, handsome, husky, and not much the worse for wear. There are things about him which set him apart from the rest of men and well above the men with whom he habitually associates. The ordinary refinements of good people, however—*SAM *doesn't know, or doesn't trouble about them. His fur coat is too furry and you and I wouldn't wear our hat quite so extravagantly. And, when he strips off the coat, he discloses a taste in jewelry which, for a man, is bizarre and then some. As to his manner, he is genial without ever stooping to the conventions of the glad hand. Innate force and instinctive wariness would always save him from that. He speaks with a mixture of Broadway, East Side, and the Ould Counthry. He has the indomitable authority of an underworld knowledge of life. As the occasion demands, he can be terrifyingly harsh or benignly mellow. This is a mellow occasion.*)

SAM: (*over his shoulder, as he enters*) Come on in, gentlemen! The water's fine! (*Immediately two other gentle-*

men follow SAM. *The first is* SERGEANT HORAN *of the Force.
The second,* LENTELLI *of the Prohibition Unit, is an oily,
curly, flashy Italian-American. They are both middle-aged.)*

GEORGE: *(speaking at the same time)* Here's Sam, now.

SAM: Happy New Year, boys!

OSCAR: *(speaking at the same time)* Hello, Sam! How did
you find the Ranch House?

SAM: That place is finished!

OSCAR: What did I tell you? I said . . .

SAM: They don't last long these days.

GEORGE: *(speaking at the same time)* Hello, there, Sergeant!

HORAN: *(speaking at the same time)* 'Evenin', George!
'Evenin', Mr. Maddox! Happy New Year!

SAM: George, shake hands with Count Lentelli of the
Prohibition Unit. He used to be an old friend of mine when
he was in the liquor business for himself. Now's he's in the
liquor business for Uncle Sam, I ain't hardly so sure of him.

LENTELLI: That's a hell of a way to talk, Sam!

GEORGE: *(shaking hands)* Lentelli, did you say the name
was?

LENTELLI: Lentelli's right. Italian.

SAM: *Count* Lentelli. George here—George Connelley—
is house manager of the Tuileries. This is Mr. Maddox, the
Tuileries bandmaster. Mr. Maddox—Count Lentelli. Count
Lentelli—Mr. Maddox.

OSCAR: Count?

SAM: *(bursting with wit)* Count "No Account!" *(Hearty
laughter from all those present.* SAM, *divested of his coat,
which* GEORGE *has taken, drops a forty-pound hand on*
LENTELLI'S *shoulder.)* Yessir. Sit down, Sergeant! This
here! This here li'l fellow's Uncle Sam's special, private,
sport-model bootlegger-sleuth, come all the way from Washington to show Broadway a dry New Year. Give him a drink,
George. *(He tosses his keys to* GEORGE.)*

GEORGE: The papers is out already announcin' a dry New
Year. *(The* SERGEANT, *seated, helps himself to* SAM'S *cigars.)*

LENTELLI: Sure they are! I give 'em the story myself.
*(*MAX, *the perfect head waiter, enters, carrying the large
reservations book. During the next scene* GEORGE *extracts
two bottles from the desk drawer. One of them is Scotch, the
other Rye. He finds glasses and ranges them with the bottles*

on the desk. He fills one of the glasses with water from the cooler.)

MAX: *(as he enters)* Good evening, Mr. McCarver!

SAM: Happy New Year, Max!

MAX: The same to you, Mr. McCarver, and many of them. I brought up the reservations for Mr. Maddox to see.

SAM: *(relieving him of the book)* What's Oscar want with 'em?

OSCAR: Ain't I got to know where my personal friends is sittin'?

SAM: You got too dam' many friends. *(He is studying the book. He calls to* LENTELLI.*)* Take a look at this, Count. Want to give you an idea of the class we cater to. *(*LENTELLI *comes up to one shoulder to inspect the chart.* OSCAR *is looking over the other.)* Them there's the table numbers, see? Now just run your eye over that list of reservations. Some of 'em was made . . . how long ago, Max?

MAX: Oh, some of those go back to last September.

LENTELLI: As long ago as that?

SAM: Yeah! As long ago as that.

OSCAR: I wouldn't have said we had reservations as long ago as that.

MAX: Oh, yes, Mr. Maddox. Easily as long ago as that.

(This much is settled, anyway.)

SAM: Look! Here's old Emma Grieber. See, Count? "Emma Grieber an' party of five." You remember old Louie Grieber?

LENTELLI: Up in the Bronx?

SAM: That's him.

LENTELLI: He's dead. This his widow?

SAM: You can guess what *she's* worth. . . . Which Kohler is this, Max? Fred or Charlie?

MAX: That's Mr. Charles Kohler.

SAM: *(to* LENTELLI*)* I guess you know who Charlie Kohler is?

LENTELLI: Charlie Kohler?

SAM: North American Steel!

LENTELLI: Oh, sure!

SAM: Don't you remember when old Senator "Whose-gum" got up against it down in Washington last year an' burnt his fingers? Last year about this time, it was. Charlie just wrote him a check for a million dollars an' tore up the old man's note.

LENTELLI: The hell!

SAM: A cool million that check was, an' Charlie never knew he wrote it.

LENTELLI: Are you well acquainted with him?

SAM: With Charlie? No. Not personally. But I seen him often. . . . Here's H. M. Le Vallier.

LENTELLI: The tobacco man? I used to know G. K.

SAM: H. M.'s a good fella, too.

OSCAR: Who was it he married?

GEORGE: Trudie Fair.

LENTELLI: On the stage, wasn't she?

OSCAR: Just as a side-line.

SAM: Trudie's gettin' on, now. How old would you say Trudie was, George?

GEORGE: Oh, I dunno. Thirty?

SAM: I'd give her more myself.

OSCAR: I see Monty Garside's got a table.

SAM: That's Garside the banker's son. Wildest Indian you ever see.

MAX: By the way, Mr. McCarver . . .

SAM: (*not hearing him as he surrenders the book to* OSCAR) Quite a line-up, ain't it?

LENTELLI: It sure is!

SAM: Oh, we get all kinds!

GEORGE: (*speaking at the same time*) Scotch or Rye, Mr. Lentelli?

LENTELLI: Rye for me. A little water.

GEORGE: Sergeant?

HORAN: No water.

(GEORGE *is pouring.*)

SAM: Short one for me, George.

OSCAR: (*studying the book*) None for me.

SAM: (*lifting his glass*) Well, boys, a happy New Year to you one an' all!

LENTELLI: Over the hot sands!

GEORGE: (*speaking at the same time*) Here's kindness!

HORAN: (*speaking at the same time*) Success to crime! (*The drinks are downed.*) Wouldn't I just once like to see a Federal Prohibition agent refuse a drink!

LENTELLI: Well, the government wouldn't never get prohibition enforced like it does without the cooperation of the police.

(They bow to one another. HORAN *goes to the cooler for a chaser, with which he washes his mouth thoroughly.)*

SAM: Don't get that way, boys! We're one big family here. Take care of the Count, George.

GEORGE: How much?

SAM: Don't buy the Capitol.

*(*GEORGE *draws* LENTELLI *aside.)*

MAX: I was just about to say, Mr. McCarver, I understand there's some difficulty over Mr. Garside's account?

SAM: Yes. He paid his last bill with a bum check.

HORAN: Oh, that's a felony!

OSCAR: His old man's kicked him out. He's broke.

SAM: I'd kick him out myself if he didn't owe me so much.

MAX: His table's been engaged for over a month. I didn't know what to . . .

SAM: *(scratching his head)* I don't want to lose Monty. The kid may be wild, but he's class. . . .

HORAN: *(munching Lifesavers)* A bad check's a felony!

SAM: That's right, Sergeant. I tell you what, Max. Don't let him sign, and shift him to the lousiest table you got. Put him right under Oscar's band.

OSCAR: Say! My band ain't as noisy as all that, Sam!

MAX: Just drop a saxophone down his neck, Mr. Maddox! *(He marks the book and goes. The transaction between* GEORGE *and* LENTELLI *ends in a transfer of bills.* SAM *notices this.)*

SAM: *(speaking at the same time)* Like to take a look-see around before you go, boys?

LENTELLI: Wouldn't mind.

SAM: New Year's Eve ain't hardly what it used to be, but we do our best. How about it, Oscar? *(He opens the door at the back. The music swells out.)* Step into my box, gentlemen. I'd hate to tell you what them decorations set me back! *(*HORAN *shares his Lifesavers with* LENTELLI.*)*

LENTELLI: *(as* HORAN *and he pass through the door)* Pretty nifty!

SAM: Yessir! I like to go out there myself an' look 'em over. Makes me feel like I'm God Almighty. *(He turns back to* GEORGE.*)* Get Mrs. Ashe.

GEORGE: *(avoiding* OSCAR's *eye)* Mrs. Ashe don't answer, Sam. I been tryin' all evening.

SAM: Try again.

GEORGE: *(very reluctant, he takes up the telephone)* Try Mrs. Ashe at the Plaza again. Mr. McCarver calling. *(The dance-music rises to a climax.* SAM *goes to the box door.)*

SAM: *(to the two officers in the box)* Excuse me, boys. . . . Telephone. . . . *(He closes the door.)*

GEORGE: *(at the telephone—diffidently)* Sam. . . .

SAM: Yeah?

GEORGE: Don't get sore. . . . I been thinkin' about Mrs. Ashe, an' . . .

SAM: *(suddenly dangerous)* Yes, George?

GEORGE: *(a glance in* OSCAR's *direction)* Nothin'. *(OSCAR has been listening avidly. Now that the situation becomes untenable, he steps quickly into it.)*

OSCAR: I wanted your opinion on my "Ave Maria" foxtrot, Sam. I got cold feet of how they'll take it.

SAM: They'll take it if you put enough kick into it.

OSCAR: Well, I'm tryin' it out to-night, just after the big noise. Listen for it. I think it's mighty cute.

SAM: I will. You better be goin' on, Oscar. It's about time.

OSCAR: *(not at all eager to go)* Yes. I was just thinkin' that. Well. . . . See you later. *(He goes by the side door.)*

SAM: *(still dangerous)* What was that you was sayin', George?

GEORGE: Oh, not a hell of a lot, I guess.

SAM: *(after a pause)* You got Mrs. Ashe all wrong. Mrs. Ashe is a wonderful little woman. She's an honest to God, hundred per cent lady. She's got more on the ball in five minutes than . . .

GEORGE: Sam, I ain't denyin' that!

SAM: Think I don't know what's on your mind?

GEORGE: All right, I can't help it if you do get sore. I got to say it anyway.

SAM: What?

GEORGE: For God's sake use your head!

SAM: I guess you mean "don't lose it."

GEORGE: Somethin' like that.

SAM: Don't worry, George. My intentions is all wool an' a yard wide.

GEORGE: *(real horror)* My God, you ain't thinkin' of marryin' her!

SAM: *(a broad grin)* Suppose I was?

GEORGE: *(genuinely alarmed)* Now listen, Sam! Pull yourself together!

SAM: *(the grin broadening)* How do you guess she'd take to the idea?

GEORGE: Damfino, but . . .

SAM: *(the lungs filled)* Shootin' pretty high for me, huh?

GEORGE: It's you I'm thinkin' of.

SAM: Me?

GEORGE: Yeah.

SAM: *(serious again)* How's that?

GEORGE: God damn it, Sam!—she ain't good enough for you!

SAM: If that wasn't funny I *would* get sore!

GEORGE: Well, it's the truth. If you knew what I know about her . . .

SAM: I know all about her. But . . . *(Solemnly.)* Why, if I could pull off marryin' her . . . !

GEORGE: What in God's name would it buy you? Tell me that! Sure, she's a swell an' a swell sport. But raisin' hell is somethin' she don't do nothin' but, an' what would it buy you to . . .

SAM: *(very sage)* I got my own ideas of what I can get outta matrimony, see? What *I* can get outta it. Because I ain't exactly what you'd call a romantic man. So you needn't worry, George. I wouldn't get roped in on no marriage except for dam' good reasons. Business reasons. I'm on the up an' up, son, an' I know what I'm after. Yeah, an' I got a dam' good hunch Mrs. Ashe can help me get it. Now see about that call.

GEORGE: *(at the telephone again)* Still no answer? *(He rings off.)*

SAM: She wired me she was comin'.

GEORGE: Want your box saved? *(MISS DOROTHY DALE enters. She is the dancing attraction and hostess of the Tuileries. She is a pretty young woman, if you don't mind hardness. At the moment, she wears dress and make-up for her number. She is evidently in a fury.)*

DOLLY: I want to speak to Sam right away.

SAM: I can't stop you, Dolly.

DOLLY: I'm not kiddin'. It's important an' it's private.

SAM: All right, Dolly. Just a minute. *(A shrug of resignation and a glance at GEORGE.)*

GEORGE: *(he opens the box door)* How's it strike you, boys?

(The two guests return. GEORGE *closes the door.)*

LENTELLI: You got some place, Sam! You certainly are on the up an' up!

GEORGE: I know you got a lot more calls to pay this evening an' business is business.

HORAN: *(speaking at the same time)* I got to get over to the precinct. . . .

LENTELLI: *(shaking hands with* SAM*)* Sam, I certainly appreciate . . .

SAM: Don't mention it, Count. Always glad to help the government.

HORAN: Good night, Sam. Happy New Year!

*(*GEORGE *gets* LENTELLI *to the door.)*

LENTELLI: *(turning back to* SAM*)* Say, Sam! Expect to get out to Salt Lake next summer to the Shrine Convention?

SAM: I'm goin' to try like hell. *(*GEORGE *takes* LENTELLI *through the door.* SAM *shakes hands with* HORAN*.)* Like hell!

*(*HORAN *laughs and goes.* SAM *closes the door.)* Well, Dolly, what's the trouble?

DOLLY: It's Jimmie again.

SAM: What about Jimmie? *(He comes over to his desk and sits down.)*

DOLLY: If I ever dance another step with *that* rat . . .

SAM: Oho!

DOLLY: I hate to say it, Sam, but the trouble's a friend of yours.

SAM: *(after a short pause)* Who?

DOLLY: Mrs. Ashe. Jimmie's plumb nuts about her an' you know Jimmie!

SAM: You leave Mrs. Ashe outta this.

DOLLY: You ask Oscar. . . .

SAM: Leave her out! . . . She's got nothin' to do with it. She don't even know Jimmie's alive.

DOLLY: All right. She ain't to blame anyway. But there's Jimmie with his tongue hangin' out like a dog's for her. . . . There's one thing I want to know right here and now. Who's hostess at the Tuileries, Mrs. . . .

SAM: *(cutting her off)* You are, Dolly. *(Through the telephone.)* Ask Jimmie Wright to step up to my office.

DOLLY: Just understand I won't have my numbers gummed for anybody. Either you get me a new partner or I break my contract, or . . .

SAM: *(pause—then)* Or what?

DOLLY: I'd rather not say. . . . I ain't mentionin' no names. But, if you don't want one hell of a row between me an' a certain lady! . . . Now, don't try to high-hat me, lookin' at me that way! . . . What are you goin' to do about it?

SAM: Not a dam' thing in the world.

DOLLY: That settles Jimmie's hash. I'll put on my South Sea solo to-night, an' begin rehearsin' a new boy in the morning.

SAM: Will you give Jimmie another chance if I talk to him?

DOLLY: So help me God, if you don't fire him, out I go.

SAM: All right. Clear outta here before he comes. *(JIMMIE bursts in. He is slight, dissolute, and excited. He wears a dress suit and the make-up for his present dance number.)*

JIMMIE: So I'm fired, am I?

SAM: Been listenin', have you?

JIMMIE: I didn't have to listen. How about my contract?

DOLLY: *(the great lady of Broadway)* You ought to ha' thought of that before!

SAM: Come on, now! None of that in here. You get out, Dolly. I want to see Jimmie alone.

DOLLY: Oh, all right. *(She sweeps out.)*

SAM: Dolly's worth more to the Tuileries than you are, Jimmie.

JIMMIE: I got a contract.

SAM: I'll use you somewheres else.

JIMMIE: It isn't that.

SAM: Well, then, what is it?

JIMMIE: *You* ought to know. You're in the same boat. Mrs. Ashe an' you . . .

SAM: I'll take just about so much from you, Jimmie.

JIMMIE: Oh, lay off! You don't get by with me for a minute. Go ahead and fire me, if you want to, but don't try to pull that stuff. I'm tellin' you . . .

SAM: When I fire a man, *I* do the tellin', see? Now you . . *(GEORGE opens the door.)* What is it?

GEORGE: Gentleman to see you, Sam.

SAM: I'm busy.

GEORGE: It's about Mrs. Ashe's table.

SAM: Mrs. Ashe's table? Oh. . . . *(JIMMIE draws himself up and laughs.* SAM *bites his lip.)* Show him up.

GEORGE: In here, sir. *(He stands aside to admit* ARCHIE ELLIS, *a personable and self-assured young rounder of undoubted breeding and some twenty-nine years.* GEORGE *goes, closing the door.)*

ARCHIE: *(to* JIMMIE*)* Mr. McCarver?

SAM: Here.

ARCHIE: I'm sorry. I think I did meet you once before, though I was a bit squiffed at the time. I'm Mrs. Ashe's cousin, Archie Ellis.

SAM: *(company speech and manners)* I remember you, Mr. Ellis.

ARCHIE: I'm sorry to be troubling you, but Carlotta—Mrs. Ashe—is down in the lobby raising bally hell about that table you gave her.

SAM: I didn't know she had a table.

ARCHIE: It's really Monty Garside's table, I suppose. He reserved it a month ago, and your head waiter's put us right under the music.

SAM: I see.

ARCHIE: Carlotta—Mrs. Ashe—is mad as fury, and the other two—Monty and another chap, a Jewish stock-broker named Burton Burton . . .

SAM: I know Mr. Burton.

ARCHIE: Silly name for a Jew, isn't it? Well, they're both tight.

SAM: Is this Mr. Garside's party?

ARCHIE: Yes. . . . Can't something be done, Mr. McCarver? It seems that my cousin and he met in Atlantic City, and came all the way up in a taxi just to get here. God knows why they wanted to get here, but now they *are* here, they're naturally disappointed.

SAM: *(at the telephone)* Tell Jerry to show Mr. Garside's party to my box. You don't mind sitting in the balcony? *(This to* ARCHIE, *who shakes his head.)* Call Max to the phone.

ARCHIE: That's frightfully kind of you.

SAM: *(holding the wire)* Don't mention it.

ARCHIE: But, I must . . . I . . .

SAM: We'll do our best to make you comfortable, Mr. Ellis.

ARCHIE: You're sure you don't *need* your box?

SAM: I was expecting a party but it's off. *(JIMMIE laughs.)*

So you're entirely welcome. *(At the telephone.)* That you Max? Put Mr. Garside's party in my box, and let me have the check. . . .

ARCHIE: I say, you needn't do that, you know. . . .

SAM: *(still through the telephone)* Take care of 'em yourself and serve 'em up that Pommery you put on ice for me. *(Rings off.)* There you are.

ARCHIE: *(staggered)* This certainly is generous of you, Mr. McCarver. I don't know what to say!

SAM: I hope you have a pleasant evening.

ARCHIE: Oh, I'm afraid I shall have a wretched time. I'm on the wagon.

SAM: There are worse places.

ARCHIE: Not with everybody tight all around you. You have to pretend you think they're as funny as they think they are themselves. . . . Haven't you noticed that? Haven't you? *(This to* JIMMIE, *who is not very attentive.)*

JIMMIE: Yeah. . . . Sure. . . .

ARCHIE: *(floundering on) I* have often. I do wish my cousin would leave me at home to sleep when she goes on these parties of hers. You see, I don't awfully enjoy drinking. And I do like to sleep. I seem to need a great deal of sleep. Some people do, you know. . . . And, if I must drink, I insist on doing it in peace and quiet. . . . In a club, or . . . Of course you call this a club, don't you? . . . Oh, I don't mean . . . I . . . You'll join us, won't you, Mr. McCarver?

SAM: Later, maybe.

ARCHIE: Oh, do. . . . They'll be wondering what's become of me. . . . I . . . Thank you so much. . . . I'll be going back to them. . . . *(He goes, vaguely.)*

JIMMIE: Are we in the same boat or aren't we?

SAM: I don't know what you're talkin' about!

JIMMIE: Oh, *don't* you!

SAM: No, an' I don't want to hear any more outta you!

JIMMIE: *Is* that so? Well, she won't look at you any more than she will at me. . . . She goes off to Atlantic City with *him,* though!

SAM: Him? Who?

JIMMIE: That goddam Monty Garside! That's who!

SAM: You're crazy!

JIMMIE: Didn't he just tell you about 'em comin' up from Atlantic City together? Well, I saw 'em goin' down to Atlantic City together.

SAM: Playin' the big detective, huh?

JIMMIE: I saw 'em goin' down together, she and Monty Garside. Yes, an' what's more, I went down there myself last Sunday an' caught 'em together. And now they come home together so they can spend New Year's Eve together!

SAM: You an' me ain't got nothin' to do with Mrs. Ashe. What she does an' where she goes ain't none of our dam' business.

JIMMIE: Don't you wish it was? She's going to marry Monty Garside, Sam! So help me, she is! I'll kill that Garside!

SAM: You'll kill nobody. Now get to hell outta here.

JIMMIE: *(speaking at the same time)* You see if I don't! You see . . . (*The box door is opened by* CARLOTTA ASHE *and we see this bone of so much contention. Some of us wonder and some of us don't. No one denies that she is a masterpiece, for it has taken centuries to produce her. Nothing so finely fashioned ever could come before the complete maturity of a race. Indeed* CARLOTTA *is, and has always been, a sort of danger-signal which nature hangs out to warn a race of its decadence. She is aristocratic in every trifle and aspect of her person and her atmosphere. She has the distinction which scorns elegance. Just now, for example, she is wearing a simple slip of a dress, and her only jewelry is a short string of small, perfectly matched and perfectly graduated pearls. She doesn't care about jewelry just as she doesn't care about make-up; she is too lazy and too busy for either. She knows, too, that such youthful loveliness as hers needs no assistance. It is beauty of every part, and unbelievably fragile and exquisite. Enchantingly incongruous, too. The dark, spritely hair above her mobile, excited face—it is cut "Lord Byron" that hair—springs upward with an outrageous vitality of its own. Her eyes catch this vitality and never lose it, whether her thought be reckless and alluring or ruthlessly cruel. The classic modelling and chiselling of her features is thrown completely off by the boyish gawkiness of her bodily movement. Her speech and her voice—one does not know quite what to say of them except that they are to be heard in and about the more expensive country clubs, drinking tea at the Plaza, slouching on the beach at Southampton. Her language is, of course, one mess of musical-comedy catch phrases. There is nothing tangibly wrong with her and yet she is, in some curious and intangible way, a little tarnished. Her great blood is there, though, and it preserves her poise. She is just twenty-eight and she can look nineteen or fifty. It depends on her mood, which depends on circumstances. Her manners are as bad as her breeding has been good. She was never disciplined in her life and nothing has ever affected her. Her eyes have that false innocence which only irresponsible wealth and an utter carelessness about money can produce. But she is undeniably and irresistibly fascinating.)*

CARLOTTA: *(as she enters)* My dear, all the way from Atlantic City in a taxi!

SAM: Good evening, Mrs. Ashe.

CARLOTTA: A yellow taxi. . . . But I did get here, Mr. McCarver!

SAM: It must have been quite a ride.

CARLOTTA: It was a panic, my dear! A perfect panic! Can you imagine! . . . But I simply must thank you, Mr. McCarver, for . . . *(Her gesture includes the box. Through the open door the supper-party can be seen as* MAX *seats its members. There is* ARCHIE *and the foolishly named stock-broker,* BURTON BURTON, *and the much-mooted* MONTY GARSIDE. BURTON *is large, middle-aged, handsome, and self-indulgent. You would not guess the Semitic secret of his ancestry before the third or fourth encounter. Then, if he had been up late the night before or happened to be angry, out it would pop at you.* MONTY, *being very drunk, is practically invisible. Drunkards have a way of becoming progressingly invisible as their speech and thought waves become progressively unintelligible. He is young. At the moment they are having a good deal of trouble with him.)*

MONTY: *(alcoholic gibberish signifying)* Let's get out of this goddam place. This isn't my table!

ARCHIE: Come on, now, Monty!

CARLOTTA: *(to Sam)* Monty can't seem to decide between not being able to stand up and not wanting to sit down.

SAM: I'm glad to see you here, Mrs. Ashe. I hoped you were going to be my guest to-night.

CARLOTTA: What was I to do with poor Monty? Look how tight he is! Isn't it too vile of him!

SAM: You're very beautiful to-night.

CARLOTTA: Thank you. Come and enjoy me while I last.

BURTON: *(coming in from the box)* Carlotta!

CARLOTTA: Yes, Bertie?

BURTON: There's champagne!

CARLOTTA: Of course, Bertie! You can always trust Mr. Sam McCarver.

ARCHIE: Coming, Carlotta?

CARLOTTA: Oh, so eagerly! . . . It's going to be a merry party after all. *(She returns to the box.* SAM *and* BURTON *shake hands in the door.)*

ARCHIE: *(speaking at the same time)* Row's over now, Monty. We're all alive and well and there's champagne. Be good and keep quiet. (CARLOTTA *regards* MONTY *distastefully.)*

SAM: Keeping up the golf, Mr. Burton?

BURTON: Eh? Oh, it's getting on to squash season. But I hope to get away South next month. Not right away. The season . . . business . . .

SAM: Sold my North American Steel. . . .

BURTON: Good gain?

SAM: Forty points.

BURTON: You were in luck.

CARLOTTA: Bertie, stop talking business and come in here. I'm sure Monty's going to be sick. (MONTY *protests loudly and unintelligibly. Laughter from* BURTON *as he goes out.* SAM *watches.)*

CARLOTTA: Oh, look at the girl in the red dress! *(She points down upon the dancing-floor. They all look.)*

ARCHIE: I say! She *is* naked!

CARLOTTA: Archie, how can you be such a fool! Could anybody resist my Archie? I ask you . . .

ARCHIE: I suppose I shall fall off the wagon.

CARLOTTA: That's right. Give in, Archie! Give in! Give that l'il girl a nice great big hand!

ARCHIE: (MAX *has been pouring champagne, and he lifts his glass)* I shall certainly fall off the wagon. . . . *(This conversation has been a considerable babble with the music swelling over it. In the office,* JIMMIE *has stood watching feverishly. Suddenly, now, he brushes the sight from his eyes and turns back toward the lobby door. As he does so he sees something in the desk drawer which startles him. It is the open drawer from which, earlier in the act,* GEORGE *took the whiskey bottles. He catches his breath in a kind of sob, reaches into the drawer and fishes out a revolver. It is at this moment that* SAM *returns to the office.* JIMMIE *slips the gun into his pocket.)*

BURTON: *(talking in the door with* SAM*)* Come into the office some day, Mr. McCarver. I'd like to have a talk with you.

SAM: I'll take you up on that, Mr. Burton. I follow the market pretty close now.

BURTON: We all have to do that.

SAM: That's the truth.

CARLOTTA: Not leaving, Mr. McCarver?

SAM: For a minute.

CARLOTTA: Be careful! It's almost time!

SAM: Don't you fret, Mrs. Ashe. I'll be back.

CARLOTTA: That's a brave boy!

SAM: *(he comes in, sees* JIMMIE, *and only partially closes the box door)* I told you to get out.

JIMMIE: I'm going.

SAM: Make it snappy.

JIMMIE: Remember what I said, that's all.

SAM: For God's sake, Jimmie, get a hold of yourself!

JIMMIE: It's nothing . . . it's nothing . . . it's only that. *(A gesture toward the box party.)*

SAM: Go on along home an' get some sleep. . . .

JIMMIE: Yes. . . . I will. . . .

SAM: . . . An' forget it. (MONTY *bursts forth anew into gibberish.* CARLOTTA *has been watching him uneasily. Now she rises, looks irritably about her, and comes into the office.)*

CARLOTTA: I'm certain Monty is going to be sick. I hate that. Getting as tight as he is spoils all the fun. *(She is distracted by the spectacle of* JIMMIE.*)* Oh. . . .

SAM: Don't mind him, Mrs. Ashe. I'll see about Monty. *(He is torn between* JIMMIE *and* MONTY. MAX *appears in the box with the first course of the supper.)* There's Max. He'll take care of Monty all right. Max, look after Mr. Garside, will you?

CARLOTTA: *(staring at* JIMMIE*)* Is there anything wrong?

SAM: No! Not a thing! You come back to-morrow, Jimmie, an' I'll fix up everything.

JIMMIE: *(brokenly—his eyes terribly burning at* CARLOTTA*)* I'm sorry. . . . It's all right. . . . *(He goes.)*

CARLOTTA: Isn't that . . . ? *(She means* JIMMIE.*)*

SAM: Jimmie Wright.

CARLOTTA: The boy who dances here?

SAM: He did dance here. I had to fire him.

CARLOTTA: Why?

SAM: He got a little out of hand.

CARLOTTA: He dances so well. *(Uproar from* MONTY.*)* I wish you'd shut that door and let me stay in here until that's over.

SAM: Certainly. *(He closes the box door. There is an uncomfortable silence.)*

CARLOTTA: I hope you don't mind.

SAM: Mind?

CARLOTTA: My staying in here.

SAM: *(pause)* Did you think I would?

CARLOTTA: *(amused)* No.

SAM: *(rushing forward with a chair)* Let me make you comfortable.

CARLOTTA: Thanks. *(She sits. There is another awkward pause.)*

SAM: Won't you take something to drink?

CARLOTTA: No. But I'll take a cigarette.

SAM: *(very effusive)* Right here. . . . *(He offers his case. She takes one. He strikes a match.)*

CARLOTTA: *(relieving him of the box)* I hate to boast, but I *can* strike a match for myself. *(She does.)*

SAM: I beg pardon.

CARLOTTA: Granted. What time's it getting to be?

SAM: About twelve.

CARLOTTA: I don't want to miss . . .

SAM: You won't. You'll hear the big noise. It always starts ahead of time.

CARLOTTA: Then I can settle back and enjoy myself.

SAM: That's the idea. I'm tickled to death to get a chance like this . . . for a little talk.

CARLOTTA: So?

SAM: Yeah! I don't get many such opportunities.

CARLOTTA: Well, make the most of this one.

SAM: Yeah! I intend to.

CARLOTTA: Good!

SAM: *(he sits on the desk. There is another awkward moment)* I don't guess I'm much like anybody you ever knew.

CARLOTTA: You're not in the *least* like anybody I ever knew.

SAM: You're not like anybody *I* ever knew.

CARLOTTA: That's your boyish innocence. "Men are nothing but little boys grown up."

SAM: Who said that?

CARLOTTA: Isn't it in the Bible?

SAM: *(deeply)* It's true—little boys grown up. . . . Until they get married.

CARLOTTA: Until they . . . ! Whoever told you that?

SAM: I thought of it myself. Just then.

CARLOTTA: I hope you're not thinking of getting married?

SAM: I am, though.

CARLOTTA: Oh, please don't, Mr. McCarver!

SAM: Why not?

CARLOTTA: It's a perfectly poisonous idea. I shan't love you any more if you get married!

SAM: Why not?

CARLOTTA: It would ruin you.

SAM: You're wrong there. It would make me.

CARLOTTA: I won't have it. You're fascinating as you are.

SAM: You don't know what I used to be.

CARLOTTA: I can guess.

SAM: Well?

CARLOTTA: Almost anything.

SAM: *(leaning toward her, suddenly expansive—all his self-consciousness lost in an autobiographical ecstasy)* I started work when I was twelve years old rustlin' drinks in a Turkish bath in Hoboken. It was some joint. You got soused at the bar an' you sobered up in the steam-room, an' then you went back to the bar to start all over again.

CARLOTTA: Doesn't it sound convenient! Did you do that? No. I suppose you were too young. *(Her interest is waning.)* I wonder how Monty is now?

SAM: Give him a minute more.

CARLOTTA: Go on. What then? I think it's really romantic.

SAM: Then twenty years of one thing an' another windin' up in this place.

CARLOTTA: How perfectly marvellous of you!

SAM: Where do I go from here? That's the question.

CARLOTTA: Anywhere you like, don't you?

SAM: Nope. When I was a kid, old Dan—he's my doorman here, now—give me my first boost. I come all this way on that boost. Now it's used up, and I need another. I gotta have another. That's what makes me think about marriage.

CARLOTTA: I never heard of anything so cold-blooded!

SAM: I can't help that.

CARLOTTA: Why, it's too awful of you!

SAM: I'm talkin' straight . . . to *you*.

CARLOTTA: *(a pause—rather dubious)* To *me*?

SAM: *(a pause—very wary)* Yeah. . . .

CARLOTTA: Why to me?

SAM: There's quite a difference between us, ain't there? *(She is at once incredulous and spellbound.) Ain't* there? . . .

CARLOTTA: I don't know. *Is* there?

SAM: It's just that difference I aim to get over.

CARLOTTA: *(the spell breaks and she rises)* I think I'd better get back to my party.

SAM: *(also rising)* What's the hurry?

CARLOTTA: Well, Mr. McCarver . . . *(But she thinks better of her explanation.)* No. . . . I shan't say another word . . . I'll . . . I'll get back to my party.

BURTON: *(as* CARLOTTA *opens the door)* Oh, there you are!

ARCHIE: Monty's passed out of the picture. *(She closes the door. The last we see of her, her shoulders are shaking with suppressed laughter.* SAM *stares after her, his face wooden.* GEORGE *enters just in time to see the box door close.)*

GEORGE: Sam!

SAM: *(not moving)* Yeah?

GEORGE: What's up with Jimmie?

SAM: Fired him.

GEORGE: Them dancin'-boys is bums.

SAM: We're *all* bums. I'm the worst bum of the lot. *(GEORGE eyes him curiously.)* Must be pretty near time. *(He looks at his watch.)*

GEORGE: Joinin' the party?

SAM: Let's have a little drink in here . . . like we used to . . . you an' me an' Dan. *(He sits down and gloomily lights a cigar.)*

GEORGE: Good idea! *(Telephone.)* Send Dan up to the office.

SAM: The three of us.

GEORGE: *(preparing the refreshments)* Take a little drink . . . make a little resolution. *(The big noise starts.)*

SAM: Yeah. . . . *(He shakes his head grimly and silently.)* An' then I'll trot along home to bed.

GEORGE: New Year's ain't what it used to was!

SAM: What is?

GEORGE: Oh, hell! A guy's got to look at things the way they're goin' to be.

SAM: New Year's is like everything else. Only it's a good time to pull yourself up an' tell yourself what a dam' fool you're makin' of yourself! *(With a savage shake of his head, he clears his mind of its recent unpleasant impressions.* DAN *enters.)* Come in, Dan, an' drink a New Year's toast.

DAN: For old time's sake, I'll do it, Sam, though ye know I'm no drinker.

SAM: We seen quite some years out an' in, ain't we, Dan?

DAN: Yes, we have. I was wishin' to-night we was back in th' old fightin' days. Wouldn't you ever be wishin' that, Sam?

SAM: *(himself again)* Not for five hundred grand, I wouldn't, Dan! Next year we're goin' to be further off than ever. What'll it be next year? A hotel? A flier in the show business? Or just plain Wall Street? There's jack on Wall Street. I ain't done half bad down there this year.

DAN: Here's hopin' your luck holds, Sam! *(The drinks are ready.* GEORGE *passes them.)*

SAM: Maybe Dan 'ud prefer champagne?

DAN: When I do drink, I drink liquor! *(They laugh and are about to drink. The big noise is punctured by a revolver-shot. The three at the desk hold their glasses suspended, listening, wondering that the back-fire from any automobile could reach them in there.)*

SAM: *(uncertainly)* Hey! *(There is the sound of a struggle just outside the box door.)*

GEORGE: What's goin' on out there?

SAM: Have a look. *(GEORGE sets down his untouched glass, goes to the box door, and opens it.* MONTY *is lying across the table dead.* ARCHIE *is struggling with* JIMMIE *for the possession of the revolver. They fairly tumble into the office.)*

ARCHIE: No you don't! *(GEORGE seizes* JIMMIE, *wrenches the gun out of his grasp and flings him bodily across the room, where he falls against the desk, whimpering abjectly.* CARLOTTA *staggers in followed by* BURTON. MAX *stands in the doorway. The music, which has faltered for a moment, resumes wildly.)*

BURTON: He's killed Monty Garside!

SAM: *(rising in consternation)* What? . . . Oh, Jesus!

DAN: *(rising, to JIMMIE)* That's the hell of a trick to play on a boss like Sam!

SAM: *(shaken, but very cool)* Have a look, George. You keep things quiet, Max. Get a doctor, Dan, an' tell somebody to go over to the precinct for Sergeant Horan. Don't say what's happened. *(The three obey immediately the orders are issued.)*

CARLOTTA: How horrible! How disgusting!

ARCHIE: It isn't pretty.

MAX: *(off stage)* Don't be alarmed, ladies and gentlemen. A fuse blew out, but there is absolutely no danger.

SAM: Good boy, Max!

ARCHIE: *(to SAM)* Give me some whiskey. Carlotta's got a heart.

SAM: Here. *(He passes ARCHIE one of the unused drinks.)*

BURTON: How the devil did it happen?

SAM: *(very depressed)* We'll find out.

ARCHIE: Come on now, Lottie. . . . *(ARCHIE and BURTON attend CARLOTTA. GEORGE returns, closing the door after him.)*

SAM: Dead?

GEORGE: Sure.

SAM: *(at the craven JIMMIE)* You poor fool!

JIMMIE: Didn't I tell you?

SAM: Keep quiet. . . . Let's see the rod.

GEORGE: *(producing it)* Here.

SAM: *(he takes it and starts with amazement)* Why, it's mine. . . . *(He sees the open drawer.)* . . . Well, I'll be God damned!

ARCHIE: If it weren't for the circumstances, I'd be glad of it.

SAM: That kind of talk don't do no good. *(DAN returns.)*

BURTON: *(to ARCHIE)* This is going to make the loudest noise since Thaw shot Stanford White. We're all in for it.

SAM: *(who has overhead this)* Say!

ARCHIE: This pretty thoroughly does for you, Lottie. Well, you've been riding for a fall. I do wish you'd left me home in bed. *(CARLOTTA does not answer. JIMMIE looks at her like a terrified dog and licks his lips. SAM watches them.)*

SAM: *(an idea striking him)* By God! . . . George, call Max. *(His eyes never leave CARLOTTA. GEORGE opens the door and calls MAX. MAX enters.)*

MAX: Yes, Sir?

SAM: *(thinking hard)* Any other witnesses?

MAX: Not a one. They couldn't have seen it from the floor. The corridor was empty.

SAM: Where's your rod, George?

GEORGE: Home.

SAM: Dan? (DAN *delivers.*) Registered?

DAN: What d'ye mean, registered?

SAM: On your permit! On your permit!

DAN: Not under any number they can trace. I'm naturally cautious with firearms.

SAM: We'll take a chance. *(He whips out his handkerchief and wipes the gun thoroughly. Then he hands it to* GEORGE, *still in the handkerchief.)*

ARCHIE: *(watching)* I say!

SAM: Print Monty's fingers all over it. . . . See if Mrs. Ashe dropped anything. (GEORGE *goes.* SAM *wipes his own gun, with which the murder was committed. He prints his own fingers all over it and slips it into his pocket.)*

ARCHIE: I say!

SAM: *(jerking* JIMMIE *to his feet)* If you ever spill a word of this I'll break your back, see? . . . Now beat it. *(Dazed,* JIMMIE *starts for the door to the lobby.)* Not that way. Out there! . . . An' out the back door, too. (JIMMIE *goes by the box door.)* Now you, Mrs. Ashe, an' the rest of you, out the same way. This is *my* funeral.

ARCHIE: What under the sun are you up to?

SAM: Never you mind that. Clear on out. Max'll show you the way. (GEORGE *returns with a scarf, vanity-box, and gloves.* SAM *hands them to* ARCHIE.)

CARLOTTA: But, you . . . I don't want to get *you* in trouble! There's no reason why you . . .

SAM: You can always turn up afterward if I don't get away with it. Clear out, now.

CARLOTTA: Oh! . . . (SAM *pushes her through the door.* ARCHIE *follows,* BURTON *next, and* MAX *brings up the rear. The sight of the dead body almost does for* CARLOTTA. SAM *closes the door after them. He is thinking so hard he fairly mutters to himself.)*

GEORGE: Here they are.

SAM: I do the talkin', see? (GEORGE *admits* HORAN *and a new cop from the lobby.)*

HORAN: Well, Sam, what's up?

SAM: Shootin' things up a bit.

HORAN: That's bad for business.

SAM: Yeah, I know it is.

HORAN: Anybody hurt?

SAM: Man named Garside. Dead.

HORAN: Who did it?

SAM: I did.

HORAN: Holy smoke! Where is he?

SAM: Out there. (GEORGE *shows the way. The two cops follow. The cops are faintly audible through the music.* SAM'S *eye rounds up his forces.* HORAN *returns.* MAX *follows him in.*)

MAX: The doctor is here, sir.

HORAN: Send him away, for God's sake. You can't blow out a man's brains an' expect a doctor to put 'em back. (*This notion tickles* HORAN'S *funny-bone.*) Who did you say he was?

SAM: Montgomery Garside.

HORAN: Relation of the banker?

SAM: Son.

HORAN: (*only a little grave*) I'm afraid this is goin' to be bad for you, Sam.

SAM: I hope not.

HORAN: So do I. How did it happen?

SAM: Self-defense.

HORAN: Oh, well, that's understood.

SAM: Sit down, Sergeant, an' have a drink.

HORAN: We don't want to be too sociable about this, Sam. There's a dead man out there.

SAM: Yeah, I know there is. (*The orchestra strikes lyrically into* OSCAR'S *"Ave Maria" foxtrot.*)

HORAN: Well! (*He takes the drink which* SAM *offers him.*)

SAM: (*he is thinking at top speed*) There's Oscar playin' his hymn tune. Hear it, boys? Not bad. Not half bad.

GEORGE: (*listening*) Not bad at all!

MAX: (*listening*) Great! (DAN *and* HORAN *nod approval.*)

SAM: Max, just ask that other copper to keep outta sight, will you? I don't want no panics more'n what I got right here. Now . . . let's see. . . . (MAX *has whispered through the back door and closed it again.*) To begin with, Garside come drunk. . . . You'll bear me out or correct me, boys? (*The gang, settling itself in perfect and plausible comfort, murmurs and nods.*) Come drunk an' just raised hell over the table we give him. Those friends of his who come with him must ha' cleared out. I didn't see nothin' of 'em. Did you, George?

GEORGE: Not me, Sam.

SAM: I guess George ought to be able to locate 'em, though. Look into that, will you, George?

GEORGE: Sure I will.

SAM: But Garside stays an' raises hell some more till I take him into my own box out there, where George an' me are passin' a quiet evenin' just watchin' things . . . with Max, too, when he had a spare moment. . . . You can see the four covers all laid out there still . . . George's an' mine an' Max's . . . an' the one Max added for Garside. George, just remember to make a list of any other witnesses the Sergeant might need.

GEORGE: I'll see to that.

SAM: Well, we got Garside quiet, an' then, by God, if he don't want to buy the place an' sign for it! I'm objectin' to that because I got a bale of his bum checks already, an' his father's kicked him out, which don't hardly improve his credit none. You remember, we was talkin' about that, Sergeant, when you was in here earlier?

HORAN: So you was!

SAM: An' me objectin' gets Garside nasty. He sure was nasty, wasn't he, George?

GEORGE: He sure was.

SAM: So George an' me comes in here, leavin' Max in charge.

GEORGE: Then Max calls us back. He couldn't handle things alone.

MAX: He got pretty violent before I called you.

SAM: I could hear him clear through the door.

DAN: Then Sam telephones down-stairs for me to come up.

SAM: There's times when you need a bouncer.

GEORGE: An' we goes out, all three of us.

DAN: The more the quieter!

SAM: An' he pulls a rod on us.

GEORGE: Just like that!

SAM: I guess his rod's still there, ain't it, George?

GEORGE: I didn't touch it.

SAM: Well, I don't take no chances on no drunk with a rod.

MAX: And he certainly was drunk!

DAN: An' the three of us jammed up in that door together.

SAM: So I just let him have it. I had to. Here's my gun. I guess you'll want it. An' that's the story. (SAM'S *gang cannot suppress an almost imperceptible movement of relief.*) A drunk who wrote bum checks an' carried a rod. Why do you suppose he carried a rod, George? I never would have expected Monty Garside to carry a rod. (*The* SERGEANT *is carefully studying* SAM'S *gun as the curtain falls.*)

ACT TWO

SCENE: The salon of a luxurious Park Avenue apartment. Just that; nothing more. Doors here and there which give on the entrance vestibule, the dining-room, the library, and the sleeping quarters. The usual lamps, davenports, and antiques. Over the mantel a portrait of a lady; period: the late eighties; style: Whistler.

It is evening. ANNIE, the maid who accompanied CARLOTTA to her first balls, comes from the hall bringing coffee. She sets the tray down and lights the lamps. Then CARLOTTA comes from the dining-room followed by BURTON. She wears a simple but very beautiful *robe d'intérieure*. BURTON wears his dinner coat.

CARLOTTA: (*speaking as she enters*) Annie, I think it might be a good idea to keep something hot for Mr. McCarver.

ANNIE: Yes, Miss Lottie?

BURTON: Won't Sam have dined on the train?

CARLOTTA: I can't be sure. He was due about seven and there might not be a diner. (ANNIE *goes into the bedroom, taking with her the tray of empty shaker and cocktail glasses left from the children's hour.* CARLOTTA *sits down to pouring the coffee.*) Of course I love your wit and wisdom, Bertie, but it wasn't for that I let you stay to dinner. You've got to come down to brass tacks, now.

BURTON: Be specific.

CARLOTTA: Sugar?

BURTON: One lump.

CARLOTTA: (*handing him his cup*) Sit down over there. You'll find cigars in that box. I want some money.

BURTON: (*settling himself*) Do you really? How much?

CARLOTTA: Twenty-five thousand.

BURTON: Hm! . . . Where do you expect it to come from?

CARLOTTA: How should I know? You handle my affairs, don't you?

BURTON: You can't have twenty-five thousand.

CARLOTTA: Why not, may I ask?

BURTON: Because you haven't got it.

CARLOTTA: Do you mean to say . . . ?

BURTON: Just that. You haven't got it. Incomes are money, not rubber.

CARLOTTA: Hell! . . . Can't you sell something?

BURTON: I've already sold everything that was sellable. (*He eyes her a moment, then decides to continue.*) You don't realize it, Carlotta, but you've been going through these crises at the rate of two a year for—well, for some time. Now you're not as rich as you were.

CARLOTTA: But . . . damn it, Bertie! . . . I've got to have it!

BURTON: Why don't you ask your husband for it?

CARLOTTA: (*a pause—then*) You don't know my Sammy on paying my bills!

BURTON: You don't seem to have much objection to my paying them.

CARLOTTA: Now, what on earth do you mean by that?

BURTON: I don't see why I should pay your bills any longer.

CARLOTTA: (*an amazed pause*) What's that?

BURTON: You were the one who said "brass tacks," not I.

CARLOTTA: Well?

BURTON: But I'm delighted. "Brass tacks" it is! You didn't have any more money for the two crises last year than you have now and I met them both out of my own pocket.

CARLOTTA: You didn't!

BURTON: Oh, I did, though. Last March, just a year ago this time, you wanted twenty thousand to go abroad on. I gave you that. Last October, when you came home, you wanted fifteen thousand more to do God knows what on. And I gave you that. You never suspected that your capital wasn't paying you just lots and lots of dividends.

CARLOTTA: May I ask what made you so infernally obliging?

BURTON: If you'll remember, I had every reason to believe that you were going to marry me after you divorced Ashe.

CARLOTTA: Whatever put that idea in your head?

BURTON: As a matter of fact, you did yourself.

CARLOTTA: I didn't!

BURTON: Oh, yes you did, though!

CARLOTTA: Oh, I couldn't have! My poor old Bertie! *(They are both intensely amused.)*

BURTON: And as long as things continue under the present auspices . . .

CARLOTTA: What *are* we going to do about it?

BURTON: I leave that to you.

CARLOTTA: You can't expect me to throw Sam over and marry you now, can you?

BURTON: I don't see that . . . that it's necessary to throw him over entirely.

CARLOTTA: *(a smiling, damnèd pause)* Isn't that remark just a trifle suggestive?

BURTON: It all depends on how you look at it.

CARLOTTA: So's your old man.

BURTON: You know how I feel about you.

CARLOTTA: You Hebrews are simply rampant about sex, aren't you? Any one would think you'd invented it.

BURTON: That's in the nature of a rejection, isn't it?

CARLOTTA: I'll call you "My Bertie" and that's all.

BURTON: I see. *(Pause. He decides to go even further.)* You don't mind my being quite frank?

CARLOTTA: Remember, Bertie, I am a woman.

BURTON: You want twenty-five thousand. I need half a million. If you'll get me what I need, I'll give you what you want. How's that for frankness?

CARLOTTA: How under the sun could I get . . . ?

BURTON: This husband of yours is making frightfully good in Wall Street.

CARLOTTA: Lucky Sam McCarver!

BURTON: That's more than a nickname, I assure you. I don't suppose you know what he's up to now?

CARLOTTA: I forget whether it's Texas or Oklahoma. You can ask him when he comes in.

BURTON: Well, he's bringing back a proposition I want very much to handle for him.

CARLOTTA: All right, handle it.

BURTON: I expect to . . . with your assistance.

CARLOTTA: Are you asking me to turn Sam over to you, signed, sealed, and delivered, for twenty-five thousand dollars? No, thank you very much, I'll do without the money.

BURTON: I'm not going to hurt him any. I get in on the ground floor of a good thing . . . you get your money, and Sam . . . well, you'd be doing Sam a real service by steering him my way.

CARLOTTA: We can skip that. I don't know about such things.

BURTON: It's very simple. You two were married under circumstances that were, to say the least, quaint. If the true story of Monty Garside's death ever leaked out, it would be uncomfortable for both of you.

CARLOTTA: Why, Bertie Burton, you blackmailing little skunk, publish and be damned!

BURTON: And send Sam up for perjury? (*Pause in the best of good humor.*)

CARLOTTA: Perjury?

BURTON: What else do *you* call it? . . . I'm being frank, Carlotta. It isn't pleasant for me to confess how badly I need help. But there you are. Now use your own judgment.

CARLOTTA: Send Sam up for perjury! Hm! Then if I don't turn Sam over to you. . . .

BURTON: If you do, it's all beer and skittles. What could be fairer?

CARLOTTA: But . . . (*The doorbell rings.*)

BURTON: That isn't Sam now?

CARLOTTA: He wouldn't ring.

BURTON: (*relieved*) Of course not!

CARLOTTA: Not exactly anxious to see him, are you?

BURTON: Don't you think you might do better with him if he didn't find me here when he came in?

CARLOTTA: How pithy you are to-night, Bertie! I had no idea you could be so pithy! (ANNIE *enters from the vestibule.*)

ANNIE: It's Mr. Archie again, Miss Lottie.

CARLOTTA: Send him away again!

ANNIE: I told him you were out. He says he'll wait till you come in.

BURTON: You'll have to see him. I can't wait here. . . .

CARLOTTA: Until Sam comes in? All right, Annie. (ANNIE *goes into the vestibule.*)

BURTON: Shall I hear from you to-morrow?

CARLOTTA: Aren't you in rather a hurry?

BURTON: Yes. Very much of one. (ARCHIE *enters. He wears his dinner coat.*)

ARCHIE: Hello, Burton!

BURTON: Hello, Archie!

CARLOTTA: Really, Cousin Archie, it's too vile of you to break in where you're not wanted!

ARCHIE: You can't very well keep me out, Cousin Lottie, if you let Burton in, can you?

BURTON: We've been talking business.

CARLOTTA: Yes. And Burton's just going anyway. (*She holds out her hand to* BURTON. *He rises, a little surprised, and takes it.*)

BURTON: Shall I hear from you?

CARLOTTA: I'll call you.

BURTON: To-morrow morning or to-night? I shall be at home all evening in case you . . . It's only a step, you know. If I keep my car waiting . . . Here, I'll just leave you my phone number. (*He scribbles it on a card which he drops on the table.*)

CARLOTTA: I'll call you. Good night.

BURTON: I'm glad you understand. Shall I have a check for you in the morning?

CARLOTTA: (*very certain*) I've lost interest in the check.

BURTON: Well, don't lose interest in . . . er . . . (*A wave of the hand.*)

CARLOTTA: (*frightened again*) I may see what I can do.

BURTON: Good night, Archie.

ARCHIE: Good night. (BURTON *goes.*) Now that I *am* here, you'll have to make the best of it.

CARLOTTA: Now that you're here . . . (*She rises and comes over to him. Their embrace is deeply affectionate.*) I believe I'm moderately glad to see you. Doesn't that sound frantic? (*She leaves him and drops listlessly in another chair.*)

ARCHIE: Three months is a long time not to see you, Lottie. . . . You look worried.

CARLOTTA: Do I?

ARCHIE: Marriage seems to be agreeing with you, though. . . . Of course, it always has.

CARLOTTA: This marriage is a regular sanitarium.

ARCHIE: Really? I should have thought being married to Sam McCarver would mean one long taxi-ride.

CARLOTTA: Sam's trying to make a lady of me.

ARCHIE: Oh! . . . Well, I suppose Sam would.

CARLOTTA: Sam really is a panic!

ARCHIE: *(uneasily beginning his business)* Er . . .

CARLOTTA: *(she eyes him sharply)* You don't need to make conversation, Archie. Something tells me you've come on a family mission.

ARCHIE: Righto.

CARLOTTA: Unpleasant?

ARCHIE: Shouldn't say so.

CARLOTTA: Odd!

ARCHIE: Oh, it's just one of those things. Of course, you knew they'd raise hell when you married Sam.

CARLOTTA: I can't possibly be bothered with what they do about anything. I got through with that years ago.

ARCHIE: Now, they want to stage some sort of a love-fest.

CARLOTTA: How vile of them, Cousin Archie!

ARCHIE: Why?

CARLOTTA: I know that tribe, my dear, and I won't have them laughing at me.

ARCHIE: God knows, I don't blame you. A duller lot of buzzards I never saw. But Aunt Alice, now. She's different.

CARLOTTA: Oh, Aunt Alice is too divine for words, of course. The old rip!

ARCHIE: Well, I'm here on Aunt Alice's account. She wants you in her box to-night.

CARLOTTA: I won't go.

ARCHIE: Why not?

CARLOTTA: My husband's out of town.

ARCHIE: He's coming back to-night. The maid told me so.

CARLOTTA: I won't go.

ARCHIE: Well, I've done *my* best.

CARLOTTA: *(she nods. Then)* Get your hat and run along. *(He turns from her, a question faltering on his lips. Her look encourages him and he brings it out.)*

ARCHIE: What *did* you do it for?

CARLOTTA: I'll try anything once. Sam did me rather a good turn, don't you think? There aren't many men who would have done what he did. Wasn't it rather up to me?

ARCHIE: Sam does belong to the white socks club.

CARLOTTA: Restrain your merriment, Archie dear. I won't have my Sammy laughed at. Sam has his points. Sam has a way with him. You do what he wants you to.

ARCHIE: Lottie, you're not getting sweet on him!

CARLOTTA: Don't play the giddy ox!

ARCHIE: Answer me! You *are* in love with him, aren't you?

CARLOTTA: *(a pause—then)* Yes . . . awfully.

ARCHIE: I thought so.

CARLOTTA: It gets worse.

ARCHIE: Happy? Tell me the truth, now!

CARLOTTA: I can contain myself. Since Sam went away to Texas ten days ago, I've been out three times. Twice to ride alone in that filthy park and once to a fitting.

ARCHIE: Good God!

CARLOTTA: It does get dull. Lonely. I don't mind admitting that to *you*. But one can't have one's cake and eat it, too.

ARCHIE: I don't see why you have to live in a convent, though.

CARLOTTA: I'm not such a fool as to try mixing Sam with . . . well, with our people. You know. So I just sit tight and wait for better days.

ARCHIE: What *do* you do with yourself?

CARLOTTA: "I have my books and my flowers and my French." . . . When Sam's home we sally forth occasionally and take in a show. He brings people to dine. Business men. Sam's on the Street, you know, making most "frightfully good." *(This quotation, as she makes it, echoes unpleasantly.)* Bertie Burton comes. . . . I'm putting Bertie up to being Sam's broker, just for old times' sake. . . . Most evenings we "sit at home by the fire and read a good book."

ARCHIE: *(very solemnly)* Cousin Lottie, you're a great woman.

CARLOTTA: Thanks.

ARCHIE: But you're trying the impossible.

CARLOTTA: I shouldn't say that.

ARCHIE: You just did say it. Isn't your being married to Sam mixing him with our people? There are differences, my dear Cousin Lottie; differences in standards and habits and everything. Even in God's country where all men are free and equal. Class differences. And they're strong as the very devil.

CARLOTTA: They're not as strong, Archie, as the difference between male and female.

ARCHIE: In the long run they are.

CARLOTTA: What I always say is: "Love conquers all."

ARCHIE: I hope it does for you, my dear, but you'll admit you've given it quite a bit to conquer.

CARLOTTA: I drive my buggy at my own gait, Archie darling. When I fall out, I lie in the mud until I'm entirely rested. Then I get back in and drive on.

ARCHIE: That's the way to talk. Won't you be good, now, and crawl out of your cocoon and show a bit of leg and all that sort of thing?

CARLOTTA: Not if hell were to freeze over for me to crawl on. I won't be made a fool of, my dear, not even to entertain the Ellis family. *(They are interrupted by the sound of voices in the hall.* SAM'S *and the voice of* CARLOTTA'S *and* ARCHIE'S *Aunt Alice, the* PRINCIPESSA STRÁ.)

PRINCESS: Is it possible?

SAM: You've got the advantage of me, lady.

PRINCESS: Of course I have!

CARLOTTA: *(rising furiously)* Did you arrange this?

ARCHIE: I give you my word. . . .

CARLOTTA: Trust Aunt Alice to get in sooner or later. (SAM *enters, opening the hall door to admit the* PRINCESS STRÁ, *a large woman of fifty-five, handsomely dressed, distressingly well-preserved.* SAM *follows her in, carrying his hat, overcoat, and valise. His appearance shows decided improvement. His English, when he speaks, has looked up. His manner alternates between a shyly bumptious formality and a boyishly pathetic ease.)*

PRINCESS: To think of our meeting in the elevator!

CARLOTTA: Is it really you, Aunt Alice! I can hardly bear it.

SAM: What do you know? Ran plumb into each other in the elevator. Glad to see me back?

CARLOTTA: Glad, Sammy? *(A defiant look toward the two Ellises.)* I'm thrilled! *(She kisses him passionately. It is about equally shocking to the* PRINCESS *and to* ARCHIE.)*

ARCHIE: Oh, Lottie!

SAM: I guess that's a pretty fair welcome home. *(The two men shake hands.)*

PRINCESS: *(to* CARLOTTA) Bad child!

CARLOTTA: Take your things into our room, Sam, and

make yourself beautiful. I want Aunt Alice to see you at your best.

SAM: My best? Say!

CARLOTTA: I know it's bad enough, Sammy, but it's all you've got. And I think it's ravishing.

SAM: Girlie! *(He goes into the bedroom.)*

PRINCESS: My dear, he's a lamb!

CARLOTTA: I'm glad you think so, Aunt Alice.

PRINCESS: He's magnificent! *(The family settles down to a quiet family quarrel.)*

CARLOTTA: If I'd wanted to be laughed at, I should have invited you.

PRINCESS: He's the most distinguished thing you've ever done! He reeks of the underworld!

CARLOTTA: I suppose you know that you're making me perfectly furious?

PRINCESS: Why not? I'm half-insane with jealousy myself. I thought I did something when I married my prince. But Guido isn't a patch on Sam. Not a patch. Even though Guido *is* a degenerate.

CARLOTTA: Listen to me before Sam comes back. This is my bed, and I'm going to lie on it.

PRINCESS: You've no idea how I envy you!

CARLOTTA: I thought I might have made it quite clear that I'm not asking for family visits?

PRINCESS: You did, my dear. Clear as print. May I ask why you are so self-conscious? If I had him, I'd flaunt him.

CARLOTTA: You don't understand.

PRINCESS: I know Sam wouldn't have to beckon twice to get me.

CARLOTTA: That's put with characteristic Ellis nastiness. Sam thinks I can teach him and help him, and maybe I can. I don't know about that. But I will not have the Ellis tribe coming in here to look at the orang-outang.

PRINCESS: You're wasting your sweetness on the desert air, my dear, and, what's more to the point, you're wasting Sam.

CARLOTTA: I'm *not!* I'm protecting him. Think of Sam and your Guido together!

ARCHIE: Aunt Alice isn't using a husband this winter.

CARLOTTA: If you don't want a real riot on your hands, you'll say good night when Sam comes back, and trot off to your damned opera.

PRINCESS: For tuppence, I'd take your husband away from you, my dear. He's worth more than . . .

ARCHIE: Careful! (SAM *returns. He stands smiling by the bedroom door. There is a dreadfully blank moment.*)

SAM: All sereno an' a lot more comfy! . . . This is *fine!* . . . Well, Archie, how's it strike you?

ARCHIE: Oh, I think it's charming. I used to know some people who lived in this house. They liked the high ceilings so much.

SAM: (*doing his level best*) We're snug as a bug in a rug here. We *love* it. We couldn't be hired to leave. So central an' . . . Can't you scrape up a few more compliments? I don't think Archie's doin' the right thing by us!

CARLOTTA: (*in agony for him*) Don't worry about Archie.

ARCHIE: You don't mean personal compliments?

SAM: Sure I do. Why not?

ARCHIE: Well, if you must! I think you've found a damned good tailor.

SAM: There now! Hear that, girlie? From Archie, too. He *knows!* (*Back to* ARCHIE, *and sinking fast.*) Your cousin found him. At least, she sicked me on to him. Your cousin's a clever girl, Archie. I always thought so. Now I *know* so.

ARCHIE: Yes. I always thought so.

SAM: (*has he said the wrong thing?*) Mind you, I don't believe a man ought to pay *too* much attention to his clothes, but . . .

ARCHIE: Don't they say clothes make the man?

SAM: (*safe, after all!*) Well, they're pretty near right if they do. A good snappy personal appearance don't hurt no gentle—*any* gentleman.

PRINCESS: You're perfectly adorable! (*And she deserts the family to make up to him.*)

SAM: What!

PRINCESS: Perfectly adorable, talking about your clothes.

SAM: (*very much taken aback*) It don't cost a man any more to look decent, an' he owes it to his wife.

CARLOTTA: (*gallant girl*) Of course he does, Sammy!

SAM: (*brightening for her assistance*) This place is Carlotta's work, too. (*He points to the portrait.*) See? Grandmother.

PRINCESS: (*to the portrait*) Dear mother!

SAM: (*he touches the little coffee-table*) Genuine antique. Over a hundred years old. Carlotta found it on Madison Avenue. (*He shakes his head. It is beyond him.*)

ARCHIE: Live and learn, eh?

SAM: Live and learn is *right!*

CARLOTTA: *(sternly)* It *is* right, Archie. (ARCHIE *curbs his wit.*)

SAM: Funny your usin' that expression! I used it myself just this afternoon, comin' up in the train. Talkin' to Charlie Kohler. You know. President of the North American Steel.

CARLOTTA: I know. I didn't know *you* knew him, Sam.

SAM: Made his acquaintance this afternoon. I seen—*saw* him come into the smoker an' I went right over an' sat down beside him. Pretty nervy, eh?

PRINCESS: Simply heroic!

CARLOTTA: I don't see that. Why shouldn't you have introduced yourself if you wanted to know him?

SAM: I said: "Mr. Kohler, my wife tells me she knows your wife an' I've long desired to make your acquaintance myself."

CARLOTTA: Oh! *(The others smile.)* Well, I do know Grace Kohler. What then?

SAM: He sent you his best. Oh, we had quite a talk. He's just as simple an' natural as anybody else. Invited me to eat dinner with him next Thursday. At the Union Club. Just a little business man's dinner. You ought to know him, Archie. You belong to the Union Club, don't you?

ARCHIE: Yes. But I shouldn't think of going there.

SAM: How's that?

PRINCESS: He'd be afraid of meeting Charlie Kohler.

SAM: Aw, say now! You don't want to be afraid of Charlie. He's a prince! . . . I guess a fellow has to be pretty prominent . . . one way or another . . . to . . . to make the Union Club, don't he—*doesn't* he?

ARCHIE: Well . . .

CARLOTTA: *(she can stand no more)* Archie and Aunt Alice are just going, Sam.

SAM: No!

PRINCESS: Come with us. I've got a box and Jeritza's singing.

SAM: Opera?

PRINCESS: Don't say no. I've fallen head over heels in love with you.

SAM: Sounds great!

CARLOTTA: Oh, Sammy! This is your first night home in over a week.

SAM: Girlie!

CARLOTTA: What a mad idea, Aunt Alice, to expect Sam and me to go out on his first night home!

ARCHIE: *(he takes pity on* CARLOTTA*)* Come along, Aunt Alice.

PRINCESS: I shan't be a bit nice to you, Archie, now that I've met Sam. I hope you don't mind my calling you Sam, Sam?

SAM: You can call me anything you like . . . Aunt Alice.

CARLOTTA: Aunt Alice's name is Princess Strá, Sam.

SAM: Princess? How come?

PRINCESS: I'm married to an Italian prince, and I live in Venice in a perfectly divine palace without any bathrooms.

SAM: *(to* CARLOTTA*)* What do I call her? Highness?

PRINCESS: Just Alice, I think, without the "Aunt."

SAM: Great!

PRINCESS: You aren't shocked at such a forward old lady?

SAM: I wouldn't call you "old."

PRINCESS: No, I should hope not!

CARLOTTA: Aunt Alice. . . . .

PRINCESS: Yes, dear?

CARLOTTA: You're just too fascinating, aren't you?

PRINCESS: Never mind, Carlotta. I want Sam to come and visit me in Venice.

SAM: Anywhere you like, Alice.

PRINCESS: That's right!

ARCHIE: Good night, McCarver.

SAM: Oh, good night, Archie. Drop in again any time. Take pot-luck with us.

PRINCESS: *(to* CARLOTTA*)* Pot-luck! Oh, my dear, stop being such a fool! You're throwing away a sensation!

CARLOTTA: Well, you can go home and have a good laugh now, can't you? *(She pushes the* PRINCESS *toward the door.)*

PRINCESS: *(taking* SAM *with her)* I'd stay forever if Carlotta would let me. I'm your slave for life.

SAM: *(as he shows them out)* I guess you're just kiddin' me a little. (ARCHIE *follows them out.* CARLOTTA *rages despairingly for a moment. Then her eye falls on that card of* BURTON'S. *She picks it up and reads the number. It sobers her. She drops wearily by the fireplace.* SAM *returns. His hand, on her neck, is terribly possessive and connubial. She submits, unhappily, but wholly.)*

SAM: I didn't hardly expect you to feel the way you do.

CARLOTTA: About what?

SAM: About me coming home.

CARLOTTA: Didn't you?

SAM: No. I always forget that, somehow. An' I'm glad we didn't go out with your aunt.

CARLOTTA: So am I. I've got something to talk to you about. . . . Oh! I told Annie to save you some dinner. Have you had dinner? (*This breaks the spell.*)

SAM: Yeah. On the train. A glass of buttermilk wouldn't go so bad though. (*She rings.*)

CARLOTTA: Did you . . . did you have a good trip?

SAM: First rate. (BURTON'S *cigarette ashes catch his eye. He tidies up the table.*)

CARLOTTA: Texas and Oklahoma, wasn't it?

SAM: Oklahoma mostly. (ANNIE *comes from the dining-room.*)

CARLOTTA: Mr. McCarver's had dinner, Annie. All he wants is a glass of buttermilk.

SAM: (*to* ANNIE) An' a piece of gluten-bread toast! (ANNIE *goes, taking the coffee-tray with her.*)

CARLOTTA: Oklahoma. . . . I hear you're going to make a lot of money out of it.

SAM: Who says?

CARLOTTA: (*she is standing behind him*) Bertie Burton.

SAM: (*sharply*) What's he know about it?

CARLOTTA: I suppose he must have heard down-town.

SAM: Been seeing him?

CARLOTTA: (*perfectly frank*) I saw him once, yes.

SAM: Where?

CARLOTTA: Here.

SAM: Came here, did he?

CARLOTTA: Yes. I sent for him to talk over some investments. I wanted some money.

SAM: Oh!

CARLOTTA: Nothing strange about that?

SAM: Not a thing. When was it?

CARLOTTA: (*surprised by his tone*) This evening.

SAM: This evening?

CARLOTTA: Yes.

SAM: What *were* the investments?

CARLOTTA: I can't remember. . . . I sent him home right after dinner so that he wouldn't stay and be a gooseberry.

SAM: That really why you sent him home, girlie?

CARLOTTA: Don't you believe me?

SAM: I believe you really *are* glad to see me back!

CARLOTTA: Certainly I am. . . . I was saying, Sam . . . Something came up while Burton was here . . .

SAM: Don't you go botherin' your little head about business, now. This ain't no time to be talkin' about business.

CARLOTTA: *(hurt)* Sam, you aren't jealous of Burton, are you?

SAM: Supposin' I was? . . . Could you blame me much?

CARLOTTA: *(frowns a moment, then)* Why don't you wear a loud tie, Sammy?

SAM: Don't you like it? *(He fingers it self-consciously.)*

CARLOTTA: I love it!

SAM: Think your aunt noticed it?

CARLOTTA: Aunt Alice wasn't in a condition to notice anything. *(A pause of perplexity. Then she throws herself on the sofa.)*

SAM: I'll give it to George. . . . Your aunt's a wonder.

CARLOTTA: Isn't she!

SAM: Funny to think of a fine woman like that married to a wop. I'd like to see Venice. I'd like to see them gondolas . . . *those* gondolas.

CARLOTTA: Venice is a poisonous sink of iniquity that smells to heaven. Aunt Alice's palace is the coldest, vilest, most loathsome house I've ever stayed in.

SAM: Oh! . . . What's the prince like?

CARLOTTA: You're too young to know.

SAM: Funny.

CARLOTTA: What!

SAM: The men you women marry.

CARLOTTA: You, for instance?

SAM: I guess so. . . . I'm steady, though. *(He comes over to sit on the sofa beside her.)* Maybe I'm a good example to you, girlie. You really *were* glad to see me?

CARLOTTA: Yes, very glad. *(ANNIE brings a tall glass of milk and two pieces of toast on a plate.)*

SAM: I'm glad I didn't pull any boners with your family. I knew how you'd feel.

CARLOTTA: *(hurt again)* Here's your milk.

SAM: Oh, thanks, Annie. That's fine.

CARLOTTA: You can go to bed, Annie.

ANNIE: Good night, Miss Lottie. *(She goes as CARLOTTA smiles toward her. SAM takes a long drink of the milk. CARLOTTA watches him.)*

CARLOTTA: Sam?

SAM: Yeah? *(He bites into the toast.)*

CARLOTTA: I was just thinking.

SAM: *(his mouth full)* What?

CARLOTTA: Oh, the way you have of going at things and getting them done so quickly and successfully, and how you're making so good down-town. I can't keep up with you.

SAM: *(his mouth very full)* Oh, yes, you can.

CARLOTTA: Burton couldn't talk about anything else tonight. *(For the fraction of a second SAM suspends chewing.)* He admires you frantically. . . . He's awfully anxious to get in on this present scheme of yours. He said he wanted to "handle" it for you. I daresay he'll be in to see you about it to-morrow.

SAM: *(again that slight suspension of chewing)* Think so?

CARLOTTA: I wish you'd let him in.

SAM: *(mouth full)* Why?

CARLOTTA: *(a pause—then)* As a favor to me. He's done so much for me, taking care of my money. He's worked so hard, and then, beside that, to-night, he said . . .

SAM: *(decisively)* Nope! *(Swallow.)* Don't like him. Don't want him. Won't have him.

CARLOTTA: But if you really are going to make so much money and get so frightfully rich, can't you . . .

SAM: I'm going to string you with diamonds like a Christmas-tree, but I got no use for Mr. Burton. . . . Oh, hell!

CARLOTTA: What's the matter?

SAM: *(he draws a jewel-case from the side-pocket of his coat)* Comin' through St. Louis I had a couple of hours to kill, an' I got you a little present. *(Opening the case he discloses a very beautiful bracelet.)*

CARLOTTA: *(thrilled)* Oh, Sam! It's wonderful!

SAM: I didn't want to come home empty-handed after the deal I made.

CARLOTTA: I can't bear it!

SAM: Let me put it on. *(He does so.)* I wish I'd remembered to give it to you while they were all here.

CARLOTTA: I'm just as glad you didn't.

SAM: *(a second's pause)* I stand corrected.

CARLOTTA: Not at all. Who am I to object to good, clean publicity?

SAM: *(stubbornly)* No. I stand corrected.

CARLOTTA: Never mind. It's the most gorgeous thing I've ever seen.

SAM: I'm glad you like it, anyway.

CARLOTTA: You're too extravagant.

SAM: Five thousand!

CARLOTTA: (*a pause—then*) I'm glad I'm worth it to you.

SAM: You're worth more than that. (*This touches her. With a swift decision she rises to find herself a cigarette.*)

CARLOTTA: Thank you. . . . Tell me something, Sam. If anybody ever told how Monty Garside really got killed, they'd accuse you of perjury, wouldn't they?

SAM: They wouldn't stop at accusin'.

CARLOTTA: You'd get in trouble, wouldn't you?

SAM: I took my chance on that.

CARLOTTA: Yes. I know you did. Just this evening I was talking to Burton, and I think I ought to tell you what he said, if you'd only stop interrupting me. (*She is taking up a cigarette and a match. His look stops her.*) What is it?

SAM: (*diffidently*) Girlie . . .

CARLOTTA: What?

SAM: I wish you wouldn't smoke.

CARLOTTA: Oh! (*Vexed, she throws the unlighted cigarette on the floor and goes savagely back to the sofa.*)

SAM: Don't get sore. Just try to understand how *I* look at things. When a man jumps from one thing to another like I done . . . (*An irritated glance from* CARLOTTA.) the *way* I done . . . the way I *did*. . . . He wants to make the jump a clean job, don't he . . . *doesn't* he? I always done that every jump I ever made since I pulled out of that Turkish bath in Hoboken like I told you about. Twenty years since, that was! I can't stand bein' reminded of what's through an' done with. (*A long drink of milk.*)

CARLOTTA: (*her anger ebbing again*) So?

SAM: Like one time when I was managin' old Dan in his fighting days. I begun to get my shoes shined then, an' I had two suits, two good suits at one time. . . . They was all right, too. I had 'em made to order. By a little Swede tailor down on Grand Street, right near the bar where I was workin' before I went in with Dan. I was livin' on Second Avenue when I was with Dan, an' I used to go down to Grand Street to the tailor's for my fittin', an' I'd walk three blocks outta my way to keep from passin' that barroom where I was workin' a month before. (*He has sunk into the roots of his past. A kind of horror creeps over* CARLOTTA.) I never could stand bein' reminded. . . . An' there used to be a fellow in the office at the Garden—Madison Square Garden, you

know. That was when I was with Dan, too. An' he spit. . . .
An' he spit just the way the bartender used to down on
Grand Street. I was in there one day an' I seen him spit—oh,
it wasn't the first time I seen him spit, but that day he kinda
got my goat just remindin' me, an' I up an' knocked him for a
cooler! Just because the way he spit made me think of a job I
wanted to forget. An' your smokin'. I know it means just
less than nothin' to you, but it takes me right back to them
women in the Tuileries, three months ago.

CARLOTTA: Sam, *please!*

SAM: Yes, it *does!* An' then I get to thinkin' how fellows
from outta town used to blow into my office—friends of
mine, you know—an' ask me "Sam, how about a quart of
liquor an' a couple of girls?" I ain't denyin' I didn't fix 'em
up. . . .

CARLOTTA: But I'm blessed if I see . . .

SAM: Maybe you don't see, but that's how I am an' I'll
thank you to remember it in the future.

CARLOTTA: *(outraged)* Sam!

SAM: You ain't never been but only one thing in your life.
You ain't got nothin' on your mind to forget. Well, I got
plenty an' I been so dam' many different things, if I couldn't
ha' kept each one separate an' wiped the slate clean every
time, where 'ud I ha' got to, I'd like to know? All mixed up
an' gettin' nowheres, that's what!

CARLOTTA: I'll never understand. It's too awful.

SAM: What's too awful?

CARLOTTA: Oh, I don't know. Your way of cutting your
life off, I suppose. It's like city blocks, isn't it, when the
neighborhood moves up-town? Every year ashamed of what
last year was! Wiping the slate clean! And what for? What
for?

SAM: What *for?*

CARLOTTA: I know. "To get ahead." But I don't understand. I never shall. Why aren't you content just to *be?*

SAM: Be what?

CARLOTTA: Well, what you are. Yourself.

SAM: Live an' learn, Archie says! We're movin' fast, you
an' me are. We're goin' to be rich. Not *just* rich. Dam' rich.
An' you know what that means. That means power. Clubs.
Travel. A yacht. Anythin'. You just watch me! *(He finishes
the milk at a draught.)*

CARLOTTA: *(giddy at the glimpse of the abyss between them)* I *am* watching you.

SAM: I was thinkin', comin' up in the train, about you an' me an' the difference between us.

CARLOTTA: The difference between us! What have I let myself in for?

SAM: I wouldn't want you to think I don't appreciate you.

CARLOTTA: I wouldn't dream of thinking such a thing.

SAM: The way you treated me with them here tonight. Just as though we'd been married ten years insteada three months, the way we was, with a dead man for a witness.

CARLOTTA: *(wild)* Oh, what's the use?

SAM: That only makes it stronger. We'll show 'em. They can't stop us.

CARLOTTA: *(the tension increasing)* I hope not. I hope not.

SAM: You're doin' your bit all right. . . . I been thinkin' of what I could do to bring your family around, well . . . around my way.

CARLOTTA: Don't worry about my family.

SAM: I'm thinkin' now that maybe I could use Archie in this Oklahoma proposition of mine.

CARLOTTA: Archie?

SAM: Yeah . . . as president.

CARLOTTA: My Archie? Are you crazy?

SAM: It's a dam' good idea. Call it "Ellis Consolidated Oil." That puts your father's name back on Wall Street. Archie'd be a figurehead, of course, but the name ought to sell stock.

CARLOTTA: My Archie to sell stock! Why, the nerve of some people's children!

SAM: Ain't it the truth!

CARLOTTA: It's too appalling! It's too perfectly appalling, really!

SAM: But . . .

CARLOTTA: I'd rather not explain. There are some things . . .

SAM: *(angry) What* things?

CARLOTTA: Oh . . . I don't know. . . . What have I let myself in for?

SAM: The scheme's absolutely on the level, if that's what you mean.

CARLOTTA: It isn't what I mean.

SAM: Well, let's have it.

CARLOTTA: It's just too appalling, that's all.

SAM: *(his patience cracking) What* is?

CARLOTTA: *All* of it!

SAM: *(rising and coming toward her none too gently)* I don't blame you for bein' stuck on that name. I'm stuck on it myself. But you ain't takin' this in the right spirit. You're my wife. . . .

CARLOTTA: Oh!

SAM: An' after the way you welcomed me home to-night, I wouldn't have expected you to. . . .

CARLOTTA: *(wild)* It isn't the name! I don't care about the name!

SAM: Then what in hell *is* the idea?

CARLOTTA: Well, I'm beginning to see what I'm worth to you! That's the idea.

SAM: Now you listen to me. You're my wife an' you're goin' to help me an' stand by me. Now you're started, you're goin' to keep right on. An' if I say it's Ellis Consolidated, then, God damn it, Ellis Consolidated it is, see?

CARLOTTA: *(a long pause—then)* There's something I'd like to find out about you.

SAM: What?

CARLOTTA: I wonder if you'd be willing to . . . *(She makes up her mind to test him.)* I'll tell you what I might do.

SAM: What?

CARLOTTA: I might make a bargain with you, if you weren't so jealous of Burton. . . .

SAM: How do you mean?

CARLOTTA: I might sell you that name.

SAM: How much?

CARLOTTA: Let Burton in . . . *(This stops him.)* Let him in and you get the name.

SAM: I tell you I got no use for him. Why are you . . . ?

CARLOTTA: Let him in or you *don't* get the name!

SAM: Say, why in hell . . . ?

CARLOTTA: Don't swear!

SAM: You know what makes me off on Burton.

CARLOTTA: Yes, I know.

SAM: Well, I'm just askin' you why. . . . *(He stops and studies her angrily and in bewilderment. She faces him down. A cynical expression comes over his features. He shrugs his shoulders.)* Oh, all right. If you insist. I need that name. I don't guess Burton can do me any harm. I'll take you. *(An awful pause.)*

CARLOTTA: I might have known you'd sell me out.

SAM: Ellis Consolidated it is! *(He holds out his hand.)*

CARLOTTA: *(taking it)* With Bertie in. *(They shake.)*

SAM: Now give us a kiss.

CARLOTTA: No! *(The kiss is intense and passionate. They separate. He watches her. She seems almost on the verge of tears. The door-bell rings.)*

SAM: Who's that?

CARLOTTA: You see. I sent Annie to bed. *(He turns to go. She takes up the telephone.)*

SAM: Who you callin'?

CARLOTTA: *(into the phone)* Butterfield 2673. . . . *(To* SAM.*)* I want Burton to come over and close this up right away.

SAM: What's the hurry?

CARLOTTA: I might weaken on the name.

SAM: Oh!

CARLOTTA: *(suddenly wild again)* God help you from now on!

SAM: Huh? *(With a long, dark look, he turns and goes out as the door-bell rings a second time.)*

CARLOTTA: *(at the telephone)* Butterfield 2673? . . . Hello, Bertie? . . . Well, I've fixed it. . . . I wish you would, yes. Right away. *(She hangs up and stands, staring into the future.)*

SAM: *(off stage)* Why, it's George!

GEORGE: *(off stage)* Hello, Sam! Surprised to see me? *(*SAM *returns with* GEORGE, *who is much as before, except that he has changed his dinner coat for a no less snappy sack suit.)*

SAM: You remember George, girlie, down at the old Tuileries.

CARLOTTA: *(the strain increasing)* How are you, George?

GEORGE: Fine, Mrs. McCarver. How are you?

SAM: First time you ever called any lady Mrs. Sam, George.

CARLOTTA: *(desperately)* Mrs. Sam!

GEORGE: Seems natural.

CARLOTTA: Yes, doesn't it!

SAM: It *is* natural. Three months married. Take a look 'round an' tell us what you think of us.

GEORGE: Pretty nifty.

SAM: High ceilings, open fireplaces, twelve rooms, four baths, an' a complete library.

GEORGE: What do you do with the library, Sam?

SAM: What do you suppose? (CARLOTTA *makes up her mind about that future.*)

GEORGE: That's what I asked.

SAM: Do you know what I wish, George? I wish my poor old mother could see me livin' here like I am. I do, George. She may have had her faults, but she was a great little woman, my mother was.

CARLOTTA: *(never so cruel before)* Oh, Sammy! You never told me about your mother!

SAM: Didn't I? (*Her unexpected mockery leaves him high in the air. He sees that cigarette she threw down earlier when he protested against her smoking. It has lain there all this time like a drawn sword between them. He takes refuge in it now, picks it up and tosses it in the fireplace. Her angry, mocking eyes follow him.*) I didn't tell you either that I'm settin' George an' Oscar up in a new place, did I, girlie?

CARLOTTA: Aren't you princely! *(To GEORGE.)* We'll come to the opening.

GEORGE: I come up about the Tuileries, Sam. We got an offer for the lease. Some used-car people want it for a show-room.

CARLOTTA: You really mustn't talk about the Tuileries before me, George. I can't stand hearing about the Tuileries. . . .

GEORGE: *(horrified at the break)* Oh, I beg pardon, Mrs. McCarver!

CARLOTTA: *(rushing on)* Whenever I hear about the Tuileries I simply want to weep. I know I'll never have a good time anywhere again. . . .

SAM: *(horrified at CARLOTTA)* Girlie!

CARLOTTA: And when I think of that dear old place being shut up just on account of a vile murder . . . Don't have any murders in the new place, will you? (GEORGE *and* SAM *are equally horrified. The door-bell rings again.*) There's Burton, now. . . . I'll answer. You take George in the library, Sam. I'll entertain Bertie until you're through. . . . *(She is going into the hall.)* You might bring us some Scotch. *(She is gone.* SAM *and* GEORGE *look after her.)*

SAM: *(after a pause)* Just a minute, George. (*He goes into the dining-room, returning immediately with a tray of Scotch, siphon, and glasses, which he sets on the table.* GEORGE, *alone, shakes his head sadly over the look of things.*) There. . . . (*He glances again toward the hall, then turns back to* GEORGE.) Come on, George. What kind of terms?

GEORGE: (*following him into the library*) Not bad. . . . Pretty fair, if you ask me. . . . (*They are gone.* CARLOTTA *returns followed by* BURTON.)

BURTON: How did you do it?

CARLOTTA: (*nostrils distended but tears in her voice*) I sold my family name . . .

BURTON: You didn't!

CARLOTTA: It's to be called "Ellis Consolidated."

BURTON: You're shameless, Carlotta.

CARLOTTA: Mix me a high-ball, duck-toes. I'm not half through with you yet. (*The drinks are made.*) I'm going to crawl out of my cocoon.

BURTON: Bravo! I'll give the first party.

CARLOTTA: (*seating herself at her ease*) You'll do more than that. I'm going to flaunt Sam!

BURTON: It will be a great sight.

CARLOTTA: Yes! Won't it! You've no idea! Neither has Sam. I've just found out what's expected of me around here and I'm going to come through. Do you know what a wife's duty is, Bertie? A wife's duty is to push her husband ahead in the world until he doesn't need her any longer in his business. I've been married four times and I never found that out until to-night. I had to fall in love to find it out, too! Funny, isn't it?

BURTON: Funny?

CARLOTTA: It's *going* to be funny . . . from now on!

BURTON: What *are* you driving at?

CARLOTTA: Flaunting Sam. That's my duty and that's where you come in.

BURTON: How?

CARLOTTA: Well, clubs, I think, for a starter.

BURTON: Clubs!

CARLOTTA: Yes, clubs! Beginning with the Union.

BURTON: Carlotta, you're crazy!

CARLOTTA: I'm not. The Union's a poisonous place, but think how Sam'll amuse those old dodoes! Sam really *is* a panic, you know.

BURTON: But, Sam, my dear girl, isn't quite up to . . .

CARLOTTA: *You* can get him in.

BURTON: Oh, can I!

CARLOTTA: *You* got in.

BURTON: Very delicately put.

CARLOTTA: *(fortissimo)* I'm going to see this through in a big way!

BURTON: What do I get out of it?

CARLOTTA: *(down again to agony)* You get Sam, my Sammy, with his money and his brains, and his Oklahoma scheme that's going to make a million. You're silly to be so proud of your vile little clubs. I'm going to have a little more fun before I die, or . . . *(She is up and after more soda. He grips her wrist.)* Careful, Bertie!

BURTON: Do you know what you do to me, Carlotta?

CARLOTTA: *(well, why not?)* I shouldn't advise you to try doing anything to me.

BURTON: I love you.

CARLOTTA: Let go of my wrist.

BURTON: You . . . *(He kisses her.)*

CARLOTTA: *(smiling)* Fool!

BURTON: *(also smiling)* That's that.

CARLOTTA: Call Sam.

BURTON: Righto! *(A long look at her, then he goes to the library door and opens it.)* Sam?

SAM: *(off stage)* Yeah?

BURTON: Carlotta seems to want you.

SAM: All right. George is just going. *(He enters. GEORGE follows.)*

CARLOTTA: *(her eyes on* BURTON*)* Good night, George.

GEORGE: Good night, Mrs. McCarver. *(As he crosses—to* SAM.*)* I can let myself out, Sam.

SAM: That's all right, George. I'll see you in the morning. . . . *(They go into the vestibule.)*

CARLOTTA: A little self-control, Bertie, and a more obliging disposition.

BURTON: I waited a long time for that kiss.

CARLOTTA: I hope you enjoyed it.

BURTON: I did. *(SAM returns, very self-conscious again about his tie, which he has changed for one of more sober hue.)*

CARLOTTA: And so my fun begins.

SAM: Sorry to keep you waiting. Has the wife taken care of you?

CARLOTTA: The best!

SAM: How about a small one in honor of . . .

CARLOTTA: Of Oklahoma and a lot more, Sam. Burton's got another great idea.

SAM: What is it?

CARLOTTA: He wants to put you up for the Union.

SAM: Me? In a Fifth Avenue club!

CARLOTTA: Just the ideal nest for him, isn't it, Burton?

BURTON: No doubt of that!

SAM: Well, if you think you can.

CARLOTTA: He got in. He can put the same old screws on for you.

SAM: I certainly appreciate that. I certainly do.

CARLOTTA: *(crescendo again)* No more convent life for Lottie, either!

SAM: *(his drink mixed)* Here's to us!

CARLOTTA: The fool I've been and the fun I'm going to have!

SAM: That's what I call mighty fine of you, partner.

BURTON: Don't mention it. The Union may take some time. But I'm glad to do what I can, Sam. For your sake and Carlotta's. (CARLOTTA *bows acknowledgment.*)

SAM: No. It *is* mighty fine of you. I don't know what to say.

CARLOTTA: *(Her eyes crackling)* Power . . . a yacht . . . clubs . . .

SAM: Girlie!

CARLOTTA: Don't say anything . . . *(To* BURTON.*)* You must go home now, Burton.

SAM: He only just came!

CARLOTTA: He's had his—drink—and now he's *de trop!*

BURTON: Oh, in that case!

SAM: Well, of course! *(He smiled uxoriously.)* Will you drop into my office to-morrow morning?

BURTON: About eleven?

SAM: Fine. I've got a lot to talk over with you.

BURTON: I'm proud to handle anything of Lucky Sam McCarver's.

SAM: I'm proud to have you. We're going to clean up on Ellis Consolidated.

BURTON: I hope so. (*To* CARLOTTA, SAM *watching him.*) Shall I see you soon again?

CARLOTTA: I'm always here.

BURTON: Good! I'll telephone. Good night.

CARLOTTA: Remember, you're giving the first party!

BURTON: I won't forget. Good night, Sam. (*He goes.* SAM *sees him out. Left alone,* CARLOTTA'S *anger flares once again. But she dismisses it and forever dismisses Sam with it. She stands quite still and looks up at that Whistler grandmother. Then she walks over to the table and deliberately and defiantly lights a cigarette. Then, with a sardonic smile, she settles herself in a chair to await* SAM'S *return.* SAM *returns, sees the cigarette, and, in his groping way, almost understands it. At any rate, it distracts him. He has to express his jealousy, but he cannot quite give rein to it. He covers his confusion with further and more detailed tidying up.*)

SAM: Has he been . . . ?

CARLOTTA: What?

SAM: Botherin' you?

CARLOTTA: Bothering me? Hell, no!

SAM: I'd kill him, God damn his soul! I used to suspect. . . .

CARLOTTA: Not Burton!

SAM: Why not? You've always had him buffaloed.

CARLOTTA: So?

SAM: What made him look at you that way?

CARLOTTA: How should I know?

SAM: Burton would as soon die as see me in one of his swell clubs.

CARLOTTA: You needn't lose any sleep over my feelings for Burton, if that's what you mean.

SAM: All right.

CARLOTTA: Turn out the lights.

SAM: All right. (*His hand on the switch, he hesitates a moment, then lets his triumph out in a great exultation.*) Ellis Consolidated! I guess I can sit pretty on that name. I guess I'm fixed whatever happens. (*He extinguishes the lights.*)

CARLOTTA: (*her head bowed*) You should be. (*There is only one lamp and that by the bedroom door.*)

SAM: I want *you* to be happy, girlie.

CARLOTTA: Restrain your dark suspicions, Samuel, and regard my happiness as flawless.

SAM: You've had a dull week.

CARLOTTA: What of it?

SAM: Nothing. I was thinkin', that's all. It doesn't hurt a man any to think about his wife.

CARLOTTA: Does it do him any good?

SAM: That's a question, too. Come to bed, girlie. (*They go out together, his arm around her waist, she leaning away from him.*)

(*The Curtain Falls*)

ACT THREE

SCENE: The salon of the Plazzo Strá in Venice. It is a large room, magnificently furnished in the style of the Venetian rococo, its gorgeous decadence accentuated by the addition of an occasional modern element, a piano, perhaps, certainly a roulette table; one small table with chairs somewhere. Windows at the back, grouped either three or five, give on a balcony which overlooks the Grand Canal. Monumental doors give on the vestibule and the dining-room. A smaller door apparently leads to a back stair to the upper apartments. It is evening.

The curtain rises upon an empty stage. After a moment, PIETRO, the gondolier-butler, enters from the dining-room. The opening of the door admits the sound of gay talk and laughter. He closes it after him, crosses the room, and goes out into the vestibule, leaving that door open. We hear his voice and the voice of CARTER ASHE speaking.

CARTER ASHE enters. He is a man of forty, manly, charming, careless. His gray hair and beard are pleasantly disarranged and his atmosphere suggests the successful and fashionable painter. He wears a Palm Beach suit and white shoes. . . . PIETRO follows him in, closing the vestibule door after him.

ASHE: Ma, silenzio, eh?

PIETRO: Si, Signor!

ASHE: Va bene! (*PIETRO goes into the dining-room. ASHE stands looking about him, nodding with slow and approving relish. He sits down to await developments.* ARCHIE *enters, flannels and blue coat, carrying his napkin.*)

ARCHIE: Good Lord, it's Carter Ashe! (*In a panic, he shuts the door behind him.*)

ASHE: Hello, Archie!

ARCHIE: Pietro wouldn't tell us.

ASHE: I told him not to. I'm a surprise.

ARCHIE: I should say you are.

ASHE: You don't seem to be very glad to see me.

ARCHIE: I'm not. If you don't mind my saying so, the sooner you clear out of here, the better.

ASHE: Why?

ARCHIE: Do you know Carlotta's with us?

ASHE: (*Gravely*) Yes.

ARCHIE: And, do you know your successor is here, too?

ASHE: (*more gravely*) Ah, I'm particularly anxious to meet him.

ARCHIE: That's like you, Carter.

ASHE: Carlotta may have divorced me, but I haven't entirely lost interest in Carlotta. Not by any means. And I've been hearing things, even in Morocco.

ARCHIE: For instance?

ASHE: Has she made such a bad mistake this time?

ARCHIE: You'll see, if you insist on staying.

ASHE: I do insist. I liked what I first heard about this fellow. And I liked her disregard of class foolishness and superficial standards. We're not a bad lot, Archie, but we see too much of each other and not enough of any one else. We're inbred, too. Look at yourself, if you don't believe me. Carlotta ought to have some children by her gunman. They'd do her good. If she's happy with him. *If* she's happy with him. I had to come and see.

ARCHIE: I shouldn't count too far on Lucky Sam McCarver's friendship.

ASHE: You don't frighten me.

ARCHIE: I don't mean to. I daresay you can take care of yourself.

ASHE: (*smiling*) I hope so. I daresay he's learned better than to be violent when he meets me. I've *some* tact. You like him, don't you?

ARCHIE: Not here, I don't. He gives me the feeling that I'm in a card house, here.

ASHE: So you are!

ARCHIE: And that he's just holding his breath to go "Poof" and blow us all to hell.

ASHE: I shall like him for that. I'm beginning to believe he and I may get on.

ARCHIE: I suppose *you* think it's amusing. A sort of Carlotta Club.

ASHE: You might call it that.

ARCHIE: I'll be interested to see how Sam takes to the idea.

ASHE: So shall I. (SAM *enters by the door from the upper apartments. He is dressed just like* ARCHIE.)

SAM: What idea? (At the sound of SAM'S voice, ASHE goes quickly through surprise, amazement and consternation, and brings up in a state of mischievous delight.)

ARCHIE: Well! *There* you are! Where the devil have you been?

SAM: (evidently embarrassed) I . . . I went out to dinner.

ARCHIE: I should say you did. You've got to make your peace with Aunt Alice. She's mad as a wet hen.

SAM: I'll have to make my peace with Carlotta, too.

ARCHIE: Oh, Lottie didn't care.

SAM: No! I don't suppose she did.

ASHE: Hello!

SAM: What are you doing here?

ASHE: Well, I more or less belong here.

SAM: In this house?

ASHE: Yes . . . I . . . (His voice goes into laughter.)

SAM: Can you beat that by much!

ARCHIE: You don't mean to say you *know* each other!

ASHE: *Know* each other!

SAM: He's the man I had dinner with! (To ASHE.) I just realized I never asked what your name was.

ASHE: Oh, we'll come to that later.

ARCHIE: And you *dined* together?

ASHE: *At* the Vapore!

SAM: (to ARCHIE) Don't let on, will you?

ASHE: No, whatever you do, Archie, *don't* let on. We met this afternoon at the Stabilimento Beach and we swam and talked together—very interesting talk it was, too!

SAM: I'll bet it was! (His discomfort tickles him and he smiles to himself.)

ASHE: And then we naturally moved on to dinner at the Vapore.

ARCHIE: Oh, this is gorgeous!

ASHE: Isn't it? *(He takes* ARCHIE'S *arm and leads him toward the dining-room.)* You go back and finish your dinner. Mr. McCarver and I have a lot more to say now that we come together in earnest.

SAM: Maybe I don't feel cheap!

ARCHIE: You're taking a bit of a chance, you know.

ASHE: He hasn't a notion of who I am.

ARCHIE: It's the damndest thing.

ASHE: Quite! Don't spoil it.

ARCHIE: I won't. (ARCHIE *goes.)*

SAM: Say! Running into you here after all I said about this place! I feel better for getting it off my chest, though.

ASHE: I'm glad to hear it.

SAM: I didn't mention any names.

ASHE: You certainly didn't. I hadn't an idea.

SAM: You know 'em all, I suppose?

ASHE: I've known them for years.

SAM: Well, they certainly get my goat. They're the God-damndest outfit *I've* ever seen. An' the funny thing is, my wife just eats 'em up! Yeah! Believe me, I'm going to grab the first chance I get to tell 'em what I think of 'em.

ASHE: That promises well.

SAM: You'll meet my wife, now.

ASHE: I already know your wife.

SAM: The hell you do!

ASHE: Yes. Smoke? *(He proffers his cigarette-case.)*

SAM: Don't care if I do. I can't even get a decent cigarette in this dump.

ASHE: You won't mind mine. They're English.

SAM: Thanks. I don't know which is worse about Venice, the cigarettes or the mosquitoes.

ASHE: Now that I know what your trouble really is, I ought to be able to set you straight.

SAM: I thought Venice was going to be a nice, quiet, old-fashioned place.

ASHE: So it was, before New York took it over. You have to think of these rich New Yorkers as a lot of degenerate pirates, who . . .

SAM: Degenerate is right.

ASHE: That accounts for the kind of conduct you were objecting to this afternoon. You see, Venice doesn't mind.

SAM: We mind at home.

ASHE: That's why people call us a race of hypocrites.

SAM: Let 'em!

ASHE: Of course! It's the highest compliment they could possibly pay us!

SAM: Did I tell you we got one bird here who carries a fan and makes up?

ASHE: No!

SAM: Yeah. I'd hate to say how many of his kind I've kicked down-stairs in my day. Say! A whole lot of this place sails right over my head, but I *know* what's the matter with him! Yeah! An' when I begin operating here, I'm starting off with him.

ASHE: Ladies find them sympathetic.

SAM: By God, if they don't! My wife likes this one fine. She thinks he's funny. Of course my wife likes the whole crew here.

ASHE: What of it! They're harmless. You and I are above them.

SAM: I'll say *I* am.

ASHE: Then why should we take them seriously and be annoyed by them?

SAM: When I ran into you this afternoon, I was ready for pretty near anything. That's a fact. I killed a man once.

ASHE: Were you planning to kill any one here?

SAM: Hell! These bimbos wouldn't be worth the trouble! That's all over now, thanks to you. But I know what I am going to do.

ASHE: What are you going to do?

SAM: I'm going to take my wife an' get out of here. I figure it's just about time for me to be moving along. You know . . .

ASHE: I think you used the phrase "Live and learn" this afternoon.

SAM: Yeah. Live an' learn is right! It's bad for my wife's health, anyway. She's got a bum heart.

ASHE: Right!

SAM: Absolutely.

ASHE: And we understand each other, don't we?

SAM: I'll say so.

ASHE: I should like to give you my notion of your situation.

SAM: Shoot!

ASHE: You're disappointed in the universe.

SAM: Is *that* all?

ASHE: That's the philosophical explanation of your troubles.

SAM: God! Have they got a philosophical explanation?

ASHE: Our relations to each other depend on our idea of the universe, don't they?

SAM: I'll bite. Never had much use for the universe. Never thought about it.

ASHE: You're wrong there. You've thought more about the universe than any man I know. Only you call it "Your Career" or "Life," or something equally personal. You look on the universe as a series of puddles, each one bigger than the last and each one made for you to jump in and be Big Frog. Well, the universe has a queer way of conforming to what any man wants of it—up to a certain point.

SAM: *(watching him craftily)* What point is that?

ASHE: The point where other people begin.

SAM: Oh!

ASHE: That's right. As long as you travelled wholly on your own, the universe worked your way. Then a time came when you couldn't make the next puddle—Carlotta's puddle—without Carlotta's help and you married her.

SAM: All right. What then?

ASHE: People don't conform. They interfere with the way universes work.

SAM: My way's a good way.

ASHE: Not for everybody, perhaps.

SAM: Everybody ain't up to my way.

ASHE: We're not discussing relative merits.

SAM: What's it all prove?

ASHE: Once a man begins to depend on other people, he has to consider them.

SAM: I don't. I'm the best friend *I* got.

ASHE: You may be your worst enemy, as well.

SAM: Think so?

ASHE: All puddles are mud at the bottom. Size doesn't make much difference. There *are* other frogs.

SAM: *(impatient)* What's it all prove, I want to know?

ASHE: That universes have to be adapted.

SAM: Not mine!

ASHE: It's the only human way, McCarver. Take it easy. You're an extraordinary man. Don't forget your wife's an extraordinary woman. It isn't her fault you don't like her puddle. She'd have stayed willingly in yours if you hadn't made her bring you here.

SAM: I'm set to move along just the same.

ASHE: Impatience is neither human nor professional.

SAM: Whatever that means!

ASHE: Think it over.

SAM: Anything else?

ASHE: Well, before they come out . . . I'll tell you who I am. Carlotta . . . your wife, that is . . . divorced me before she married you. I'm Carter Ashe. *(Long pause.)*

SAM: Well, I'll be damned!

ASHE: I came here to meet you to-night, and I'm heartily glad I met you as I did this afternoon, and I wish you every kind of luck where I failed. . . .

SAM: That's damned nice of you.

ASHE: I hope you think so because I mean it.

SAM: I wouldn't like to say that your comin' here strikes me as funny.

ASHE: You have a perfect right to say it, but here I am.

SAM: *(reverting a trifle)* Yeah! . . . An' what am I goin' to do about it? . . . Is that the idea?

ASHE: It's part of the idea, isn't it?

SAM: *(with elegant sarcasm)* You seem to be lookin' for trouble. Do you think you can get away with comin' here when my wife's here! Oh, hell, you're just like the rest of this crew! *(He withdraws in disgust as the door opens to admit* TUDOR RAEBURN, *an aesthetic young American, with steady, moist eyes, dressed like* ARCHIE *and the rest of the company.)*

ASHE: Now, just a minute, my dear fellow. I didn't come here to pick a fight with you or to make you pick a fight with me. I came here to . . .

SAM: Well?

ASHE: I'm beginning to wish I hadn't come at all.

RAEBURN: Where did *you* come from, Carter?

ASHE: *(turning from* SAM) I came from Morocco, Tudor.

RAEBURN: Been painting there? Well, don't paint here. I'm sick of pictures of Venice. *(*MIRIAM HALE *enters, a hard young American, beautifully dressed, and smoking a cigarette in a holder.)*

MIRIAM: Who's dropped in on us now?

RAEBURN: It's only the ashman.

MIRIAM: Hello, Carter!

ASHE: Hello, Miriam!

MIRIAM: I say, does Carlotta know?

ASHE: No, Miriam. I'm a surprise.

MIRIAM: You're the makings of a jolly good row. Alice! *(The* PRINCESS, *dressed in her notion of what a rococo palace demands of its mistress, enters.)*

PRINCESS: Yes?

MIRIAM: Tell Carlotta that both her prodigals have come home to roost.

PRINCESS: Oh, my God!

RAEBURN: Don't say that. Miriam wants a row. It's too hot for a row, Miriam!

MIRIAM: It's never too hot for a row.

PRINCESS: *(bearing down on* ASHE*)* You and Sam!

ASHE: We've been dining together.

PRINCESS: You and Sam?

ASHE: Sam and I.

PRINCESS: I can't bear it! What will Carlotta say?

MIRIAM: Something monstrous. Carlotta!

ASHE: Please don't call her. I'm just going.

MIRIAM: You're not!

PRINCESS: Oh, yes, he is.

RAEBURN: Sam's falling down on him. What's the matter, Sam? Won't you fight?

SAM: Who do you want me to fight?

MIRIAM: Carter, of course.

PRINCESS: Now we aren't going to have any trouble, are we? Carter's here, and Carter's going, and . . .

RAEBURN: It's the best thing he *could* do. He's only interrupting Pudge's story. . . . Pudge!

PUDGE: *(in the dining-room)* Coming!

MIRIAM: Good night, Carter. Come and see us.

ASHE: Who is "us"?

MIRIAM: Tudor and me.

ASHE: *Tudor* and you?

MIRIAM: My man's off with Alice's living in . . .

PRINCESS: They don't matter. Good night, Carter. It wasn't nice of you to come.

ASHE: You'll admit it's nice of me to go. . . . *(He is shaking hands preparatory to leaving.)*

SAM: *(very comfortably) I* won't admit any such thing.

PRINCESS: Sam!

SAM: *I* think he better stick around.

ASHE: Why?

SAM: Carlotta might want to see him. When I came in a little while ago I heard Archie and him talking about a Carlotta Club.

PRINCESS: A Carlotta Club!

MIRIAM: How horrible!

SAM: I guess this is it. I guess we better have the convention. I wouldn't want it called off on my account.

PRINCESS: (*pause—then softly*) Don't, Sam!

SAM: (*pause—then*) I haven't decided what I'm going to do yet, so I guess he'll stick around.

ASHE: (*pause—then*) Why, yes . . . If you like. . . .

MIRIAM: (*to* RAEBURN) Let's call Carlotta.

RAEBURN: I'm bored with Carlotta and her husbands. Pudge!

PRINCESS: Sam, please, *please* be good . . .

SAM: Don't you fret. (PUDGE *appears. He is small, young, and vivacious. He wears a dinner coat of black watered silk with red sandals and a fan to match them. He stands flourishing the fan.*)

PUDGE: Calling me?

RAEBURN: Yes. . . . I want to hear the rest of that story.

PUDGE: What story? (*He sees* ASHE *and flits over to him.*) Oh, hello, Carter! How well you're looking! (*To the* PRINCESS.) Isn't it gorgeous, these two together? Shall I call Carlotta?

PRINCESS: No, for heaven's sake, don't!

PUDGE: Oh, all right! It'll be funnier later because she's having a love-fest with Archie. (*To* RAEBURN.) You mean the story about the Laceys and Minnie Rastignac?

RAEBURN: (*as they group around the table*) Do you call her Minnie to her face, Pudgie?

PUDGE: What if she is a princess! Don't we both come from Detroit?

RAEBURN: Never mind Detroit.

PUDGE: Then don't interrupt. . . . (*His mind back to the two husbands.*) Oh, this is grand! This is gorgeous! Well, this is the story. . . . I saw Reggie Lacey drinking at the Luna when I went over to the Palazzo Rastignac for dinner, so I *know* he was squiffy. Well, it seems that when he came home to the Grand, Elinor just refused to dine with him, and it seems she sent word over to ask could she come and dine with Minnie and me. And it seems Reggie said she wasn't to go near Minnie, and said things about her that everybody knows, of course—poor Minnie—but Elinor insisted and began to dress, and so Reggie went back to the Luna and just drank on.

MIRIAM: Reggie would!

PRINCESS: Oh, Reggie!

PUDGE: Well, but Elinor came right on over, because she's always welcome, and you know what they say about *that*. Though I don't think so. Um-um. Not Minnie and Elinor.

PRINCESS: Of course not!

MIRIAM: Never. *(Laughter from RAEBURN.)*

PUDGE: Well, we were just sitting down, the three of us, when Reggie appeared. Oh, it seems the Princess's man wouldn't let him come up-stairs, so he sent up a note to her, calling her just every name you could think of, which she is, only I don't think Reggie ought to say such things. Not to an older woman.

ASHE: Oh, Pudge! Pudge! *(General laughter at the table.)*

PUDGE: So then he went around to the back and broke in the kitchen door, and threw all our dinner out into the canal, and we had to go over to Florian's.

MIRIAM: *(roaring with laughter)* What *did* the Princess do?

PUDGE: My dear, you should have *heard* that woman laugh!

RAEBURN: I think it's awfully funny!

PRINCESS: Poor Minnie!

ASHE: I saw her at the Excelsior to-day. She was walking on the beach with a girl. . . .

RAEBURN: *(excited)* The sunburnt one with pearls around her neck?

ASHE: A beauty!

MIRIAM: A beautiful beast!

RAEBURN: Just that! I've never seen such arms!

PUDGE: Don't, Tudor! Arms *always* make me shudder.

SAM: Oh, my God! *(All eyes to SAM where he sits apart and ponders.)*

PUDGE: What's that, Sam?

SAM: Nothing.

PUDGE: Sam doesn't get one bit of thrill out of arms!

SAM: I don't get your kinda thrill outta anything.

PUDGE: Poor Sam! What a dull life you must lead! *(He*

turns laughting to MIRIAM *as* CARTER *goes over to* SAM, *the* PRINCESS *following.*) My dear, I must tell you about Minnie's dress. It was cut down to . . .

MIRIAM: Shut up, Pudge! Listen to them! (*She points toward* SAM, *to whom* ASHE *is already speaking.*)

ASHE: Look here, McCarver. . . . I apologize for coming here and I agree with everything you think about me. Now be a good sport, and come along over to the Piazza with me, and we'll bury the hatchet.

SAM: No, thanks.

PRINCESS: Do, Sam. There's music in the Piazza to-night.

SAM: I'd rather stay here.

ASHE: Why?

SAM: You'll see, if you stay, too.

PRINCESS: Oh, dear! There's been one killing in this marriage already.

ASHE: (*to the* PRINCESS) Perhaps I'd better stay. (CARLOTTA *enters, quickly and gaily.* ARCHIE *follows her.*)

CARLOTTA: It's no go, Cousin Archie. . . . You ought to be ashamed. . . . Archie's been trying to carry me off on a petting party. It's such a long time since I've been on a petting party, I really can't remember what one feels like. It'll be the most terrific thrill when I do go on one again. But then, I don't suppose I ever shall go on one again because my Sammy is such an iconoclast. (*Then she sees* CARTER, *and it is a tense moment before she collects herself.*) Is iconoclast the word I want, Carter?

SAM: (*grimly*) I'll bite. Is it?

CARLOTTA: Why, there's my Sammy, too! We missed you at dinner, Sammy. I was worried. I was afraid you might have been annoyed at something I did. I hope she was nice.

SAM: Who?

CARLOTTA: I had such an idyllic picture of you on the beach with one of those fascinating little beach tarts. They are *so* sweet.

PUDGE: Oh, she's grand! She's gorgeous! She's marvellous!

SAM: (*self-control*) You had me wrong, girlie. I was having dinner with your . . . your former husband. . . .

CARLOTTA: My former . . . (*To the room.*) Isn't Sammy too stately for words! (*Her hands on* CARTER'S *shoulders.*) Did you talk about me, Carter? Did you tell Sammy how to manage me, and what a blissful old time you and I used to have together?

SAM: *(moving toward her in horror)* Girlie!

CARLOTTA: Look at my strong, silent he-man! He's a better bet than you were, Carter!

ASHE: Much. . . . *(Baffled and wounded, SAM turns away. The PRINCESS lays her hand on his arm. There is a general smile.)*

PUDGE: Rover's going into his corner to lick his wounds.

CARLOTTA: Oh, Pudge, what a bewitching name for him! What do you think he is, an English bull?

PUDGE: Oh, no! I think he's a great, big, wonderful police dog.

CARLOTTA: Perhaps you're right. I'm so deathly tired of police dogs. *(Then, like a tigress, she is at ASHE once more.)* Damn you for turning up! What the devil did you come here for?

ASHE: *(a little sternly)* To see, my dear, what had become of you.

CARLOTTA: I hope you've seen?

ASHE: I've seen that you're behaving very badly.

CARLOTTA: So?

ASHE: You used to be game. Now you're only reckless.

CARLOTTA: *(one of those wild bursts of hers)* I'll show you whether I'm game or not! *(A general murmur and movement.)*

ASHE: I hope so.

CARLOTTA: *(a long, tremulous pause)* You haven't changed much, have you? *(She looks at him and at SAM, standing sullenly apart. Something out of the past comes back. She bursts into tears and flings herself out through the window onto the balcony. ASHE, MIRIAM, and ARCHIE follow her. SAM starts. The PRINCESS, through the exclamations of the others, restrains him. PUDGE watches.)*

PRINCESS: Sam.

SAM: What?

PRINCESS: Come over here, I want to talk to you.

SAM: What about?

PRINCESS: Why can't you be like the rest of us and get some fun out of life?

SAM: What do you want me to do?

PRINCESS: Give Carlotta as good as she gives you.

SAM: Pick up tarts at the Lido? Let's pretend it's because I don't talk Italian.

PRINCESS: You're hopeless!

ARCHIE: *(he comes away from the window where*

CARLOTTA *and* ASHE *are talking on the balcony, and takes* PUDGE *by the arm to the roulette table, where* RAEBURN *is idling with a deck of cards)* Want to deal a few cold hands, Tudor?

RAEBURN: Don't mind. . . . Coming in, Pudge?

PUDGE: Yes, if you give me lots of aces.

PRINCESS: *(speaking at the same time)* I can't do anything with you.

SAM: Well, I can do a few for myself!

PRINCESS: For instance?

SAM: I'd rather not say.

PRINCESS: Tell me and I'll advise you.

SAM: *(indicating* ASHE*)* He just gave me quite a bit of advice.

PRINCESS: If it was good, take it.

SAM: I had my mind made up already.

PRINCESS: Made up to do what?

SAM: To get Carlotta out of here.

PRINCESS: Poor lamb!

SAM: I got nothing to complain about. If I had, I could do better than complain.

PRINCESS: I won't have anything violent, Sam! If you shoot anybody, I'll never speak to you again.

SAM: I haven't got a gun.

PRINCESS: Thank heaven!

RAEBURN: *(to the poker game)* How many?

ARCHIE: Three.

RAEBURN: Pudge?

PUDGE: Oh, go on about your business!

SAM: *(speaking at the same time)* What did he come here for?

PRINCESS: To see you and annoy Carlotta.

SAM: She's glad to see him!

PRINCESS: *(very wisely)* No, she isn't, Sam. She doesn't like being reminded any better than you do.

ARCHIE: *(sweeping up his winnings)* What a measly kitty!

SAM: What did she marry me for?

PRINCESS: You love her, don't you?

SAM: Why shouldn't I?

PRINCESS: And she loves you.

SAM: She's got a funny way of showing it.

PRINCESS: I know . . . it's only in books, Sam, that love conquers all!

SAM: Is that so?

PRINCESS: You poor lambs, both of you!

SAM: Thanks!

PRINCESS: I'd go to the ends of the earth for you, Sam McCarver, so I would. This very night as ever was! Now you're embarrassed. I'm only trying to brace you up.

SAM: She's tired of me.

PRINCESS: What a man! What a man! What a man!

SAM: Didn't she say so just now?

PRINCESS: Answer me this: what did *you* marry *her* for?

SAM: Because she . . .

PRINCESS: Because she stood for everything you wanted that you couldn't get without her.

SAM: Is that your idea, too?

PRINCESS: Mine and Archie's. Are we wrong?

SAM: No, you're not!

MIRIAM: *(to those at the roulette-table)* Stop playing poker!

ARCHIE: What'll it be? Roulette?

PUDGE: Oh, yes!

PRINCESS: Run along now and play roulette and keep your temper.

PUDGE: *(counting chips)* Five . . . ten . . . fifteen . . . twenty . . . twenty-five . . . thirty . . .

MIRIAM: How much are we buying?

PUDGE: Two hundred!

SAM: Do you think she'll go away with me?

PRINCESS: Ask her. Are you afraid?

SAM: No!

PRINCESS: Oh, well, keep your head whatever happens.

SAM: Whatever happens, I won't lose it.

PRINCESS: I suppose you think that's comforting! Well, run along now. I'm too old to steal you, and you're too rich for me to buy, and that's that. They're waiting for you over there. Aren't you waiting for Sam, children?

ARCHIE: If it's roulette, I'm not the bank.

SAM: Who did you say figured that out about why I married Carlotta?

PRINCESS: Archie and I.

SAM: I suppose you think I got what I was after?

PRINCESS: Haven't you?

SAM: Yes. You bet your life I did! I learned a lot, that's sure. Now I'm through. I can do better than this, you know.

I can do a lot better than this. *(A wave of* SAM'S *hand encompasses the room and its inmates.)*

PRINCESS: I should be the last to deny that, Sam.

SAM: And so it's up to Carlotta. Does she want to play ball or don't she?

PRINCESS: *(she shakes her head, then with her hand on his sleeve)* Please don't be bad to-night? Please? *(SAM looks at her without answering.* CARLOTTA *and* ASHE *re-enter from the balcony.* MIRIAM *turns to them.)*

MIRIAM: All right now, Carlotta?

CARLOTTA: Oh, yes, I'm all right, now.

PUDGE: Come on, Sam, you can be bank.

RAEBURN: I'm bored with roulette.

MIRIAM: What else is there to do in Venice?

ASHE: You'll be good now, won't you?

CARLOTTA: You take me right back to our honeymoon in Sicily.

ASHE: We spent our honeymoon in England.

CARLOTTA: I know we did. I only said that to make it harder. . . . You always make my Sammy bank, Pudge.

SAM: That's because I'm the only one who's got any money. *(He goes to the table. The game begins.* ASHE *comes idly down stage.* CARLOTTA *idly watches the game.)*

ASHE: That's the truth.

CARLOTTA: Sammy's a regular Monte Carlo.

PUDGE: Why shouldn't you have money, you great oil baron, you! You ruthless Wall Street Wizard!

MIRIAM: Faites vos jeux, Messieurs!

ARCHIE: Coming in, Aunt Alice? *(The Princess joins them.)*

PUDGE: I feel so reckless, I could stake my pants on the red.

SAM: Go ahead—you don't need 'em.

PUDGE: Don't be vulgar!

RAEBURN: *(as he pitches his counters out)* There!

PUDGE: Play three sides, Tudor. You win three times, divided by half, and at thirty-six to one. . . .

MIRIAM: Shut up, Pudge. Rien ne vas plus.

PUDGE: Archie wins. Wouldn't you know Archie would win?

RAEBURN: I had that hunch. I'm doubling.

MIRIAM: Come on.

PRINCESS: There's a limit on doubling. There's got to be a limit on doubling, hasn't there, Sam?

(Wearily CARLOTTA *leaves the roulette game and goes to* ASHE.*)*

CARLOTTA: Give me a cigarette, Carter.

(He obeys.)

SAM: Why aren't you people playing?

CARLOTTA: Oh dear! Must we?

PRINCESS: Never mind them, Sam.

MIRIAM: Rien ne vas plus. *(The roulette table becomes absorbed in the ball.)*

ASHE: *(to* CARLOTTA*)* As I was just saying outside, you've got to stop some day, you know. May I advise you to stop here? You could do a great deal worse. As you said, he probably is a better bet than I was.

PUDGE: Oh, nobody won a thing!

PRINCESS: *(comes over for a cigarette)* If I'm to play roulette on the brink of a volcano . . . wait for my bet, Sam!

RAEBURN: *(tossing his counters out)* If you stick to your guns, you can't lose.

PUDGE: Archie, that's my number.

ARCHIE: All right, here's another.

MIRIAM: Rien ne vas plus.

CARLOTTA: *(suddenly rising, almost hysterical)* I'm bored.

ASHE: Is that the best excuse you can offer?

CARLOTTA: For what?

ASHE: You can still make this marriage work if you give him a real chance. He thinks you're swindling him. Surely you're clever enough to . . .

CARLOTTA: I like that! Swindling him!

ASHE: *(amazed at her outburst)* My dear!

CARLOTTA: Carter, if you knew! *(She bursts into tears. He tries to comfort her. She pushes him off. He sits perplexed and horrified.)*

MIRIAM: I've won!

PUDGE: But I've lost. . . . We've all lost. . . . I'm ruined. . . . Excuse me while I change my luck. *(He runs around the table.)* Give me some more, Sam.

SAM: How much?

PUDGE: A thousand.

SAM: Liras or dollars?

PUDGE: Lire, silly. I'm so excited I don't care *what* I do!

RAEBURN: I'm through. I always loathed roulette.

MIRIAM: You loathe any game you don't win.

RAEBURN: So do you. . . .

PUDGE: Somebody give me a pencil so I can write Sam a chit!

ASHE: *(to* CARLOTTA*)* Why don't you slip away to your room? I'll go and play roulette.

CARLOTTA: Go ahead. I'll be all right. *(Perplexed, he goes to the table.)*

PRINCESS: *(offering a bill)* I want two hundred more, Sam.

ARCHIE: *(offering a bill)* So do I.

SAM: *(to* ASHE*)* You coming in this time?

ASHE: I thought I would. Give me two hundred, too.

SAM: I'll give you the show of your life, my friend.

ASHE: *(startled by his tone)* Eh?

PUDGE: *(as* SAM *serves them he presents his chit, which he has written with* ARCHIE'S *pencil)* Scare-cats, with your measly two hundreds! There's mine for a thousand.

SAM: *(quite calmly, eying* CARLOTTA*)* I don't want any more of your chits. They're no good. *(This makes a real sensation. The players draw back from the table in a kind of alarm.)*

PUDGE: What? Why I never in all my life. . . . Carlotta!

CARLOTTA: What? *(She turns and meets* SAM'S *eye.)*

PUDGE: Did you hear what your husband said then?

CARLOTTA: No!

SAM: *(increasing calm and good humor)* I said I didn't want any more of his damned rubber chits.

ARCHIE: Oh, Sam, come on now!

PRINCESS: *(to* ASHE *and* CARLOTTA*)* For heaven's sake . . . stop this, you two. . . . This is your fault. . . .

CARLOTTA: Our fault, Aunt Alice?

PUDGE: I've never been spoken to so in my life. Never! Did *you* hear, Alice?

PRINCESS: Yes, of course, I heard.

SAM: I said I didn't want any more of his chits, and I don't. They're no good. I've got fifty thousand liras worth now. Let him pay up or get out of the game.

PUDGE: How dare you insinuate . . . ?

SAM: I've thrown plenty of your kind down-stairs in my life. If you don't keep quite I'll throw you out the window.

PUDGE: You'll do nothing of the kind. We let you into a decent house and treat you as though you were a gentleman, and . . .

SAM: All I have to do is take your chits and keep quiet. . . .

PUDGE: You think I can't make my chits good!

SAM: I know you can't. Here they are. Fifty thousand liras worth of a fairy's calling-cards. *(He tosses the handful on the table, his eye on* CARLOTTA. *The guests all draw back. There is a moment of complete silence.* SAM *seems the only living creature in the room.)*

CARLOTTA: Really, Sam!

PRINCESS: Sam, I'm sure they're all right. . . . But perhaps we hadn't better play any more to-night, Pudge.

SAM: I don't care about 'em. I don't want 'em. I give 'em back, see? Now you don't have to treat me like a gentleman any more, an' I can use my own judgment about how I treat you. *(A faint scream from the* PRINCESS. *Again silence.)*

CARLOTTA: Oh, what's the use?

SAM: What's that?

PUDGE: Never in my life. . . . *(He bursts into tears.)*

PRINCESS: If I could think of a prayer, I'd say it.

CARLOTTA: *(speaking at the same time, her arms around* PUDGE'S *shoulders)* Never mind, Pudgie, darling, what difference does it make?

PRINCESS: Oh, dear me! Dear me! Dear me!

ARCHIE: *(speaking at the same time)* Sam. . . . Come along out with me and have a look at the moon or something.

SAM: I want to talk to Carlotta.

CARLOTTA: Haven't you talked enough?

MIRIAM: *(all this while she has been standing at the window with* RAEBURN) Here's Minnie Rastignac's motorboat stopping at the door, Alice.

PUDGE: Minnie! How lovely!

ASHE: For God's sake, don't let *her* come up!

RAEBURN: *(calling down over the balcony)* Hello! Minnie! *(A voice answers unintelligibly from below.)*

ARCHIE: It's no go, Sam. . . . Come along. That's a good fellow. . . .

SAM: When I'm ready, I'll paint the town red with you. But I'm not ready yet.

PUDGE: *(speaking at the same time)* Minnie'll lay him out cold. He wouldn't dare talk that way to me before Minnie. She'll lay him out cold.

RAEBURN: *(still leaning over the balcony)* What?

MIRIAM: She wants to take us all over to the Excelsior to dance!

ASHE: Saved!

PRINCESS: Oh, bless Minnie! Yes . . . say we'll be right down.

RAEBURN: Fine! We're coming down.

CARLOTTA: Give me a cigarette, Carter.

ASHE: *(to* CARLOTTA*)* Alice's volcano erupted on schedule.

CARLOTTA: Yes. Didn't it!

RAEBURN: *(coming to* PUDGE*)* There now, Pudge, we'll take you to the Excelsior and you can dance your tears away!

PUDGE: I'm never coming to this house again. Never . . . never . . . never. . . . *(He breaks from* RAEBURN *and rushes out into the vestibule.)*

PRINCESS: Sam. . . . *(She hesitates and then thinks better of it.)* Oh! . . . Dear me! . . . Dear . . . me. . . . *(She turns to* MIRIAM.*)* Your things are in my room, Miriam. *(As she goes out.)* I've never been through anything so dreadful.

MIRIAM: *(speaking at the same time)* Yes, I know they are. Don't worry, Alice. It'll quiet down.

(They go out into the vestibule.)

CARLOTTA: I'll get my coat. *(She goes out by the door to the upper apartment.* SAM, *who has stood by surlily spinning the wheel, moves to follow her.)*

ARCHIE: Steady!

RAEBURN: Come along, Carter.

ASHE: Just a minute. *(He walks over to* SAM.*)* Before I go, I should like to say . . .

SAM: Well, say it!

ASHE: Simply that I was acting like a fool to come here, and . . . don't draw any wrong conclusions, will you?

SAM: Well?

ASHE: If you want any satisfaction, of course . . .

SAM: If I want it, I'll take it. . . .

ASHE: Right!

SAM: I'm sorry I can't agree with you about universes.

ASHE: I'm *very* sorry. *(He glances at* ARCHIE, *who nods to him to go.* RAEBURN, *already at the door, goes out.* ASHE *follows him. They close the door after them.)*

SAM: Ugh!

ARCHIE: Exactly. But what's the use of kicking?

SAM: None.

ARCHIE: Then keep your shirt on and leave things be. They're never as bad as they seem.

SAM: That's true!

ARCHIE: Will you come out with me on a private expedition? (SAM *shakes his head.* CARLOTTA *returns, wearing her cloak, still smoking her cigarette.*)

CARLOTTA: Have they all gone?

SAM: All but us, and we ain't going.

CARLOTTA: *We* ain't?

SAM: You and me ain't.

CARLOTTA: (*she smiles and moves toward the door*) Coming, Archie?

SAM: Archie can go. You're goin' to stay an' talk to me.

CARLOTTA: (*she turns, and their eyes meet for a blazing second—then*) Archie, tell them to wait for me. I'll be down in a jiffy.

SAM: They'll have to wait a long time.

ARCHIE: Lottie . . . do you think I'd better?

CARLOTTA: Run along! Run along! Do as I tell you! (ARCHIE *goes, closing the door after him.*)

SAM: Now. . . .

CARLOTTA: What a bloody ass you have made of yourself!

SAM: Well, I guess I kinda busted things up here, all right, all right, all right, all right! I've stood all I'm goin' to stand. (*Silence from* CARLOTTA.) I ain't goin' to let any wife of mine lead me the kind of a dance you're tryin' to lead me. I guess I got a right to make some demands on my wife's actions? (*Silence from* CARLOTTA.) You're goin' to do what I say now! (*More silence.*) Do you hear? (*Still silence. He waits for an answer, then plunges on.*) Do you expect me to sit still an' watch you an' him get together again? What do you an' him take me for? (*Again he waits for an answer. There is none forthcoming.*) Do you think I don't know what he come here for? Do you think I don't know all about you an' all you're up to?

(*A long pause.*)

CARLOTTA: Not quite all, Sammy. (*Her tone is ice and banter and fury, all humorously blended.*)

SAM: No?

CARLOTTA: You're absolutely wrong about Carter.

SAM: *Am* I?

CARLOTTA: I never go back over old ground. . . . The trouble with you, Sammy, is your innocence. If you only kept your eyes open, you might see something really worth

while. . . . Oh, yes! I've trod the primrose path of dalliance.
. . . You didn't know I was so poetic, did you?

SAM: I guess maybe there is quite a lot about you I don't know, but there ain't much I don't suspect.

CARLOTTA: And you just grin and bear it!

SAM: Now you're coming away with me outta this.

CARLOTTA: Oh, no, I'm not!

SAM: Either you're my wife, or . . .

CARLOTTA: Go on, call me harsh names!

SAM: You're not puttin' a thing over on me!

CARLOTTA: Aren't you getting a little *too* fretful?

SAM: I got as much outta you as I ever expected to get, an' then some. Now I'm givin' you your last chance. Do you stick or don't you?

CARLOTTA: No! Not if sticking means sticking to you, you cold-blooded thug! I'm so bored with you this minute, I could see you in hell!

SAM: Is that so? Well, the hell with you an' your whole tribe! I got a bellyful of 'em.

CARLOTTA: I've seen the time when you weren't so fussy.

SAM: What do you mean, fussy?

CARLOTTA: Aha! All set for the big show-down, aren't you? What you really mean is you've got all you could possibly get out of me! My God, what a fool I was not to see through you in the beginning, you damned Broadway Babbitt! And I married you because I thought I owed you something! Oh, my God!

SAM: Yah! You're not worth a decent man's attention.

CARLOTTA: So? Who's the decent man? You, I suppose. I wish I thought that. . . . Do you think I've any respect left for you? Oh, don't say you don't give a damn. I know you don't. It doesn't matter, now. . . . I wonder how much there is to choose between my "tribe" and you. I dare say there must be something. I've never seen any tribe yet that wasn't somehow better than the man who was too good for it. . . . People weren't meant for stepping-stones. At least, I don't think they were. My tribe has its points. Its only sin is being useless and I'm not sure that isn't a virtue. There's more and better in this world than the main chance, Sam. You'll never understand that, but it's so. The main chance did for you and me. I'm sorry, too. We might have got on well enough, if it hadn't been for the main chance. You've never done anything "useless," have you? You should, sometime. Just once. . . . Oh, hell, what's the use!

SAM: Don't make me laugh. Your tryin' to put me in the wrong strikes me as funny after all I've stood from you.

CARLOTTA: Well, I stood you and your little ways until I couldn't stand any more. I put up with you, my friend, until you sold me out to Burton, just to get my name to sell stock. Then I caught on to how you'd been buying me in and selling me out from the beginning. Then I cut loose. But you didn't mind. Oh, no! Not as long as you were still getting ahead. Not as long as you could still use me. You did the sticking then, my friend.

SAM: I ain't denyin' I knowed what I was after, but by God . . .

CARLOTTA: For God's sake, talk grammar! *(An awful pause.)* There's your show-down. From now on I drive my buggy at my own gait, young man. What are you going to do about it?

SAM: For two cents I'd break your damned degenerate neck.

CARLOTTA: Just like that?

SAM: *(moving toward her)* Just like that.

CARLOTTA: *(drawing back a little)* Look out, Sam. . . . Don't do anything silly. . . . Help! Archie! Archie! *(They have been waiting outside for something of this sort. Now ARCHIE and ASHE burst in, with the PRINCESS close behind them. For a moment nobody moves. Then SAM charges ASHE. They mix it in real earnest, ASHE giving a good account of himself. PIETRO comes. SAM is overpowered and held. The Princess squeals. SAM laughs harshly. CARLOTTA stands trembling with fear and outraged fury.)*

ARCHIE: I shouldn't have left you, Lottie.

PRINCESS: Sam, you promised to be good!

CARLOTTA: Do you suppose I could get a room at the Grand, Aunt Alice?

SAM: Don't bother. I'll go. I'm through here, anyway.

PRINCESS: *(an hysterical wail)* But I don't want you to go, Sam! I don't want you to go!

CARLOTTA: Keep him. I don't want him!

ASHE: *(as they release SAM)* Well, you *can* "move along" now, can't you?

SAM: Ain't it the truth! *(He walks quickly out.)*

(The Curtain Falls)

The curtain rises again as soon as possible to show the living and dining room of a small apartment on the upper West Side of New York City. The furniture is pretty, but drearily undistinguished. Close by the gas-grate is a large easy chair which faces the audience. It is seven months later; the following March.

A moment after the curtain rises an elevator door is heard to slam. Then the outer door of the apartment is opened with a latch-key and CARLOTTA enters, dressed in street attire. She isn't quite as gay as she used to be. She is pale, and she moves with a wary precision of convalescence. But she is more than ever beautiful. She stands a moment by the door, shivering weakly.

CARLOTTA: Are you there, Annie? (ANNIE *enters quickly.*)

ANNIE: Dear me, Miss Lottie! I never heard you come in at all! (CARLOTTA *does not answer.* ANNIE *takes the fur coat.* CARLOTTA *wrenches her hat off and throws her purse down on a table. Then she drops exhausted into the easy chair by the grate.* ANNIE *continues.*) You shouldn't have gone out to-day in this nasty March weather. The doctor told you to be careful. . . . Running around in your state of health all day on a day like this. . . . I've a good mind to tell on you. . . . Would you drink a hot cup of tea if I made it for you?

CARLOTTA: I might. I really might.

ANNIE: Then you sit right there. The kettle's all boiled. (ANNIE *is going.*)

CARLOTTA: I want a cigarette.

ANNIE: You know what the doctor said about smoking?

CARLOTTA: All right. Damn the doctor. (ANNIE *goes.* CARLOTTA *sits deep in thought. She rises and goes for her purse. She brings it to her chair. She opens it and takes out a large piece of paper which she studies a moment. She folds this up and thrusts it into the side of the chair. She follows this with a green booklet which looks surprisingly like an American passport. Then she pulls out a roll of bills and counts them carefully. She is just putting them back when* ANNIE *returns with the tea things.*)

ANNIE: There's a toasted muffin for you, too.

CARLOTTA: Annie, that cash I gave you last week? How much is left of it?

ANNIE: There's well over two hundred dollars left.

CARLOTTA: (*half to herself*) With my three hundred, that

makes five hundred and something. I need five hundred more, at least. (ANNIE *has got the tea things on the little table beside the chair.*)

ANNIE: Drink your tea, now.

CARLOTTA: (*turning her attention to the tea*) Five hundred and something. It's all there is. It will have to do. . . . We're sailing for Europe Saturday, Annie.

ANNIE: Sailing?

CARLOTTA: On the *Conte Verde*. Straight off for Genoa.

ANNIE: We ain't. Oh, Miss Lottie, you certainly are sudden about your movements.

CARLOTTA: (*smiling*) We'll stay all summer. Maybe longer.

ANNIE: Now that's just splendid! Excuse me, Miss Lottie, for askin', but are we goin' alone?

CARLOTTA: Yes.

ANNIE: I'm perfectly delighted. It'll do you a world of good.

CARLOTTA: Yes, won't it? (*The elevator door again, then the door-bell.*)

ANNIE: Oho! Will that be Mr. Burton callin' to-day?

CARLOTTA: (*shaking her head*) No. . . . I don't think so. . . . See who it is. (ANNIE *goes to the door. It is* ARCHIE.)

ARCHIE: Hello, Annie!

ANNIE: It's Mr. Archie, ma'am.

ARCHIE: Hello!

CARLOTTA: Hello, Archie. Want some tea?

ARCHIE: (*coming in*) Not me. How are you feeling?

CARLOTTA: All right. Like hell. I don't mind.

ANNIE: Mr. Archie, she's been out all day.

CARLOTTA: It didn't hurt me any. Run along, Annie. (ANNIE *goes.*)

ARCHIE: You ought to know better . . . a day like this. . . .

CARLOTTA: I had business.

ARCHIE: (*dubiously*) Can you stand a shock?

CARLOTTA: I'd love one.

ARCHIE: All right. . . . (*Calls through door.*) Come in. She won't bite! (SAM *appears on the threshold; quite an altered* SAM, *a* SAM *who would grace any company and be a credit to any tailor, a* SAM *who is just a trifle conscious of his advance in the world, a* SAM *who has gained dignity and grown just a little ridiculous about it. He comes in.*

CARLOTTA *looks up and sees him and instinctively smooths back her hair. They look at one another for a moment. It is a very serious moment for both of them.)*

CARLOTTA: It's my Sammy, after all these months! . . . *(She goes over to him, all her defenses down. She speaks, though, to* ARCHIE.*)* I'm indebted to you for this visit, I suppose?

ARCHIE: I don't deny it.

SAM: *(recovering himself)* I was perfectly willing to come. I can't stay long. I've got an important engagement at six. *(He looks at his watch.)* A very important engagement with Mr. Charles Kohler of the North American Steel. At six, so I can't stay. But I was perfectly willing to come.

CARLOTTA: *(however much she may be hurt, she manages to see the funny side)* When are you going to divorce me?

SAM: I'm not.

CARLOTTA: Take off your coat, Sammy. If you don't you'll catch cold when you go out. *(Back to the chair.)* Haven't I sinned enough? I'm too sick to sin any more.

ARCHIE: Don't, Lottie!

CARLOTTA: I should think that nine months of desertion ought to be enough to satisfy any man, let alone Sam's previous complaints.

ARCHIE: Now, Lottie, please lay off. I brought Sam here and I want you to be polite and listen to what he has to say.

SAM: *(his coat removed)* I'm sorry you've been sick.

CARLOTTA: Thank you!

SAM: Same old heart?

CARLOTTA: Much the same, thank you.

SAM: *(looking about him as he sits down)* This isn't much of a place.

ARCHIE: All it wants is a Gideon Bible.

CARLOTTA: It's the best I can afford.

SAM: What are you living on?

CARLOTTA: About my usual diet. Hasn't Sam developed a charming bedside manner? *(This last to* ARCHIE.*)*

ARCHIE: Now there's no good in bluffing, Lottie. I told Sam you're broke.

SAM: I guessed Burton's crash wouldn't do you any good.

ARCHIE: I hate to think what Burton did with her money.

SAM: I used to know Burton. I started a deal with him

once. I had to crowd him out. It was the only square thing he ever touched—Ellis Consolidated.

ARCHIE: Wasn't I president until you crowded *me* out?

SAM: I'm out myself now. It did make a million. (CARLOTTA *buries her grin in her teacup.*) I used to tell you you'd get yours for trusting him, but you wouldn't listen to me because he always made so much money for you. Now he's going to jail. It's the place for Burton. The square deal's the only deal that pays in the long run.

CARLOTTA: *(emerging from her teacup)* Archie, I want you to write that out fifty times so that you'll never, never forget it.

SAM: What do you mean by that?

CARLOTTA: *(the sibyl)* You seem to have done pretty well by yourself on square deals. They tell me Lucky Sam McCarver's the smartest thing on Wall Street, and I'm *so* proud when I hear that! I don't know but I *will* let you do something for me.

ARCHIE: Now you're talking! That's what I brought him here for. I said to him: She won't take a penny of yours from your lawyers. But if you come yourself, it will be like seeing the cash, and she certainly needs the cash.

SAM: You know I'll do anything I can—within reason.

CARLOTTA: *(wincing)* It must be wonderful to do and say and be everything "within reason"!

SAM: What do you expect?

CARLOTTA: *(a pause—then)* Nothing. Go on.

SAM: I repeat: I'll do anything I can—within reason.

CARLOTTA: Would you give Archie a job, then? I was just thinking how nice it would be if Archie could look after me. I've spent all Archie's money, you know, being so sick.

ARCHIE: Now don't try that on. It was damn decent of Sam to come.

CARLOTTA: So decent it almost makes me ill.

SAM: I don't understand your attitude.

CARLOTTA: Don't you? *(She turns to* ARCHIE*)* I wonder what Sam would say if I were to tell him this is Burton's flat?

SAM: What!

CARLOTTA: That's what it is! . . . Burton used to keep these little *pied-à-terre* all over town so that every variety of lady friend could feel perfectly at home. . . . Before his crash, that was. . . . I've always imagined he reserved this one for his stenographic flames. Oh, you can't mistake it.

Here to-night and back at the office in the morning with a forty-dollar wrist-watch.

ARCHIE: Fie, Lottie! Sam'll think Burton is . . .

SAM: I might have known you'd come to it.

CARLOTTA: Didn't you rather hope I should? . . . I'm sorry to disappoint you, Sammy. My status here might be described as living on Burton but not with him.

SAM: Gold-digging, eh?

CARLOTTA: In a small way. Somebody had to help me out. When I left the hospital, I had nowhere to go and Burton so kindly offered me this.

SAM: You could have come to me for help.

CARLOTTA: That *would* have been gold-digging. . . . Somehow I don't mind stringing Burton along. I despise him, but I'm rather fond of him. I don't despise you, Sam.

SAM: And you're not rather fond of me.

CARLOTTA: *(pause—then)* You *have* risen in the world, haven't you?

SAM: You treat me as if I'd done you an injustice. *(Again* CARLOTTA *retreats to her teacup.)* Look here, Archie. You remember that night in Venice. Do you think I did wrong that night?

ARCHIE: *(on the horns of a dilemma)* Well . . .

CARLOTTA: *(more sibylline than ever)* Doing right or wrong depends entirely on what you're after, Sammy.

SAM: You *would* think that!

CARLOTTA: *I* would?

ARCHIE: Now, stop it! This isn't the point. The point is, will you take the allowance Sam offers you?

CARLOTTA: I'll take it as alimony.

SAM: You won't get alimony.

CARLOTTA: If you've come here in that state of mind, you might just as well run along to your appointment.

SAM: I've come here to do my best for you.

CARLOTTA: Within reason. It's a little bit late for you to do that.

SAM: I know you think so. But I don't. So you'd better be—reasonable. You're sick and you're hard up. . . .

CARLOTTA: Divorce me and I'll soon be healthy, wealthy, and wise. I'm not so unreasonable. I shouldn't even suggest alimony if I could get along without it and if I didn't know that "money is no object" to Lucky Sam McCarver. Think of yourself. Get rid of me and you can marry a rich lady from

Cleveland and have lots of children who'll get ahead just as you got ahead until, presently, they'll be just like Archie and me. Won't you be proud, then?

SAM: Oh, this business is too much for me! *(He rises.)*

ARCHIE: Lottie, for Heaven's sake!

SAM: I'm going.

CARLOTTA: Well, Sammy, you haven't entirely wasted your time coming here. You couldn't have hoped for a better judgment on me than this . . . sick and poor and beaten . . . could you? Isn't it just what you came to see? *(This last is the most sibylline of all.)*

SAM *(to ARCHIE)* If you'll call at my office in the morning, I'll settle for any expense Carlotta may have caused you.

CARLOTTA: How really magnanimous!

ARCHIE: That won't be necessary.

CARLOTTA: Oh, you needn't worry about me, either of you. I'm sailing off for Europe on Saturday. Yes, Archie dear, I've patched things up with Aunt Alice, and I'm joining her in Nice. I've been buying my passage and getting my passport to-day. Here they are.

ARCHIE: Good God!

CARLOTTA: Aunt Alice only just sent me the money, or I should have told you, Archie. She's got a villa with a beautiful young movie actor in it and she's gone in for the prevention of infantile paralysis because there's a beautiful young English doctor in that. I don't know whether I'll draw the doctor or the actor, but either one will do. Perhaps we'll share the doctor and settle down as philanthropists in Paris. I've always known that Aunt Alice would wind up as a philanthropist. It's the only thrill she hasn't tried.

SAM: I wish you a pleasant voyage.

CARLOTTA: Be sure to let me hear from you after you make the Union, won't you?

SAM: *(looks at her a moment, then turns to ARCHIE)* I'll . . . I'll leave the field to you. *(He takes up his hat and coat. He hesitates. They watch him.)*

CARLOTTA: Good-by, Sam. . . . Won't you say good-by? *(He puts down his hat and coat and comes over face to face with her.)*

SAM: I renew my offer to you.

CARLOTTA: Your offer of marriage?

SAM: My offer of twelve thousand a year for the balance of your life.

CARLOTTA: For the balance of my life! What a dreary sound that has!

SAM: I'm serious.

ARCHIE: Lottie, for God's sake take it.

CARLOTTA: (not all mockery) Do you still love me sweetly, madly?

SAM: (controlling more than his temper) Will you take it?

CARLOTTA: (he wouldn't say it) I'll take a cigarette. I'm a bit groggy from so much conversation.

ARCHIE: Stop talking. (ARCHIE gives her a cigarette from the mantel. She fluffs the first match and apologizes with a smile. The second works. She thanks him with a smile.)

CARLOTTA: (she will give him another chance) Why do you want me to take your money, Sam?

SAM: Because you're my wife. That's reason enough for me.

CARLOTTA: I'm not convinced by it.

SAM: Well. . . .

ARCHIE: Lottie, please. . . .

CARLOTTA: (a wild crescendo) No! NO! NO! (Quite decidedly.) Thank you very much indeed. . . . No. . . . (Then.) I've half a mind to tell you why. . . .

SAM: Why?

CARLOTTA: Because . . . (But she is too proud, and he wouldn't understand in any case. She gives it up.) Well, because.

SAM: (all the pomp gone) What's going to happen to you, girlie?

CARLOTTA: (smiling at the old nickname) I haven't an idea.

SAM: Look here . . . if twelve thousand isn't enough, I'll double it.

ARCHIE: Oh, Lottie!

CARLOTTA: (as if money mattered) Would you take me back?

SAM: I . . . I might . . . that is, if you would . . .

CARLOTTA: And there you are, because I never will.

SAM: Hear that, Archie? I'd like to know what more I can have to say after that?

CARLOTTA: There's nothing more for any one to say, so do let's cut this short.

ARCHIE: Yes, I think we'd better.

SAM: *(belligerent)* When I'm good and ready. I'm meeting you half way . . .

CARLOTTA: You think you are, but we can't either of us give in and there isn't so much as one little square inch of ground where we can ever meet. There isn't anything that either of us can do or say or want that doesn't outrage and infuriate the other. The world's your oyster, Sammy, and my Waterloo. Well, you like oysters and I don't much mind Waterloos.

SAM: You think you're too dam' good for the world, that's your trouble.

CARLOTTA: I dare say neither you nor I amounts to a hill of beans if the truth were known.

SAM: There you go! Trying to put me in the wrong again! Well, you're not going to get away with it this time.

CARLOTTA: I'm not trying anything of the sort. I haven't any hard feelings left any more. It all comes down to the kind of a man you are and the kind of a woman I am. You can take advantage of everything that happens to you. I have to make a mess of everything that happens to me. You're a go-getter. I'm a runner-away. I admire you, on the whole. I don't mind telling you that. . . . Oh, I know a lot now that I never used to know. It's being sick, I guess. Isn't there something in the Bible about losing your soul to find it? I never read the Bible and I never shall read it. . . . What you are in the end is what you were born to be in the beginning. Where or how doesn't make the least difference. . . . Run along, now, and be a howling success. I'll read about you in the papers.

SAM: I've offered you twelve thou . . .

CARLOTTA: *Please* don't talk any more about money.

SAM: What do you expect me to do? Make love to you?

CARLOTTA: *(this strikes home)* Oh, no! . . . No . . . not that. I don't expect anything like that.

SAM: That's lucky.

CARLOTTA: I do wish you'd go now.

SAM: I'd like to give you both a piece of my mind for bringing me 'way up here on this wild-goose chase. I'm sorry it isn't in my nature to be sentimental, but I'm too busy. I'm ready to do my duty but, by God, the pair of you seem to think . . .

CARLOTTA: If you get wrought up, Sammy, you'll only increase your blood-pressure.

SAM: I can't help getting wrought up. A man has his duties. You're one of mine. I've always lived up to my duties. Never shirked one of 'em. That's what put me where I am to-day.

CARLOTTA: I put you where you are to-day.

SAM: You! Don't kid yourself, girlie! Hard work and a level head and knowing what I was after and trusting in my judgment . . . and my luck. . . . They put me where I . . .

ARCHIE: If I were you, I'd save that kind of talk for *The American Magazine*. It's a long way from the Tuileries to this, Sam. You wouldn't have made it alone in a single year. You wouldn't even have learned to dress yourself alone. Don't brag. Lottie's right.

SAM: I'm not saying . . .

CARLOTTA: *(settling herself in the big chair once more)* Don't interrupt the sermon, Archie. This is Napoleon's farewell to Josephine. Let him get through with it.

SAM: *(furious)* That's like you! That's like you! You won't even give a man credit for a decent feeling. You're a fake and you always were one. I'd have done better to marry one of the tarts on old Doorman Dan's booty list. Why, when I think of the harm a woman like you can do in the world!

(ARCHIE is about to protest in physical violence.)

CARLOTTA: Now, now, Archie! Never mind! It doesn't matter.

SAM: Little Jimmie Wright ought to have shot you instead of Monty Garside.

ARCHIE: *(his eyes blazing at SAM)* It's a long way from the Tuileries just the same.

SAM: And where are we at? I'm fixed. Yes. But look at her! And do you think I'm going to let her go on and do more damage? Give her a divorce the way her other husbands did, and turn her loose again? Like hell! I'll take care of her . . . I'll see that she's well fixed. But, by God, she's going to be responsible to me.

CARLOTTA: *(her voice weak for all its mockery)* Oh, Sam, you really *are* a panic!

SAM: *(rushing on)* Am I? Oh, it isn't as though I wouldn't take you back, girlie, and forgive and forget everything. I've always tried to do the fair and square thing, and I hope to God I always will. That put me where I am to-day—nothing else, see? An' I come here to say all this, generous as you please—you'll have to admit that—and what kind of a line of talk do you hand me back?

CARLOTTA: So's your old man! (*A spasm of pain contracts her face. Her hand makes a fumbling movement toward her heart. Then both hands fall, and she lets her head drop wearily back.*)

SAM: Just what I might have expected from you. Frivolous, that's what you are! From the ground up. You're a parasite. You're worse than a parasite. I don't know what you are! But, by God! when I think . . .

ARCHIE: (*irritably*) That's all very well, Sam, but have a heart. Lottie's still sick.

SAM: Excuse me. I forgot. I guess I was getting a little bit excited.

ARCHIE: A little bit! It's all a lot of bunk, anyway!

SAM: *What* is?

ARCHIE: All of it! I'm damned if I see where you've got anything to preach about.

SAM: Preach!

ARCHIE: (*who is growing angrier and angrier*) Yes, preach!

SAM: (*blazing up again*) By God, if that isn't just like you Ellises! Is there anything you won't sneer at! Just let a man like me get up in the world and begin to make a success of things, and you . . . Yah!

ARCHIE: (*cutting him off*) I don't think so much of your kind of success.

SAM: What do you mean, my kind of success?

ARCHIE: Oh, well, as Lottie says, "it all depends on what you're after." . . .

SAM: (*in disgust*) Yah!

ARCHIE: You may be a howling success, Sam, but there's one thing you'll never be.

SAM: What's that?

ARCHIE: You can guess.

SAM: (*he does, and it hurts*) I made my mistake when I got married.

ARCHIE: (*exploding*) You filthy bounder! You ought to get down on your knees and thank God for Lottie's marrying you. Lottie's a great woman. Lottie plays the game. Don't you, Lottie?

SAM: I'm damned if she hasn't fallen asleep!

ARCHIE: What? (*He goes over to her. He sees that her jaw has fallen.*) Good God!

SAM: Has she fainted?

ARCHIE: *(examines her eyeballs—then)* She's . . . look! . . .

SAM: *(looking)* You'll have to call a doctor, anyway.

ARCHIE: There's one on the next floor. I'll fetch him. *(He runs out, leaving the door open.)*

(SAM *stands dumbly staring at his dead wife. The cigarette still smokes in her hand. He sees it, takes it away from her and extinguishes it. Then he looks again at the beautiful, still face. After a moment, he reaches out and touches it. Then, passionately, he presses her hand to his lips. Then he draws back and considers matters.*

He looks his god in the eye, so to speak, and is relieved to ascertain that he, at least, has nothing to be ashamed of.

Then, suddenly, a clock somewhere strikes six and he remembers that appointment he mentioned earlier. He looks at his watch. He really ought to go. He doesn't quite like to leave CARLOTTA *this way, and he glances uneasily in her direction as though to tell her so. Just the same, he is a busy man with great responsibilities.*

He glances toward the door, wondering how much longer ARCHIE *is going to be about that doctor. He would like to stay until they come. He stands tapping his foot and calculating just how long it will take him to drive to . . .*

He looks at his watch again. He is already late. He makes up his mind to the inevitable.

He goes over for his coat. He takes up his hat. He is just settling it on his brow when his eye once more falls upon the dead woman. He remembers the respect due the dead, and walks out uncovered.

He walks out as though he were going to a funeral— solemnly, without haste, but firmly. He will telephone AR- CHIE *in the morning about arrangements for* CARLOTTA'S *interment, and, of course, he will pay all the bills. But he will never again doubt his own self-sufficient power and destiny.)*

The curtain falls as he disappears.

COMMENTARY

According to John Mason Brown in *Upstage* (1930), *Lucky Sam McCarver* is Sidney Howard's best work. This is high praise indeed for a play that closed after only twenty-nine performances. Brown's estimation is further substantiated by such critics as Joseph Wood Krutch and Burns Mantle. The latter even considered including *Lucky Sam McCarver* as one of the ten best plays of the year and is quoted as saying that the play "suffered a quick and, to me, undeserved failure." Krutch was not as enthusiastic as Mantle but did consider the play an honorable and honest attempt at fine theater.

The characters of Sam and Carlotta are two of the most realistic characters in the American theater, and through them Howard's ironic iconoclasm is clearly visible. The idealistic view of the lower class as a repository of virtuous labor and character building, and of the upper class as a place for sweet-tempered, utterly dignified ladies and gentlemen is ruthlessly shattered by Howard, thus part of the irony of the title *Lucky Sam McCarver*.

The characters battle each other on a personal as well as a class level. Howard taunts the idle decadence of the wealthy class through Carlotta and scorns the greed and avarice of the lower class through Sam. Sam's hunger for sexual reward and material success at any price collides with Carlotta's need to be loved yet have total self-control. They are true to life and never make any compromises with their instincts that relate to their respective classes, needs, and ambitions.

One has only to look back on the graft and corruption of the Harding Administration to see the validity of Howard's characters. George, Dan, and the policeman are straight out of the speak-easy world of New York. And Pudge and the Princess mirror expatriate types found in Venetian society of the period. Howard's contribution to realistic characterization in the American theater is obviously quite substantial and significant.

Another dimension of the realism of the 1920s was the interrelationship of character and setting. In a Darwinian sense, a relationship is established between environment and character. As the characters were utterly real, so too were their backgrounds—the speak-easy for Sam, the apartment for Carlotta, the palace for upper-class, jaded foreigners in Venice.

In the original production the twenty-four-year-old set designer, Jo Mielziner, tried in the third act to create an absolutely real baroque palace in Venice. In so doing he upset the balance by putting the actors in a setting in which they could neither be seen nor heard. One might note that too much detail of setting can be self-defeating and destroy the illusion necessary to realism. Mielziner admitted that his set for the Venice scene overwhelmed the actors.

Although in his preface Howard assumed his play was plotless, there is careful foreshadowing of Carlotta's heart trouble leading to her death at the play's end. The melodramatic device of killing Monty in Act I and the heightened action of the fight scene in Act III are clear manifestations. Similarly, the use of the stockbroker, Burton, as a foil for Sam is an obvious plot device. Yet, in spite of these carryovers from the old realism, Carlotta's death is absolutely justified on the basis of the events of the play. Here death grows out of her conflict with Sam, for when Carlotta discovers that Sam doesn't love her and merely wants to use her name to garner material advantage, she reverts to her earlier, decadent self and rapidly deteriorates. She dies largely because she really did love Sam and couldn't contend with his cold contempt. Some critics took exception to this ending and may be one reason the play was not well accepted.

Howard wanted to demonstrate that the universal desire for material reward should be challenged and questioned. He asked what we gained or lost when we achieved material success. His answer was that we lost self-realization, feeling, and sentiment. Certainly Howard did not believe that one could return to the older morality, and he emphasized that the truth of life was to be true to ourselves. Sam couldn't be himself because he needed success too much and he was willing to sacrifice anything for it. Carlotta couldn't be herself because she had already been seduced by success; she had been born with too much money and power, and she used it for trivial purposes. But she did have one thing that Sam could never have—true upper-class élan.

The vacuousness of the American upper class is pilloried ruthlessly in the play, as is the clumsy, determined assault on wealth and power by lower-class Sam. Howard slams the American "aristocracy" by placing the third act in the midst of Venetian decadence. This scene change is important and its significance was lost on most of its critics. Venice, in the 1920s, was ideal for exposing the empty "petting party" mentality of that time and place. Pudge, the effeminate American, is contrasted with the sinister virility of Sam McCarver. The emptiness of life in Venice is attacked over and over by Howard and perhaps explains why the predominantly upper-class theatergoing public of New York did not take gently to the play, nor care to embrace its cutting edge.

The play also assaults lower-class materialistic dreams through Sam's crassness in Venice. McCarver is the immigrant Irish type used earlier in the American theater, and he is attacked for his rise-at-all-costs attitude. Howard is clearly a social critic of American manners and morals, using theme as well as character as the basis for dramatic composition. Certainly, Sam and Carlotta are strong characterizations, but Howard gets at their lives through theme. Both lose sight of the ethical commitment that went with achieving the American Dream. Sam has riches but no morality.

The play is antiromantic and differs markedly in this regard from O'Neill's *Anna Christie*. Howard's emphasis is on accommodation in the marriage from the very beginning. In his Preface to the play, Howard states that his characters came together through instinct, that they used each other with very little sentimental palaver about love. Because the instincts have to do with sex and power, Howard's debt to Freud is unmistakable.

Howard believed that his play was somewhat experimental in that it explored upper- and lower-class levels of society strictly through dialogue between the representatives of those two classes, Carlotta and Sam. Indeed, a major contribution of Howard to American realism can be seen by his utter emphasis upon showing the inner workings of these two extraordinary characters.

Perhaps Howard was too ambitious for the theater of his day, for the play failed at the box office despite his experimental fine-tuning of the characterizations. Certain critics assailed it as being "cryptic" and "obscure," even "sketchy" and "elliptical." Alexander Woollcott in the *New York Morning World* (October 22, 1925) ridiculed Howard for a line that Howard had quoted in the program: "And the lonesome traveler derives a sort of comfort and society from the presence of vegetable life." Woollcott thought that it must have come from a "seed catalog." That may be amusing, but it insensitively avoids Howard's point. It referred to the fact that the play did not have the customary plot that most theatergoers were used to but that an audience could take "comfort and society" from watching the slow growth of two keenly aware characters over the course of their passionate contact with life. For a society out of touch with the soil, with natural life, Howard prescribes observation of the slow, organic development of "vegetable life."

Finally, it is imperative that the acting of the production be noted, since Howard made much over the fact that he wrote for the actors. John Cromwell, in playing Sam, was warmly received by audience and critics, while Clare Eames was not. Could it have been that the play was not as well cast as Howard would have us believe? Could it have been that audiences of that time simply could not understand nor empathize with Carlotta, while they only too clearly understood Sam?

Howard's general disappointment in Broadway was exacerbated by the lack of critical acclaim for *Lucky Sam McCarver,* a play he rightly felt was superbly conceived and written. The language is witty, provocative, and brightly touched by excellent characterizations. It makes a welcome evening for a "lonesome traveler."

IN ABRAHAM'S
BOSOM
by
Paul Green
(as edited by Franklin D. Case)

BACKGROUND

As Sidney Howard was a product of the times, the whirlwind forces that shaped the American character during the 1920s, so Paul Green was a product of place, of the farms and earth of North Carolina. If Howard's dramas showed how Americans struggled with materialism and old taboos in order to find their self-identity, Green's dramas demonstrated that man and nature were in a constant battle for survival, which man could win providing he had the "tools" as well as conviction and spirit.

Paul Green had a long and fruitful career as a playwright, novelist, poet, teacher, and humanitarian. In 1926 when he was beginning to receive attention, Barrett H. Clark, while editing and writing an introduction for a collection of Green's one-act plays, asked him for a biographical sketch. This is what Green returned:

Born on a farm near Lillington, N.C., March 17, 1894. Farmed in the spring and summer and went to country school a few months in the winter. Later went to Buie's Creek Academy, from which he was graduated in 1914. Taught country school two years. Entered the University of North Carolina in 1916. Enlisted in the army in 1917. Served as a private, corporal, sergeant and sergeant-major with the 105th Engineers, 30th Division. Later as a Second Lieutenant at Paris. Served four months on the

Western front. Returned to the University of North Carolina in 1919. Was graduated from there in 1921. Did graduate work at his alma mater and at Cornell University. At present he is a member of the faculty at the University of North Carolina.

However, these facts do not give us the warmer description of Green's daily life while a professor at the University of North Carolina that is provided by Howard Mumford Jones in *Southwest Review* (Autumn 1928): "A venerable Ford draws up to the curb and the driver, a squarely built, badly dressed young man, with the body of a farmer and the head of a dreamer, gets out and mounts the steps with the slow, awkward walk of a man brought up to plowed fields, and hog and hominy."

By that time, he had written a score of one-act plays, several of which had already been published, and two full-length plays still in manuscript. Green was instructed about playwriting, or at least he was encouraged to write plays, by Frederick Koch, founder of the Drama Department at the University of North Carolina and of the Carolina Playmakers. Koch was one of a group of pioneers who were instrumental in establishing theater and drama in the universities and colleges during this time. (Of course, George Pierce Baker and Brander Matthews were *the* pioneers who established programs at Harvard, Yale, and Columbia. Thomas Wood Stevens at Carnegie Institute of Technology created the first degree program in theater; Thomas Dickinson organized the Wisconsin program; E. C. Mabie was active at the University of Iowa; Kenneth Rowe was developing theater and drama at the University of Michigan; and Glenn Hughes was the organizer of the School of Drama at the University of Washington).

According to Vincent Kenny, whose biography, *Paul Green* (1971), is useful and instructive, Koch taught his students to write with "enthusiasm, spontaneity, accurate observation and honesty. He brought to his students a respect for the folk play, for an art form which challenges the sensitive probing artist to achievements beyond the scope of commercial theater" (p. 1).

In 1926 The Provincetown Playhouse produced *In Abraham's Bosom,* and the play was awarded the Pulitzer Prize for the 1926–27 season. Consequently Green and the play received national attention. Soon other plays were being produced, including *The Field God* (1927); *The House of Connelly* (1931), which launched the Group Theater; *Roll, Sweet Chariot* (1934); *Johnny Johnson* (1936, with music by Kurt Weill); and *Native Son* (1941, an adaptation of the novel by Richard Wright).

After 1937 Green turned to writing a form of drama that became known as symphonic. Green said that these pieces, which were written for outdoor production, were developed because "the narrow confines of the usual Broadway play and stage are not fitted to the dramatic needs of the American people." Usually referred to as outdoor spectacles, the symphonic dramas have been very popular, leading to the founding of the Outdoor Drama Association affiliated with the University of North Carolina. Some of the best known of these dramas are *The Lost Colony,* at Roanoke, Virginia; *The Common Glory,* at Williamsburg, Virginia; and *Wilderness Road,* at Berea, Kentucky.

In addition to writing a number of novels, Green was a successful screen writer, having provided the scenario for *State Fair* (1945) and other scripts for actors Bette Davis, Greer Garson, and Clark Gable.

He received many honors and awards, including a Guggenheim Fellowship in 1928; he was elected president of the National Theater Conference in 1940; he was appointed to UNESCO in 1950, and elected to membership in the National Institute of Arts and Letters. He died in May, 1981, at his home in Chapel Hill.

Green's accomplishment in the drama is twofold. First, he is the most influential of the folk writers in the American drama (his contribution to the folk drama will be discussed further in the Commentary section), and second, he is primarily responsible for releasing the black character—in the drama written by white playwrights—from the shackles of stereotype in which he had been cast for so many generations. Prior to 1920 the stage black commonly was a servant with one of two personalities: a grinning, watermelon-loving buffoon who invariably massacred the English language, or, less frequently, a lovable, gentle, sentimental "Uncle Tom" or "Aunt Jemimah." If the character was not a servant, which was very rare, the individual usually was a quadroon or octoroon who appeared to be white. Not only were the characters stereotyped, but they were enacted by white actors in "blackface." The tradition of the comic servant and the use of "blackface" was influenced by the minstrel show, which was a predominant form of entertainment between 1842 and 1870; although, black characters did appear in the drama prior to 1830. In any case, black actors did not appear on stage with whites. There were no integrated casts in straight plays until the 1920s, and even at that time a public outcry was heard.

Integration began with musicals, and the first black performer to appear with a white company was the talented Bert Williams, who was hired by Abe Erlanger in 1910 to sing and dance, as well as perform his comic routines, in *Follies*. It was said that Williams:

> blazed a pathway from the minstrel house to the legitimate theater; he unlocked the door, which had, for centuries, shut out colored performers from white shows. He lessened discrimination by conquering the prejudice of managers and producers. He overcame much of the hostility of the press against mixed casts and he reformed and refined the art, so-called, of the (white) black-face comedians, by teaching them to substitute drollery and repose for roughness. (Charles Anderson, quoted in Edith J. R. Isaacs, *The Negro in the American Theater* [1947], p. 42)

Booker T. Washington said, "Bert Williams has done more for the race than I have. He has smiled his way into people's hearts. I have been obliged to fight my way" (ibid., p. 42).

In keeping with their purpose, the Provincetown Players provided the initial opportunity for integration in the straight drama. When O'Neill wrote *The Emperor Jones*, it was apparent that a black actor was needed, and so Charles Gilpin, who had acted at the Lafayette Theater, a producing organization for black actors, writers, and audiences, was located by Jig Cook. Gilpin's performance as the tormented and bewildered Jones was nothing short of sensational, and in essence broke the color line; however, when O'Neill brought to The Provincetown Playhouse his *All God's Chillun Got Wings* in 1924 with Paul Robeson, it presented a new crisis. The play dealt with a marriage between a black man and a white woman. At one point in the play, the woman kisses her husband's hand. The history of the event has been reported by Deutsch and Hannau in *The Provincetown, A Story of a Theater* (1931):

> "All God's Chillun Got Wings" opened on May 15th to an accompaniment of poison pen letters, telegrams to O'Neill threatening his life and the lives of his children, and an anonymous promise of a bomb in the cellar. District Attorney Banton, a Southerner, had not read the play but knew that its author was the man who had written "The Hairy Ape" and "The Emperor Jones." He declared that he would "get" O'Neill. (p. 111)

He got the mayor to refuse to issue acting permits for the children in the cast. O'Neill rewrote the scene in which they appeared, and the show went on. In 1947 when writing *The Negro in the American Theatre*, Edith J. R. Isaacs observed:

> As we look back upon ALL GOD'S CHILLUN GOT WINGS after twenty years, it is clear that its importance lay chiefly in its repercussions, in the critical analysis of the drama and the acting that it stimulated. Practically every question relating to the future of the Negro in the American theater came to the surface there: Is the Negro actor an artist? . . . Has Negro life anything of importance to contribute to the mainstream of American drama? Or is the drama of Negro life a separate thing, insofar as it exists at all? (p. 78)

All God's Chillun Got Wings was really a weak play as far as depicting black character, although it was surely significant for its time. With it O'Neill had cracked the door open to realistic portrayal of blacks. Two years later in the same theater Green smashed the whole door down and went rushing in with *In Abraham's Bosom*. Thus the American theater and the American public at large owe another debt to that vital theater on MacDougal Street in Greenwich Village. In passing, it is interesting to note that by 1924 the focal point of the management had changed. The official name of the organization was The Experimental Theater, Inc., and Robert Edmund Jones and Kenneth MacGowan were preoccupied with methods of production. In keeping with their plans, they leased another theater, the Greenwich Village. In their prospectus they announced:

In these two playhouses a beginning will be attempted toward a true repertory company. A single group of players will appear at both theaters. They will be given the security of permanent employment and the advantages of constant work together. Each actor will play a wide variety of parts. All will work toward a creative ensemble.

By 1926 The Provincetown Playhouse had undergone another change in management and ideology. Actually looking back to the days of George Cram Cook, James Light and M. Elizabeth Fitzgerald wanted to find new playwrights. Thus, MacGowan and Jones, more interested in experimentation with the "new stagecraft," managed the Greenwich Village Theater, and the Playhouse itself was given to Light and Fitzgerald. O'Neill tried to serve all masters. When Barrett Clark presented the new managers with *In Abraham's Bosom*, they were not overly enthusiastic because of the many problems the play presented, particularly the difficulty of finding an all-black cast. In addition, the play had already been rejected by over twenty producers. Nevertheless, plans for the production went forward. Jasper Deeter was hired to direct the play and Cleon Throckmorton was to provide the settings. From Harlem came Julius Bledsoe, Rose McClendon, and Abbie Mitchell to play Abe, Goldie, and Muh Mack. The play opened on December 30, 1926, and Edith Isaacs reported:

> It is difficult to remember scenes in any play that were more compelling than the tragic scenes in which these three players appeared together—all artists, all with long theater training, all understanding that unity among players which the Russians call "communion." (*The Negro in the American Theatre*, p. 80)

Brooks Atkinson, who had just become the featured critic for the *New York Times,* saw the play the second night after it had moved to the Garrick Theatre six weeks later and wrote:

> On last Tuesday evening the opportunity for which every muted understudy prays earnestly every day came to Frank Wilson, in the cast of "In Abraham's Bosom." Julius Bledsoe, the leading player in that uncommonly

adroit cast, did not appear at the usual hour and did not communicate with the management. Actors and audience both waited patiently for about thirty minutes. Then Mr. Wilson, who had been playing a minor part in the first scene, walked on as Abraham McCranie and gave a performance not only almost letter perfect, but also swift, direct, and extraordinarily moving. Inasmuch as "In Abraham's Bosom" is the "biography of a negro in 7 scenes," the leading player is on stage almost without interruption, and he sets the key of the entire production. Mr. Wilson suffused the drama with a passionate sincerity that pulled together the tattered scenes and gave a lucid meaning to the theme. He is the sort of understudy that strikes terror into the hearts of leading players. As the result of what the management considered Bledsoe's contractual defection, Mr. Wilson has been given the leading part permanently. . . . After six weeks at The Provincetown Theatre, this fine tragedy by Paul Green has moved as far north as the Garrick, where it has more room in which to flaunt its beauties. . . . Played by a group of excellent negro actors, who communicates perfectly the individual and racial characterizations of the text, "In Abraham's Bosom" is the most penetrating, unswerving tragedy in town, and surely one of the most pungent folk dramas of the American stage. No wonder devious rumors already whisper that the Pulitzer judges regard it with high favor. . . . It comes, not from a theatrical workshop, but from the heart of the author. (February 20, 1927)

When Paul Green won the Pulitzer Prize for drama with *In Abraham's Bosom,* the theatrical world was astounded. The other plays that had been considered included *The Silver Cord* by Sidney Howard, *Broadway* by George Abbott, *Saturday's Children* by Maxwell Anderson, and *The Road to Rome* by Robert Sherwood. The complete honesty and power of Green's characters had obviously caught the judges.

Green's contribution to the American theater is inestimable, for it was he who at long last showed white audiences how valid black theater could be. Indigenous black theater had existed in America for generations, but it had been available only in back alleys for black audiences. A favorite

pastime for white toughs was to vandalize the places of
performance and terrorize the audiences. Prodigiously talented actors like Ira Aldridge were run off to Europe, where
they found fame and fortune. But Paul Green, by his un-
daunted courage in writing for blacks, made it clear that
black life was something whites could understand. It was, in
fact, a part of mainstream America. Paul Green had flung
open the door and in stepped the talented black writers and
actors of the Harlem Renaissance on their way to Broadway.
Following on their heels, almost a generation later, came
playwrights James Baldwin, Lorraine Hansberry, and Amiri
Baraka (Leroi Jones).

IN ABRAHAM'S BOSOM
The Biography of a Negro
in Seven Scenes
(1926)

CHARACTERS

ABRAHAM MCCRANIE—*a Negro.*
GOLDIE MCALLISTER—*his sweetheart and later his wife.*
MUH MACK—*his aunt.*
BUD GASKINS ⎱
LIJE HUNNEYCUTT ⎰ *Turpentine hands for the*
PUNY AVERY ⎰ *Colonel.*
DOUGLASS MCCRANIE—*Abraham's son.*
EDDIE WILLIAMS ⎱
LANIE HORTON ⎰ *Students to Abe.*
NEILLY MCNEILL ⎰
COLONEL MCCRANIE—*a Southern gentleman, once the
    owner of slaves.*
LONNIE MCCRANIE—*his son.*

SCENES

SCENE I. The turpentine woods of eastern North Carolina, the summer of 1885.

SCENE II. In Abraham McCranie's cabin, spring, three years later.

SCENE III. The school house, winter of the same year.

SCENE IV. A house in Durham, winter, fifteen years later.

SCENE V. The same as Scene II, an autumn evening three years later.

SCENE VI. On a road near his home in Scene II, an hour later.

SCENE VII. The same as Scene II, about thirty minutes later than Scene VI.

SCENE ONE

In the turpentine woods of Eastern North Carolina, forty years ago, near a spring at the foot of a hill. The immediate foreground is open and clear save for a spongy growth of grass and sickly ground creepers. In the rear a wide-spreading tangle of reeds, briars, and alder bushes shuts around the spring in a semicircle. At the right front the great body of a pine, gashed and barked by the turpentine farmer's axe, lifts straight from the earth. To the left a log lies rotting in the embrace of wild ivy. Maples, bays, dogwoods and other small trees overrun by tenacious vines raise their leafy tops to shade the spot. Through interstices in the undergrowth one can see the pine forest stretching away until the eye is lost in a colonnade of trees. The newly scraped blazes on the pines show through the brush like the downward spreading beards of old men, suggestive of the ancient gnomes of the woods, mysterious and silently watchful.

At the left front four tin dinner pails hang on a limby bush. The sound of axes against the trees, accompanied by the rhythmically guttural "han—n—h! han—n—n—h!" of the cutters comes from the distance. One of the laborers breaks into a high mournful song—

> Oh, my feets wuh wet—wid de sunrise dew,
> De mawning stah—wuh a witness too.
> 'Way, 'way up in de Rock of Ages,
> In God's bosom gwine be my pillah.

Presently there is a loud halloo near at hand, and another voice yodels and cries, *Dinner time—m-m—e! Git yo' peas, ev'ybody!* Voices are heard nearer, a loud burst of laughter, and then three full-blooded Negroes shuffle in carrying long thin-bladed axes, which they lean against the pine at the right. They are dressed in nondescript clothes, ragged and covered with the glaze of raw turpentine. As they move up to the spring they take off their battered hats, fan themselves, and wipe the streaming sweat from their brows. Two of them are well-built and burly, one stout and past middle age with some pretension to a thin scraggly mustache, the second tall and muscled, and the third wiry, nervous and bandy-legged. They punctuate their conversation with great breaths of cool air.

YOUNG NEGRO: Monkey walking in dis woods.

OLDER NEGRO: Yah, Jaboh progueing round and 'bout m.

LITTLE NEGRO: While us res' he roos' high in pine tree.

YOUNG NEGRO: Fall on Puny's back 'bout th'ee o'clock, it um down, Hee—hee.

PUNY: Ain't no monkey kin ride me, tell you.

They stand fanning themselves.

OLDER NEGRO: Dat nigger tough, ain't you, Puny?

PUNY: Tough as whitleather, tough 'y God! (*He gets own on his belly at the spring.*) Mouf 'bout to crack, kin rink dis heah spring dry.

OLDER NEGRO: (*Slouching his heavy body towards the ool.*) Hunh, me too. Dat axe take water same lak a saw-ill.

He gets down flat and drinks with the other. The water an be heard gluking over the cataract of their Adam's pples. The YOUNGER NEGRO *opens his torn and sleeveless ndershirt and stands raking the sweat from his powerful hest with curved hand.*

YOUNG NEGRO: (*After a moment.*) Heigh, Puny, you'n .ije pull yo' guts out'n dat mud-hole and let de engineer take drink.

With a sudden thought of devilment he steps quickly orward and cracks their heads together. PUNY *starts and alls face foremost in the spring.* LIJE, *slow and stolid, saves imself, crawls slowly upon his haunches and sits smiling ood-naturedly, smacking his lips and sucking the water rom the slender tails of his mustache.*

LIJE: (*Cleaning his muddy hands with a bunch of leaves.*) Junh—unh, not dis time, my boy.

LITTLE NEGRO: (*Scrambling to his feet, strangling and puttering.*) Damn yo' soul, why you push me, Bud Gaskins?

BUD: (*A threatening note slipping into his laugh.*) Hyuh, yuh, don't you cuss at me, bo.

PUNY: Why'n't you 'pose on somebody yo' size? Bedder ry Lije dere.

BUD *gets down and begins drinking.*

LIJE: (*Drawling.*) Don't keer 'f 'e do. Ducking good foh ou dis hot weather.

PUNY: (*Helplessly.*) Allus picking at me. Wisht, wisht—

BUD: Heah I is lying down. Come on do whut you wisht.

(PUNY *makes no reply but turns off, wiping his face on hi*
shirt sleeve, and staring morosely at the ground. BUD *gets t*
his feet.) Yah, reckon you sail on me and I jam yo' haid i
dat spring lak a fence post and drownd you.

PUNY: (*His anger smouldering.*) Talk is cheap, blac
man, cheap!

Suddenly afraid of his boldness in replying, he turns an
looks at BUD *in a weak pleading defiance.*

BUD: (*Making a frightening movement towards him.*
Mess wid me a-jowing and I knock yo' teef th'ough yo' skull

LIJE: Hyuh, Bud, you let Puny 'lone.

He moves over to his bucket, gets it and sits down on th
log at the left.

BUD: (*Turning for his bucket with a movement of dis*
gust.) Sho' I ain't gwine hurt him—po' pitiful bow-legs.

PUNY *clenches his hands as if stung to the quick, an*
then beaten and forlorn reaches for his bucket, the wea
member of the herd. He throws off his overall jacket, reveal
ing himself stripped to the waist, and sits down at the pin
tree.

LIJE: (*Laying out his food and singing.*)

> 'Way, 'way up in de Rock of Ages
> In God's bosom gwine be my pillah.

BUD: (*Looking at* PUNY'S *bony bust.*) Uhp, showing of
dat 'oman's breas' o' yo'n, is you? Haw-haw.

PUNY: (*In sheer ineffectuality answering him blandly.*
Gwine cool myse'f.

LIJE: Me too, peoples. (*He loosens his belt, pulls out hi*
shirt-tails, undoes his shirt, and pats his belly.) Lawd, Bud
you sho' led us a race dis mawning on dem dere boxes
Musta sweat a peck er mo'.

BUD: (*Taking his bucket and sitting on the ground nea*
the center.) Race? Hunh, wait till fo' o'clock dis evening
you gwine call foh de ca'f rope, sho' 'nough. (*Tickled at th*
tribute to his powers.) And po' Puny, de monkey have ri
him to deaf.

PUNY: Putt us in de cotton patch, and I kin kill you off d
way a king snake do a lizard.

BUD: Picking cotton! Dat 'oman and chillun's job. N
reg'lar man mess wid dat. (*Waving his hand at the wood*
behind him) Turpentiming's de stuff.

They fall to eating heartily, peas, side-meat, molasses poured in the top of the bucket-lid from a bottle, bread and collards. The axe of a fourth hand is heard still thudding in the forest.

LIJE: *(Jerking his bread-filled hand behind him)* Whyn't Abe come on? Time he eating.

BUD: Let him rair. 'On't hurt hisse'f a-cutting. Gitting to be de no 'countest hand I ever see.

LIJE: Useter could cut boxes lak a house afiah.

PUNY: And hack! Lawd, dat nigger could hack.

LIJE: De champeen o' de woods and de swamps.

PUNY: Bedder'n Bud, bedder'n all. Knowed him to dip eight barrels many day.

BUD: Cain't he'p whut has been. Ain't wuth my ol' hat now. Colonel Mack say so too. And I heahd Mr. Lonnie talking rough to him over at de weaving house day 'fo' yistiddy 'bout his gitting trifling heah lately.

PUNY: Been gitting no' count since two yeah' 'go. De time when de white folks hang dat Charlie Sampson on a telegram pole—him whut 'tacked a white 'oman, and dey shoot him full o' holes, ayh!

BUD: Dey did. And dat Abe gut his neck stretched hadn't been foh de Colonel. Fool went down dere in de night and cut dat nigger down and bury 'im hese'f.

LIJE: *(Looking around him)* 'Twon't do to mess wid white folks and dey r'iled up.

They lapse into silence under the touch of worry, something undefinable, something not to be thought upon. They swallow their food heavily. Presently LIJE *stops and looks at the ground.*

LIJE: Abe ain't safe.

BUD: Eyh?

LIJE: *(Gesturing vaguely behind him)* Abe talk too much.

BUD: *(Nodding)* He do, talk too much to white folks.

PUNY: Cain't he'p it, I bet.

BUD: Kin too. Didn't talk much 'fore dat boy wuh hung. Worked hard den and say nothing.

LIJE: Sump'n on he mind. Sump'n deep, worry 'im, trouble—

BUD: Trouble 'bout de nigger, wanter rise him up wid eddication—fact!

PUNY: Hunh, rise him up to git a rope roun' his neck. Nigger's place down de bottom. Git buried in he own grave-yard, don't mind out.

BUD: Raght on de bottom wid deir hand and legs, muscle power, backbone, down wid de rocks and de shovels and de digging, dat's de nigger. White man on top.

LIJE: You's talking gospel.

PUNY: Abe say he gwine climb. I heah him tell de Colonel dat.

BUD: Fo' God! Whut Colonel say?

PUNY: He ain't say nothing, des' look at 'im.

LIJE: Abe is bad mixed up all down inside.

BUD: White and black make bad mixtry.

LIJE: Do dat. (*Thumping on his chest*) Nigger down heah. (*Thumping his head.*) White mens up heah. Heart say do one thing, head say 'nudder. Bad, bad.

PUNY: De white blood in him coming to de top. Dat make him want-a climb up and be sump'n. Nigger gwine hol' him down dough. Part of him take adder de Colonel, part adder his muh, 'vision and misery inside.

LIJE: Ssh!

PUNY: (*Starting and looking around*) Colonel Mack he daddy, everybody knows. Lak as two peas, see de favor.

BUD: (*Bitingly*) Talk too much! Little bird carry news to de Colonel and he fall on you and scrush you. Ain't nigger, ain't white whut ail him. Dem damn books he gut to studying last yeah or two. Cain't go to de woods widdout 'em. Look up dere on his bucket, foh Christ sake. (*He points to the remaining tin bucket in the bush. A small book is lying on the top under the handle. Snorting.*) 'Rifmatic I bet. Give a nigger a book and des' well shoot him. All de white folks tell you dat.

PUNY: (*Pouring molasses on his bread*) He sma't dough, in his haid. Dat nigger gut sense.

LIJE: Has dat. Gitting so he kin cipher raght up wid de Colonel.

PUNY: (*Looking at* BUD) Bet some day Colonel Mack put him woods boss over us.

BUD: Ain't no nigger gwine boss me, hoss-cake. Split his haid open wid my axe.

LIJE: (*Leaning back and emitting a halloo*) Heighp, you, Abe! Dinner! Gwine cut all day?

BUD: Gi' him de full title and he'll heah you.

LIJE: (*Grinning*) Aberham, Aberham McCranie!

PUNY: Yeh, you, Aberham Lincoln, whut drapped de nigger he freedom from de balloon, you better git yo' grub!

An answering shout comes out of the forest.

BUD: Trying to cut past time, mebbe us'll think he sma't.

PUNY: Don't keer whut you think, Bud, gitting so he look down on you and de rest of us.

BUD: Damn yo' runty soul, whut you know 'bout it? Ain't no nigger living kin look down on me and git by wid it. Do, and I make 'em smell o'dat.

He clenches his heavy fist and raises it to heaven; lowering it, he crams a handful of cornbread into his mouth.

PUNY: Hunh, and you was one o' de fust to brag on him foh goin' on sho't rations so de Colonel buy him books and learn 'im to teach school.

BUD: Sho't rations. Ain't no sho't rations, and dat Goldie gal bringing him pies and stuff eve'y day. Be here wid a bucket in a few minutes, I betcha. Fool love de ve'y ground he squat on! And he look down on her caze her ign'ant. And teach school! Been heahing dat school teaching business de whole yeah. He ain't gwine teach no school. Niggers 'on't send to him, dey s'on't. Niggers don't want no schooling.

PUNY: Mought. Abe tol' me dis mornin' dat de Colonel gwine fix it wid de 'missioners or something in town today. I know whut de matter wid you, Bud. Hee-hee.

BUD: Whut?

PUNY: *(Hesitating)* Abe come riding by in de two-hoss coach. Us'll be bowing and a-scraping. Us'll pull off'n our hats and be "Howdy, Mister Aberham." (BUD *turns and looks at him with infinite scorn, saying nothing.*) And Bud? (BUD *makes no answer.*) Bud?

BUD: Whut?

PUNY: Dat Goldie business whut worrying you, hee hee. She love Abe and—

BUD: *(Bounding up and kicking* PUNY'S *bucket and foot into the bushes.)* Damn yo' lousy soul, minner mind stomp you in de dirt! *(He towers over the terrified* PUNY, *who lies flat on his back whimpering.)*

PUNY: Don't hit me, Bud. Foh God's sake! I des' joking.

LIJE: Go at it, fight it out. *(Singing as he watches them.)*

> De bones in de grave cried Ca'vary
> De night King Jesus died.

BUD: *(Kicking dirt at* PUNY *and going back to his bucket.)* Done told him now. Ain't gwine say no mo'! Next time be my first rammed down his th'oat, and turn him wrong side out'ards.

ABE *comes in at the right, carrying his axe. He is a young Negro, with a touch of the mulatto in him, of twenty-five or six, tall and powerfully built, dressed much like the others in cap and turpentine-glazed clothes. He puts his axe by the pine at the right, pulls off his cap and fans himself, while he pinches his sweaty shirt loose from his skin. His shaggy head, forehead and jaw are marked with will and intelligence. But his wide nostril and a slumbrous flash in his eye that now and then shows itself suggest a passionate and dangerous person when aroused. From the change in the actions of the others when he enters it is evident that they respect and even fear him.*

ABE: What's de trouble 'tween you and Puny, Bud?

BUD: *(Sullenly)* Ain't no trouble.

PUNY: *(Crawling around on the ground and collecting his spilled food.)* Ain't nothing, Abe, I des' spilled my rations.

ABE *gets his book down and seats himself in the shade at the left. He begins working problems, using a stub of a pencil and a sheet of crumpled paper.*

LIJE: Puny, I got some bread left you kin have.

He pulls a harp from his pocket and beings to blow softly.

PUNY: I don't want nothing else, Lije. Et all I kin hold. *(After a moment.)* Putt yo' bucket up foh you.

He gets LIJE'S *bucket and hangs it along with his own in the limby bush.* BUD *eats in silence, puts up his bucket, gets a drink from the spring, and resumes his seat, hanging his head between his knees.* PUNY *goes to the spring and drinks.*

BUD: *(Pouring snuff into his lip)* Don't fall in an' git drownded, Puny.

PUNY: Want some water Lije?

He goes to the log, curls himself up in the shade beside it and prepares to sleep.

LIJE: *(Stirring lazily)* Believe I does.

He goes to the spring and drinks, returns to the pine tree and sits down.

PUNY: Ain't you g'in' eat no dinner, Abe?

ABE *makes no reply.*

LIJE: Call him again. *(Touching his head with his finger)* Deep, deep up dere.

PUNY: Heigh, Abe, bedder eat yo' grub.

ABE: *(Starting)* You call me?

PUNY: You so deep stud'in' didn't heah me. Bedder eat yo' dinner. Git full o' ants settin' up dere.

ABE: I goin' to eat later.

BUD: Yeh, when Goldie come.

ABE: Hunh!

BUD: You heahd me.

ABE: *(Irritably)* Don't let me heah no mo'.

BUD: Hunh?

ABE: You heahd me. (PUNY *snickers from his log with audible delight.* LIJE *waits a moment and then lies down.* BUD *reaches out and tears a bush from the ground and casts it angrily from him.*) I'll eat my dinner when it please me, you gentlemens allowing. *(There is a touch of anger in his voice which he apparently regrets on second thought, for he goes on more kindly.)* Goldie said she goin' to fetch me sump'n t' eat to-day. I got to work dis problem. Been on it two days now. Cain't git it out'n my head. Ain't been able to sleep two nights. (BUD *sits staring and spitting straight before him. Presently* LIJE *begins to snore, then* PUNY *follows.* ABE *goes on with his figuring.* BUD *turns over on the ground and goes to sleep.* ABE *becomes more and more absorbed in the problem he is working. He mutters to himself.*) How many sheep? How many sheep? *(He clutches at his hair, gnaws his pencil, and turns to the back of his book.)* Answer say fifteen. Cain't make it come out fifteen, cain't, seem lak, to save me. Man must have answer wrong. Six go into fo'teen, three, no, two times and—two over. *(His voice dies away as he becomes lost in his work. Presently his face begins to light up. He figures faster. Suddenly he slaps his knee.)* Dere whah I been missing it all de time. I carried two 'stid o' one. Blame fool I is. *(He hits the side of his head with his knuckle. In his excitement he calls out.)* Puny, I gitting dat answer. *(But* PUNY *is snoring away. In a moment he throws down his book with beaming face.)* I got it, folkses, I got it. Fifteen! Dat white man know whut he doing, he all time git dem answer right. *(He turns expectantly towards* LIJE.) I got it Lije. (LIJE *makes no answer. He turns towards* PUNY *again, starts to speak but sees he is asleep.*) Bud! *(But* BUD *makes no answer. The heavy breathing of the sleepers falls regularly upon his ears. His face sinks into a sort of hopeless brooding.*) Yeh, sleep, sleep yo' life away. I figger foh you, foh me, foh all de black in de world to lead 'em up out'n ignorance. Dey don't listen, dey don't heah me, dey in de wilderness, don't wanta be led. Dey sleep, sleep in bondage. *(He bows his head between his knees.)* Sleep in sin. *(Presently.)* Time me to eat.

He reaches for his bucket and is about to open it when a loud shout comes from off the left.

ABE: Stop yo' laughing, I heah somebody hollering.

A second halloo comes down the hill.

PUNY: Dat de Colonel and Mr. Lonnie!

BUD: Sound lak 'em. Da's who 'tis.

ABE: *(Going off at the left)* Heah we is, Colonel Mack, at de spring eating dinner! *(He comes back.)* Colonel Mack and Mr. Lonnie coming on down heah.

PUNY: Co'se. Gut to see how many boxes us cleaned up dis mawning.

ABE: He tell me 'bout de school now. *(He stirs around him in his excitement.)* Mebbe dat his main business heah in de middle o' de day.

BUD: Hunh, mebbe. Gut some special work want done. Wanter hurry us to it, dat's whut.

The sound of voices is heard approaching from the left, and almost immediately the COLONEL *and his son* LONNIE *come in. The* COLONEL *carries a riding whip. He is a stout, run-down old Southerner with all the signs of moral and intellectual decadence upon him. Lechery, whiskey, and levity of living have taken their toll of him, and yet he has retained a kind of native good-naturedness. His shirt front and once pointed beard are stained with the drippings of tobacco juice. There is something in his bearing and in the contour of his face that resembles* ABE. *His son, a heavyish florid young man of twenty-three or four, walks behind him.*

COLONEL: *(In a high jerky voice)* Snoozing, hanh?

ABE: Just finishing our dinner, suh.

PUNY: Us 'bout to wuk over-time to-day, Colonel.

COLONEL: Not likely, I reckon. Say, I want you fellows, all four of you, to get over to the swamp piece on Dry Creek. Boxes there are running over, two quarts in 'em apiece, prime virgin. *(They begin to move to their feet.)* No, I don't mean to go right now. Gabe's coming by on the big road here *(Jerking his whip towards the rear.)* with a load of barrels and the dippers in about a half-hour. Meet him out there.

LONNIE: Yeh, we want to git the wagons off to Fayetteville to-night.

COLONEL: How you get on cornering this morning, Bud?

BUD: Purty good, suh. Us fo' done 'bout all dat pastuh piece, suh.

COLONEL: Fine, fine. That's the way. Puny and Lije stay with you?

BUD: Raght dere eve'y jump.

LIJE: Yessuh, yessuh!

PUNY: When he gi' de call we gi' 'im de 'sponse eve'y time, suh. Yes, suh, us kept 'im crowded.

COLONEL: We got to git on, Lonnie. Want to see how the scrape's coming over on Uncle Joe's Branch. Be up on the road there in half a' hour.

LONNIE: *(Stopping as they go out)* Got so you doing any better work lately, Abe?

ABE: *(Starting)* Suh!

LONNIE: You heard me.

ABE: I didn't understand you, Mr. Lonnie.

LONNIE: You understood me all right. *(Pointing to the book on the ground.)* Let them damned books worry you still?

COLONEL: Come on, Lonnie.

ABE: *(Stammering)* I dunno—I——

COLONEL: Still holding out on short rations, ain't you, Abe?

There is the least hint of pride in the COLONEL'S *voice.*

ABE: *(Somewhat confused)* I studying whut I kin, slow go, slow go.

COLONEL: Stick to it. You the first nigger I ever see so determined. But then you're uncommon! *(The* COLONEL *moves on.)* Come on, Lonnie.

ABE: *(Following somewhat timidly after him)* Colonel Mack, did di—you—whut'd dey say over dere 'bout that little school business?

COLONEL: Bless my soul, 'bout to forgit it. I talked it over with the board and most of 'em think maybe we'd better not try it yet.

ABE: *(His face falling)* When dey say it might be a good time? I gitting right 'long wid dat 'rithmetic and spelling and reading. I kin teach de colored boys and gals a whole heap right now, and I'll keep studying.

COLONEL: *(Impatiently)* Oh, I dunno. Time'll come mebbe. Mebbe time won't come. Folks is quare things y'know.

He moves on.

ABE: Cain't you git 'em to let me try it awhile? Reckon—

COLONEL: I don't know, I tell you. Got my business on my mind now.

LONNIE: He's done told you two or three times, can't you hear?

ABE: (*His eyes flashing and his voice shaking with sudden uncontrollable anger*) Yeh, yeh, I hear 'im. Dem white folks don't keer—dey——

LONNIE: (*Stepping before him*) Look out! none of your sass. Pa's already done more for you than you deserve. He even stood up for you and they laughing at him there in town.

ABE: (*Trembling*) Yeh, yeh, I knows. But dem white folks don't think—I going to show 'em, I——

LONNIE: (*Pushing himself before him*) Dry up. Not another word.

ABE: (*His voice breaking almost into a sob*) Don't talk to me lak dat, Mr. Lonnie. Stop him, Colonel Mack, 'fore I hurt him.

The other Negroes draw off into a knot by the pine tree, mumbling in excitement and fear.

COLONEL: Stop, Lonnie! Abe, don't you talk to my son like that.

LONNIE: By God, I'm going to take some of the airs off'n him right now. You've gone around here getting sorrier and more worthless every day for the last year. What you need is a good beating, and I'm gonna give it to you.

He steps backwards and snatches the whip from his father's hand.

COLONEL: Stop that, Lonnie!

LONNIE: Keep out of this yourself. (*He comes towards* ABE.) I'll beat his black hide off'n him.

ABE: Keep 'im back dere, Colonel Mack. I mought kill him! Keep 'im off.

LONNIE: Kill him! All right, do it. There, damn you!

He strikes ABE *across the face with his whip. With a snarl* ABE *springs upon him, tears the whip from his hands and hurls him headlong into the thicket of briars and bushes. Then he stands with his hands and head hanging down, his body shaking like one with the palsy.*

PUNY: (*Screaming*) You done kilt Mr. Lonnie! Oh, Lawdy, Lawdy!

COLONEL: (*Running to* LONNIE *who is crawling up out of the mud with his clothes and skin torn. He is sobbing and cursing*) Are you hurt? How bad are you hurt?

LONNIE: Let me git at that son of a bitch and I'll kill him dead. *(Moaning.)* Oh, I'll beat his brains out with one o' them axes.

COLONEL: If you ain't dead, you'd better keep your hands off'n him. I'll fix him. *(He reaches down and picks up the whip. Thundering.)* Git down on your knees, Abe! Git down, you slave! I'm gonna beat you.

ABE *jerks his head up in defiance, but before the stern face of the* COLONEL *his strength goes out of him. He puts his hands up in supplication.*

ABE: Don't beat me, Colonel Mack, don't beat me wid dat whip!

COLONEL: Git down on your knees! I've beat many a slave, and I'll show you how it feels.

He strikes him several blows.

ABE: *(Falling on his knees)* Oh, Lawd, have muhcy upon me!

The COLONEL *begins to beat him blow upon blow.* PUNY, BUD *and* LIJE *stand near the pine in breathless anxiety.*

PUNY: De Colonel'll kill 'im!

BUD: *(Seizing his arm)* Shet dat mouf, nigger!

COLONEL: *(As he brings the whip down)* Let this be a lesson to you to the end of your life!

ABE: *(His back twitching under the whip, his voice broken)* Muhcy, Colonel Mack, muhcy!

COLONEL: You struck a white man, you struck my son.

ABE: *(Raising his tear-stained face)* I yo' son too, you my daddy.

He throws himself down before him, embracing his feet. The COLONEL *lowers the whip, then drops it behind him.*

LONNIE: *(His voice husky with rage)* You hear what he say? Hear what he called you?

He seizes the whip and in a blind rage strikes the prostrate ABE *again and again.*

COLONEL: *(Stepping between them)* Stop it! Give me that whip. (LONNIE *nervelessly hesitates and then reluctantly hands him the whip.)* Go on back out to the road and wait for me. Trot! (LONNIE *in disgust and rage finally goes off at the left nursing his face and his arms.)* Get up, Abe. Get up, I say.

ABE *sits up, hugging his face between his knees. The* COLONEL *wets his handkerchief in the spring, and with his hands on* ABE'S *head bathes the bruises on his neck and shoulders.*

ABE: *(In a voice grown strangely dignified and quiet)*
Thank 'ee, thank 'ee, Colonel Mack.

COLONEL: *(Breathing heavily)* Thanky nothing. I had to
beat you, Abe, had to. Think no more about it. Dangerous
thing, hitting a white man. But this is the end of it. Won't be
no law, nothing but this. Put some tar and honey on yourself
to-night and you'll be all right to-morrow. *(The bushes are
suddenly parted at the rear and a tall sinuous young mulatto
woman bounds through. She carries a bucket in her hand. At
the sight of the* COLONEL *bathing* ABE'S *head and neck she
rushes forward with a low cry. The* COLONEL *turns towards
her.)* Now, Goldie, ain't no use cutting up. Abe been in a
little trouble. Nothing much.

GOLDIE: *(Moaning)* I heahd de racket and I 'fraid somebody being kilt. Is you hurt bad, Abe, honey babe? *(She
bends tenderly over him, her hand running over his hair.)*
Who huht you, honey, who huht you?

COLONEL: *(Handing* GOLDIE *his handkerchief)* Look after him, Goldie. *(He goes out at the left calling.)* Wait a
minute, Lonnie!

GOLDIE: Whut dey do to you, Abe? Who huht you? *(All
the time she is rubbing his neck, dabbing his shoulders with
the handkerchief, and cooing over him.)* Why'n you kill dem
white mens if dey hurt you? You kin do it, break 'em lak
broomstraws.

ABE: *(Standing up)* Ain't nobody hurt me. I crazy dat's
whut, crazy in de haid. Ain't nobody hurt me.

GOLDIE: *(Clinging to him)* You is hurt, hurt bad. Look at
yo' po' neck and shoulders. Look at 'em beat wid great
whales on 'em!

ABE: *(Growling)* Ain't nobody hurt me, I tell you.

GOLDIE: Lay yo'se'f down heah and let me smoove off
yo' forehead and put some cold water on dat mark crost yo'
face. Please'm, Abe.

ABE: *(Suddenly crying out in a loud voice)* I ain't nothing,
nothing. Dat white man beat me, beat me like a dawg. *(His
voice rising into a wail.)* He flail me lak a suck-egg dawg!
(He rocks his head from side to side in a frenzy of wrath.)
Lemme git to him! *(He falls on his knees searching in the
leaves and finds a stone.* GOLDIE *stands wringing her hands
and moaning. He jumps to his feet, raising the stone high
above his head.)* Lemme git to him, I scrush his God-damn
head lak a egg shell!

He moves to the left to follow the COLONEL. GOLDIE *throws her arms around his neck.*

GOLDIE: No, no, you ain't gwine out dere, Abe, Abe!

PUNY: (*Crying out*) Stop him, Bud! Lije, keep him back!

LIJE: (*Coming from the pine tree*) Hyuh, now you, Abe, stop dat.

BUD: (*Moving quickly before him and blocking his path*) Stop dat, fool. You gwine fix it to git yo'se'f hung up on a telegram pole. Body be so full o'holes, sift sand.

GOLDIE: (*Sobbing*) Don't do it, Abe, sugar babe.

She throws herself upon his breast.

BUD: (*Reaching toward her*) Seem lak you take yo'se'f off'n dat man!

ABE: (*Pulling her arms from around him*) Lemme loose, lemme loose. (*After a moment he throws the stone down.*) I ain't going do nothing.

He sits down on the log at the left, holding his head in his hands.

GOLDIE: (*Bringing her bucket*) Hyuh, eat sump'n, Abe, you feel better. I gut some pie and some cake in heah foh you.

ABE: (*Pushing* GOLDIE *away*) I ain't want nothin t' eat, ain't hongry.

GOLDIE *drops on her knees beside him and laying her head in his lap clasps her arms around him.*

GOLDIE: (*Sobbing softly*) Oh, boy, boy, why dey beat you up so? Whut you do to 'em?

ABE: Fool, fool I is. Crazy, dat's it.

BUD: (*Sharply*) He g'in Mr. Lonnie and de Colonel back talk. Cain't sass white mens and git 'way wid it. Abe orter know better.

LIJE *wanders over to the right blowing his harp softly and forlornly.*

PUNY: (*Sitting down on the ground*) Cain't be done, Abe. Cain't.

BUD: (*Stripping leaves from a bush and watching* GOLDIE *as she carries on over* ABE.) Hyuh, 'oman, stop dat rairing. (*Muttering to himself.*) Nevah see two bigger fools.

ABE *puts his hands mechanically on* GOLDIE'S *shoulders and begins stroking her.*

ABE: Stop it, baby. Ain't no use to cry.

PUNY *sits with his mouth open in astonishment watching them.* LIJE *lays himself back on the ground and blows his harp, apparently no longer interested.*

BUD: *(Jealousy rising within him)* Heigh, Goldie, git up from dat man's lap. He ain't keer nothing foh you. (GOLDIE's *sobs die away and she is quiet.)* He say you foolish many time. He look down on you.

GOLDIE: *(Raising her tear-stained face)* How you know? You jealous, Bud Gaskins. He better man dan you. Wuth whole town of you. *(Catching ABE by the hand and picking up her bucket.)* Come on, come on, honey, le's go off dere in de woods and eat our dinner by ourse'ves!

BUD: *(Coming up to her)* Hyuh, you stay out'n dat woods wid him, nigger.

ABE: *(Standing up)* Yeh, yeh, I come wid you.

He moves as one in a dream, and reaches out and pushes BUD *behind him.*

GOLDIE: *(Her face alight, a sort of reckless and unreal abandonment upon her)* I knows where dere's a cool place under a big tree. And dey's cool green moss dere and soft leaves. Le's go dere, boy. I gwine tend to you and feed you. *(She moves across towards the right, leading ABE like a child.)* We make us a bed dere, honey. (LIJE *sits up watching them.)* Us forgit de 'membrance o' all dis trouble. *(A kind of ecstasy breaking in her voice.)* Dere de birds sing and we hear de little branch running over de rocks. Cool dere, sweet dere, you kin sleep, honey, rest dere, baby. Yo' mammy, yo' chile gwine love you, make you fohgit.

ABE: *(Moved out of himself)* Yeh, yeh, I come wid you. I don't keer foh nothing, not nothing no mo'. You, des' you'n me.

GOLDIE: Ain't no worl', ain't no Lije and Bud, nobody. Us gwine make us a 'biding place and a pillah under dat green tree. *(In sweet oblivion.)* Feel yo' arms around me, my lips on yo'n. We go singing up to heaben, honey, togedder—togedder.

They go off, her voice gradually dying away like a nun's chant.

BUD: *(Breaking a sapling in his grasp)* Gwine off, gwine off in de woods togedder dere lak hawgs.

PUNY: *(Bounding up, his body shaking in lascivious delight)* I gwine watch 'em—hee-hee—I gwine watch 'em.

LIJE: *(Knocking him back)* Bedder stay out'n dat woods. Abe kill you.

PUNY: *(Standing up by the pine tree)* Kin see 'em, her still a-leading 'im.

LIJE: (*Standing up and peering off to the right*) Dere on de cool moss and de sof' green leaves.

BUD: (*Stripping the limbs from the top of the broken sapling*) Ain't gwine look. Dey fools, bofe fools. (*Raging out.*) Dere she go playing de hawg. Didn't know she lak dat. (*He sucks in his breath with the sound of eating something.*) Wisht to Gohd I knowed she lak dat. I de man foh her. Bud Gaskins. I tame her, Gohd damn her, I tame her down and take dat speerit out'n her.

He crowds out his chest and walks up and down.

PUNY: (*Grasping* LIJE's *arm*) Cain't hardly see 'em no mo', kin you?

LIJE: Kin hardly.

BUD: (*His anger and jealousy disappearing in physical emotion and vulgar curiosity.*) Whah dey now?

LIJE: (*Pointing*) Dere, dere, dey crossing de branch now.

PUNY: (*Breathlessly*) I see 'em. I see 'em. He arm 'round her now, her head on he shoulder. (*He capers in his excitement.*) Lawd! Lawd!

BUD: (*With a loud brutal laugh as he slaps* LIJE *on the back*) On de sof' green moss.

LIJE: (*Laughing back and dragging his harp across his mouth*) Whah de leaves is cool.

PUNY: Cain't see 'em no mo'. (*He whirls about and turns a handspring.*) Whoopee, folkses! Gwine run away wid myse'f!

BUD: (*His eyes shining*) Down whah de branch water run.

He shuffles a jig among the leaves.

LIJE: (*Blowing upon his harp*) Singing raght up to heaben!

He plays more wildly as they all drop into a barbaric dance that gradually mounts into a dionysiac frenzy.

PUNY: Heaben!

BUD: Jesus, Lawd, Fadder and Son!

LIJE: (*Singing loudly as they dance, the music running into a quick thumping rhythm*)

> My feets wuh wet wid de sunrise dew,
> De mawning stah wuh a witness too.
> 'Way, 'way up in de Rock of Ages,
> In God's bosom gwine be my pillah.

They gambol, turn and twist, run on all fours, rear themselves up on their haunches, cavort like goats.

PUNY: In God's bosom—hanh!

BUD: In who bosom?

LIJE: In who bosom, bubber!

*A loud halloo comes down from the hill in the rear,
unnoticed by them.*

PUNY: In Goldie's bosom. Hee-hee-hee.

BUD: and LIJE—Haw-haw-haw! Hee-hee-hee! In God's
bosom gwine by my pillah.

The halloo is repeated.

LIJE: Hyuh, dere dat Gabe calling us. Better git, or de
Colonel have dat stick on our back.

They gather up their buckets and axes. PUNY *clambers
up the pine a few feet and drops to the ground.*

BUD: Kin see?

PUNY: See nothing. Hee-hee!

LIJE: Gut to leave 'em now. Abe ketch it 'gin don't mind
out. He not coming wid us.

BUD: He done foh now. Dat gal gut him hard and fast.
(Snorting scornfully) Books, books! Rise 'em up, lak hell!

LIJE: I done told you. Heart say dis, head say dat. Bad
mixtry. Bad. Crazy!

PUNY: *(Shouting)* Heigh, you Gabe! Coming! *(They move
out at the rear up the hill, singing, laughing and jostling
each other.)*

> 'Way, 'way down by de sweet branch water
> In her bosom gwine be he pillah!

Hee-hee—haw—haw—!

*Their loud brutally mocking laughter floats back behind
them.*

SCENE TWO

A spring day about three years later, in ABRAHAM MC-
CRANIE'S two-room cabin. The room is roughly built of
framed material and unceiled. To the right front is a fireplace
with a green oakwood fire going. A wood box is to the right
of the chimney. To the left rear of the room is a bed, and at
the left center rear a door leads out to the porch! To the right
of the door a window gives a view of wide-stretched cotton
fields. Below the window close to the wall is a rough home-
made chest with several books on it, and hanging between it

and the door is a sort of calendar, with the illustration of a slave leaving his chains behind and walking up a hill towards the sunrise. There is a caption at the top of the print in large letters—"WE ARE RISING." Several old dresses, bonnets, and coats hang on the nails in the joists in the right rear. A door in the right center leads into the kitchen. At the left front is a dilapidated old bureau, small pieces of wood taking the place of lost casters. The top drawer is open, sagging down like a wide lip, with stray bits of clothing hanging over the edge. A bucket of water and a pan are on the bureau. There are several splint-bottomed chairs and a rocker in the room.

When the curtain rises MUH MACK is sitting by the fire rocking a bundle in her arms. She is a chocolate-colored Negress of near sixty, dressed in a long dirty wrapper, and barefooted. Her graying hair is wrapped in pigtails and stands around her head Medusa-like. A long snuff-stick protudes from her mouth, and now and then the fire sputters with a frying noise as she spits into it. GOLDIE's long gaunt form lies stretched on the bed at the left partly covered by a sheet, her head hanging off on her arm. She is constantly raising in her languid hand a stick with a paper tied to it to shoo away the flies. MUH MACK rocks and sings.

MUH MACK:

> Oohm—oohm—hoonh—oohm—oohm—
> Dis heah baby de pu'tiest baby,
> Pu'tiest baby in de lan'.
> He gwine grow up champeen sojer,
> Mammy's honey, onlies' man.
> Oohm—oohm—hoonh—oohm—oohm—

GOLDIE: *(In a tired voice)* How he coming now?

MUH MACK : *(Shaking her finger and wagging her head at the bundle)* Done seen um grow. Look at me lak he know me.

GOLDIE: *(With a long sigh)* I so tiahed, tiahed. Seem lak I kin sleep forever.

MUH MACK: Lie and sleep, sleep. Git yo' stren'th.

GOLDIE: I tiahed but cain't sleep. *(She lapses into silence. The old woman rocks and sings. Presently GOLDIE raises her head.)* Whut day to-day?

MUH MACK: Sa'd'y.

GOLDIE: Seem lak I cain't 'member nothing. Whut day he come?

MUH MACK: He come a-Chuesday.

GOLDIE: Dat make him—le's see, how old?

MUH MACK: Fo' day now.

GOLDIE: (*Suddenly sitting up with a gasp*) Dem udder two die, one th'ee days, udder'n fo'.

MUH MACK: Nanh—nanh, lie back down. Dis heah baby live be hundred. He strong, he muscled. Dem udder po' little 'uns puny, bawn to die. Do mark was on 'em f'om de fust.

GOLDIE: (*Bending her head between her knees and weeping softly*) Dey was so pitiful and liddle. I cain't fohgit how dey feel and fumble foh me wid deir liddle hands and dey hongry.

MUH MACK: (*Irritably*) Bless Gohd, crying adder dem, and gut dis fine 'un heah. Lay yo'se'f down on dat bed and res'.

GOLDIE: Cain't fohgit 'em, cain't.

MUH MACK: Hunh, mought as well and dey done plowed in de ground.

GOLDIE: (*Her tears beginning to flow again*) Yeh, yeh, dey is! Abe didn't try to keep Mr. Lonnie f'om cutting down dem plum bushes and plowing up dat hedgerow. I hold it a'gin him long as I live.

MUH MACK: Why foh? De dead's de dead. Let de earf hab 'em. Let cotton grow over 'um. No use mo'ning. Think on de living.

GOLDIE: Po' Abe, 'on't his fault dough. He proud, stand by see white mens plow over 'em, say nothin', 'on't beg foh his babies.

MUH MACK: Cain't blame 'im! He stiff neck. God break his spirit. Gi' 'im two dead 'uns to fetch 'im down. He bedder humble now. (*Talking half to herself*) He talk proud lak, gwine raise up big son, leader 'mong men. Fust 'un come thin, liddle lak rat. He hate 'im. He die. God call 'im. Second come, Ol' Moster keep him liddle, thin. He die too. Abe gitting down to sackcloff and ashes. God see him down crying foh muhcy, He send dis 'un, strong. Israel man. He gwine flourish, he gwine wax.

GOLDIE: (*Stretching herself out on the bed*) Abe say dis 'un gwine die too, same lak de udders. He don't look at 'im, pay no 'tention.

MUH MACK: Hunh, he will dough when he sees 'im fleshen up wid he sucking.

GOLDIE: Whah he?

MUH MACK: Went down in de new ground planting cawn. Won't make nothing dough and it de light o' de moon. He be heah directly foh he dinner.

GOLDIE: Po' Abe wuk too hard.

MUH MACK: *(Snorting)* Wuk too hahd de mischief! Ain't wuk whut ail him. He studyin' ol' books and mess too much. Crap shows it.

GOLDIE: He don't look well, neiver.

MUH MACK: Cain't look well and worry all time. *(A step is heard on the porch)* Dere he now. Take dis baby. Gut to put dinner on de table.

She takes the baby over to GOLDIE, *lays it by her side, goes out at the right, and is heard rattling dishes and pans in the kitchen.*

GOLDIE: *(Crooning over her baby)* Now you go sleep, res' yo'se'f, git strong and grow gre't big.

ABE *comes in at the rear carrying a hoe and a file. He is barefooted and dressed in overalls, ragged shirt and weather-stained straw hat. Sitting down near the center of the room, he begins filing his hoe.*

ABE: *(Without looking around)* How you come on?

GOLDIE: Better, I reckon. *(With s sharp gasp)* Hyuh, why you fetch dat hoe in de house?

ABE: *(Paying no attention to her query)* Baby still living, hunh?

GOLDIE: Abe, take dat hoe out'n dis house. Mought bring bad luck on you. *(Raising herself up in bed)* Mought bring sump'n on de baby.

ABE: Cain't swub dem new-ground bushes wid no dull hoe.

GOLDIE: *(Pleading)* Take it out'n de house, I say.

ABE: When I damn ready.

GOLDIE: *(Calling)* Muh Mack! Muh Mack!

MUH MACK: *(Coming to the door at the right)* Whut ails you? *(She sees* ABE *filing his hoe.)* Lawd he'p us! Throw dat thing out, throw it out! Ain't gut no sense. Goldie too weak to be worried up.

ABE: Aw right den. I finish wid it now. Set o' fools. Eve'ything got a sign 'tached to it. Ign'ant, bline!

He throws the hoe out through the rear door and gets a book from the chest and begins reading.

MUH MACK: Back at dem books, Lawd, never see sich. *She goes scornfully back to the kitchen.*

ABE: *(Half growling)* Says heah niggers gut to git out'n dem 'spicions and being 'fraid. Ain't no signs wid evil and good in 'em. I read dat last night. *(Reading and halting over the words.)* "The Negro is a superstitious person. There are signs and wonders in the weather, some fraught with evil, some with good. He plants his crops according to the moon, works and labors under the eye of some evil spirit of his own imagining." *(Closing the book with a bang.)* Heah dat?

GOLDIE: I heah but don't mind it. Mean nothing. White man wrote it, and he don't know.

ABE: Dat's jest it; he do know. Nigger one don't know. Dat book wrote foh you, Muh, and all de rest of de bline.

GOLDIE: Put up dem ol' books. Seem lak you keer mo' foh 'em dan you do dis heah baby, and he a fine boy chile.

ABE: *(Throwing the book back on the chest)* What he nohow? Ain't 'rested in 'im. Ain't no use being. He be dead in week. God done cuss me and my household. No luck at nothing. Cain't raise chillun, cain't raise crap, nothing. Ain't dry weather, wet. Ain't wet, dry. Heah May month and cold 'nough foh freeze. *(He stretches his feet to the fire.)* De damn crows down dere on de creek pulling up my cawn faster'n I kin plant it. *(He rocks his head.)* Jesus!

GOLDIE: *(Pleading)* Abe, honey, don't git down. Things coming better now. Dis boy gwine make you feel better. Heah he lie now des' smiling lak he onderstand me. *(Bending over the baby.)* Yeh you is gwine grow up and take trouble off'n yo' po' daddy. Yeh, you is.

ABE: *(Holding his head in his arms)* Listen to dat talk, listen dere. *(Bitterly.)* 'Oman know. She know. Heah I am wid no money to buy me shoes. *(Holding up his dust-stained foot.)* Dere you is, foot, cut wid glass, full o' b'rars, wo' out stumping de roots and snags, and I can't buy nothing to kiver you wid.

GOLDIE: De Colonel give you shoes, you ax him.

ABE: Ain't gwine ax him nothing, not nothing. *(Suddenly clenching his fist and hitting his thigh)* Dat man beat me, beat me at de spring th'ee yeah ago, I ain't fohgit. *(He gets up and strides over to the bed and looks down at the suckling infant.)* Dere you lie drinking yo' grub in. Whut you keer? Nothing.

He lays his hand roughly on the baby and pinches him. The child lets out a high thin wail.

GOLDIE: *(Beating his hand off)* Quit dat pinching dat baby. Quit it.

ABE: *(Laughing brutally as he walks up and down the floor)* Yeh, you fight over 'im now and he be plowed in de ground lak de udders in a month. Hee-hee! Ain't dis a hell of a mess! It sho' God is. And us ain't got 'nough to feed a cat. You'n Muh cook and slay and waste fast I make it. Note at de sto' done tuck up, crap done all mortgaged up 'head o' time. Cain't make ends meet, cain't. *(Throwing his hands out hopelessly.)* I ain't no farmer.

GOLDIE: *(Wretchedly)* Oh, Abe, we git on somehow, us will. And Muh'n me don't waste. I be up wid you in de fields by de middle o' de week. Po' chile, you need sleep, need rest.

ABE: Make no difference. Wuk our guts out do no good. I tell you, gal, de Nigger is down, down. De white man up dere high, setting up wid God, up dere in his favor. He git eve'ything, nigger git de scraps, leavings. *(Flaring out)* Ain't no God foh de nigger, dat's white man's God. Dat come to me down in de new ground.

He sits down again, tapping his feet on the floor.

GOLDIE: *(Wiping her eyes)* Honey, you gut to stop talking lak dat. Cain't be bad luck allus. I'se 'feared when you talk dat wild talk. God heah it he do. *(MUH MACK comes and stands in the door.)* He mought be doing all dis to make us good, make us humble down befo' him.

ABE: Humble down, hell! Look at de udder nigger den. Dey shout and carry on in de church, pray and pay de preachers in deir blindness. Dey humble. What do God do? Starve 'em to deaf. Kill 'em off lak flies wid consumption. Dey dying 'long de river same as de chillun in de wilderness.

MUH MACK: You blaspheaming, da's whut you doing. No wonder Gohd take yo' babies 'way, no wonder he make yo' mule die, blast down yo' plans and send de crows and cold weather and root lice to destroy yo' craps. *(Her eyes flashing)* You gut to change yo' ways. Some day he gwine re'ch down from de clouds and grab you by de scruff o' de neck and break you cross he knee. He gi'n you fine baby chile, you don't thank him. You gut to fall down, pray, git low, git humble. *(Her voice rises into a semichant.)* You dere, Jesus, heah my prayer. Dis heah sinner, he weeked, he blaspheam. Save him and save dis po' liddle baby.

GOLDIE: (*Weeping over the child*) Do, Lawd, heah our prayer.

ABE *sits down in his chair and stares moodily into the fire.*

MUH MACK: (*Crying out*) Dem dere ol' books cause it, da's whut. Burn um up, burn um wid fiah. Yo' wild talk gwine make de Upper Powers drap lightning on dis house, gwine destroy all of us. (*She wraps her arms before her, mumbling and swaying from side to side. Suddenly she raises her head and striding over to the chest shakes her fist at the books and kicks them.*) You de trouble. I hates de sight o' you, and I wish dere wa'n't nary one o' you in de worl'.

ABE: (*Throwing her back*) Look out 'oman! Don't you tech my books!

MUH MACK: You mash my arm!

With a wail she goes out at the right and is heard sobbing in the kitchen.

GOLDIE: Oh, you struck huh! Abe—Abe——

She sits up in the bed rocking the baby and quieting him. A heavy step sounds on the porch. ABE *sits before the fire smoothing out the leaves of a book, as a voice calls from the outside.*

VOICE: Heigh, you, Abe!

GOLDIE: (*Quickly*) Dat de Colonel out dere, Abe.

ABE: (*Going to the door*) Yes, suh, dat you, Colonel Mack?

COLONEL: (*Coming in*) Yes. How you come on, all of you? (*He looks around the room and at the bed. Three years have worked a great change in him. He is stouter, his face mottled, and he walks with difficulty, propped on a stick.*) Been wanting to see that fine baby, Abe.

ABE: (*Quietly*) Yes, suh, yes, suh.

MUH MACK: (*Coming in*) And he sho' is a fine 'un. (*Standing near the* COLONEL.) Fine and strong same lak Abe when he wuh bawn.

COLONEL: What's the matter, Goldie? Ain't been fighting, have you all? Who was that making a racket in here?

GOLDIE: (*Keeping her head lowered*) I all right, Colonel Mack.

MUH MACK: (*Wiping her eyes*) Ain't no row, Colonel. Want you to 'suade dat Abe git rid o' dem ol' books. 'Nough trouble come on us 'count of um.

COLONEL: (*Laughing*) The devil, let him keep his books. He's the only nigger in the whole country worth a durn. Let me see the baby. (GOLDIE *shows the baby.*) That's a fine un, Abe. He'll live. Let me feel him. (*Holding him up.*) Heavy, gracious!

MUH MACK *looks at him intently and there is the vaguest touch of malice in her voice as she speaks.*

MUH MACK: Lawd, it all comes to me ag'in. Jest sech a day as dis thirty yeah ago you come down heah and hold Abe-up dat-a-way.

COLONEL: (*Looking through the window a long while*) Time hurries on, it goes by in a hurry. (ABE *looks before him with an indefinable expression on his face. A constrained silence comes over them and the* COLONEL *takes a sort of refuge in gazing intently at the child. Once or twice he clears his throat.*) Yes, Callie, we're getting old.

For an instant all differences are passed away and they are four human beings aware of the strangeness of their lives, conscious of what queer relationships have fastened them together.

MUH MACK: (*Starting*) Yes, suh, we ain't gut much longer.

Then the baby begins to cry and the COLONEL *smiles.*

COLONEL: Here, take him, Goldie. Favors Muh Mack, don't favor you, Abe.

ABE: Yes, suh.

COLONEL: (*Drawing a heavy, folded paper from his pocket slowly and with weighty dignity*) I got a little surprise for you'n Goldie, Abe. (*He puts on his spectacles, opens the paper and starts to read.*) "Whereas"—(*He stops as if convulsed with pain, and presently goes on.*) "I devise to Abraham McCranie a house and tract of land containing twenty-five acres and formerly known as the 'Howington place,' to him and his heirs forever." (*Hesitating a moment and folding the paper together.*) Then follows a description of the place in course and distance, Abe, which I won't read. It's all signed up and recorded in the court-house.

He feels around him heavily for his stick.

ABE: (*Incredulously*) Whut dat? Dat foh me?

COLONEL: Yes, for you. A deed to this house and twenty-five acres of land, yours.

He holds out the paper to ABE.

ABE: (*Taking it with trembling hands*) Lawd, Colonel Mack, whut I gwine say?

COLONEL: Say nothing. Say thanky if you want to.

ABE: *(Overcome)* Thanky, suh, thanky, suh.

COLONEL: Shake hands on it, Abe.

ABE: *(Wiping his hand on his coat)* Thanky, suh.

The COLONEL *looks at his bent head with strange intentness, and then drops* ABE'S *hand.*

GOLDIE: Oh, Colonel Mack!

Her eyes are shining with thankfulness.

MUH MACK: Abe, you's gut land, boy, you owns you a piece o' land, Glory!

She runs up to the COLONEL *and covers his hands with kisses.*

COLONEL: *(Waving her off)* Nothing, nothing to do for him. He deserves it. *(Looking straight at* ABE.*)* You do, boy. I want to see you go forward now. You had a hard time the last three years.

GOLDIE: He has, po' boy. He had it hard since de day he married me.

COLONEL: Hunh. He couldn't a done better nowhere. I know. *(The* COLONEL *picks up his stick which he has laid across the bed.)* Well, I got to move on. *(He stops near the door.)* And, Abe, how's your book business coming on?

ABE: I—I studying and reading now and den. Most too tiahed every night dough to do much.

COLONEL: Don't give up like Lonnie. Sent him to school, and sent him to school, even tried him at the university, won't stay. He ain't worth a damn, that's what. *(Turning towards the door and stopping again.)* Well, I've got another little surprise for you in celebration of that fine boy.

He looks down and taps on the floor.

ABE: *(Excitedly)* Whut is it, Colonel Mack, suh?

COLONEL: How'd you like to try your hand at teaching a little school next fall?

MUH MACK *throws up her hands.*

GOLDIE: *(Breathlessly)* Oh, me!

ABE: *(In confusion)* Teach school? Yessuh, I——

COLONEL: I'm going to have that old Quillie House fixed up and put some benches in it and a blackboard. I'll get two Negroes to serve with me on the school board and we'll try you out. *(Smiling queerly.)* I been reading your books, too, Abe.

ABE: *(With a great breath)* I gwine teach school—at last!

COLONEL: *(Going shakily out at the door)* Yes, at last.

Now don't forget your crop, Abe, and study yourself to death.

ABE: *(Following him)* Colonel Mack, you, you—I—I——

COLONEL: Take care of that baby. Raise him up right. And, Abe, don't forget you ain't gonna have no easy time. I'll get a lot of cussing for this, well as you. Go on eat your dinner. *(He stops on the porch and calls.)* Here, Goldie, take this fifty cents and buy the boy a stick of candy. *(He steps to the door and throws the coin on the bed.)* Take care of him and don't kill him on collards and beans.

He goes off.

ABE: *(Calling after him)* I ain't, Colonel, I gwine raise him. I gwine make a man——*(He stops and stands watching the old man going in the lane. Then he turns and stumbles into the room with shining face.)* I—I fohgives him all. I don't 'member dat beating by de spring no mo'.

GOLDIE: *(Reaching out from the bed and grasping his hand)* Oh, honey babe, our troubles's ended. We gwine—we gwine have 'nough t' eat and you gwine be happy.

She turns over in the bed and begins to cry softly.

ABE: *(Patting her shoulders)* Dere, dere, don't you cry, chile. *(He wipes his eyes with his sleeve.)* I been mean man. *(In a husky voice.)* I treat my gal mean, blaspheam 'gin de Lawd. I gwine do better, I——

A sob chokes in his throat.

MUH MACK: *(Coming up to him and clasping her arms around him)* Bless de Lawd, you gwine do bedder now.

She sits down in a chair and bows her head in her lap.

GOLDIE: He good man, de Colonel. He too good to us. Raise us up, help us.

ABE: *(Vaguely)* Up! Lift me up! Up tow'd de sun! *(He glances at the calendar. Then thumping on his breast.)* Ain't no mo' bitter gall in heah. Peace. It come all suddent over me. *(He suddenly falls on his knees by the bed in a sobbing burst of prayer.)* O God, God of de po' and of de sinful!

MUH MACK: Yea, our God.

ABE: De black man's God, de white man's God, de one and only God, heah me, heah my prayer.

MUH MACK: *(Swaying and moaning)* Heah 'im, Jesus!

GOLDIE: *(Softly)* We dy chillun, Lawd.

ABE: Dy little chillun, and you pow'ful. You de Almighty, us de dust in dy hand. Us po' and weak, us nothing. Lak de grasshopper, lak de po' fee-lark, swept away in de storm.

Man gut no stren'th in um, no muscle kin raise him, 'cepting yo' power. He walk in de wind, de wind take 'im away. Man cain't stand. He lost, lost. Shet in de grave, shet till de judgment.

MUH MACK: Jesus! Jesus!

GOLDIE: *(Piteously)* Jesus!

ABE: *(His voice rising into a chant)* Dey gone at de planting, gone at de harvest. De hoe dull wid rust, de harness wait on de peg, de bridle hand, de collar hang dere useless. Dey ain't no mo' hoeing, ain't no mo' plowing, no shoe track in de furrow. Man gone, same lak a whisper, hushed in de graveyard, in de deep grave.

MUH MACK: Oh, ha' muhcy 'pon us.

GOLDIE: Muhcy!

ABE: *(Raising his head up, his eyes closed)* Heah us, heah us, heah me dis day, heah my po' prayer. Fohgive me my sins, my blaspheamy. Wipe out de evil o' my weeked days. Now heah I do humble down, I do cohnfess. Lift me, raise me, up, up!

MUH MACK: Hallelujah!

GOLDIE: Amen.

ABE: *(Bowing his head in a storm of grief)* Re'ch down yo' hand and gimme stren'th. Now I draw nigh, I feel yo' sperit. Save me, save me now! *(*MUH MACK *and* GOLDIE *pray and moan aloud. Presently* ABE *stands up and cries out exultantly.)* He save me, he done save me! He done fohgive me!

MUH MACK: *(Clapping her hands wildly)* Bless de Lawd, bless um!

ABE *is silent a moment, his face working with emotion. He turns and bends down over the bed.*

ABE: *(Puts his arms around* GOLDIE *and she clings to him)* Honey chile, I changed. I gwine take new holt. From dis day I begins. *(He loosens her arms from around his neck and stands up, a strange set look on his face.)* I gwine keep heart now, look up, rise. I gwine lead. *(Looking down at the baby.)* I gwine raise him up a light unto peoples. He be a new Moses, he bring de chillun out of bondage, out'n sin and ign'ance.

He turns suddenly and goes to the bucket at the left, pours some water out in a pan and sets it on the bed. Then he bends down and lifts the baby in his hand.

ABE: *(Dipping his hand in the water and holding the child aloft, his face lighted up in a beatific smile)* On dis day I names you Douglass. You gwine be same lak him. Yeh, better. You gwine be a light in darkness, a mighty man. *(He dips his hand into the water and sprinkles the child.)* I baptize you and consecrate you to de salvation ob my people dis day! Amen!

The women stare at him transfixed, caught out of themselves. He bends his head and stands with the child stretched before him as if making an offering to some god.

SCENE THREE

Winter of the same year. The old Quillie House, a Negro cabin of one bare room, now fitted up as a school-house. At the left center is a squat rusty cast-iron stove, the pipe of which reels up a few feet and then topples over into an elbow to run through the wall. A box of pine knots rests on the floor by it. Four or five rough pine benches, worn slick by restless students, stretch nearly the length of the room, ending towards a small blackboard nailed to the wall in the rear center. Between the benches and the blackboard is the teacher's rickety table with a splint-bottomed chair behind it. A heavy dinner bell with a wooden handle is on the table. To the right rear is a small window, giving a glimpse of brown broomsedge stretching up a gentle hill, and beyond, a ragged field of stripped cornstalks, gray now and falling down in the rot of winter rains. To the left rear is a door opening to the outside.

The curtain rises on the empty room. Presently ABRAHAM MCCRANIE comes in, carrying a tin lunch bucket and two or three books. He is wearing an old overcoat and a derby hat, both making some claims to a threadbare decency. He sets the bucket and books on the table and hangs his coat and hat on a nail in the wall at the right; then comes back to the stove, revealing himself dressed in baggy trousers, worn slick with too much ironing, heavy short coat, cheap shirt, and a celluloid collar with no tie. With his pocket-knife he whittles some shavings from a pine knot and starts a fire in the stove. He looks at his watch, beats his hands together from cold, and stirs about the room, his brow wrinkled in thought and apparent worry. Again and again he goes to the door and stares out expectantly. Looking at his watch the second or third time, he takes up the bell and goes out and rings it.

ABE: *(Shouting towards the empty fields)* Books! Books! Come in to books! *(He returns and sits down by the stove.)* No scholars in sight. *(With a sigh.)* Oh, me! *(He goes to the board and writes laboriously across the top:* "January 21. An idle brain is the devil's workshop." *While he is writing, three Negro students come in carrying a bucket and a book or two each—a lazy slumbrous girl of eighteen or twenty, a stout thick-lipped youth about the same age, and a little serious-faced ragged boy of ten.* ABE'S *face brightens at the sight of them.)* Good morning, chillun. Late. Everybody a little late.

STUDENTS: *(Standing uncertainly around the stove)* Good morning, Mr. Mack.

ABE: *(Finishing his writing)* This will be our motto foh to-day. (ABE'S *speech has improved somewhat. When he speaks with conscious deliberation he substitutes "this" for "dis," "that" for "dat," and so on. But when in a hurry or excited he drops back into his old methods. He addresses the little boy.)* Read it, Eddie, out loud.

EDDIE: *(Eagerly.)* I kin read it, Mr. Mack. *(In a slow and halting voice he reads.)* "A' idle brain is the devuh's wuk-shop."

ABE: Good, fine, Kin you read it, Neilly?

NEILLY: *(Boldly.)* Yeh, suh, read it raght off.

ABE: And how 'bout you, Lanie?

LANIE: *(Dropping her heavy-lidded eyes.)* I kin too.

She and NEILLY *look at each other with a fleeting smile over some secret between them.* EDDIE *gazes up at them, his lips moving silently as if over something to be told which he dare not utter.*

ABE: *(Pulling out his watch.)* Twenty minutes to nine. Whah the other scholars? *(No one answers.* NEILLY *gives the girl a quick look and turns deftly on his heel and kicks the stove, sticking up his lips in a low whistle.)* You see the Ragland chillun on the road, Lanie?

LANIE: *(Enigmatically.)* Yessuh, I see 'em.

ABE *goes to the door and rings his bell again.*

ABE: Books! Books! Come in to books! *(He puts the bell on the table and stands pondering.)* How 'bout the Maffis chillun?

NEILLY: Ain't coming!

ABE: Dey say so?

NEILLY: Yessuh.

ABE: (*Shortly.*) Take yo' seats. We'll go on wid our lessons if nobody else don't come.

He turns to his table.

EDDIE: (*Pulling excitedly at* LANIE'S *dress.*) G'won, ax him whut he gwine do.

LANIE: (*Snatching herself loose from him.*) Shet up. Ain't my business.

ABE: Put yo' buckets up and take yo' seats and listen to the roll-call. All the late ones ketch it on the woodpile and sweeping up the school-yard. (*Eyeing them.*) I said take yo' seat.

EDDIE *hurries to his seat.*

NEILLY: Ain't gwine have no school, is we?

ABE: Hunh?

NEILLY: Ain't gwine be no mo' school.

LANIE *giggles.*

ABE: (*With a worried note in his voice.*) Going have school same as usual. Seem lak all of 'em late dough. Take yo' seats, time foh the spelling lesson. Won't have de scripture reading dis mawning.

NEILLY: De rest of 'em done quit school.

LANIE *giggles again.*

ABE: Stop dat giggling and go to yo' seat.

LANIE *moves to her seat sulkily.*

EDDIE: (*In a high frightened quaver.*) Mr. Mack, dey all say de school ain't gwine run no mo' and dey ain't coming.

ABE: How dey hear it? I ain't heard it. (*No one answers.*) Whah'd you folks get all dis news, Neilly?

NEILLY: Dey was all talking it down de road. We wouldn't a-come eiver, but Eddie dah beg me and Lanie so hard to come wid 'im. Ain't no mo' folks coming dough.

ABE: (*Hitting the table with his fist.*) Sump'n' up. Dey got to show me fo' I quits, dey got to show me. Putt up yo' buckets and things, we going have school. (*They reluctantly set down their buckets near the wall and stand waiting.*) Take yo' seats, I say, and listen to yo' name. (*He pulls out a cheap arm-and-hammer memorandum book and begins calling the roll.*) Lanie Horton.

LANIE: Presunt.

She looks around at the bare seats and gives her senseless giggle.

ABE: Vanderbilt Jones, absent; 'Ona May Jordan, absent;

Jane Matthews, absent; Sister Matthews, absent; Jennie McAhlister, absent; Neilly McNeill.

NEILLY: Present.

He smiles at LANIE.

ABE: Arthur Ragland, absent. Didn't 'spect him back nohow. Dora Ragland, absent; Nora Ragland, absent; Eddie Williams.

EDDIE: Prizzunt.

ABE: (*Sits drumming on the table and staring before him. The students twist about on their seats in embarrassment.*) I'll put the writing lesson up while you study. (*They go to their seats.*) Lanie, you look wid Eddie in his book. (*He turns to the board and begins to write down the copy models. As he writes, the students mumble over their words in a drone.* NEILLY *and* LANIE *begin talking to each other in low whispers.* EDDIE *is lost in his book.* LANIE *suddenly giggles out loud, and* ABE *turns quickly from his board.*) Heigh you, Lanie, stand up in dat corner over thah. School isn't out yit.

LANIE: I ain't done nothing. (*Half audibly.*) "Isn't!"

ABE: Don't talk back. Stand in de corner wid yo' face to de wall. Hyuh, Eddie, you read in dis reader and let her have yo' book.

LANIE *creeps over to the corner and mouths over her lesson.* ABE *finishes his apothegm,* "A Wise man will rise with the sun, or before it." *He is finishing another,* "Wise children will imitate the manners of polite people," *when there is a stir at the door and* PUNY AVERY *comes in, swallowed up in a teamster's coat and carrying a long blacksnake whip in his hand.*

PUNY: Good mawning.

ABE: Good morning, Mr. Avery.

At the appellation of "Mister" PUNY *stuffs his cap against his mouth to hide a grin.*

PUNY: How you come on, Mr. McCranie? Kin I warm my hands a minute? Freezing col' setting on dat waggin seat.

He moves up to the stove and stretches his hands above it.

ABE: Help yo'se'f. Be a snow fo' night, I believe.

PUNY: Yeh, or—look lak it.

He warms himself, and ABE *sits at the table watching him questioningly. Now and then his gaze drops upon the whip.*

ABE: Hauling lumber over the river?

PUNY: Is dat. (*Looking at* LANIE *in the corner.*) Whut she do?

ABE: Misbehaved.

PUNY: Seem lak yo' school kinda thin. (ABE *says nothing.*) Been gitting thinner ev'y since Colonel died last fall, ain't it?

ABE: Been dropping off some since then.

PUNY: Whah all de rest o' de scholars?

ABE: Haven't showed up yet.

PUNY: Uhm.

ABE: Why you want to know, might I ask.

PUNY: (*Authoritatively.*) Already know. And foh yo' own good I come by to tell you and to bring you a message.

ABE: (*Looking at him intently and then waving his hand at the three students.*) You chillun kin go out and have recess now. Mr. Avery wants to see me on a little business. (LANIE *and* NEILLY *get their coats and walk out.* EDDIE *remains crouched in his seat, unconscious of his surroundings.*) What message you got foh me?

PUNY: You des' well quit de school business raght heah and now. Dey ain't gwine send to you no mo'.

ABE: What's the trouble?

PUNY: Trouble! You gone and done it, you has, when you beat Will Ragland's boy yistiddy. Will so mad he kin kill you.

ABE: (*Anger rising in his voice.*) Needn't think I'm skeahed of him.

PUNY: I knows you ain't. But you wants to keep on teaching, don't you?

ABE: Yeh, and I'm going to.

PUNY: Nunh-unh, you ain't neiver. Will went 'round last night and gut everybody to say dey won't gwine send to you no mo'. Dey ain't gwine stand foh no nigger beating deir young 'uns.

ABE: (*Angrily.*) I had a right to beat him. I couldn't make him work no other way, and 'sides he told a lie to me. Said he didn't eat up po' little Sis Maffis' dinner. Several of 'em seen him do it.

PUNY: Cain't he'p it. You beat 'im so dey had to have a doctor foh him, and Will done gone to de sher'ff to git out papers foh you.

ABE: (*Starting out of his chair.*) Gwine have me 'rested?

PUNY: He is dat. And mo', I reckon. And my advice to

you is to git f'om heah. As a member of de school boa'd I say, bedder leave.

ABE: He think he kin run me 'way?

PUNY: Don't know what he think. Know I wouldn't lak to lie in no white man's jail-house, dat's me.

ABE: De otheh members of the boa'd know 'bout it?

PUNY: Us had a meeting last night.

ABE: What dey say?

PUNY: (*Fumbling in his pockets.*) Dey all side wid Will, 'count o' de beating and 'count o' dat speech you made in chu'ch last Sunday.

ABE: Wuh Mr. Lonnie dere?

PUNY: He dere and he send dis heah writing to you.

He pulls a note from his pocket and hands it to ABE, *who opens it excitedly.*

ABE: (*Clenching his fist.*) Dat man say heah—God—He say de boa'd done all 'cided de school got to stop. (*He tears the note to pieces and throws it in the stove.*) He say dere he know a good job in Raleigh at public wuk he kin git me. (*Bitterly.*) Say I do better at dat dan farming or school. (*Pacing the floor, he throws his hand above his head.*) Nanh, anh—suh, I sets a oaf on high, I ain't going let 'em run me off. Dey cain't skeah me. Dey cain't run me off lak I stole sump'n'. (*He turns on* PUNY *with blazing eyes and* EDDIE *watches him terrified.*) Why you all vote dat way? Whyn't you stand up and vote foh me? You know I trying do right. You weak, coward, no backbone.

PUNY: (*Backing towards the door.*) I ain't gut nothing 'gin you, Abe. Why you 'buse me?

ABE: Git out o' heah. All o' you down on me. (*Crying out.*) I ain't gwine give in. Dey cain't run me. You cain't run me. I fight 'em. I stay heah. Let 'em putt me in de jail, I last till de jail rot down. (*He moves menacingly towards* PUNY, *who flees through the door and slams it after him.*) I come through deir bars, deir iron won't hold me. I'll git dere, I'll come. My flesh will be as tough as deir iron! (*He goes to the table and picks up his books. He opens the Bible and stands thinking. Dropping into his chair, he sits with his elbow on the table and his chin in his hand, gazing into the distance. The anger and bitterness gradually pass from his face.*) Dat man's talk, proud. Cain't push through 'thout help—(*Putting his hand on the Bible.*) 'thout help from up there. (*He bows his head on the table.* EDDIE *begins to sob and, leaving his seat timidly, approaches* ABE'S *bent form, gulping and wiping his nose and eyes with his sleeve.* ABE *looks up and puts his arm around him.*) Son, this heah's the last of this school. But we cain't stop, we got to keep on. (EDDIE *leans his head against him, his sobs increasing.*) Got to keep studying, got to keep climbing. (*After a moment he stands up and writes across the board,* "This School is stopped for a while." LANIE *and* NEILLY *come inquiringly in.*) Chillun, ain't goin' to be no mo' school till mebbe next yeah. You kin go home. (LANIE *giggles and* NEILLY *looks at him with familiar condescension.*) But I wants to dismiss with a word of prayer. (*At a sign from him,* EDDIE *falls on his knees by the table. He gets down at his chair.*) Our Father, where two or three is gathered—(NEILLY *and* LANIE *look at him, pick up their buckets and scurry out giggling and laughing loudly.* ABE *springs to his feet, his face blank with astonishment. He calls after them furiously.*) Heigh, heigh, you!

They are heard going off, their sharp laughter softening in the distance.

NEILLY: 'Fo' Gohd, he down on his knees!

LANIE: (*Her voice growing faint.*) Yeh, and he 'bout kilt Arth yistiddy.

NEILLY: Haw—haw—haw.

LANIE: Hee—hee—hee.

Their voices die away.

SCENE FOUR

Fifteen years later. A room in the poverty-stricken Negro section of Durham, North Carolina, as it was then. When the curtain rises, GOLDIE is washing at a tub placed on a goodsbox at the left of the room. MUH MACK is seated at the fireplace at the right, bent under a slat bonnet and dozing. Pots and pans are piled around the hearth and a kettle is singing on the fire. Several garments are hanging on chairs before the fire drying.

To the left rear is a bed with a pile of rough-dried clothes on it. A door at the center rear leads into another room. To the right of the door is a low chest with books and dishes set upon it. At the right front by the chimney is a small window letting in the sickly light of a dying winter day. In the center of the room is a small eating-table covered with a greasy, spotted oil-cloth.

For several minutes neither of the women says anything. GOLDIE washes heavily at the tub, her body bent and disfigured with the years of toil and poverty and the violence of childbirth. She wrings out a garment and takes it to the fireplace.

GOLDIE: (*Lifelessly*) Move yo'se'f, Muh. Lemme hang up dis shirt.

MUH MACK: (*Testily as she moves her chair with her body*) Lemme 'lone. Cain't sleep, rest—nothing.

GOLDIE *drags up a chair, hangs the shirt on it and returns to her washing. Her movements are slow, oxlike, and in her eyes now and then comes a sort of vacant look as if some deadening disease has had its way within her brain or as if trouble and worry have hardened her beyond the possibility of enthusiasm or grief any more. Between her eyes a deep line has furrowed itself, a line often found on the foreheads of those who think a great deal or those who are forgetting how to think at all. And her mouth has long ago fastened itself into a drawn anguished questioning that has no easeful answer in the world. She washes away at the tub, the garment making a kind of flopping sound against the board. After a moment she calls to* MUH MACK.

GOLDIE: Gitting neah 'bout day-down, Muh. Time to start supper.

MUH MACK: (*Whom age and poverty have made meaner than before*) Yeh, yeh, it is, and I gut to git it, I reckon.

GOLDIE: (*Making an effort to hurry*) Yeh, Mis' Duke got to have her clothes to-morrow, I done said.

MUH MACK: (*Getting slowly to her feet*) Oh, me my! My leg done gone to sleep! (*She fumbles among the pans on the hearth*) Yo' water hyuh all gwine bile 'way.

GOLDIE: Gimme hyuh! (*She takes the kettle and pours the water into the tub and then goes on scrubbing the clothes*)

MUH MACK: Whut I gwine cook?

GOLDIE: Make some cawn bread, and dey's a little piece o' Baltimo' meat in de chist.

MUH MACK *arranges her pan on the fire with much grumbling and growling and goes over to the chest.*

MUH MACK: (*Knocking the pile of books off with a bang, opens the chest and pulls out a small piece of white meat*) Hunh, look at dis, will you? Ain't mo'n 'nough to fill my old hollow toof. Cain't us git sump'n' else foh supper? I et dat old meat and cawn bread till it makes me heave to look at it.

GOLDIE: Dat all dey is.

MUH MACK: Dat won't make a mou'ful foh Abe. Whut we gwine eat?

GOLDIE: Abe won't eat it nohow, and I don't want nothing. You'n Douglass kin eat it.

MUH MACK: Bofe of you gwine die if you don't eat. Dat Abe been living off'n cawfee and bread two weeks now. No wonder he look lak a shadow and cain't ha'f do his work.

GOLDIE: Cain't eat when you ain't gut it.

MUH MACK: Well, starving ain't gwine give you stren'th to git no mo'. How you gwine keep washing foh folks and you don't eat?

GOLDIE: (*Bowing her head in weariness over the tub, her voice rising with sudden shrillness*) Oh, Lawd Gohd in heaven, I don't know.

MUH MACK: Calling on Gohd ain't gwine he'p you git no supper eiver. (*Throwing the meat back into the chest and slamming the lid*) Well, I ain't gwine cook dat old mess. I'll set right heah by dis fiah and starve wid you and Abe.

GOLDIE: (*Drying her hands on her apron*) I gut des' one mo' fifty-cent piece in dat pocketbook. I'll git it and run out and buy some liver den. Po' Abe gut to live somehow. (*She goes out at the rear and returns immediately holding an empty ragged purse in her hand*) Whah my ha'f dollar! Whah is it?

MUH MACK: (*Dropping into a chair by the fire*) Hunh, needn't ax me. Ain't seed it.

GOLDIE: (*Sitting down and rocking back and forth*) Somebody stole it. (*Turning upon* MUH MACK) You done gin it to dat Douglass.

MUH MACK: Ain't.

GOLDIE: Yeh, you has, you has.

MUH MACK: (*Beating the floor with her foot*) Ain't, I tell you.

GOLDIE: (*Staggering to her feet*) And he off somewhah's spending it foh ice-cream and mess.

MUH MACK: Don't keer 'f I did. Po' boy do widdout all de time.

GOLDIE: (*Falling on the tub with renewed vigor*) Cain't cry now!

MUH MACK: G'won down dere and git dat man to let you

have sump'n on a credit. You can pay 'im to-morrow when Mis' Duke pay you.

GOLDIE: He done said he ain't gwine let us have no mo' widdout de money.

MUH MACK: Mebbe Abe fetch sump'n' when he come.

GOLDIE How kin he and dey don't pay 'im off till to-morrow evening?

MUH MACK: (*Suddenly crying out with a whimper*) Look lak us gwine starve spite of all. I wants to go back home. I wants to go back to home. Mr. Lonnie won't let us do widdout.

GOLDIE: I been wanting to go back for fifteen yeah, but Abe's gwine die fo' he go back.

MUH MACK: (*Beating her hands together in her lap*). Crazy, crazy! He de biggest fool in de whole world. He gitting down lower eve'y day. Gitting sick wuss all de time. Oh, me, whut'll become of us all! (*Her voice falling into a sort of hypocritical whine.*) Heah I is all laid up wid rheumatiz and cain't see how to trabbel no mo' and 'bout to starve. Starve, heah me!

GOLDIE: (*Dropping into her chair again*) You ain't de on'y one.

MUH MACK: Reckon I knows it. But dat don't keep my stomach f'om cutting up.

GOLDIE: We doing de best we kin by you.

MUH MACK: (*Somewhat softened*) I knows it, chile, but dat Abe, dat Abe, I say! He de trouble at de bottom of it all.

GOLDIE: Needn't keep talking 'bout Abe. Why don't you say dat to his face. He doing de best he kin.

MUH MACK: (*Her anger rising*) I will tell him. Dere you set, Goldie McCranie, and say dat, after he done drug you f'om pillar to post foh fifteen yeah. Doing de best he kin! He ain't nothing, des' wuss'n nothing! He des' a plumb fool. But he mammy wuh a fool befo' 'im. Da's how come he in dis worl'.

GOLDIE: Stop dat. He sick, been sick a long time, po' fellow, and he keep trying.

MUH MACK: Sick! He wa'n't sick back dere when he got into co't and lost all his land trying to git dem lawyers to keep 'im out'n jail, and he beat dat Will Ragland's boy ha'f to death. (GOLDIE *bows her head in her hands, swaying from side to side.*) De devil in him! Dat's whut.

GOLDIE: (*Wretchedly*) You done sot dere by dat fiah and

told me dat same tale time and ag'in, day in, day out. I don't want to heah it no mo'.

MUH MACK: Unh-unh. And I reckon you will dough. Wuh he sick, and he cutting up a rust in Raleigh and de niggers and white folks runnin' him out'n dere? It was old Scratch in him dere too. I tells you.

GOLDIE: Dey didn't treat 'im raght over dere.

MUH MACK: Hunh. No, dey didn't. And dey didn't treat him raght in Greensboro, did dey? Same old tale dere, gitting in a row wid somebody and ha' to leave. He's mean, mean lak sump'n' mad at de world.

GOLDIE: *(Tossing her head about her)* I dunno. I dunno. He orter nevah married me and gut tied down. Seem lak things all go wrong, crosswise foh him.

MUH MACK: *(Staring at her)* Hunh. Things'll be crosswise wid 'im till dey straighten 'im out in de grave. Dem's my words. *(Blowing her nose in her skirt and half weeping.)* If all dat shooting and killing in Wilmington wouldn't make 'im do better, nothing in de Gohd's world kin.

GOLDIE: *(Moaning)* Stop dat talking. I cain't beah it.

MUH MACK: Co'se you gwine stay by 'im—and starve too. Foh dat's whut you'll do. Whut he don't spend on medicine he do on dem old lodges and sich and books and newspapers. And gits turned out'n eve'y one of 'em foh his speeches and wild talk, he do. *(With grim satisfaction.)* Shoveling dat coal down at de power house reckon'll hold him down foh a while. *(With an afterthought.)* Hold 'im down till somebody crack his haid wid a shovel and tu'n 'im off. *(Stirring the fire and then folding up her hands.)* I done said my say-so now. Do no good, 'caze you so wropped up in de fool.

GOLDIE: *(Flaring out)* No, it won't do no good. I gwine stick by him. *(Rising and turning to her work again.)* Dey ain't never done 'im right. Dey all been down on him f'om de fust.

MUH MACK: *(Shrilly)* And 'll be till de last. Otheh niggers makes a living foh deir fambly. Why don't he? Allus gut his eyes on sump'n else.

GOLDIE: He gwine be a big man yit. Dem udder niggehs do de dirty work and take whut dey kin git. Dey de low-down trash. *(Her voice trembling)* He gwine git him a big school some dese days.

MUH MACK: *(Laughing scornfully)* Hee-hee—hee. Listen

at him. He cain't teach nothing. De niggeh school teachers round hyuh know mo'n a minute dan Abe do in a week. Dey been to college at Raleigh and Greensboro and no telling whah. And dey gut some sense 'sides deir learning. Dat li'l Eddie Williams has. He done gone th'ough dat Shaw school in Raleigh and is off doing big wuk. Why couldn't Abe do sump'n lak dat!

GOLDIE: *(Her voice breaking)* Shet up, I tell you.

MUH MACK: *(Sulkily)* Aw right den, but dat talk don't fill yo' stomach.

Pulling a walking stick from the chimney corner, she groans and creaks to her feet.

GOLDIE: Wait'll Douglass come f'om school and I'll git him to go down to de cawner and git some meat f'om dat man.

MUH MACK: Done past time foh Douglass to be heah. Mought not come till late.

GOLDIE: *(Drying her hands again and patting her hair)* I'll go den. You putt de kittle on foh some cawfee and set de table and I'll be right back. *(Far off a muffled whistle blows.)* Dere's de power-house whistle. Abe be heah soon. Light de lamp and putt on de table. *(She goes out.)*

MUH MACK: *(Somewhat mollified, calling after her)* Aw raght.

She puts her stick back in the corner, fills the kettle and stirs stiffly about her, bringing plates to the table and laying out the knives and forks. She hobbles into the room at the rear and returns with a lamp without any chimney, which she lights at the fireplace and places on the table. While she is engaged in making coffee over the fire, DOUGLASS *strolls in. He is a young Negro in short trousers, fifteen or sixteen years old, black as* MUH MACK *and with something of a wild and worthless spirit already beginning to show in his face. He carries two ragged books under his arm.*

DOUGLASS: *(Dropping the books by the door and kicking them near the chest)* Heigh!

MUH MACK : *(Jumping)* Who?—hee—hee, you skeahed me, honey. *(She stands up and looks at him indulgently.)* Whah you been so late?

DOUGLASS: Oh, round and about. Stopped by de hot dawg stand awhile, chewing de rag wid some fellows.

MUH MACK: She knowed you tuck dat money soon's she found it gone.

DOUGLASS: *(Alarmed)* Pap don't know, do he?

MUH MACK: Not yit. He ain't come f'om wuk. *(He turns back into the room at the rear and reappears with a guitar. Sitting down wonderfully at ease, he begins strumming.)* Lawd, Lawd, honey, gi' us a piece 'fo' yo' daddy comes. *(He falls to playing and* MUH MACK *begins to pat the floor and skip happily now and then as she moves about the fireplace.)* Hee-hee—dat beddern'n eating.

DOUGLASS: *(Hugging up the "box" and throwing back his head in abandon)* Hee-hee—ain't it dough! *(He turns and scowls at the books lying on the floor, and begins singing to them.)* Dem old books—*(Strum, strum.)* lying in de corner, *(Strum, strum.)* Dem old books—*(Strum, strum.)* lying in de corner—*(Strum, strum.)* Lie dere, babies, lie dere! Hee-hee—Muh Mack, I kin make music raght out'n my haid. *(He goes on throwing his fingers across the strings.)*

MUH MACK: You kin, honey, you sho'ly kin.

She sits listening happily. He wraps himself over the guitar, his fingers popping up and down the neck of the instrument with marvelous dexterity. His bowed head begins to weave about him rhythmically as he bursts into snatches of song.

> Look down, look down dat lonesome road,
> De hacks all dead in line.
> Some give a nickel, some give a dime
> To bury dis po' body o' mine.

MUH MACK: *(Staring at him)* I declah! I declah! Listen at dat chile.

DOUGLASS: Ne'h mind, ne'h min' me. *(Modulating with amazing swiftness from key to key)* And dere was po' Brady. Po' old Brady.

MUH MACK: Yeh, Brady, dey laid him down to die.

DOUGLASS: *(Singing)*

> Oh, Brady, Brady, you know you done me wrong,
> You come in when de game was a-goin' on!
> And dey laid po' Brady down.
>
> Wimmens in Gawgy dey heard de news
> Walking 'bout in deir little red shoes,
> Dey glad, dey glad po' Brady dead.

When I close my eyes to ketch a liddle sleep,
Po' old Brady about my bed do creep,
One mo', des' one mo' rounder gone.

While he is singing and playing, ABE *comes suddenly in at the rear dragging a heavy wooden box in one hand and carrying a dinner-pail in the other. He is dirty and begrimed with coal dust.*

ABE: *(Shouting)* Put up dat box! (DOUGLASS *bounds out of his chair as if shot and backs away from him.*) Putt down dat damn guitah, you good-foh-nothing!

ABE *hangs his cap and dinner-pail on a nail by the door and comes heavily across to the fire. His face is haggard and old and his shoulders have grown humped with the going of time.* DOUGLASS *slips out with his guitar and presently creeps in and sits stealthily on the chest.* ABE *lays the goods box on the floor and breaks it up and places pieces of it on the fire. Then he sits down and stretches out his feet and stares moodily before him.* MUH MACK *hurries around making bread, frying the hated side meat, and arranging the table.*

MUH MACK: *(Tremulously)* How you feeling? You come quick adder de whistel—

ABE: Ah, feel lak I'll stifle in heah. *(He strikes his breast once and then follows it with a fury of savage blows)* Cain't get no wind down in dat b'iler house. *(He drags his hand wearily across his brow and shakes his head as if clearing his eyes of a fog.)* Whah Goldie?

MUH MACK: Gone out to de cawner to git some meat. Time she back.

ABE: How long fo' supper?

MUH MACK: Soon's she gits back and we kin cook de meat.

ABE: *(Pulling off his shoes and setting them in the corner.)* I'm going to lie down a minute till my head clears up. Feel lak it'll blow off at de top. *(Grasping his chair, he staggers to his feet and goes across the room. At the door he stops and looks down at* DOUGLASS.) I' going to tend to you in a little bit.

DOUGLASS *quails before him. He goes out and slams the door.*

MUH MACK: Whut de name o'God ail him now? Wus'n ever.

DOUGLASS: *(Whimpering)* He gwine beat me! He'll kill me.

The bed is heard creaking in the rear room as ABE *lies down.*

MUH MACK: Whut'n de world foh?

She stands tapping her hands together helplessly.

DOUGLASS: He done heahed sump'n' on me. Oh, he gwine beat me to deaf.

ABE *is heard turning in his bed again, and he immediately appears in the door.*

ABE: Shet up dat whimpering. Git over dere and start washing on dem clothes foh yo' po' mammy. *(DOUGLASS darts over and begins rubbing at the board and sniffling.)* Dry up, I tell you.

ABE *turns back to his bed.*

MUH MACK: *(Sitting to the fire and rocking back and forth in her anxiety.)* Oh, Lawd,—Lawd!

She hides her head in her skirt grumbling and moaning. Presently GOLDIE *comes in.*

GOLDIE: *(Coming over to the tub)* Look out, son, lemme git at 'em.

She falls to washing feverishly.

MUH MACK: *(Looking up)* Whah dat meat, Goldie?

GOLDIE: Dat man look at me and laugh, dat's whut. *(Turning angrily towards* DOUGLASS You went and—

MUH MACK: *(Throwing out her hand in alarm)* Nanh, nanh, Goldie. *(Lowering her voice and nodding to the rear.)* Abe in dere. He find out 'bout dat, he kill de boy. Done say he gwine beat 'im foh sump'n' 'nother.

GOLDIE: When he come?

MUH MACK: He des' dis minute gut heah.

GOLDIE: *(In alarm)* He wuss off, I bet. *(She hurries into the room and is heard talking softly and kindly to* ABE. *He answers her with indistinct growls. In a moment* GOLDIE *returns.)* Putt whut you gut on de table and le's eat. *(She goes on with her washing.)* Abe ain't feeling well. Hadder eat whut he kin, I reckon.

MUH MACK *puts the bread, coffee and meat on the table.*

MUH MACK: Come on, you all.

GOLDIE: Come on in, Abe. *(*ABE *enters in his undershirt and trousers.)* G'won and eat, I don't want nothing.

ABE: *(Almost falling in his chair.)* Come on and set whedder you can or not. *(*GOLDIE *takes her place at the table.)* Come on, Douglass.

DOUGLASS: I don't want nothing eiver.

MUH MACK *draws up her chair.*

ABE: Don't make no difference. I said come on. (DOUGLASS *gets a chair and takes his place.* ABE *surveys the fare before him.*) Dis all you got foh a working man and he sick?

GOLDIE: I didn't have no money and——

She gulps and drops her head to hide her tears.

ABE: (*Kindly as he reaches out and touches her shoulders.*) Neveh mind, honey chile. (*He closes his eyes with weariness and sits brooding. Presently he raises his head.*) Well, neveh you mind, I ain't hungry. (*Looking at her sadly.*) But you must be plumb wore out wid all dat washing and all. (*Dropping his head.*) Le's have de blessing. Oh, Lawd, we thank Thee foh what we have befo' us. Make us truly thankful foh all Thy gifts and save us at last, we humbly beg, foh Christ's sake, Amen! (*After the blessing is over* GOLDIE *still keeps her head bowed, her shoulders heaving with sobs.* MUH MACK *pours out the coffee and hands it round.* ABE *calls to* GOLDIE.) Come on eat sump'n', Goldie, you feel better, you git yo' stren'th back. Drink some this coffee. (GOLDIE, *bursting into wild sobs, goes and sits by the fire.*) What's de matter, chile?

GOLDIE *stands up and looks towards the table with anguished face.*

GOLDIE: Abe, Abe honey babe, whut us gwine do?

She buries her face in her hands.

ABE: You done heahed sump'n', ain't you?

GOLDIE: Yeh, yeh, Liza told me. Jim done come f'om de power house and told her.

ABE: (*Dully.*) Neveh mind. Come on drink some coffee. We talk 'bout dat directly. I got sump'n' else to tell you, too.

MUH MACK: (*Staring at him in fear.*) Whut dat happen at de power house?

ABE: (GOLDIE *wipes her eyes and returns to the table to drink her coffee.*) Befo' we gits on what happened wid me, I got a question to ax dis young gentleman. (*Looking across at* DOUGLASS.) Why don't you eat?

DOUGLASS: (*Falteringly.*) I ain't hongry.

ABE: Try and see do you want anything.

DOUGLASS: I cain't eat nothing.

ABE: How come?

DOUGLASS: I des' don't want nothing.

ABE: *(Bitterly)* I reckon I know how come. Dis evening I pass on the other side of de street and see you down dere at dat drink stand setting up dem wuthless niggers wid yo' mammy's good money. *(Savagely.)* Oh, yeh, I know dat's whah you got it. I see you last night watching her putt it away.

GOLDIE: Please don't have no mo' row, Abe.

ABE: I ain't gwine beat 'im foh dat, nunh-unh. Sump'n' else he's goin' to ketch it foh. *(Raging out.)* De teacher stop me on de street and tell me you doing wuss'n ever in yo' books and she done had to putt you back in third reader. *(Swallowing his third cup of coffee down with a hunk of bread, he stands up and stares into the distance.)* Heah we done labor and sweat foh you, fix foh you to rise up and be sump'n'. Eight yeah you been going to school and you won't work, you won't learn. *(He strikes the table with his fist, and the lamp flickers and almost goes out.)* You ain't no good. Onct I thought you gwine go on, climb, rise high and lead.

He seizes him by the collar and, lifting him from the floor, shakes him like a rag.

DOUGLASS: *(Sputtering and choking.)* Pap, papa!

MUH MACK: *(Whining in terror.)* Stop dat! You kill him!

ABE: I teach you to fool wid dem low niggers! I git you out'n dem trifling ways or I'll break yo' back in two. *(He sits down and jerks the boy across his knee and begins beating him blindly.)* I name you foh a great man, a man what stand high lak de sun, and you turn out to be de lowest of de low! Change yo' name, dat's what you better do. *(With a cuff on the cheek he hurls him across the room, where he falls sobbing and wailing on the floor.)* Shet dat fuss up! DOUGLASS' *sobs gradually cease.* GOLDIE *starts toward him, but* ABE *jerks her back.)* Let 'im lie dere, de skunk and coward.

GOLDIE *turns despairingly to her washing again.* ABE *moves to the fire and sits down, pulling a wrinkled newspaper out of his pockets, while* MUH MACK *rocks and slobbers and moans.*

MUH MACK: You need de law on you, Abe McCranie. You beat dat po' baby——

ABE: You what gwine ruin him. He takes adder you and yo' trifling.

MUH MACK: Oh, I gwine leave heah, find me nudder place to stay.

ABE: We all got to git another place to stay.

GOLDIE: Le's go back home, Abe! Le's go back.

MUH MACK: Ha' we gut to leave 'caze whut you done down at de power house? (*Wringing her hands.*) Whut you do down dere? Oh, Lawd!

ABE: Ain't no use waking up de neighborhood wid yo' yelling. I didn't do nothing but stand up foh my rights. A white man sass me and I sass back at him. And a crowd of 'em run me off. Won't be able to git no other job in dis town. God damn it! (*Standing up and shaking his fist.*) God damn de people in dis town! Dem wid deir 'bacco warehouses, and cotton mills, and money in de bank, you couldn't handle wid a shovel.

MUH MACK: Le's go back home. De Colonel fix it in his will so us could have a place to come back to. Mr. Lonnie'll rent us some land.

GOLDIE: (*Coming over to* ABE'S *chair and dropping on her knees beside him.*) Abe, Abe, le's go back. Please do. Le's go back whah we growed up. Ain't no home foh us in no town. We gut to git back to de country. Dat's whah we belong.

She lays her head in his lap.

ABE: (*Looking down at her tenderly.*) Yeh, yeh, honey. We is gwine back. Adder all dese yeahs I knows now de town ain't no place foh us. Fifteen yeah we been trying to make it and couldn't Dat's what I was going to tell you. Back home de place foh us. Back in our own country. (*Staring before him and a smile suddenly sweetening the hardness of his face.*) We go back dere and take a new start. We going to build up on a new foundation. (*His voice rising exultantly.*) Dere's whah my work is cut out to be. (*Standing up.*) Seem lak sump'n' spoke to me and said go back down on de Cape Fair River. I heard it plain lak a voice talking. "Dese streets and dese peoples ain't yo' peoples. Yo'n is de kind what works and labors wid de earf and de sun. Dem who knows de earth and fullness thereof. Dere's whah yo' harvest is to be." And den when I come face to face wid de ruining of my boy, in my anger I see de way clear. We going back, we going back. And dere at last I knows I'm going to build up and lead! And my boy going to be a man. (*Looking at* DOUGLASS *with a hint of pleadingness.*) Ain't it so?

But DOUGLASS *only stares at him coldly.*

GOLDIE: *(Softly, the tears pouring from her eyes.)* Yeh, yeh.

ABE: And all dis sin and tribulation and sorrow will be forgot, passed away, wiped out till de judgment, won't it, chile?

GOLDIE: It will, oh, I knows it will. We done suffered our share and Old Moster gwine be good to us now.

ABE: Good! Yeh, good!

He sits with bowed head.

SCENE FIVE

Three years later. The same as Scene Two, in ABE's cabin on the MCCRANIE farm. The room shows some sign of improvement over its former state. There is a lambrequin of crêpe paper on the mantel, a wooden clock, and at the right a home-fashioned bookcase with books and magazines. On the rear wall is the same colored print with the caption of the rising slave.

ABE is seated at a table near the front writing by a lighted lamp. He is better dressed and more alert than formerly. Further back and to the left of the fireplace sits MUH MACK dozing and quarreling in her rocking chair. Her head and face are hid under the same slat-bonnet, and a dirty pink "fascinator" is draped over her bony shoulders. Her huge snuff brush protrudes from her lips and now and then describes a sort of waving motion when she moves her jaws in sleep. Between her knees she clasps her walking-stick.

Through the window at the rear come bright streaks from the orange afterglow of the west. The November sun has set and the sky near the horizon is fading into a deep gloom under an approaching cloudiness. In the oaks outside the sparrows going to roost pour out a flooding medley of sharp calls resembling the heavy dripping of rain from eaves. For a moment ABE continues his writing and then lays down his pencil and replenishes the fire. He returns to his chair and sits drumming absently on the table.

ABE: When Goldie coming back, Muh?

His speech is gentle and more cultivated.

MUH MACK: *(Starting out of her sleep.)* Whut you say?

ABE: When Goldie coming back from Mr. Lonnie's?

MUH MACK: When she git done o' dat washing and arning, po' thing.

ABE: Seem like it's time she was back.

MUH MACK: Whut you keer 'bout her and you setting dere all day wuking at dat old speech mess. Po', po' thing, wid all her trouble wonder she able to cook or work or do anything.

She turns to her snoozing and ABE *picks up his pencil again and gnaws at it as he works on his speech. Soon he stops and begins tapping on the table.*

ABE: What trouble she got now?

MUH MACK: *(Astounded.)* You ax dat and you fixing to bring mo' trouble on us wid yo' schooling and mess. And wid Mr. Lonnie down on you 'bout de crap ag'in. Lawd, Lawd! And who dat won't let his po' boy putt foot in de home? Keep 'im driv' off lak a homeless dawg.

She wipes her eyes with a dirty rag.

ABE: You talk, but this time they won't be no failing. The school is going through. Then I can talk to Mr. Lonnie. Six men done already promised a thousand dollars. Cain't fail this time, nosuh.

MUH MACK: You don't 'serve nothing, and won't let po' Douglass come back to see his mammy. *(Brightly.)* Dem men mebbe ain't promised. Dey talking.

ABE: *(Sharply.)* I know. . . . You needn't say another word about it. *(Concerned with the speech.)* I won't let Douglass darken my door.

MUH MACK *stirs from her doze and sniffles into her rag, wiping the rheumy tears from her eyes.* ABE *turns to his writing. He writes more and more rapidly as he nears the end. Presently he throws down his pencil and stretches his arms back of his head with a weary yawn. He looks towards* MUH MACK *and speaks exultantly.*

ABE: That's the best I've ever done. They can't go against that, they can't this time. That crowd's going to listen to me to-night.

MUH MACK: Mebbe dey will, but you's talked yo' life away, and it hain't come to nothing.

ABE: *(Looking at the speech.)* I've done my best this time. All I got from books and experience is there, and the truth's in it. *(He gathers the closely written sheets together.)* I tell 'em——*(He turns to his speech and begins to read as he rises from his chair.)* I say, ladies and gentlemen, *(He does not notice the movement of disgust* MUH MACK *makes as she turns away from him.)* this night is going to mean much in the lives of each and every one of us, big and little.

MUH MACK: Hit won't ef dey treats dey chil'en lak you treats yo' one.

ABE: *(Hurrying on.)* It marks the founding of the Cape Fair Training School, an institution that will one day be a light to other institutions around about. It is to be our aim here to offer education to the colored children amongst us and offer it cheap. *(He turns toward* MUH MACK *and speaks with more spirit, as if his audience were directly before him. But she turns her back to him and blinks into the fire.)* Looking over the country, ladies and gentlemen, we see eight million souls striving in slavery, yea, slavery, brethren, the slavery of ignorance. And ignorance means being oppressed, both by yourselves and others.

He picks up his pencil and crosses out a word.

MUH MACK: *(Sarcastically.)* Dey hain't nobody been in slavery since de surrenduh. Ef dey is, how cum?

ABE: *(Continuing his speech without noticing her.)* Ignorance means sin, and sin means destruction, destruction before the law and destruction in a man's own heart. The Negro will rise when his chareckter is of the nature to cause him to rise—for on that the future of the race depends, and that chareckter is mostly to be built by education for it cannot exist in ignorance. We have no other way. *(He strides in front of the old woman, who has dozed off again under his eloquence. She raises her head with a jerk when he thunders at her.)* A little over forty years ago the white man's power covered us like the night. Through war and destruction we was freed. But it was freedom of the body and not freedom of the mind. *(Throwing his arm out in a long gesture.)* What we need is thinking people, people who will not let the body rule the head. I been accused of wanting to make the Negro the equal of the white man. Been run from pillar to post, living in poverty because of that belief. But it is false. I never preached that doctrine. I don't say that the colored ought to be made equal to the white in society, now. We are not ready for it yet. But I do say that we have equal rights to educating and free thought and living our lives. *(Caught up in the dreams of his life, he pours out a roll of words and beats the air with his fists.)* With this one school-building we can make a good start. Then we can get more teachers later on, and

some day a library where the boys and girls can read about
men that have done something for the world. *(Forgetful of
his written page, he shouts.)* And what will stop us in the end
from growing into a great Negro college, a university, a light
on a hill, a place the pride of both black and white. *(He
stands a moment, lost in thought. Turning through the
leaves of his speech, he looks toward* MUH MACK, *who sits
hid under her bonnet.)* Ain't that the truth, Muh Mack? Ain't
it? *(Anxiously.)* They can't stand out against that, can they?
Ain't that a speech equal to the best of the white, ain't it?
    He coughs.

MUH MACK: Lawd Jesus! You's enough to wake de daid.
And you brung on yo' cough ag'in.

ABE: *(Fiercely.)* I tell you it's going through. I believe the
people here are with me this time.

MUH MACK: *(Bitterly.)* You's made dem dere speeches
from Wilmington and Greensboro to I don' know where. It's
foolishnesses, and you knows it. (ABE *arranges the leaves of
his speech without listening to her.)* Time you's learning dat
white is white and black is black, and Gohd made de white to
allus be bedder'n de black. It was so intended from de
beginning.

ABE: *(Staring at her and speaking half aloud.)* We been
taught and kept believing that for two hundred years. *(Blazing out.)* But it's a lie, a lie, and the truth ain't in it.

MUH MACK: *(Going on in her whining, irritating voice.)*
Ef you'd a putt as much time on picking cotton lately as you
has on dat speech, you wouldn't have Mr. Lonnie down on
you de way he is. De truf's in dat all right.

ABE: *(Trying to control his nervousness and anger.)* I
ain't a farmer. My business is with schools. *(Hotly.)* Can't
you learn nothing? You dribbling old——, here for twenty
years you've heard me talk the gospel and it ain't made no
impression on you. *(He turns away, realizing the vanity of
his words to her. He speaks to himself and the shadows of
the room.)* That speech is so! It's so, and I got to speak it
that-a-way. *(He looks about him with burning eyes and
pleads as if with an unseen power.)* The truth's there. Can't
you see it? *(His nostrils quiver and he goes on in a kind of
sob, calling to the unbeliever hiding within the dark.)* God
A'mighty knows they ain't no difference at the bottom.
Color hadn't ought to count. It's the man, it's the man that
lasts. *(Brokenly.)* Give us the truth! Give us the truth!

He coughs slightly, and a queer baffled look creeps over his face. For the moment he seems to sense ultimate defeat before a hidden, unreachable enemy.

MUH MACK: *(Looking at the clock and snapping.)* Thought you's bound to be at de Quillie House by six o'clock. It's done near 'bout time. Git on. I wants my nap.

She pours snuff into her lip and turns to her snoozing again. With a hurried look at the clock, ABE *crams his speech into his pocket, gets a plug hat from the desk, and blows out the lamp. The room is filled with great leaping shadows from the darting flames of the fireplace.*

ABE: *(At the door.)* You remember what I said about Douglass.

MUH MACK: Git on, git on. *(Whining sarcastically.)* Sho' you'll be a light on de hill and de pride o' de land—and you won't even let a po' old woman see her boy.

ABE: *(Turning back.)* Damn him! If he puts his foot in this house he'd better not let me get hold of him. They ain't no man, flesh of my flesh or not, going to lie rotten with liquor and crooks around me. That's what I been talking against for twenty years. I drove him off for it and I'd do it again. Just because a little time's passed ain't no reason I've changed.

MUH MACK: He mought a changed and want to do bedder.

ABE: *(Coming back into the room.)* Changed enough so he like to got arrested in town yesterday and it his first day back.

MUH MACK: *(Pleading in a high quavering voice.)* But I gut to see him. He's been gone two yeah.

ABE: Let him come if he dares. You ruint him with your tales and wuthless guitar playing and I don't want nothing more to do with him.

MUH MACK: *(Mumbling to herself.)* I's gwine see him 'fo' he goes 'way back yander ef I has to crawl slam over de river.

ABE: *(With brightening eye.)* You heard me. He ain't no longer mine, and that's the end of it.

MUH MACK: *(Bursting into a rage.)* And yo' ain't none o' mine. You's gut all de high notions of old Colonel Mack and de white folks and don't keer nothing foh yo' own. Git on. *(He stands looking at the floor, hesitating over something.)* Whut you skeered of, de dark?

ABE: *(Shuddering and going across the room and getting*

an old overcoat from a nail.) Yes, I'm afraid of it. You're right, I'm none of yours, nor my own mother either. You know what I am—no, I dunno what I am. Sometime I think that's de trouble. *(Sharply.)* No, no, de trouble out there, around me, everywhere around me. *(The despondent look comes back to his face and he speaks more calmly.)* I'll cut across the fields the near way. And tell Goldie not to worry. I'll be back by ten with the school good as started. *(At the door he turns back again and calls to the old woman earnestly.)* Muh Mack, don't let her worry, don't. *(But the old woman is asleep.)* Let her sleep, let us all sleep.

He goes out softly, closing the door behind him.

SCENE SIX

An hour later the same evening. A sandy country road twists out of the gloom of scrubby oaks and bushes at the rear and divides into a fork, one branch turning sharply to the left and the other to the right. The moon has risen low in the east, casting a sickly drunken light over the landscape through the flying clouds. To the left in a field of small loblolly pines the dim outline of a barn can be seen. The tops and the branches of the larger trees move like a vast tangle of restless arms, and the small bushes and grasses hug the earth under the wind's blustering. Down the road in the distance come the sounds of running footsteps. And farther off, almost out of hearing, the halloo as of someone pursuing. The footsteps thump nearer, and presently ABE staggers up out of the darkness and falls panting in the edge of the bushes at the right. His hat is gone and his clothes torn. The shouts sound fainter in the night and gradually die away.

ABE *crawls to his knees and stares back at the road, his breath coming in great gasps. His learning and pitiful efforts at cultural speech have dropped away like a worn-out garment and left him a criminal.*

ABE: Reckon, reckon dey leave me 'lone now, de damn cutth'oats! *(Holding his sides with his hands and rocking his head in pain.)* Oh, my breast feel lak it'll bust. Yeh, I outrun you, you po' white trash. *(Clambering wildly to his feet and staring up the road.)* But you done fix me now. You done got all de underholt and lay me on de bottom. *(Looking up at the sky and raising his fist above his head.)* Dere dat moon looking on it all so peaceful lak. It don't know, it can't feel what dey done to me. *(Bursting out with a loud oath.)* God damn 'em to hell! Dem white sons of bitches! Dey don't gi' me no chance. Dey stop every crack, nail up every do' and shet me in. Dey stomp on me, squash me, mash me in de ground lak a worm. *(His voice breaking into a sob.)* Dey ain't no place foh me. I lost, ain't no home, no 'biding place. *(He throws himself down on the ground and lays his cheek to the earth. Unseen by him, a light begins to twinkle at the barn. He sits up and looks intently at the ground.)* Seem lak dis earf feel sweet to me. It warm me lak it feel sorry. *(Laying his hand on it as if it were a being.)* Ground, you is my last and only friend. You take me in, you keep me safe from trouble. Wisht I could dig me a hole now and cover me up and sleep till de great judgment day, and nobody never know whah I gone.

LONNIE MCCRANIE, *stout and middle-aged, comes in at left with a lantern.*

LONNIE: Heigh there!

ABE: *(Bounding up.)* Keep back, whoever you is. Stay back dere, white man.

LONNIE: *(Peering forward.)* Who's that cutting up crazy here in the night?

ABE: Ain't nobody, nobody.

LONNIE: Well, by God, Abe, what's the matter?

ABE: That you, Mr. Lonnie?

LONNIE: Yeh. What'n the world's the matter? I was out there at the barn and heard the awfulest racket. Somebody talking like they was crazy.

ABE: Trouble, Mr. Lonnie, trouble.

LONNIE: Trouble, what sort of trouble? *(Coming closer and holding up his light before ABE.)* Great goodness, you're wet as water.

ABE: *(Straightening up.)* I all right now. Got to go on.

He makes a drunken step on the road towards the right. LONNIE *gets quickly before him.*

LONNIE: Where you going?

ABE: I going to leave heah, going clean away.

LONNIE: No, you're not. Tell me what's the matter.

ABE: Dem white men run me away from the Quillie House.

LONNIE: That's what the shouting was about, was it?

ABE: Mebbe so, suh.

LONNIE: Uh-huh. You were down there 'bout your school business, anh?

ABE: I wa'n't doing no harm. I was going to talk to 'em 'bout our school foh next year, and when I got there dey was a crowd of low-down white men dere——

LONNIE: Look out, mind how you talk.

ABE: I minding all right. When I got there they done run them lazy niggers off and told me I had to go. *(Grimly.)* Dey couldn't skeer me though. I went on in de house and started my speech. And den——*(Throwing out his arms wildly.)* Mr. Lonnie, help me git back at 'em. Help me git de law on 'em.

LONNIE: What'd they do?

ABE: Dey fell on me and beat me and told me I got to git out of de country. And dey run me off. But I reckon some of 'em got dey heads cracked. *(His body swaying with weakness.)* What I going to do? I don't know what?

LONNIE: Go on home and behave yourself.

ABE: *(His voice almost cracking.)* I ain't done nothing. I tell you.

LONNIE: *(Roughly.)* Serves you right. I've told you time and again to quit that messing about and look after your crop and keep in your place. But you won't, you won't. I reckon you'll stay quiet now awhile.

ABE: *(Pleading with him.)* But I done right. I ain't done nothing to be beat foh.

LONNIE: The devil you ain't! I've been off to-day all around the country trying to get hands to pick out your cotton. It's falling out and rotting in the fields.

ABE: But I ain't lost no time from the cotton patch, 'cepting two or three days and I was sick den. I been sick all to-day.

LONNIE: You needn't talk back to me. If you're sick what are you doing out to-night and getting yourself beat half to death? Yeh, I reckon I know such tales as that. And you needn't fool with the crop no more. I done levied on it and am going to have it housed myself.

ABE: *(Moving towards him.)* You mean you tuck my crop away from me?

LONNIE: Don't talk to me like that, I tell you. *(A fit of coughing seizes ABE.)* Call it taking away from you if you want to. I'm done of you. Next year you can hunt another place.

ABE: (*His face working in uncontrollable rage.*) Den you's a damn thief, white man.

LONNIE: (*Yelling.*) Stop that!

ABE: (*Moving towards him.*) Now I'm going to pay somebody back. I going to git even.

LONNIE: Stop! I'll kill you with this lantern.

ABE: (*With a loud laugh.*) Yeh, yeh, hit me. Yo' time done come.

He makes a movement towards LONNIE, *who swings his lantern aloft and brings it crashing down on his head. The light goes out and the two rocking forms are seen gripping each other's throats under the moon.*

LONNIE: Let go—let go——

ABE *gradually crushes him down to the ground, choking him.*

ABE: (*Gnashing his teeth and snarling like a wild animal.*) I choke you, I choke yo' guts out'n yo' mouf. (*He finally throws* LONNIE'*s limp body from him, and then falls upon it, beating and trampling the upturned face.*) Dere you lie now. Dead! (*His voice trails high into a croon.*) I wipe out some de suffering of dis world now! (*Standing up and drawing away from the body.*) I—I—git even, I pay 'em back. (*He begins wiping his hands feverishly upon his trousers.*) Blood! Blood, de white man's blood all over me. (*Screaming out in sudden fear.*) I done kilt somebody! Oh, Lawd, Mr. Lonnie! Mr. Lonnie! (*He falls on his knees by the body.*) What's de matter? Wake up, wake up! . . . Pshaw, he's asleep, fooling. (*Springing to his feet.*) He's dead, dead. (*The wind groans through the trees like the deep note of some enormous fiddle and then dies away with a muffled boom across the open fields.* ABE *stands frozen with horror.*) Listen at dat wind, will you! Mercy, dat his spirit riding it and crying! (*He falls prone upon the earth moaning and rocking. In a moment he sits up and holds his head tightly in his hands.*) O—oh, seem lak my head done turnt to a piece o' wood, seem lak cold as ice. (*He slaps his forehead queerly with his open palms.*) De whole world done seem turnt upside down, everything going round me lak a wheel. (*As he stares wonderingly around and gropes before him like one dreaming, the branches of the trees seem to change their characteristics and become a wild seething of mocking, menacing hands stretched forth from all sides at him. He snatches up a piece of broken fence rail and snarls at them.*) Don't tech me, I kill you! (*He *stands in an attitude of defense and the branches seem to regain their normal appearance. Stupefied, he lets the rail fall to the ground and then wraps his arms spasmodically across his face.)* O Lawd, I going crazy, dat's what! *(He bends over jerking and shivering. Presently from the left he sees appear a shadowy cortege of raggle-taggle country gentry, men and boys carrying muskets, sticks and stones. Their faces, illumined by the moon, are set and frozen in the distortion of hate and revenge. In the midst of them is a young Negro being dragged along with a rope around his neck.* ABE *starts back with a gasp.)* What's dis? Whah am I? *(Suddenly terrified.)* Lawd, dat's a lynching! . . . It's de night o' dat lynching. And dat dere's Charlie—Charlie Sampson. *(Seizing the rail.)* What you white mens doing? *(Crying out.)* Dat you, Charlie! I come save you! *(The group appear to pass silently down the road at the rear, the prisoner throwing out his arms and clawing the air as he is dragged onward.* ABE *springs forward at them and swings his rail through the air. It lands on the ground with a thud. He shrieks.)* Ghosts! Dey's ha'nts! Dey ain't no peoples! *(Jerking up his head and looking queerly around him.)* Jesus, mebbe dat's me dey hanging! *(He stands rooted in his tracks as they disappear down the road. After a moment out of the underbrush at the left steal two shadowy figures dressed in the fashion of the late fifties. One is a young good-looking Negress of twenty, the other a dandified young white man about thirty. As they move across the scene at the rear, the man looks guiltily around him as if in fear of being surprised. The woman stops and points to the thicket at the right. He nods and motions her to move on.* ABE *looks up and sees them stealing away. He leaps to his feet and stares at them in stupefaction.)* Who dat 'oman and white man? *(With a joyous cry he rushes forward.)* Mammy! Mammy! Dat you! Dis heah's Abe, yo' boy! Mammy! *(The figures begin entering the thicket.)* Mammy! Dat you, Colonel Mack? Whah you going? Stay heah, help me, I——*(The man and the woman disappear in the bushes.* ABE *stands with his mouth open, staring after them.)* Whut's all dis? Must be anudder dream—a dream. Sump'n' quare. *(He moves cautiously forward and parts the bushes and starts back with a loud oath.)* God damn 'em! Dey dere lak hawgs! *(The fearful truth breaks upon him and he shrieks.)* Stop it! Stop dat, Mammy, Colonel Mack! *(Rushing towards the bushes again and stopping as if spellbound)* Stop dat, I tell you, dat's me! Dat's me!

He stumbles backward over the body of LONNIE MCCRA-NIE *and, shrieking, rushes down the road at the left.*

SCENE SEVEN

Thirty minutes later. DOUGLASS has arrived and with MUH MACK before the fire is giving an account of his travels. He is now about nineteen years old, and has developed into a reckless dissipated youth, dressed in the cheap flashy clothes of a sport.

DOUGLASS: *(Turning towards* MUH MACK *with a bitter smile.)* Yeh, I says it and I says it ag'in. Let dem dere Norveners putt Pap in print foh what he's trying to do foh de niggers. Ef dey could see him now down a po' dirt fahmer dey'd not think he's such a sma't man. Let him read his books and git new ide's. Dey won't change de nigger in him, not by a damn sight. He's raght down working a tenant and dat's where he belongs. Git me? Ah, him off to-night making his speeches. I bet to Christ dis heah's his last 'un.

MUH MACK: Foh God's sake don' carry on so. Come on and tell me some mo' 'bout de places you been since you left heah. *(He sits looking in the fire.)* Whut—whut's de matter? You hain't been usual so ficey-lak wid yo' pap. You been drinking?

DOUGLASS: *(Laughing sweetly.)* Yeh, I been drinking. And I gut cause to cuss de whole works out. *(Looking at her fiercely.)* Listen heah. Let dis slip in yo' yur, foh you'd heah it soon enough. You never has swung a' eight-pound hammer, steel driving day adder day in the br'iling sun, has you? And you hain't never done it wid a ball and chain on you ca'se you is marked dang'us, has you? and dat foh a whole yeah long? Well, I has.

MUH MACK: *(In astonishment)* You been on de roads since you left?

DOUGLASS: *(Recklessly)* I has dat and wo' de convict clo'es des' ca'se in my drunkenness I 'gun to preach some o' his doctrines 'bout dere being no difference 'twixt de cullud and de white. I knowed bedder. But I was drunk and had hearn so many o' his speeches. De judge said he'd des' stop my mouf foh a month. And I gut a knife one day and stabbed a gyard to de hollow. And dey gin me twelve months foh dat.

MUH MACK: *(Admiring his prowess)* You allus was one whut fou't at de drap o' de hat.

DOUGLASS: *(Disgustedly)* Yeh, a damn fool, and I ain't fohgit how he run me off'n heah and beat me! *(Bursting out with shining eyes)* Hain't I gut cause to hate him and want to git him down?

MUH MACK: Gittin' on de roads ain't much, Douglass.

DOUGLASS: No, it ain't much to lie in de jug, is it? You do it and you ain't never gwine have no more peace. De cops is allus watching you. You gits de look and dey knows you. Dey tried to 'rest me yistiddy over dere, and I hadn't done nothing. And de old man was knowing to it too. But I's learnt what he'll never learn and it's dis—dat we belongs down wid de pick and de sludge hammer and de tee-arn and de steam shovel, and de heavy things—at de bottom doing de dirty work foh de white man, dat's it. And he ain't gwine stand foh us to be educated out'n it nuther. He's gwine keep us dere. It pays him to. I sees it. And adder all dese yeahs Pap keeps on trying to teach dat men is men. Some white man's gwine shoot his lights out one dese days, see ef dee don't. *(With a reckless forgetfulness)* And so I says gimme a fast time, a liddle gin to drown down all my troubles in, and den—*(He goes over to the door and gets his guitar)* A liddle music to top it off wid. How about it, Muh Mack?

MUH MACK: *(Straining her eyes through the shadows)* Whut you gut dere? *(Jubilantly)* Lawd, Lawd! Ef you ain't brung yo' box wid you! And I ain't heerd nothing but dem sporrers by de do' and dat old rain crow in de hollow since you left two yeah back. Play her, boy, play her.

By this time he has sat down by the fire strumming.

DOUGLASS: *(Turning up while MUH MACK sits in a quiver of excitement)* Lemme play yo' old piece. My 'oman in Rocky Mount said 'twas de onliest chune.

MUH MACK: Dat's it! Dat's it! Lawd, gimme de "Band." I useter be put in de middle every time foh dat step. Dance all day, dance all night, des' so I's home by de broad daylight. Chile, I c'd natch'ly knock de wool off'n 'em. *(As DOUGLASS plays she chuckles and whines with delight and almost rises from her seat. He starts in a quiet manner gradually working up to a paroxysm of pantomime and song. MUH MACK begins doing the Jonah's Band Party step with her heels and toes while sitting. DOUGLASS spreads his wriggling feet*

*apart, leans forward with closed eyes, and commences the
"call," with the old woman's quavery slobbering voice
giving the "sponse.")*

CALL: Sech a kicking up san'!

SPONSE: Jonah's ban'!

*This is repeated; then comes the command to change
steps.*

> "Hands up, sixteen, and circle to de right,
>   We's gwine git big eatings heah to-night.
>
> "Sech a kicking up san'! Jonah's Ban'!
>   Sech a kicking up san'! Jonah's Ban'!
>
> "Raise yo' right foot, kick it up high,
>   Knock dat Mobile buck in de eye.
>
> "Sech a kicking up san'! Jonah's Ban'!
>   Sech a kicking up san'! Jonah's Ban'!
>
> "Stan' up, flat-foot. Jump dem bars.
>   Karo backwards lak a train o' cyars.
>
> "Sech a kicking up san'! Jonah's Ban'!
>   Sech a kicking up san'! Jonah's Ban'!
>
> "Dance roun', 'oman, show 'em de p'int,
>   Dem yudder coons don'ter how to coonj'int."

By this time DOUGLASS *is playing a tattoo on the wood of
his box and carrying on the tune at the same time.* MUH
MACK *has risen from her chair. With her dress to her knees,
defying her years, she cuts several of the well-remembered
steps. At sight of her bare and thin dry shanks the delirious*
DOUGLASS *bursts into loud mocking guffaws and only plays
faster.*

The door opens at the right and GOLDIE *comes timidly in.
Her face is worn and haggard, and the strained vacant look
in her eyes has deepened.* MUH MACK *stops and creeps
guiltily to her chair.* DOUGLASS *tapers off his music and
stops. For a moment* GOLDIE *stands astonished in the door,
holding a bulky tow-sack in her hand. She drops the sack
and hurries over to* DOUGLASS.

GOLDIE: Muhcy me! I knowed 'twas you soon's I heard
de guitar. And sech carrying-ons!

DOUGLASS: *(Rising confusedly as she comes up to him)*
How you, Mam?

She puts her hand shyly on his arm and then clings convulsively to him, her shoulders heaving with restrained sobs. He lays one arm around and stands looking tenderly and somewhat foolishly down at her. It is evident that in his way he cares for her. She suddenly raises her head, dries her eyes with her apron, and fetches wood from the box.

GOLDIE: *(Punching the fire)* Whyn't you let me know Douglass'd come, Muh Mack?

MUH MACK: He des' come.

DOUGLASS: *(Laying his box on the bed)* Mam, you set in dis char. You must be cold.

She sits down wearily, and he stands with his back to the fire. MUH MACK *picks up her snuff-brush and slyly begins to dip from her tin box.*

GOLDIE: *(With a sudden start of terror)* You hain't seed yo' pap, has you?

DOUGLASS: No'm, I ain't seed 'im. I found out he done gone to de Quillie House 'fo' I come. I slipped in heah and found Muh Mack asleep. Lawd, I skeahed her wid a fiah coal.

GOLDIE: *(Suddenly reaching out and clutching his hand to her face)* Don't you and yo' pap have no trouble. Don't agg him on. He—he—ain't well and might rile easy. We—we kin see one 'nother off.

DOUGLASS: Oh, I'se gwine be partickler. Now don't worry no mo'. It's awright.

GOLDIE: *(Slowly getting up)* You all set while I fix you some supper. I got something good foh Abe and de rest of us. Lemme show you. *(She brings the bag, sits down in the chair and takes out a big meaty ham-bone.* MUH MACK *eyes it hungrily. Naïvely)* Ain't dat de finest dough? And I gut a hawg haid, too, and collards and cracklings.

DOUGLASS: *(Angrily)* Dat's de way wid dem damn—wid dem white folks. Dey works you to death and den shoves dey old skippery meat off on you foh pay.

GOLDIE: *(A worried look coming over her face)* You hand't ort to say dat, Douglass. Mr. Lonnie gi'n me it—all of it. And he paid me cash foh my work. Abe'll have a new bottle o' medicine Monday. *(She fingers the food childishly, and* DOUGLASS *turns away with a smothered oath. Putting the food back into the bag, she stands up)* Now I'll git you some supper.

DOUGLASS: I cain't stay foh no supper. I promised to eat down de road wid Joe Day. Le's set and talk, ca'se we don't have much time and you can cook adder I'm gone.

GOLDIE: *(Hesitating)* Well—lemme put dese heah in de kitchen den. *(She goes out at the right)*

DOUGLASS: What makes Mam act so quare?

MUH MACK: *(Surprised)* Do how? She acts awright.

DOUGLASS: She don't. She acts sort o' lost lak—wropped up in something. *(He scratches his head perplexed)*

MUH MACK: Ef dey's anything wrong wid her it's 'count o' trouble, I reckin.

DOUGLASS: De hell-fi'ed fool! He's drug her to death wid his wildishness.

MUH MACK: And ef it's trouble dat ails her, I reckins as how you's done yo' shur in bringing it on.

He swallows his reply as GOLDIE *comes in. She lights the lamp, then sits down and begins staring in the fire.*

DOUGLASS: *(After turning from one side to the other)* Mammy, whut's de matter wid you?

GOLDIE: *(Brushing her hand across her face and looking up as she wipes the tears from her eyes)* Lawd bless you, chile, dey ain't nothing. I's des happy to be wid you. *(She catches his hand and holds it a moment, then drops it and begins to look in the fire again.* DOUGLASS *watches her intently a moment and then turns away as if somewhat awed by her manner. There is a noise of someone's coming up on the porch.*

MUH MACK: *(Crying out in fear)* Dat's him, Douglass! I knows his step. Dat's yo' pap.

GOLDIE *stands up, wringing her hands and crying silently as* DOUGLASS *gets his guitar and hurries into the kitchen. The door at the left opens and* ABE *enters.*

GOLDIE: *(Leaning forward and rousing the fire)* Did everything turn out—(MUH MACK *suddenly screams.* GOLDIE *looks up and cries out)* Oh!

ABE *comes towards the fire. His face is bruised, his clothes torn to shreds, and he sways as he walks.*

MUH MACK: *(Rising from her chair)* Dey's been adder him! Dey's been adder him!

ABE: *(Snarling at her)* Shet up yo' damn yowling, will you? and don't be rousing de neighborhood. I'm not dying yit.

GOLDIE *stands a moment terror-stricken and then runs up to him.*

GOLDIE: You's hurt, hurt bad, Abe, po' baby!

ABE: *(Pushing her back)* Ain't hurt much. No time to doctor me now. *(He stands before the fire.* MUH MACK *collapses in her chair. He is no longer the reformer and educator, but a criminal, beaten and hunted)* I come to tell you to git away—*(Panting)* to—to leave, leave!

GOLDIE: *(Sobbing and burying her face in her hands)* Whut's happened! Whut's happened!

MUH MACK: *(Swaying in her chair and crying to herself)* Lawdy-a-muhcy on us! Lawd-a-muhcy!

For a moment he stands before the women silent, with closed eyes.

ABE: *(He staggers and grips the mantel and stands listening as if to far-away sounds. He turns desperately to the cowering women)* Git your clothes and leave. You got to go, I tell you everything's finished at de end.

GOLDIE: *(Wailing)* What happened at de schoolhouse?

ABE: *(Pushing his bruised hand across his forehead)* I cain't, cain't quite think—yeh, they was a crowd of white men at de door with dough-faces over their faces. Said wa'n't going to be no meeting. Dey beat me, run me off. And dey give me till to-morrow to git outen de country. You got to git away, foh it's worse'n dat—oh, it is! *(Calmly and without bitterness)* Who you reckon set 'em on me? Who you think it was told 'em about de trouble I been in before? Yeh, and he made it out terribler'n it was. Douglass told 'em. . . . He done it. My own flesh and blood. No! No! he was but ain't no more! *(Gloomily)* But I don't blame him—dey ain't no blaming nobody no longer.

GOLDIE: *(Fiercely)* He didn't—he wouldn't turn ag'in' his own pa.

ABE: *(Sternly)* Hush! He did though. But it don't matter to-night. And you got to leave. *(Half screaming and tearing at the mantel)* Now! Now, I tell you.

GOLDIE: *(Between her sobs)* Did you—who hurt you?

ABE: I tell you I've done murder, and dey coming for me.

MUH MACK *sits doubled up with fear, her head between her arms. With a sharp gasp* GOLDIE *ceases weeping and sits strangely silent.*

MUH MACK: Murder! Oh, Lawd-a-muhcy!

She mumbles and sobs in her rag.

ABE: Dey drove me away from de meeting. I come back by the road mad. *(He gasps)* Every white man's hand ag'in' me to de last. And Mr. Lonnie come out to de road when I passed his house and begun to abuse me about de crop. He struck at me, and I went blind all of a sudden and hit him wid my fist. Den we fou't. *(His voice growing shrill)* And I hit him and hit him. I beat his head in. I killed him dead, dead! I beat on and on until all de madness went out of me and de dark was everywhere. Den I seed a sight—*(He stops, aghast at the remembrance)* I left him dere in de night dead on de ground. Dey done found 'im—I heah 'em crying up dere in de night. Dey's coming to git me. *(He holds out his bruised hands)* His blood's still shining on dem hands.

He turns his head away in fear.

MUH MACK: *(In a high whine of terror)* My God a-mighty! You kilt yo' own flesh!

ABE: *(Turning wrathfully upon her)* Yeh, yeh, some bitch went a-coupling wid a white man! And I seed it—seed it! *(He drops his hands helplessly. A sort of terror comes upon him)* Oh, Lawd God! I'm anudder Cain. I tell you I—I scrushed his head in and beat it till I put out de stars wid blood. Mercy! Mercy! *(With his hands still held before him, he stands with bowed head. After a moment he looks up and speaks calmly, almost resignedly, his dignity coming back to him)* This is the way it was meant to be, and I'm glad it's ended. *(He stands with his fists to his temples, and then flings out his arms in a wide gesture)* Oh, but damn 'em! Don't dey know I want to do all for de best. *(Shaking his fist at the shadows)* I tell you, I tell you I wanted—I've tried to make it come right. *(Lowering his head)* And now it's come to dis.

DOUGLASS *comes in from the kitchen and stands away before him, his face filled with shame and fear.* ABE *looks at him without interest.*

DOUGLASS: Befo' God, Pap, I—I didn't mean no sech happenings. I never thought—

ABE: *(Eyeing him coldly.)* Who you? *(More loudly)* A leader, a king among men! *(To the women)* Here's Douglass and you can go wid him.

DOUGLASS *turns back into the kitchen and instantly runs out. His eyes are staring with fear.*

DOUGLASS: *(In a throaty whisper)* Come on, Mam! *(Twisting his cap in terror)* Dey's coming. I heerd 'em from de kitchen do'. Dey's coming. Run, Pap! God have muhcy!

MUH MACK *hobbles to him and tries to pull him through the door at the right. He looks back towards his mother.*

MUH MACK: Come on! Come on!

DOUGLASS: Mam, Mam, don't stay heah!

ABE: *(Raising* GOLDIE *from her chair)* Go on wid him. You ain't to blame foh nothing.

He pushes her towards DOUGLASS. *But she turns and throws her arms around him, clinging silently to his breast.*

MUH MACK: *(Pulling* DOUGLASS*)* I heahs 'em. Dat's dem coming.

With an anxious look at GOLDIE, DOUGLASS *hurries with* MUH MACK *through the door and into the fields.* ABE *places* GOLDIE *back in her chair and stands looking at her. He catches her by the shoulders and shakes her.*

ABE: Tell me, what is it, Goldie! What ails you, gal? *(She sits looking dumbly at him and he draws away from her. Presently there is a sound of stamping feet outside, and voices slip in like the whispering of leaves. A stone is thrown against the house, then another and another. One crashes through the window and strikes the lamp. The room is left in semi-darkness.* ABE *with a sob of overwhelming terror falls upon his knees. Twisting his great hands together, he casts up his eyes and cries in a loud voice)* God, God, where is you now! Where is you, God! *(He begins half sobbing and chanting)* You has helped befo', help me now. Is you up dere? Heah my voice! *(Fear takes possession of him)* Blast me, Lawd, in yo' thunder and lightning, if it is yo' will! Ketch me away in de whirlwind, foh I'm a sinner. Yo' will, yo' will, not mine. Let fiah and brimstone burn me to ashes and scatter me on de earf. *(Gasping)* I've tried, I've tried to walk de path, but I'm po' and sinful. . . . Give me peace, rest—rest in yo' bosom—if it is dy will. Save me, Jesus, save me!

He falls sobbing to the floor.

VOICE: *(Outside)* Come out of there, you dirty nigger! *(A shudder runs through him, and his sobs grow less violent)* Come out! Come out!

Another stone crashes through the room. As if ashamed of his weakness, ABE *rises from the floor. He speaks firmly to the shadows.*

ABE: In the end it was so intended. *(Looking around him)* And I end here where I begun. *(He bursts out in a loud voice.)* Yet they're asleep, asleep, and I can't wake 'em!

VOICES:

He's in there.

I hear him talking.

He's done talking now, goddam him!

We'll show him the law all right.

He's got a gun!

Shoot him like a dog.

ABE: (*Wiping his brow and again speaking in the rôle of the educator trying to convince his everlastingly silent hearers*) But they'll wake up, they'll wake—a crack of thunder and deep divided from deep—a light! A light, and it will be! (GOLDIE *still sits hunched over in her chair. As he speaks he goes to the door at the left*) We got to be free, freedom of the soul and of the mind. Ignorance means sin and sin means destruction. (*Shouting*) Freedom! Freedom! (*Lifting up his voice*) Yea, yea, it was writ, "Man that is born of woman is of few days and full of trouble. . . ." Lak de wind wid no home. Ayh, ayh, nigger man, nigger man—(*He opens the door*) I go talk to 'em, I go meet 'em—

VOICE: Hell! Lookout! There he is!

ABE: Yea, guns and killings is in vain. (*He steps out on the porch*) What we need is to—to— (*His words are cut short by a roar from several guns. He staggers and falls with his head in the doorway*)—and we must have—have—

At the sound of the guns, GOLDIE *springs to her feet. For an instant everything is still. Then several shots are fired into* ABE'S *body.*

VOICE: Quit the shooting. He's dead as a damned door! Now everybody get away from here—no talking, no talking. Keep quiet—quiet.

There is the sound of shuffling footsteps and men leaping the fence.

GOLDIE *moves toward the door where* ABE *lies. Halfway across the room she stops and screams and then drops down beside his body.*

The wind blows through the house setting the sparks flying.

CURTAIN

COMMENTARY

Much of Paul Green's early acclaim is the result of his Pulitzer Prize–winning drama, *In Abraham's Bosom*. As a play derived entirely from folk roots, it has a unique place in the development of native American drama. Green sought to capture the truth of the American folk character. Where the local colorists included both city and rural ethnic types, in folk drama only the rural types are treated. Green once said, "It seems to me the folk are those living closer to a terrible and all-wise nature."

Up until the time of *In Abraham's Bosom*, the black had appeared on the Broadway stage only as a one-dimensional stereotype. But Green showed a full-dimensioned black human being, instead of an unreal "Yassuh-Massa" shuffle-footed Negro type. Green wedded the two things: black man as symbol and as three-dimensional character. Green shows the tragedy of blacks striving for individual and collective justice. Abe, however, is the only black in the play who sees himself as a person born to something more than servility.

This play is the most realistic black folk drama—almost perfectly capturing the dialect and idiom of the region—that had appeared up to 1927 in the New York theater. The rural black man is seen in the deprivation of his borrowed cabin habitat—hungry and hopeless. *In Abraham's Bosom* is a lyrical lament for the injustice suffered by American blacks. Its voices rise out of the post–Civil War South to emphasize that the pattern of white oppression did not end with Appomattox but continued long after. In order to make his point about black suffering, Green, more than other American dramatists of his time, wrote tragedy. Abe fails partly because he has too much wrath and pride, which is his tragic flaw; yet his stubbornness is understandable. His father, the Colonel, beats him, humiliating him in front of his black friends. (A scene reminiscent of Alex Haley's recent novel, *Roots*.) Action is merely a function of Abe's will to change his life, to be educated, and as a result to change society. Unfortunately, his blind insistence on this direction is at the expense of everything else. His death is consequently a foregone conclusion.

Paul Green wrote of the strengths and failings of both races in the struggle for individual recognition. Abe thought that education was the key to true equality between the races. Therefore, all he wanted was to be educated and to educate other blacks. For that dream, his body was riddled with bullets as he stood in the doorway of his cabin. Had he become sophisticated enough through proper education, Abe would not have been the tragic figure in the doorway, but, instead, a man able to control his emotions so that he could deal with the prejudice around him. His failure stands as eloquent testimony to the terror that ignorance can bring to the human heart—both black and white.

A newspaper columnist in 1931 wrote that Green "keeps his feet firmly planted in the real world where women have babies and men slave for bread and everybody fights and hates and loves." Green also believed absolutely that man was imbued with a transcendental spirit but was held back by brutality, ignorance, and greed. In that respect, Green was a traditionalist, who was, therefore, out of step with O'Neill and Howard. In fighting against McCarthyism, he once observed that "truth still remains the truth, right still the right, justice still remains justice, and human hearts still aspire upward."

Although he was a traditionalist in theme, Green was an experimenter in that he used ritualistic and expressionistic devices. For example, at the end of Scene II, Abe goes through a prayer session in which he releases pent-up emotions. He thanks God for the land, a child, and a chance to teach school. This ritualistic device drawn from the life of the American black is also used at the end of Scenes I and IV.

In Scene IV, expressionistic technique is employed. In expressionism the playwright reveals the inner feelings and emotions of his characters by showing how they perceive reality. And since people think in flashes, fragments, and images, the drama must mirror these natural (if often bizarre) manifestations of the mind. For the expressionist, time and space do not exist. Rather, through the use of clipped language and an ignoring of linear development, a theme is erratically presented. There is even a revival of the soliloquy, which was one of the devices of the romantic drama that was targeted for extinction by the realists. Whenever the audience is asked to look at reality as perceived through a character's distorted or demented mind, expressionism is being used. That is precisely what occurs when Abe sees figures from his past looming up around him just after he has been beaten and run off by the KKK in Scene VI. As Abe experiences a mental breakdown, the audience sees things through Abe's tormented eyes. The result is expressionistic. Obviously, Green was more of an experimenter than is generally recognized. O'Neill had already introduced expressionism, and Green put it into good practice.

Despite the innovations and exceedingly well drawn characters, reviewers found the play "stark" and "faulted but beautiful, too episodic." One reviewer said: "Paul Green has put into his picture a searching and passionate sympathy for all those who seek to help humanity in spite of itself. Unfortunately, he has also reproduced much of the tedium of this experience with a detailed fidelity which only the magic of sustained emotion could make good stagecraft. The results are isolated moments of true tragedy and interminable stretches which even the excellent cast could not sustain." This has generally been the tenor of criticism over the years. But what Paul Green succeeded in doing was to show the entire life of the folk in his region. On stage, that had never been done before quite so well, and his doing it even in a flawed work is a splendid achievement. His perfect ear for folk dialect in the play is rewarding for the playgoer. In addition to his completely faithful use of the spoken word of his region, he was completely faithful in representing the physical details of Abe's rural environment—clothes, cabins, utensils, and so forth.

According to Mrs. Rhoda Wynn, Administrative Assistant to Paul Green Dramas, the play has never been produced south of the Mason-Dixon Line. In fact, the play has rarely been produced in recent years. This may be because of racism, or simply embarrassment at the intensity of white–black relations in the play. Or perhaps directors are wary of the play because of its use of dialect. But that shouldn't be a problem because Green published a revised version of the play in *Five Plays of the South*, in which he rewrote all the most difficult-to-understand parts of the dialect. He retained the original scenes but made the language clearer. Still, the play did not find ready producers, and that is a sad fate for a Pulitzer Prize–winner. One suspects that the play's unfortunate reviews, its courageous attack on racism, and its precise rendering of dialect all made production difficult. Whatever the reasons may be, it is time that the play is brought once again to the public's attention.

Mrs. Paul Green graciously consented to publication of an edited version of the original version of the play in this book. She was aware of the editors' need to include the original version that won the Pulitzer Prize in drama so that the dialect could be preserved and accurately reflect the drama of the 1920s. Green's later edition, which made the text more literary, would not be representative of his work in the 1920s. Mrs. Green also kindly agreed to the many cuts made in this edited version in order to tighten the dramatic action. The drama's tragic rhythm remains, and its lyricism is as beautiful as ever.

Paul Green was a sensitive, kind man who understood the suffering poor of his region as well as anyone. Listen to his words from *Lonesome Road* about blacks:

> For more than a hundred years he has built roads there, leveled hills and forests, plowed the fields, sweated and groaned forth the great brag crops of naval stores, of cotton, tobacco, and corn, with little or no reward, material or otherwise. Living in the vilest of huts, the prey of his own superstitions, suspicions and practices, beaten and forlorn before God Almighty himself—he has struggled helplessly in the clutch of affliction and pain. He has perished by the thousands in the long servitude of his white master. Unceasingly, he has matched his strength with the earth that bore him, going forever in the end to rot unnoticed in the land he's tilled, ... Such is his story before imagined justice. (*Lonesome Road: Six Plays for the Negro Theater*, New York, 1926, p. xix).

Epilogue

In the fifteen years from 1915 to 1929, American drama and theater evolved into a significant artistic medium. Although there was much experimentation with avant-garde forms, realism was the dominant motif. What had the realists accomplished? They stood back and looked at the world with an objective eye and attempted to catch the moving panorama of American life in all its variety. As a result, the stage was populated with diverse figures from all walks of life. Thus the realists were primarily reporters. Consequently, the everyday (as well as the bizarre) details of life were of considerable interest to them. The manner in which characters dressed, moved, thought, and talked had to be depicted on stage. In addition, the world in which the characters lived had to be duplicated with some accuracy. Above all, everything these characters thought about, needed, and desired was now dramatically viable.

These realistic playwrights were not content to show a superficial world à la Belasco; rather they attempted to reach into the minds and hearts of their characters, without the benefit of a priori knowledge. Consequently, preaching was replaced by insight into the dark nature of the conscious and unconscious in their furious combat. Such playwrights wanted to find out what haunted the inner world of man and why. New focus was placed on the female character, and stock types (like the stage Irishman) were abandoned. The black character finally became three-dimensional.

Having fulfilled their primary obligation as reporters, the most insightful of these writers became historians—they attempted to interpret the facts. They became involved with the consequences of behavior. Having studied the characters, having placed them in dynamic and disturbing situa-

413

tions, they tried to determine the ultimate results of those experiences.

Although these realists were the descendants of James A. Herne, Eugene Walter, Augustus Thomas, they were also influenced by Ibsen, Strindberg, and other experimentalists from Europe. The impact of these avant-garde writers was most pronounced on O'Neill, who, having started with realism in his sea plays and *Beyond The Horizon,* immediately shifted to expressionism in *The Emperor Jones, The Hairy Ape,* and *The Great God Brown.* O'Neill above all wanted to find the most dynamic method of expressing man's inner torment. In shifting to expressionism, he attempted to objectify inner experience, and as a result these later plays often focus on the "world" of one person who is terribly disturbed.

One finds, therefore, that the expressionistic play is often as much monologue as dialogue. Because the play and the situations are the result of the experiences that occur in the subconscious or unconscious mind of one character, we note distortions and dreamlike events on stage. Often the characters and the distortions that they perceive become symbols; therefore, objects and characters have more connotative than denotative meaning. It is easy to see that the expressionist writer reveals truth by looking out from the character's mind, contrary to realism, where the audience finds truth by looking into the scene with its own eyes. For the expressionist, reality becomes subjective; for the realist, it is objective. The realistic writer tries to observe the effect of experience on consciousness, whereas the expressionist very often deals with the power of the subconscious and the unconscious.

The theater of the 1920s was a barometer of the times and showed how Americans were trying to maintain their individuality while searching for success, personal identity, and fulfillment. Morals were questioned, old standards and values were challenged. Each character in his own way tried to come to terms with personal survival in a materialistic society.

When the stock market collapsed October 29, 1929, an era and a way of life came to an end. The consequences were revealed in the plays of the 1930s, many of which advocated a new way of life. Social justice became the theme on and off the American stage. Radical theatrical organizations mushroomed, advocating social change, and for the first time in the history of the United States, the Federal government went into the business of financing the arts.

In Volume 2 of *Modern Drama in America,* we will demonstrate how the new wave of social-protest drama was integrated with realism. As the new realists of the 1920s used the new stagecraft to express their ideas, the realists of the 1930s further refined theatrical techniques and devices.

Look for these popular titles from Washington Square Press at your bookseller now

Toni Morrison
THE BLUEST EYE
An unusual, haunting, and profound novel of yearning and despair in black America by the award-winning author of Song of Solomon and Tar Baby.
44720-3/$2.75/160 pp.

John Sayles
UNION DUES
A National Book Award nominee, Union Dues is a novel about the life and love, the corruption and survival of a father and son.
82109-1/$2.50/400 pp.

Wallace Stegner
THE BIG ROCK CANDY MOUNTAIN
The Pulitzer Prize-winning author's first major novel, the story of a drifter who throws everything away in search of a magic land where he can be himself.
82804-5/$2.75/640 pp.

Don DeLillo
END ZONE
A brilliant novel of love, death, and the new gladiators by "the writer Vonnegut, Barth and Pynchon were once oddly and variously taken to be"—Washington Post.
82012-5/$1.95/208 pp.

John Irving
THE HOTEL NEW HAMPSHIRE
The bestselling author of The World According to Garp follows the eccentric Berry family across two continents in this "startlingly original" (Time) novel.
44027-6/$3.95/560 pp.

WSP
WASHINGTON SQUARE PRESS
Published by Pocket Books